# Urdu Vocabulary

گنجینۂ معنی کا طلسم اس کو سمجھیے
جو لفظ کہ غالب مرے اشعار میں آوے

Think of it as an enchanting spell with a treasury of meaning—
Each word that appears in my poems, Ghalib.

# Urdu Vocabulary

## A Workbook for Intermediate and Advanced Students

Gregory Maxwell Bruce

EDINBURGH
University Press

Edinburgh University Press is one of the leading university presses in the UK. We publish academic books and journals in our selected subject areas across the humanities and social sciences, combining cutting-edge scholarship with high editorial and production values to produce academic works of lasting importance. For more information visit our website: edinburghuniversitypress.com



Edinburgh University Press Ltd
The Tun—Holyrood Road
12 (2f) Jackson's Entry
Edinburgh EH8 8PJ

Typeset in 14/16 Myriad Arabic by
IDSUK (DataConnection) Ltd, and
printed and bound in Great Britain

A CIP record for this book is available from the British Library

ISBN 978 1 4744 6719 3 (hardback)
ISBN 978 1 4744 6720 9 (paperback)
ISBN 978 1 4744 6721 6 (webready PDF)
ISBN 978 1 4744 6722 3 (epub)



Published with the support of the University of Edinburgh Scholarly Publishing Initiatives Fund.

# Contents

# Acknowledgments

This book is the result of sixteen years of language studies in Arabic, Hindi-Urdu, Persian, and Sanskrit that began at the University of California, Santa Cruz and continued at the American Institute of Indian Studies, Delhi University, and the University of Texas at Austin. My first Hindi-Urdu teacher, John Mock, remains a major source of inspiration to me. I am likewise grateful to all the teachers at the American Institute of Urdu Studies' program in Lucknow for their patience and for introducing me to the world of Urdu literature. I am especially grateful for the many hours that I spent discussing Urdu words with Fahmida Bano, Wafadar Husain, Ahtesham Khan, and Sheba Iftikhar. At the University of Wisconsin, Madison, I was lucky to assist and observe the late Qamar Jalil, whose pedagogical insights are reflected throughout this text. At the University of Texas at Austin, I had the great fortune to study with some of the greatest teachers of language and literature in the world. Syed Akbar Hyder provided me with a broad and rigorous instruction in Urdu literature. Michael Hillmann spent years training me in the intricacies of Persian. Many of the ideas and insights in the Arabic and Persian units of this book are the direct result of his mentorship. I am also grateful to Rupert Snell, with whom I spent eight years studying Hindi, for exposing me to the many joys of Hindi-Urdu words and the intellectual rewards of applied philology.

This book is also the result of eleven years spent teaching Urdu at the Universities of California, Berkeley, Texas at Austin, and Wisconsin, Madison. I initially conceived of the project at the South Asia Summer Language Institute at UW Madison in 2008 and benefitted from conversations with students and colleagues, including Qamar Jalil and Faraz Sheikh. I developed the basic structures of the units and many early drafts of the lessons while teaching in the Hindi-Urdu Flagship at UT Austin. I taught many talented students there over the years, but am especially grateful for the feedback of Ayana D'Aguilar and Courtney Naquin, who worked through many early drafts of the exercises with me in my final year in graduate school. I have spent the past four years developing and teaching the materials to students at UC Berkeley. Their feedback has inspired what seem now like countless rounds of revision. Special thanks are due to the following students, who have worked through substantial portions of the book in its final stages of preparation for publication: Hammad Afzal, Khudeeja Ahmed, Hammad Ali, Aparajita Das, Elizabeth Gobbo, Salil Goyal, Shazreh Hassan, Caylee Hong, Zain Hussain, Talib Jabbar, Maryam Khan, Adeel Pervez, Omar Qashoa, Adnan Rawan, Ahmad Rashid Salim, Nawal Seedat, and Fatima Tariq. Special thanks are also due to Sally Goldman for her helpful feedback and suggestions on the Sanskrit unit and to my friend and colleague Walter Hakala for his learned comments on the units in a late stage of revision. Their feedback has considerably improved the quality of the book. All errors and oversights are, of course, mine alone.

It would not have been possible to carry this project to completion without the support and expertise of the editors and staff at Edinburgh University Press. Special thanks are due to Adela Rauchova for supporting the project from the outset. Thanks are also due to Eddie Clark, Bekah Dey, Zuzana Ihnatova, Emma Rees, Kirsty Woods, and the team of typesetters. I am also grateful to the anonymous peer reviewers whose comments have improved the utility of the book and to the many anonymous Urdu instructors from around the world who responded to Edinburgh's preliminary survey with enthusiasm for the project. Finally, many thanks to my teacher and friend Hamidreza Ghelichkhani for the beautiful calligraphy on the cover.

The lessons in this book took around ten years to design, compile, and edit. I did most of the work between other academic writing projects, late at night, on weekends, over dinner, and while traveling for work and pleasure. I am deeply grateful to my family and friends for supporting and encouraging me as I excused myself from conversations to jot down notes about words.

# A Note on Transliteration

This book follows the system of transliteration used by the *Journal of Urdu Studies* (Brill). (See the chart below.) On occasion, it deviates from the system to reflect Urdu pronunciation more accurately; for example, فعل [fel] instead of [fi'l]. Such deviations are explicitly noted in the text or clarified by context. The sections discussing Sanskrit and Hindi, and the Hindi books listed in the bibliography, use a slightly modified version of the transliteration system used by McGregor in his Hindi dictionary. The modifications avoid confusion with those in Urdu and more intuitively approximate pronunciation. They include sh for ś (श), ṣh for ṣ (ष), ṛi for ṛ (ऋ), and n, ñ, and m for nasals. By contrast, transliterations of the titles of Hindi books listed in the bibliography follow the standard system to facilitate cross-reference with library catalogues.

| ا | a, i, u, ā | | | | | | | | |
|---|---|---|---|---|---|---|---|---|---|
| ب | b | پ | p | ت | t | ٹ | ṭ | ث | ṡ |
| ج | j | چ | ch | ح | ḥ | خ | ḳh | | |
| د | d | ڈ | ḍ | ذ | ż | | | | |
| ر | r | ڑ | ṛ | ز | z | ژ | zh | | |
| س | s | ش | sh | | | | | | |
| ص | ṣ | ض | ẓ | | | | | | |
| ط | ṭ̤ | ظ | ẓ̤ | | | | | | |
| ع | ' | غ | ġh | | | | | | |
| ف | f | ق | q | | | | | | |
| ک | k | گ | g | | | | | | |
| ل | l | م | m | | | | | | |
| ن | n | ں | ñ | | | | | | |
| و | v, ū, o, au | | | | | | | | |
| ہ | h | ھ | h | | | | | | |
| ی | ī | ے | y, e, ai | | | | | | |
| ء | ' | ة | t | | | | | | |
| iẓāfat | -e | | | | | | | | |

# INTRODUCTION AND HOW TO USE THIS BOOK

*Urdu Vocabulary: A Workbook for Intermediate and Advanced Students* is the first textbook in English to give students the knowledge that is required to obtain a large Urdu vocabulary quickly. Originally titled *A Treasury of Meaning*, it is designed for English-using students of Urdu at the intermediate to advanced levels. Its content and methods have developed from years of experience teaching Urdu in the University of Wisconsin, Madison; the Hindi-Urdu Flagship Program at the University of Texas, Austin; and the University of California, Berkeley. The goal of the book is to be both academic and accessible. It introduces students to the rules by which Urdu vocabulary is derived from relevant languages. The explanations, examples, and exercises are varied, ranging from philological connections through morphological information to idioms. Its method draws from linguistic research in Urdu, applied linguistics, and the vocabulary acquisition methods. It is fast-paced and self-contained, and can be used either in the Urdu classroom or as part of a self-study course. Although designed with American college students and research scholars in mind, it can be used profitably by students of Urdu in a variety of learning contexts and across a range of ages and levels.

The methods of the book draw on research indicating that instruction in etymology and morphology is an effective means of vocabulary acquisition. Etymologically informed approaches have been shown to be more effective than simply looking up words in a dictionary and lead to greater rates of retention and greater confidence in dealing with unfamiliar vocabulary (Hosseini et al. 2012). The same study shows that when students do not recognize cognates and morphologically related terms, they have much more difficulty retaining and recognizing unfamiliar vocabulary. The importance of etymologically informed studies are confirmed by a number of case studies (Harley 1996). Students with morphological and etymological knowledge are more likely to infer successfully the meaning of unfamiliar words than students who guess the meaning of words from context alone (Morrison 1996). A recent study challenges popular language-acquisition methods by presenting evidence that decontextualized, list-based learning can lead to greater retention over time than contextual learning (Qian 1996). One study of university-level students in a beginning French class has shown that word analysis activities focused on cognates and designed to be read in conjunction with regular course materials led to positive advantages in vocabulary acquisition (Tréville 1996). Likewise a lack of etymological and morphological knowledge may hinder acquisition. According to one study, students who do not recognize cognates and morphologically related words may have more difficulty understanding and retaining unfamiliar vocabulary (Reynolds 2015).

The information in each unit applies to all types of Urdu language study by focusing on the methods of acquiring a large vocabulary for the purpose of reading. Research has shown that a sufficient vocabulary, more than syntax or general reading ability, is the best predictor for student success in reading (Laufer 1997). To date, Urdu pedagogical material has given students opportunities to read across a wide range of registers, genres, and contexts. But it has been shown that while extensive reading alone does develop a student's vocabulary, intentional vocabulary learning in conjunction with reading results in quantitatively higher levels of vocabulary acquisition and qualitatively more advanced levels of understanding (Paribakht and Wesche 1997).

*Urdu Vocabulary* is intended to facilitate rapid progress to advanced levels of comprehension. To the extent possible, the words used in the examples and vocabulary exercises have been selected by correlating the most extensive Urdu word counts available (Ahmed 1973; Barker et al. 1969) with the vocabulary thresholds formerly used by the the Common European Framework of Reference for Languages (CEFR) (Milton and Alexiou 2009) and the competency standards of the American Council on the Teaching of Foreign Langauges (ACTFL). The selection of vocabulary is intended to provide students with the foundational vocabulary required to reach the advanced level and the linguistic knowledge that will carry them into the advanced and superior levels. This method is supported by recent research in language acquistion, which suggests that it is helpful for students to limit vocabulary in the beginning to allow them to read widely (Coady 1997). There is also evidence that, especially at the advanced level, exposure to rare words and metalinguistic knowledge are necessary (Arnaud and Savignon 1997). For this reason, I have also included some rare vocabulary words that neatly demonstrate the paradigms discussed in the lessons. The effectiveness of this combined approach is confirmed by my anecdotal experience teaching Urdu to students at the UC Berkeley, UT Austin, and UW Madison.

Conventional wisdom holds that students must spend at least a year studying each of the major languages that contribute to Urdu word-building (Arabic, Persian, and Sanskrit) in order to gain command of Urdu vocabulary and idioms, especially at the literary level. The intention of the present book is to remove the need to do so by training students in the relevant structures of these languages as they are used in Urdu across a range of registers and contexts, from everyday vocabulary to literary maxims and quotations. Students who develop command of the concepts covered in the lessons in this book will not need to spend years studying these languages. But they will have laid a solid foundation in them, and it is hoped that the book will encourage them to pursue further study.

Although Ahmed and Barker's word counts are the best available for Urdu, they are slightly outdated, and, more significantly, they draw primarily from the language of Urdu newspapers, which are dominated by the Perso-Arabic registers of the language and often exclude informal registers, including slang and profanity, as well as Sanskritic and colloquial Indic registers. In selecting examples for the Hindi-Urdu and Prakrit-Sanskrit units, I have relied on my own informal word count conducted using internet searches and a small body of texts chosen specifically for their inclusion of these registers. I have noted them at the end of the unit. It should be noted that the unit on shared etymologies does not strictly follow the above-mentioned thresholds, since the purpose of the unit is to present readers with as many potentially familiar words as possible and to explore the myriad connections between English and Urdu without regard for frequency. That said, although some rare English words have been chosen for the sake of illustration, most of the words selected are glossed in the *New Oxford American Dictionary*. The etymological relationships have been taken from the *Oxford English Dictionary* (*OED*) or deduced from comparison and cross-referencing the *OED* with etymological information included in Urdu and Hindi dictionaries by Platts and McGregor and Sanskrit dictionaries by Monier-Williams and Apte.

This book is divided into five units. The first unit examines English-Urdu cognates across a range of linguistic traditions to familiarize English-language readers with the Urdu they already know, so to speak. There is good evidence that explicit instruction in cognate recognition, particularly cognate recognition across scripts, accelerates vocabulary acquisition (Helms-Park and Perhan 2016) and that explicit training in word forms improves student learning (Elgort and Warren 2014). It has also been argued that vocabulary acquisition should be of two kinds: awareness and retention; and that awareness must involve metalinguistic knowledge (Arnaud and Savignon 1997). The unit is thus designed to facilitate recognition of Urdu-English cognates for this purpose. But it is also designed to draw readers' attention to the interconnectedness of the two languages across a range of temporal and geographical contexts. Challenging any form of exclusivism, it demonstrates this interconnectedness with examples of borrowing and highlighting shared histories that Urdu, like English, has been part of a long history of global exchange across a range of languages. It also argues that Urdu, like English, cannot be reduced to any particular community (religious or otherwise), geographic region, linguistic tradition, or nation state.

The following units introduce students to the ways in which Arabic, Hindi-Urdu, Persian, and Prakritic-Sanskritic morphologies generate vocabulary in Urdu. Unit 2, "The Arabic Element," is the longest in the book and typically requires close and repeated study. Students will find that by spending time learning the system of Arabic word-building at a relatively early (intermediate-advanced) stage of language learning, they will be able to acquire a larger vocabulary faster than if they do not. The patterns or paradigms from which Arabic derives vocabulary from a root (usually triliteral) are especially important for Urdu students, since they produce vocabulary spanning a wide range of registers. By learning the twenty or so word-building patterns, the various ways that Arabic forms plurals, and the concepts related to Arabic roots covered in the unit, students will be in a position to develop familiarity with, even command of, of a large number of words relatively quickly. For example, the root concept نظر (to see) generates around thirty words in Urdu; and that number does not include various plural forms of derived nouns. By spending time studying and memorizing how the patterns in the unit affect meaning, students can, in effect, gain familiarity with an average of around two dozen words for free, so to speak, for each commonly used root that they learn.

Unit 3, "The Hindi Element," surveys the patterns of word-building in the vernacular language that, for at least the past six centuries or so, has been called Dakkini (Deccani), Khari Boli, Hindi, Hindustani, and Urdu. Indeed, as late as the mid-nineteenth century, poets and writers used the word "Hindi" to refer to a language and literary tradition that would only be called "Urdu" today. Like all shifts in naming, these changes have always been contingent on context. In recent history, they have largely been related to the long history of language-related and communal politics in South Asia. In this book, "Hindi" is used in its literal Perso-Arabic meaning of "Indian" or "Indic," but with specific reference to the patterns of word-building that distinguish Hindi-Urdu from other Indic languages such as Panjabi, Gujarati, and Bengali. Urdu, then, refers in this text to the language sometimes identified grammatically as Hindi-Urdu, usually written in the Nastaliq script, and whose vocabulary draws from Arabic, Hindi, Persian, Prakrit, and Sankrit, as well as a a wide range of other languages, many of which are discussed in Unit 1.

Unit 4, "The Persian Element," similarly guides students through the morphology of Persian. Students typically find the Persian lessons easier than the Arabic material. Efforts to familiarize oneself with Persian verbs and master their many derivations are rewarded with a wide range of everyday words, idioms, phrases, and aphorisms in Urdu. The unit accordingly takes readers from basic everday elements of Persian present in Urdu to the appreciation of Persian proverbs and literary fragments that they are likely to encounter in a wide range of contexts, from Bollywood films to academic articles. To this end, the unit concludes with a basic introduction to Persian grammar.

Unit 5, "The Prakrit-Sanskrit Element," guides students through Sanskrit word-building, the relationship between Sanskrit and Prakritic languages, and briefly introduces students to Sanskrit grammar. Urdu pedagogy across the globe has been dominated for more than a century by Perso-Arabic studies to the exclusion of Sanskrit, effectively rendering invisible to Urdu students not only the historical and linguistic relationships between Urdu and Sanskrit, but also the relationship of Urdu to other Indic languages. For reasons that have much more to do with politics than language, registers of Urdu that include Sanskrit vocabulary have been increasingly associated exclusively with Hindi. This book rejects this exclusivism and examines the most important relationships between Sanskritic and Urdu. From personal names to Indian television shows, from classical Urdu poetry to Urdu works on Sanskrit philosophy, Sanskrit borrowings and Sanskritic vocabulary is found across a wide range of literary genres and discursive contexts. These registers and words form the core of the lessons in the unit.

Lessons and sections in each unit follow a standard structure. First, readers are introduced to a key concept through explanation and example. Next, exercises guide the student from recognition through formal reproduction and semantic understanding to meaning-prediction. Once the basics of word-building in Arabic, Persian, and Sanskrit/Prakrit have been covered, a series of advanced lessons introduce students to grammars of the languages. The purpose of these advanced lessons is to facilitate comprehension of idioms and quotations that students are likely to encounter as they advance to superior levels of proficiency. The lessons in this book are designed to complement any reading program, but I have included at the end of each unit a short list of Urdu books that readers will find useful when reviewing the exercises therein.

## How to Use this Book

Regardless of the context in which one uses this book, the materials in it can be integrated into a range of study contexts at the intermediate and advanced levels. Any student preparing for intermediate-level study should read the introductory sections of each unit to become familiar with the building blocks of Urdu vocabulary. By the end of an ideal intermediate Urdu course focused on developing reading skills, students should be able to identify obvious Arabic, Persian, Hindi, and Sanskrit vocabulary in Urdu and recognize commonly encountered suffixes, prefixes, patterns, and other word-building elements. For the Arabic element, this includes common Form I patterns (nouns, active participles, agentive nouns, nouns of place), Forms II and III of the verbal noun, and broken plurals. For Persian, this includes a handful of verbal noun patterns, *iẓāfat*, and conjunctions. For Hindi, this includes the most common verbal nouns. For Sanskrit, this includes the information about *sandhi* and *vṛiddhi*. By the end of an advanced course, students should be familiar with all the word-building patterns in the book. In some cases, students developing advanced skills will also find it helpful to have developed familiarity with the grammatical units, too. The introductions to Arabic, Persian, and Sanskrit grammars, idioms, and proverbs are designed to help students develop superior-level skills. They are also intended to encourage students to pursue study of the languages, too.

The explanations, examples, and exercises in this book are written in a way that allows the book to be used for self-study or as part of the curriculum in Urdu language and literature courses. Reading passages are not included, since the purpose of the present book is to give students the verbal background required to develop a large vocabulary quickly as they read Urdu texts spanning a wide range of genres, periods, and styles. Users will find this book most effective when combined with regular reading program, be it in an Urdu language or literature classroom or in conjunction with a self-directed program of study. Instructors may find it effective to assign units for homework or incorporate them into lesson plans as warm-up exercises in preparation for reading. Students may also find it useful to scan reading passages for examples of the general concepts covered in the lessons and to record or to use the charts in the appendices as models for a vocabulary journal. Here follow several ways in which the units in this book can be incorporated into formal classes and private programs of study.

The most direct way to integrate the materials in this book into formal Urdu courses is to use them as supplementary exercises in at the intermediate and advanced levels. In intermediate courses, teachers might assign the first sections of each unit, which introduce students to the sources of Urdu vocabulary and acquaint them with the basics of Urdu etymology and word-building. The exercises can be reinforced with word-hunt exercises in primary texts. For example, when reading a text in which a large number of Arabic words is found, teachers might assign the first section of the Arabic Element, which teaches them to recognize Arabic words. They might also ask students to scan an intermediate-level text to identify the Arabic words in it.

Another way for teachers to integrate the materials in the book into existing courses is to assign specific topics in relation to particular reading assignments. For example, one of the readings in my first-semester intermediate course includes three Arabic nouns of place (*maktab*, *madrasah*, and *maḥfil*). I assign the nouns of place lesson as supplementary homework and ask students to find nouns of place (and recognize their root and ties to other vocabulary) in their reading and subsequently in class. The same method may be applied in an advanced course with the more advanced concepts at the end of each unit as appropriate. For example, students reading short stories in which Persian idioms or poems are quoted may find it helpful to work through some of the exercises in the basics of Persian grammar.

Another way to integrate the materials is to assign the lessons and exercises as a structured part of a syllabus and course of study. I have found when using the materials in this way that it is best to set clear goals for students before the semester begins (see suggestions below). I then create a schedule of regular homework assignments and incorporate the materials into quizzes and exams. For example, if students in an advanced course are reading texts that draw extensively from Perso-Arabic registers, teachers might arrange to cover those units completely in the course of the class. The students in one of my advanced Urdu courses at UC Berkeley recently completed both units in their entirety in the course of a single semester alongside a text that engaged topics in Sufism, philosophy, and history. Ideally, the students would have worked through the materials in the course of an entire year. I gave the students a schedule of exercises to do for homework. We set aside 20–30 minutes each week to cover the exercises in class before proceeding to read and discuss the text. The benefit of this method is that it prepares students to make connections in unfamiliar contexts without relying on any particular text to dictate which lessons are studied.

A third way to integrate the material into courses is to use it as reading practice. This applies in particular to the materials in the first unit on shared etymology. I have assigned materials from the first unit in particular to students who have only recently learned the script. Single words make excellent reading practice, since they do not require students to understand both vocabulary and grammar. Since the unit reviews shared histories through shared etymology, it also facilitates recognition even of unfamiliar words. If the teachers and students who use this book are anything like me and my students, they will also find that the cultural and historical information about Urdu inspires interesting discussions about the language and the way that it has been represented.

A fourth way to incorporate the material is to make it the main focus of an advanced seminar. The materials in the text are easily adaptable to short-term, intensive seminars or semester-long seminars and study groups. In my experience, it takes around twenty hours of classroom time to work through all the exercises in this book when they are assigned as homework and selectively assessed in class. This makes the book an ideal coursebook for week-long, intensive seminars in Urdu vocabulary acquisition with 25–30 hours of classroom time. A semester-long course on Urdu words would allow instructors to select and integrate readings that complement the lessons in each unit. Since most semester-long courses in American universities offer 40–45 hours of classroom time, a neat balance can be struck between the exercises in the book, secondary readings, and classroom activities.

Reading practice and communicative tasks are two effective methods for students to apply and master the materials in this book. Readers who require a refresher course on the Urdu script might consult Delacy (2001). For introductions to Urdu grammar, Schmidt (1999), Matthews and Dalvi (1999; 2003) or its recent revision by Masud (2014) are perhaps the best-suited for self-study. The present book occasionally includes the Devanagari or Nagari script for comparative purposes. Although it is not necessary to read Nagari for present purposes, readers who wish to read the few Nagari portions may find the introduction to the script by Snell (2000) especially helpful.

In the reading practice method, teachers select and assign readings in tandem with the lessons in each unit, preferably those available in English translation. Another good choice would be to use one of the dozen or so Urdu readers for English-language learners. Those by Barker et al. (1968, 1975, 1977), Khan and Azim (1962), Naim (1965), Narang (1967), Shackle and Snell (1990) are classics. They also include explanations of Urdu vocabulary that students may find helpful to compare with the explanations in this book. The books listed at the end of each unit are suggested as advanced-level readings that illustrate the concepts covered in the unit. One way to use them is for students to complete a lesson, then proceed to scanning and "gisting" exercises in the texts. For example, they might complete the lesson on the Form II verbal noun in Arabic تفعیل and then scan a long passage in Nażīr Aḥmad's *Ibn ul-Vaqt* to find examples of its use, not familiar vocabulary, and estimate the meaning of unfamiliar vocabulary through a combination of etymological and contextual analysis. The teacher might focus attention on one or two examples, give them information about key words, and then ask them to work in pairs to estimate the meaning of the words in context. By applying the rules in the lesson, they will be better equipped to summarize or translate the passage, and will also find it easier to use and discuss unfamiliar vocabulary in it. The English translation can be used to help resolve issues. It can also be the subject of a discussion about the word or passage in question. Self-study users might profitably scan a substantial sample of Urdu text (e.g. a newspaper, short story, long poem) for examples of the word forms discussed here. Many of the units in the present book contain miniature versions of "word-hunts" of this kind that prepare students for scanning and studying longer passages.

Teachers may also use the lessons in this book as the bases of communicative exercises. For example, once the students have completed the final exercises in a lesson, teachers might ask them to interview each other about a given topic and use five words from the lesson in their questions and answers. Alternatively, they might ask them to answer a question or series of questions about a reading, stipulating that students use specified words or types of words in their responses.

The concepts in this book are not exclusive to Urdu. Hence, in principle, there is no reason why some of the units and lessons need be restricted to Urdu students alone. The units on Arabic and Persian, for example, are relevant to students of any Persianate language, including Ottoman Turkish, Panjabi, Pashto, and Persian, inter alia. I recently convened a seminar of graduate students from Near Eastern Studies, South & Southeast Asian Studies, and the Haas Business School at UC Berkeley interested in Arabic, Persian, and Urdu to work through the exercises in the units on Arabic and Persian. The units on Hindi and Sanskrit may be of interest to Indologists and students of other South Asian languages that use the Arabic script and incorporate Sanskritic vocabulary, such as Sindhi and Punjabi. Likewise, the units on Arabic and Persian may be of interest to students of languages that are not typically written in the Urdu script, but which borrow a substantial number of words from the languages (Bangla and Gujarati, for example).

This book may also be used as a primer or handbook for self-study. The explanations, examples, and exercises in this book are designed both for use in the classroom and for self-study. The unit on shared vocabulary can be fruitfully studied at any level and with any purpose in mind. Students at the intermediate level should familiarize themselves with the introductory material in each unit before progressing to the more advanced topics. At the advanced level, the choice as to which units to study will depend on the interests of the student. If the student wishes to read contemporary Urdu newspapers written in Pakistan, the sections on the Arabic, Hindi, and Persian elements will be helpful. Students who have studied Hindi and are new to Urdu may find that the unit on shared etymology and those on Hindi and Sanskrit provide the best introductions and reading practice. Students might begin each session with two to three lessons and exercises, then proceed to whatever text they are studying and scan for examples of the lessons covered in the book. I recommend working with texts that have been translated into English.

This book can also be used to facilitate and accentuate the use of a word journal. One of the most effective ways to use this book is in conjunction with a word journal. Word journals are among the best ways for students to develop and retain vocabulary, since they help them to relate new words and concepts to meaningful cultural and linguistic contexts. They can also be used in thematically focused courses as well as in general survey courses. In my intermediate Urdu course, which surveys a wide range of readings, I require that students choose five topics at the beginning of the semester for which they want to develop a richer and more nuanced vocabulary. In thematic courses, I have asked students to choose five topics relevant to the course focus. Throughout the semester, students collect words, phrases, and idioms from their readings and log them in their journals, relating them to their chosen topics and to other words to which they are etymologically related. Students are required to note relevant words, look for synonyms and antonyms, record examples of their use, and use this information to build sentences of their own. They are also encouraged to group words into categories based on etymology, concept, topic, context, register, and so on. I also require them to produce a course-final assignment in which they incorporate the vocabulary into a project or presentation. In the past, such course-final assignments have included skits, essays, personal reflection papers, formal presentations, and interviews.

The vocabulary and exercises in this book can provide material for journals in a number of ways. I require my students to organize their journal in part by grouping related words. They may also use the patterns in this book to derive related words or search for new words in dictionaries. They may also incorporate words from this book itself into their journals. For example, a student interested in science or education might encounter the word *ʿilm* (knowledge) and record it under that heading. Then, while completing the exercises in this book, the student may encounter the related words *ʿālim* (scholar) and the pattern that allows the student to derive *muʿallim* (teacher or educator) from *taʿlīm*. The student may also discover that all these are related to the commonly used *maʿlūm* (known) and add it, too, to the list in the journal. The purpose is thus not only to collect words under thematic headings, but to teach students to see how those words relate to each other and how other words might therefore relate to words that they already know. Teachers might also assign a particular pattern or patterns (for example, the Arabic Form I active and passive participles فاعل and مفعول) and ask students to record all the words in them that they encounter throughout the semester and learn the meanings of their roots. A feasible goal might be to see if any patterns in meaning emerge and to encourage to students to note the relationship of words in these patterns to other words that they encounter.

Finally, sections of this book can be used as readings in cultural studies and translation courses. The units in this book are designed to encourage critical and nuanced thinking about the history of Urdu. This book is intended to serve dual purposes as both a language-learning textbook and as a work of postcolonial studies. As such, parts of it can be adapted for and incorporated into courses focused on colonial and postocolonial studies, translation theory, and cultural surveys of Islam and South Asia. The first unit, for example, explores the connections between Urdu and English through their shared histories and vocabularies. In doing so, it challenges essentialist and reductive narratives that tie Urdu exclusively to any particular community, historical period, literary tradition, religion, and nation state. It also discredits the east-west binaries that have characterized orientalist and neo-orientalist approaches to Urdu and English literature. Instead, it paints a picture of two languages connected by myriad historical processes stretching from preliterate times through antiquity to the postcolonial period. In deconstructing civilizational binaries and demonstrating the historical contingency and interdependency that characterize the relationship between English and Urdu, it joins an ever-growing body of scholarship that divorces the study of language and culture from essentialist and reductivist epistemologies.

The units that follow develop this anti-esssentialist and anti-reductive thesis through close analysis of words that reflect the richness and plurality that characterize Urdu language and literature. The couplet by Ġhālib that inspired the working title of this book, *A Treasury of Meaning*, beautifully illustrates this approach to language. At the center of the couplet is the *t̤ilism* (cognate with the English talisman) of Urdu fantasy and adventure literature; *t̤ilisms* are enchanted worlds that often trap heroes in their wondrous, often even confusing and mystifying, labrynths. Ġhālib claimed that each word in his collected works was a t̤ilism hiding untold treasures. Far from reducing the words in his poetry to single meanings, Ġhālib suggests that each word opens a door to a t̤ilism-like world of enchanting connections and seemingly endless treasuries filled with meaning. I hope that the readers of this book will conclude that Ġhālib might just as well have been speaking about the Urdu language itself.

## Bibliography


Ahmed, Hasanuddin (1973). *Urdu Word Count*. Hyderabad: Villa Academy.

Arnaud, Pierre J. L. and Sandra J. Savignon (1997). "Rare Words, Complex Lexical Units, and the Advanced Learner." In *Second Language Vocabulary Acquisition: A Rationale for Pedagogy*, ed. James Coady and Thomas Huckin, 157–73. Cambridge: Cambridge University Press.

Barker, Muhammad Abd-al-Rahman, Shafiqur Rahman, Saphikura Rahamana, Hasan Jahangir Hamdani (1968). *An Urdu Newspaper Reader*. Montreal: McGill University Press.

Barker, Muhammad Abd-al-Rahman, Hasan Jahangir Hamdani, Khwaja Muhammad Shafi Dihlavi (1969). *An Urdu Newspaper Word Count*. Montreal: McGill University Press.

Barker, Muhammad Abd-al-Rahman, Hasan Jahangir Hamdani, Khwaja Muhammad Shafi Dihlavi, and Shafiqur Rahman (1975). *A Course in Urdu*. 3 vols. Ithaca, NY: Spoken Language Services.

Barker, Muhammad Abd-al-Rahman, Shah Abdus Salam, and Muhammad Akbaruddin Siddiqi (1977). *A Reader of Classical Urdu Poetry*. 3 vols. Ithaca, NY: Spoken Language Services.

Coady, James (1997). "L2 Vocabulary Acquisition through Extensive Reading." In *Second Language Vocabulary Acquisition: A Rationale for Pedagogy*, ed. James Coady and Thomas Huckin, 225–38. Cambridge: Cambridge University Press.

Delacy, Richard (2001). *Beginner's Urdu Script*. Lincolnwood, IL: NTC/Contemporary Pub.

Elgort, Irina and Paul Warren (2014). "L2 Vocabulary Learning From Reading: Explicit and Tacit Lexical Knowledge and the Role of Learner and Item Variables." *Language Learning* 64, no. 2 (June): 365–414.

Harley, Birgit (1996). "Introduction: Vocabulary Learning and Teaching in a Second Language." *Canadian Modern Language Review* 53, no. 1 (October): 3–12.

Helms-Park, Rena and Zhanna Perhan (2016). "The Role of Explicit Instruction in Cross-Script Cognate Recognition: The Case of Ukrainian-Speaking EAP Learners." *Journal of English for Academic Purposes* 21 (March): 17–33.

Hosseini, Effat, Shahrzad Sarfallah, Fateme Bakhshipour, and Hamid Reza Dowlatabadi (2012). "The Impact of Using Etymological Analysis on Teaching Vocabulary to EFL University Students." *Theory and Practice in Language Studies* 2, no. 9 (September): 1868–76.

Khan, Masud Husain and Abdul Azim (1962). *A Second-Year Urdu Reader*. Berkeley, CA: Center for South Asia Studies.

Laufer, Batia (1997). "The Lexical Plight in Second Language Reading: Word You Don't Know, Words You Think You Know, and Words You Can't Guess." In *Second Language Vocabulary Acquisition: A Rationale for Pedagogy*, ed. James Coady and Thomas Huckin, 20–34. Cambridge: Cambridge University Press.

Matthews, David and Mohamed Kasim Dalvi (2003). *Teach Yourself Urdu*. London: Hodder Headline, 1999. Rev. and repr. New York: McGraw-Hill.

_____ (2014). *Complete Urdu*. Rev. Timsal Masud. London: Hodder and Stoughton.

Milton, James and Thomaï Alexiou (2009). "Vocabulary Size and the Common European Framework of Reference for Languages." In *Vocabulary Studies in First and Second Language Acquisition: The Interface between Theory and Application*, ed. Brian Richards et al., 194–211. London: Palgrave Macmillan.

Morrison, Louise (1996). "Talking about Words: A Study of French as a Second Language Learners' Lexical Inferencing Procedures." *Canadian Modern Language Review* 53, no. 1 (October): 41–75.

Naim, C. M. (1965). *Readings in Urdu: Prose and Poetry*. Honolulu, Chicago: East-West Center Press, South Asia Language and Area Center, University of Chicago.

Narang, Gopi Chand (1967). *Readings in Literary Urdu Prose*. Madison: Department of Indian Studies, University of Wisconsin. Reissued by New Delhi: National Council for Promotion of Urdu Language, 2001.

Paribakht, T. Sima and Marjorie Wesche (1997). "Vocabulary Enhancement Activities and Reading for Meaning in Second Language Vocabulary Acquisition." In *Second Language Vocabulary Acquisition: A Rationale for Pedagogy*, ed. James Coady and Thomas Huckin, 174–200. Cambridge: Cambridge University Press.

Qian, David D (1996). "ESL Vocabulary Acquisition: Contextualization and Decontextualization." *Canadian Modern Language Review* 53, no. 1 (October): 120–42.

Reynolds, Barry Lee (2015). "The Effects of Word Form Variation and Frequency on Second Language Incidental Vocabulary Acquisition through Reading." *Applied Linguistics Review* 6, no. 4 (November): 467–97.

Schmidt, Ruth Laila (1999). *Urdu: An Essential Grammar*. London, New York: Routledge.

Shackle, Christopher and Rupert Snell (1990). *Hindi and Urdu Since 1800: A Common Reader*. London: School of Oriental and African Studies.

Snell, Rupert (1991). *The Hindi Classical Tradition: A Braj Bhāṣā Reader*. London: School of Oriental and African Studies.

_____ (2000). *Teach Yourself Hindi*. Lincolnwood, IL: Teach Yourself Books.

Tréville, Marie-Claude (1996). "Lexical Learning and Reading in L2 at the Beginner Level: The Advantage of Cognates." *Canadian Modern Language Review* 53, no. 1 (October): 173–90.

# UNIT 1
# URDU AND ENGLISH: SHARED HISTORIES, SHARED VOCABULARIES

Before beginning this unit, please keep the following points in mind. First, the etymology of a word does not determine its meaning. Etymology can be a useful tool for predicting the meaning of a word and in some cases can even clarify connotative differences among words with similar denotations. Still, linguists, philologists, philosophers, and translators often remind us of the dangers of the etymological fallacy, that is, believing that a word's history either predicts or limits its meaning. They also remind us that many cognates are "false friends"; that is, they are similar in form because they are related, yet differ significantly in meaning. Use and context have important roles to play. A good example is the English-Urdu cognate pair "syrup" and شراب [sharāb] (wine, liquor). Etymologically speaking, they are the same word, but, obviously, their meanings are quite different. Urdu poetry does not celebrate the mystical qualities of syrup and Americans do not pour شراب on their pancakes.

Second, this unit surveys a large number of cognates common to English and Urdu. It is not an exhaustive list of such words, nor does it touch on all the words borrowed into each language from the languages surveyed here. Urdu borrows a considerable number of words from Portuguese, but this unit only deals with the ones to which an English word is also related. For example, it is believed that Urdu borrows its words for "pineapple" and "bucket" (اَنَنّاس [anannās] and بالٹی [bālṭī]) from the Portuguese *ananás* and *balde*, but since these words do not have familiar cognates in Standard American English, they are not discussed in this unit.

Third, this unit is not exhaustive. Many Urdu words have been borrowed into English and appear in standard English dictionaries, but are not included here. In general, the following units prefer words with high frequencies as indicated in the *Oxford English Dictionary* (*OED*); although, in some cases, highly specialized terminology has been cited for the purpose of illustration.

Fourth, while this unit divides Urdu words into sections according to their language of origin, it is important to remember that the origin of many Urdu words is either uncertain or contested. For example, Urdu may have been borrowed پستول from either English or Portuguese, though the latter is more likely.

Finally, and perhaps most significantly, it is always important to keep in mind that the notion of a word having a distinct origin can be misleading. Words travel from one language to another, are borrowed, exchanged, lexicalized, delexicalized, relexicalized, and so on. For the sake of ease, this unit has identified the etymological origins of words according to philological convention. However, these etymons (that is, the word from which a later word is derived) are themselves outgrowths of linguistic traditions that are not necessarily identical with the one in which they are found. This complex relationship of etymology and history, with special reference to the case of English and Urdu, is nicely illustrated by the English words "pilau" and "pilaf." Cognate with the Urdu پُلاؤ, [pulā'o] these words appear to have been borrowed from Persian and Turkish. Platts' dictionary identifies the Urdu word as borrowed from Persian or Hindi and related to Sanskrit. The *New Oxford American Dictionary* identifies "pilaf" as a borrowing from Persian through Turkish. However, the etymon of all three words is ultimately uncertain. As the entry for pulao in the *NOED* indicates, the etymon may lie in Sanskrit and proto-Indo-European languages or perhaps a Dravidian ancestor of Tamil.

## 1.1 English in Urdu

Urdu has borrowed and adapted English vocabulary since at least the eighteenth century. Some English words have become so deeply absorbed into Urdu that they are hardly recognized today as borrowings.

Recognizing English words in Nastaliq is essential for developing speed as a reader. Here are some helpful tips.

Urdu spelling and pronunciation typically follow the English closely:

| | | |
|---|---|---|
| مِمبر | ← | member |
| نمبر | ← | number |

But sometimes English words are difficult to recognize and may reflect the influence of non-rhotic English accents. Also, note the characteristic sound change from z to j in the first example.

| | | |
|---|---|---|
| دَرجَن | ← | dozen |
| دَراز | ← | drawers |

Urdu typically renders the English "t" and "d" as retroflex ٹ and ڈ:

| | | |
|---|---|---|
| ڈاکٹر | ← | doctor |
| ڈِگری | ← | degree |

But there are exceptions. Scholars infer that the following words therefore may not have been borrowed into Urdu from English, but from other European languages.

| | | |
|---|---|---|
| تَولیا | ← | towel |
| بوتل | ← | bottle |

Pronouncing English words correctly in Urdu can also be challenging. Keep the following points in mind:

Urdu tends to avoid initial consonant clusters, often infixing or prefixing a vowel:

| | | |
|---|---|---|
| [gilās] گِلاس | ← | glass |
| [isṭeshan] اِسٹیشن | ← | station |

*A. Match the Urdu words to the English words.*

| | | | | | | |
|---|---|---|---|---|---|---|
| ۷۔ گِلٹی | ۶۔ رپورٹ | ۵۔ بیرا | ۴۔ گارڈ | ۳۔ بِل | ۲۔ بسکٹ | ۱۔ ڈَبل |
| double۔ج | gilding۔ث | guard۔ٹ | bearer۔ت | report۔پ | bill۔ب | biscuit ۔ا |

Because the legacy of British colonialism and military and political rule in South Asia, Urdu has a large number of English loanwords related to the military, law, finance, and civic administration. The British were not the only European power in South Asia, of course; some philologists therefore believe that the following word comes from French, reflecting the presence of French military presence in South Asia during the colonial period:

| | | | |
|---|---|---|---|
| (a rank of soldiers) | لام | ← | l'arme |

*B. Match the Urdu military terms to the English words from which they are borrowed.*

| | | | |
|---|---|---|---|
| platoon | ا | ___ | ۱۔ اَردَلی |
| company | ب | ___ | ۲۔ میجر |
| colonel | پ | ___ | ۳۔ لفِٹنٹ |
| lieutenant | ت | ___ | ۴۔ رنگروٹ |
| major | ٹ | ___ | ۵۔ کمپنی |
| recruit | ث | ___ | ۶۔ کمان |
| command | ج | ___ | ۷۔ کَرنَل |
| general | چ | ___ | ۸۔ کپتان |
| orderly | ح | ___ | ۹۔ پَلٹَن |
| captain | خ | ___ | ۱۰۔ جَنرَل |

*C. Match the Urdu terms related to law with their English sources.*

| | | | |
|---|---|---|---|
| judge | ا | ___ | ۱۔ سمن |
| summons | ب | ___ | ۲۔ پولِس |

| | | | |
|---|---|---|---|
| police | پ | ___ | ۳۔ جیل |
| warrant | ت | ___ | ۴۔ اپیل |
| magistrate | ٹ | ___ | ۵۔ ایکٹ |
| appeal | ث | ___ | ۶۔ کورٹ |
| court | ج | ___ | ۷۔ وارنٹ |
| act | چ | ___ | ۸۔ مجسٹریٹ |
| jail | ح | ___ | ۹۔ جج |

*D. Match the loanwords related to commerce and finance.*

| | | | |
|---|---|---|---|
| roll (a revenue catalogue) | ا | ___ | ۱۔ نوٹ |
| note | ب | ___ | ۲۔ فیس |
| check | پ | ___ | ۳۔ رجسٹر |
| bank | ت | ___ | ۴۔ پِنشَن |
| fees | ٹ | ___ | ۵۔ بنک |
| pension | ث | ___ | ۶۔ چک |
| register | ج | ___ | ۷۔ رول |

*E. Match terms related to government.*

| | | | |
|---|---|---|---|
| policy | ا | ___ | ۱۔ کانگریس |
| league | ب | ___ | ۲۔ کمیٹی |
| congress | پ | ___ | ۳۔ گورنمنٹ |
| parliament | ت | ___ | ۴۔ پارٹی |
| committee | ٹ | ___ | ۵۔ چیف |
| government | ث | ___ | ۶۔ لیگ |
| leader | ج | ___ | ۷۔ کونسل |
| party | چ | ___ | ۸۔ لیڈر |
| council | ح | ___ | ۹۔ پالیسی |
| chief | خ | ___ | ۱۰۔ پارلیمنٹ |

*F. Match terms related to civic administration.*

| | | | |
|---|---|---|---|
| deputy | ا | ___ | ۱۔ کمیشن |
| permit | ب | ___ | ۲۔ کمیشنر |
| in charge | پ | ___ | ۳۔ کلکٹر |
| assessor | ت | ___ | ۴۔ ڈِپٹی |
| commission | ٹ | ___ | ۵۔ پرمٹ |
| officer | ث | ___ | ۶۔ کمیٹی |
| commissioner | ج | ___ | ۷۔ اسیسر |
| committee | چ | ___ | ۸۔ افسر |
| collector | ح | ___ | ۹۔ ایجنٹ |
| agent | خ | ___ | ۱۰۔ اِنچارج |

*G. Match terms related to the railroad and transportation.*

| | | | |
|---|---|---|---|
| rail | ا | ___ | ۱۔ انجن |
| brake | ب | ___ | ۲۔ ریل |
| train | پ | ___ | ۳۔ اسٹیشن |
| railway | ت | ___ | ۴۔ کنڈکٹر |
| station | ٹ | ___ | ۵۔ بریک |
| conductor | ث | ___ | ۶۔ ٹرین |
| motor | ث | ___ | ۷۔ ریلوے |
| engine | ث | ___ | ۸۔ موٹر |
| tram | ح | ___ | ۹۔ پٹرول |
| petrol | خ | ___ | ۱۰۔ ٹرام |

*H. Match terms related to education.*

| | | | |
|---|---|---|---|
| professor | ا | ___ | ۱۔ کالج |
| conference | ب | ___ | ۲۔ کانفرنس |
| class | پ | ___ | ۳۔ یونیورسٹی |
| college | ت | ___ | ۴۔ کلاس |
| university | ٹ | ___ | ۵۔ پروفیسر |

Urdu and English borrow the names of countries and other geographical terms from many languages. Urdu often follows the orthography of other languages that use the Arabic script such as Arabic and Persian. For example:

| | |
|---|---|
| Algeria | الجزائر |
| Azarbaijan | آذَربائجان |
| Morocco | مراکش |
| Gibraltar | جبل طارق |

*I. Match the Urdu names for countries and regions with their English cognates.*

| | | | |
|---|---|---|---|
| France | ا | ____ | ۱۔ بُلغار |
| China | ب | ____ | ۲۔ تاجِکستان |
| Palestine | پ | ____ | ۳۔ فَلَسطِین |
| Israel | ت | ____ | ۴۔ چِین |
| Bulgaria | ٹ | ____ | ۵۔ اِسرائیل |
| Portugal | ث | ____ | ۶۔ فَرانس |
| Iraq | ج | ____ | ۷۔ بَرطانیہ |
| Cyprus | چ | ____ | ۸۔ پُرتگال |
| Britain | ح | ____ | ۹۔ قُبرِص |
| Tajikistan | خ | ____ | ۱۰۔ عِراق |

*J. Practice recognizing the Urdu names for countries. Give the English cognates of the Urdu words.*

۱۔ نیپال　۲۔ سَعودی عَرَب　۳۔ جاپان　۴۔ آسٹریلیا　۵۔ مالی

۶۔ آسٹریا　۷۔ میکسیکو　۸۔ عُمان　۹۔ ایران　۱۰۔ مڈغاسکر

*K. Practice recognizing English loanwords in Urdu. Read the following words aloud and give their English source-words.*

۱۔ ٹکٹ　۲۔ پینسل　۳۔ سوسائٹی　۴۔ میم　۵۔ اَسپتال

۶۔ بکس　۷۔ اِنچ　۸۔ مِسٹَر　۹۔ بِل　۱۰۔ پریس

*L. Read the section headings of the appropriately named Urdu daily آج and underline the words borrowed from or shared with English.*

| | | | | | |
|---|---|---|---|---|---|
| کالم | بلاگ | ویڈیوز | دلچسپ و عجیب | سائنس و ٹیکنالوجی | شوبز |
| صحت | کھیل | بزنس | انٹرنیشنل | پاکستان | صفحۂ اول |

## 1.2 Urdu in English

Because of overlapping histories of commercial exchange, colonialism, imperialism, and globalization, English has borrowed a substantial number of words from Urdu. The following words have fascinating etymologies:

cushy ← خوشی

English borrowed the word "cushy" from Urdu in the nineteenth century (Urdu itself having borrowed it from Persian). Scholars guess that it acquired its common sense of "undemanding" or "easy" because of its association with the etymologically unrelated word "cushion." In Urdu, of course, خوشی means "happiness" or "delight."

Equally interesting is the etymology of the word "punch." Note that not all Urdu words in English are Often mentioned in European travelogues to India in the seventeenth century, punch is so named because of its five (پانچ) ingredients.

| English | Sanskrit | Urdu |
|---|---|---|
| punch (drink) | panca | پانچ |

Here is another fascinating etymology. English borrows the word "cheese" meaning "great or important thing" (as in "the big cheese") from the Urdu چیز (thing), a word which Urdu itself borrows from Persian. This "cheese" bears no etymological relation to the word meaning a food made from curds.

"the big **cheese**" ← چیز

*A. Match the English loanwords to the Urdu sources. In some cases, the sense of the Urdu word differs from that of the English. Look up the Urdu words in a dictionary and note any differences that you find particularly interesting.*

| | | | |
|---|---|---|---|
| raj | ا | ____ | ۱۔ جَنگل |
| thug | ب | ____ | ۲۔ مگرمچھ |

| | | | |
|---|---|---|---|
| ganja | پ | ____ | ۳۔ راج |
| toddy | ت | ____ | ۴۔ ٹھگ |
| cheetah | ٹ | ____ | ۵۔ کھاٹ |
| jungle | ث | ____ | ۶۔ چیتا |
| shampoo | ج | ____ | ۷۔ لُوٹ |
| mugger (animal) | چ | ____ | ۸۔ تاڑی |
| loot | ح | ____ | ۹۔ چانپو |
| cot | خ | ____ | ۱۰۔ گانجا |

Many of the food names that have entered English through Urdu come from Persian and Arabic. For example, English borrowed the following words from Urdu, and we are told that Urdu borrowed them from Persian:

naan ← نان

paneer ← پنیر

Here is an Urdu word commonly found on American food labels:

guar (gum) ← گوار

*B. Match the Urdu food names with the English. If any of the food items are unfamiliar, visit a grocer or a restaurant to learn more about them. When it comes to food, first-hand experience is always the best teacher.*

| | | | |
|---|---|---|---|
| chutney | ا | ____ | ۱۔ نان |
| daal | ب | ____ | ۲۔ بریانی |
| samosa | پ | ____ | ۳۔ دال |
| lassi | ت | ____ | ۴۔ گھی |
| korma | ٹ | ____ | ۵۔ چٹنی |
| naan | ث | ____ | ۶۔ لَسّی |
| tikka | ج | ____ | ۷۔ روٹی |
| biryani | چ | ____ | ۸۔ قُرمہ |
| roti | ح | ____ | ۹۔ تِکّا |
| ghee | خ | ____ | ۱۰۔ سموسہ |

The English word "kulfi" (a special kind of ice cream) has an interesting etymology. Though borrowed from Urdu, it ultimately traces to the Arabic word قفل [qufl] (lock, seal). This is because kulfi is prepared by sealing a mixture of milk, sugar, and flavorings in small containers, which are then submerged in ice. The inversion of the letters follows idiomatic use and has parallels in other Urdu words.

kulfi ← قلفی ← قفلی ← قفل

Equally interesting is the history of the word تندور ("tandoor" in English). Scholars believe that English borrowed it from Urdu, Urdu perhaps from Turkish, and Turkish from Arabic or Persian (in which it is written and pronounced تنور [tanūr]).

tandoor ← تندور ← تنور

Incidentally, the noor [nūr] in تنور is believed to be related to the Semitic word for fire نار [nār].

*C. Match the Urdu loanwords to the English. Look up any unfamiliar words in a dictionary to familiarize yourself with their use and etymology.*

| | | | |
|---|---|---|---|
| teapoy | ا | ___ | ۱۔ ڈنگی |
| bandana | ب | ___ | ۲۔ ڈکیت |
| dinghy | پ | ___ | ۳۔ چھینٹ |
| bangle | ت | ___ | ۴۔ تِپائی |
| cowrie | ٹ | ___ | ۵۔ چارپائی |
| dacoit | ث | ___ | باندھنوں / باندھنا |
| charpoy | ج | ___ | ۷۔ کوڑی |
| chintz | چ | ___ | ۸۔ بنگڑی |
| dixie (pot) | ح | ___ | ۹۔ دائی |
| dai | خ | ___ | ۱۰۔ دیگچی |

*D. Practice recognizing Urdu words that have been borrowed into English. Read the following words aloud and give the English borrowings.*

۱۔ رُوپیہ ۲۔ خاکی ۳۔ شال ۴۔ پنڈت ۵۔ مَست

Keep in mind that the words that English borrows from Urdu have often themselves been borrowed into Urdu from other languages. For example, the words "khaki" and "dixie" (pot) were both borrowed into English from Urdu, but are themselves loans or derivations from Persian.

Here are some examples of other Persian words that have been borrowed into English by way of Urdu:

| | | | |
|---|---|---|---|
| purdah | ← | (covering, veil, curtain) | پردہ |
| pashmina | ← | (woolen cloth) | پشمینہ |
| ispaghula | ← | (lit. horse-ear) | اسپغول |

## 1.3 English, Urdu, and Portuguese

Many everyday Urdu words are borrowed from Portuguese. For example, according to the author of the Urdu dictionary نور اللغات, the Urdu word for Englishman [انگریز] [angrez], colloquially European or Euro-American, is likely borrowed from the Portuguese word *Inglés* (English), from which also the Urdu word for the English language [انگریزی] [angrezī] is also derived. Likewise, the names of the months of the year in Urdu were mostly borrowed from Portuguese and therefore reflect Portuguese spelling and pronunciation, though some seem to have been influenced by English, too.

اکتوبر ← October Outubro

The following word is likely borrowed from the Portuguese, rather than the English, since it lacks the retroflex consonant ٹ characteristic of English borrowings and is closer to Portuguese in pronunciation.

اسپتال ← hospital (Portuguese)

The following Portuguese borrowing shows a change from "l" to "n," which occurs in other Urdu words as well.

(auction) نیلام ← leilám

*A. Read the Urdu names of the months aloud. Then read the Portuguese names. Note the lack of the retroflex consonants* ٹ *and* ڈ *in the Urdu names for the months of the Gregorian calendar. This is good evidence that the words were not borrowed from English. In some cases, (October, for example), the name of the month is believed to be a hybrid of the Portuguese and the English.*

جنوری فروری مارچ اپریل مئی جون جولائی اگست ستمبر اکتوبر نومبر دسمبر

Compare with the Portuguese:

Janeiro, Fevereiro, Março, Apri, Maio, Junho, Julho, Agosto, Setembro, Outubro, Novembro, Dezembro.

*B. Match the English cognates of the Portuguese loanwords in Urdu. The Portuguese sources of the Urdu are given in italics. English glosses are given in parentheses. Note that some Urdu words may have more than one cognate in English, since most are derived from Latin.*

| | | | |
|---|---|---|---|
| ۱- *padre* | ← | پادری | (priest) |
| ۲- *másto* | ← | مَستُول | (mast) |
| ۳- *pistola* | ← | پستول | (towel) |
| ۴- *pipa* | ← | پیپا | (cask) |
| ۵- *chave* | ← | چابی | (key) |
| ۶- *caju* | ← | کاجو | (cashew) |
| ۷- *cámara* | ← | کمرا | (room) |
| ۸- *igreja* | ← | گرجا | (church) |
| ۹- *sabonete* | ← | صابن | (soap) |

| | | | | | |
|---|---|---|---|---|---|
| a. soap | b. clavier | c. ecclesial | d. camera | e. pistol | f. clavicle |
| g. father | h. chamber | i. pipe | j. spade | k. cashew | l. mast |

*C. See if you can guess the English cognate(s) of the following Urdu words borrowed from Portuguese. English glosses of the Urdu are given in parentheses.*

| | | | |
|---|---|---|---|
| ۱- *mestre* | ← | مستری | (mechanic, tradesman) |
| ۲- *carraguem* | ← | کرانچی | (cart) |

## 1.4 English-Urdu Cognates—Arabic

English and Urdu borrow and derive a great deal of vocabulary from Arabic, though often through different traditions. Urdu takes many Arabic terms either directly from Arabic or via Persian, while English borrows much of its Arabic vocabulary directly or indirectly from post-classical Latin. A large number of scientific terms were borrowed from Arabic through Latin into English. Urdu borrows these terms, too, often through Persian.

| English | | Urdu | | Arabic |
|---|---|---|---|---|
| alchemy | (chemistry) | کیمیا | ← | الكيميا |
| elixir | (the philosopher's stone) | الاِکسیر | ← | اِکسیر |
| algebra | (arithmetic) | جبر ومقابلہ | ← | الجبر |
| zero, cypher | (zero) | صِفر | ← | صِفر |

| | | | | |
|---|---|---|---|---|
| zenith, azimuth | (direction) | سمت راس | ← | سمت الراس |
| nadir | (likeness, opposite; parallel) | نظیر | ← | نظیر السمت |

The first three examples in English retain the Arabic definite article ال [al-] (the), which is seldom retained in borrowings in Urdu. This article is retained in various forms in English.

| English | | Urdu | | | Arabic |
|---|---|---|---|---|---|
| alcove | (dome) | قُبّہ | ← | (dome) | القبة |
| lute | (wood) | عود | ← | (oud) | العود |
| alcazar | (fortress) | قصر | ← | (fortress) | القصر |

Multiple English words are derived from the following Arabic word, which is commonly used in Urdu:

| English | | Urdu | | | Arabic |
|---|---|---|---|---|---|
| emir, emirate, amir, admiral | (wealthy, ruler) | امیر | ← | (ruler) | امیر |

The *-al* ending of the English word "admiral" is the Arabic definite article ال (the) and reflects a shortening of a longer Arabic phrase امیر الامرا [*amīr ul-umarā*] (amir of the amirs). This explains why the spelling and pronunciation of this word has varied in English over time, from amiral to admirail, and, most recently, admiral.

Other terms reflect the long history of contact, through trade, between speakers and users of Arabic and those of European languages. The Arabic word shown here, the aptly named city of Mosul (lit. site of contact), is related to a set of Urdu words built on the same root وصل (to join). English borrows it as the name of cloth associated with the city. And it also borrows it as the place name, of course.

| English | Urdu | | | Arabic |
|---|---|---|---|---|
| Mosul, muslin | موصِل / وصل / وصال | ← | (Mosul) | موصل |

## A Cautionary Note on the Myth of Origins

Keep in mind that although words are said to be traceable to an etymon, this does not mean that the etymon itself is not borrowed from, or derived from still other etymons. For example, although it is said that the etymon of the following English and Urdu cognates (both of which are equally rare and technical words) is the Arabic word خولنجان, which is said to have been borrowed from Persian. According to the *Oxford English Dictionary*, the Persian word most probably comes from a Chinese word meaning ginger from either Ko in Canton or Gaoling.

| English | Urdu | | Arabic |
|---|---|---|---|
| galangal | خولنجان | ← | خولنجان |

Likewise, the spelling of the Urdu word for Constantinople, the now archaic name for the city of Istanbul, marks it as an Arabic word, but, of course, Arabic borrowed it from the Greek or Latin.

| English | Urdu |
|---|---|
| Constantinople | قسطنطنیہ |

*A. Match the Urdu and English cognates from Arabic. Use a dictionary with etymological information to facilitate recognition of the semantic and orthographic relationship between the Urdu and the English.*

| | | | | |
|---|---|---|---|---|
| tariff | ا | ____ | (sugar) | ۱۔ شکر |
| sequin | ب | ____ | (treasury, storehouse) | ۲۔ مخزن |
| gazelle | پ | ____ | (travel) | ۳۔ سفر |
| ghoul | ت | ____ | (praise, definition, name) | ۴۔ تعریف |
| magazine | ٹ | ____ | (coin) | ۵۔ سِکّہ |
| hakim | ث | ____ | (jinn) جن (jinn) | ۶۔ جنّی |
| tare | ج | ____ | (deer, fawn) | ۷۔ غزال |
| sugar, saccharine | چ | ____ | (demon) | ۸۔ غول |
| genie | ح | ____ | (physician) | ۹۔ حکیم |
| safari | خ | ____ | (foundation, manner) | ۱۰۔ طرح |

The following commonly used chess term has been in use in English since the fourteenth century. Note that the Arabic etymon includes both an Arabic [مات related to موت meaning death] and a Persian [شاہ meaning king] element:

| English | | Urdu | Arabic |
|---|---|---|---|
| checkmate | شاہ مات | ← | (the king is dead) شاہ مات |

The following Arabic term is the source of an Italian word through which the English borrows it:

| | | English | Arabic |
|---|---|---|---|
| arsenal | ← | (lit. house of manufacture) | دار الصناعۃ |

A large number of Urdu words include or are related to both the words that you see in this Arabic compound. Here are some examples:

دار [realm, house]

| | | |
|---|---|---|
| ← | دار الشفا | (hospital; lit. "house of healing") |
| ← | دار الحکومت | (capital city; lit. "seat of government") |

صناعت [industry, craft, trade]

| | | |
|---|---|---|
| ← | مصنوعی | (artificial) |
| ← | صنائع بدائع | (poetical devices) |

Students of the history of science will be interested to know that a large number of English terms related to mathematics, physics, biology, chemistry, and other branches of learning were borrowed and adapted from Arabic into Latin. For example, the English word "algorithm" is borrowed from a Latinization of the name of the influential mathematician محمد بن موسیٰ الخوارزمی Muḥammad bin Mūsā al-Ḳhvārizmī (d. ca. 847). The name al-Ḳhvārizmī refers to the region of Khvārizm (Khwarazm) in Central Asia. The name for the science entered English in the seventeenth century via Latin, in which it had been used (with various spellings) in the sense of numerical notation since at least the thirteenth century.

الخوارزمی ← algorithm

This history of borrowing explains why English retains a large number of Latinate spellings of Arabic names.

*B. Match the Arabic-language philosophers with their Latinized equivalents.*

| | | | |
|---|---|---|---|
| ۱۔ ابن سینا | ____ | ا | Avempace |
| ۲۔ ابن رشد | ____ | ب | Avicenna |
| ۳۔ ابن باجہ | ____ | پ | Averroes |
| ۴۔ الفارابی | ____ | ت | Razes |
| ۵۔ الرازی | ____ | ٹ | Algazel |
| ۶۔ الکندی | ____ | ث | Alkindus |
| ۷۔ الغزالی | ____ | ج | Alpharabius |

English-language scholars began to abandon these Latinized forms in the twentieth century, preferring instead to use transliterations closer to the Arabic. Write the name of the corresponding Arabic (Urdu) name from the list above. Note that names beginning with Ibn (son of) in Arabic are pronounced "ibn-e," with the Persian *iẓāfat* [-e], in Urdu (hence, Ibn-e Rushd). The Arabic spellings are given here, since they are typically used in English.

| | | | |
|---|---|---|---|
| 1. Ibn Rushd | 2. al-Ghazali | 3. al-Razi | 4. Ibn Bajja |
| 5. al-Farabi | 6. al-Kindi | 7. Ibn Sina | |

## Astral Terminology

Students familiar with the language of astronomy, astrology, and subjects related to the astral sciences will be interested to know that both English and Urdu borrow the names of many stars from Arabic. For example, the name of the giant star Aldebaran, which is among the brightest in the sky, is derived from the Arabic الدبران (the follower). This word, with its triliteral root د ب ر (following, turning one's back; elapsing, passing, going by) is related to the following Urdu words, all of which contain the same three root letters in the same order:

| | |
|---|---|
| (defection, retreat; misfortune) | اِدبار |
| (counsel; strategy; remedy) | تدبیر |
| (the backside, buttocks) | دُبُر |
| (the west wind, zephyr) | دَبُور |
| (counselor; prudent) | مُدَبِّر |
| (one who retreats; retiring) | مُدبِر |

*C. The following exercise reviews many of the Arabic names for stars and their English forms. It lists only those Arabic astral names which are also commonly-used Urdu words. The relevant meaning of the Arabic word has been given in parentheses. The most common Urdu meaning has also been given when it differs from the Arabic.*

| | | | | |
|---|---|---|---|---|
| Izar | ا | ____ | (eye) | ۱۔ عین |
| Alphard | ب | ____ | (weight) | ۲۔ وزن |
| Muphrid | پ | ____ | (middle [of the sky]) | ۳۔ وسط (السماء) |
| Wezen | ت | ____ | (falling, occurring) | ۴۔ واقع |
| Wasat | ٹ | ____ | (sword) | ۵۔ سیف |
| Ain | ث | ____ | (solitary) | ۶۔ مفرد |
| Vega | ج | ____ | (girdle, trousers) | ۷۔ ازار |
| Alnilam | چ | ____ | (the string; U: نظام [system]) | ۸۔ النظام |
| Saiph | ح | ____ | (chair, stool) | ۹۔ کُرسی |
| Cursa | خ | ____ | (the lone one; U: فرد [individual]) | ۱۰۔ الفرد |

## Islamic Terminology

Both English and Urdu borrow technical terms related to Islam from Arabic. The most obvious example is the word "Islam" itself:

| English | Urdu | | Arabic |
|---|---|---|---|
| Islam | اسلام | ← | اسلام |

*D. Match the English and Urdu loanwords from Arabic that are closely tied to the Islamic tradition.*

| | | | |
|---|---|---|---|
| houri | ا | ____ | ۱۔ عید |
| hadith | ب | ____ | ۲۔ فتویٰ |
| hajj | پ | ____ | ۳۔ حور |
| Ramadan | ت | ____ | ۴۔ مسلم |
| zakat | ٹ | ____ | ۵۔ قرآن |
| Quran | ث | ____ | ۶۔ رمضان |
| Kaaba | ج | ____ | ۷۔ زکات |
| Muslim | چ | ____ | ۸۔ حدیث |
| fatwa | ح | ____ | ۹۔ حج |
| Eid | خ | ____ | ۱۰۔ کعبہ |

## Spanish Names

A considerable number of Arabic words that have been borrowed into Urdu are familiar to English speakers as proper names of places in Spanish.

One of the most ubiquitous examples is the Spanish *guad-*, derived from the Arabic وادی [valley; river], which appears at the beginning of a large number of Spanish place names. Many of these names were originally the names of places in Andalusia and later brought to the Spanish colonies.

| | | Spanish/English | Arabic |
|---|---|---|---|
| Guadalajara | ← | (valley of stone) | وادی الحجارة |
| | | | Urdu |
| | | (valley) | وادی |
| | | (stone) | حجر |

The largest river in Spain likewise takes its name from the same source:

| Spanish/English | | | Arabic |
|---|---|---|---|
| Guadalquivir | ← | (the great valley) | الوادی الکبیر |

| | Urdu |
|---|---|
| (valley) | وادی |
| (large, great) | کبیر |

It is not surprising that the following Spanish/English term derives from Arabic, since it is located between the Iberian Peninsula and Morocco.

| Spanish/English | | | Arabic |
|---|---|---|---|
| Gibraltar | ← | (Mountain of Tariq) | جبل طارق |

| | Urdu |
|---|---|
| (mountain) | جبل |
| (a proper name; lit. "morning star") | طارق |

The common personal name طارق (striker; night-time visitor; morning star), which is related to the verbal root طرق (to beat) is itself related to a number of Urdu words:

| | | |
|---|---|---|
| ("the beaten path"; way, method; road) | طریقہ | طریق |

The following name of a famous Spanish knight is also derived from Arabic:

| Spanish/English | | | | Arabic |
|---|---|---|---|---|
| El Cid | ← | (the lord) | [al-sayyid] | السید |

| | Urdu |
|---|---|
| (honorific title identifying descendants of the Prophet) | سید |

The following is a contested etymology, but one that is considered plausible nonetheless:

| English | | Spanish | | | Arabic |
|---|---|---|---|---|---|
| California | ← | … | ← | (caliph) | خلیفہ |

In Urdu, the word خلیفہ (whence the English word caliphate) means a successor, for example, in a hereditary lineage of master teachers or artists.

## Arabic, Hebrew, and Amharic

Since Arabic and Hebrew are cousins within the family of Semitic languages, it is not surprising to find that many English words borrowed from Hebrew (either directly or indirectly through Yiddish) are cognate with Arabic words that often have similar meanings.

An especially good example of this is the word "menorah," whose Arabic cousin is the etymon of the English minaret and the Urdu منار / منارہ.

| | Urdu | English | Arabic | Anglicized Hebrew |
|---|---|---|---|---|
| (minaret) | منارہ | minaret | منارة | menorah |

Another good example is the word "Yom" in the name of the Jewish holiday Yom Kippur, which is cognate with the Arabic يوم [day], which Urdu borrows in a number of phrases.

| | Urdu | | | Arabic | | Anglicized Hebrew |
|---|---|---|---|---|---|---|
| (Independence Day) | یومِ آزادی | ← | (day) | يَوم | (day of atonement) | **Yom** Kippur |

Fewer English words have been borrowed from Amharic, which is another cousin, but it, too, provides interesting points for comparison. The following Hebrew and Amharic words borrowed into English contain an element that is cognate with the Arabic word from which the Urdu word and its relatives are derived.

| | Urdu | | Arabic | Anglicized Amharic | Anglicized Hebrew |
|---|---|---|---|---|---|
| (head / headman) | راس / رئیس | (head) | رَأس | **Ras**tafari | **Rosh** Hashanah |

Incidentally, the Hebrew term contains another word, anglicized as *shanah* (year), which has Arabic and Urdu cousins.

| | Urdu | | Arabic | Anglicized Hebrew |
|---|---|---|---|---|
| (year) | سن / سَنَت | (year) | سَنَة | Rosh Ha**shanah** |

Other examples remind us that English is tied to Hebrew and Arabic through religious connections, too. The word "Babel," as well as its relative "Babylon," (lit. the gate of god), for example, can be traced to an Akkadian word comprising two parts, both of which are cognate with Hebrew, Arabic, and Urdu words:

| | Arabic and Urdu | | | | (from Akkadian) |
|---|---|---|---|---|---|
| (god) | الله | (gate) | باب | (the gate of god) | Babylon |

The second component of Babel, el/lah/ilah, appears again in the following Hebrew word, which is cognate with the Arabic and Urdu. The Hebrew is in fact a plural term, which is used in the singular.

| | Arabic and Urdu | | | | Anglicized Hebrew |
|---|---|---|---|---|---|
| (God) | اللہ | (god) | الٰہ | (god[s]) | Elohim |

Another example is the name of the city Bethlehem (Hebrew: house [*beth*] of bread [*lehem*]). The first element, Beth (house) is unsurprisingly found in the names of Jewish temples. It is also found in proper names, such as Bethesda and Bethany. In Urdu, its cognate بیت most commonly refers to an internal couplet in a poem, though it may also refer to a house in proper names. The second element لحم means meat or flesh in Arabic and the same in Urdu, though in Urdu it is typically only used in specialized contexts.

| | | Arabic and Urdu | | |
|---|---|---|---|---|
| (meat) | لحم | (house) | بیت | Bethlehem |

There are other common pairs, too, that reflect the close relationship of Hebrew and Arabic, and the consequent connections between both languages and Urdu. The first of the pairs below both mean "son." The pair of Arabic words ابن / بن are regularly used in Arabic personal names. In Urdu, the first of the pair, ابن [ibn], is always used when it is the first word in a name and may be used in the middle of names, and is always used with the Persian by iẓāfat; thus, the pen name adopted by the famous Urdu writer of detective fiction, Ibn-e Ṣafī (lit. "Son of Ṣafī). In Arabic, the second, بن [bin], is used when it appears between two names. Hence, رستم بن زال [Rustam bin Zāl], the Arabicized name of the hero of the Persian *Shāhnāmah* (book of kings) and a regular presence in Urdu literature and culture, from the marṡiyah poetry of Mīr Anīs and the Dāstān-e Amīr Hamzah to the title of wrestling champions in India and Pakistan (Rustam-e Hind; Rustam-e Pakistan).

| Arabic and Urdu | | Anglicized Hebrew | |
|---|---|---|---|
| (son) | ابن / بن | (son) | Ben |
| (lord) | ربّ | (lit. my lord) | rabbi |

The connection between Arabic and Hebrew (and through them English and Hebrew) is made clearer by the following Arabic phrase, which is often affixed to the front of homes in South Asia. Compare the final ربّی (my lord) with the Hebrew rabbi (lit. my lord):

| | |
|---|---|
| (this by the grace of **my lord**) | ہذا من فضل ربی |

As a final example of the shared histories of English and Urdu as seen through the shared histories of Hebrew and Arabic, consider the second element in the following. There is a handful of related Urdu words, but I list only two here.

| | | Arabic and Urdu | | | Anglicized Hebrew |
|---|---|---|---|---|---|
| (excellent; a tree in paradise) | طوبیٰ | (good) | طَیّب | (congratulations) | mazel**tov** |

The following word, borrowed through Yiddish, is probably derived from a Hebrew word meaning "to hear," which is itself related to a number of Urdu words through Arabic.

| | | Arabic and Urdu | | Yiddish |
|---|---|---|---|---|
| (listeners) | سامعین | (hearing) | سماعت | schmooze |

A more obvious parallel is found in the following:

| | Arabic and Urdu | | Anglicized Hebrew |
|---|---|---|---|
| (peace be upon you) | السلام علیکم | (peace [be upon you]) | shalom (aleichem) |

These examples are only those which are found in English. Since Arabic and Hebrew are cousins, they contain a substantial number of cognates. Pairs such as کلب (dog) and the Hebrew *kelev* (dog); کَبِیر (great) and *kabbir* (great) are just the tip of the iceberg.

## Divergent Paths, Winding Roads

Just as Urdu borrows a great deal of its Arabic terminology through Persian, English borrows much of its Arabic vocabulary indirectly, typically by way of French or medieval Latin. Despite passing through different linguistic traditions at different times, many cognates retain similar if not identical senses.

| English (via French ambre) | Urdu (via Persian?) | | Arabic |
|---|---|---|---|
| amber | عنبر | ← | عنبر |

| English (via Portuguese tufão) | Urdu (via Persian?) | | Arabic (perhaps from Greek) |
|---|---|---|---|
| typhoon | طوفان | ← | طوفان |

By contrast, some English-Urdu cognates of Arabic origin differ considerably in meaning, though context and history sometimes make the semantic relationship discernable. Consider the following example. Bear in mind that this etymology is contested.

| English (via Italian *maschera* [mask]) | | Urdu | | Arabic |
|---|---|---|---|---|
| mascara | (jester) | مَسخَرہ | ← | مسخرة |

The root of the Arabic word مسخرۃ means "to laugh, mock, or make fun." Urdu retains the sense of the Arabic. Philologists hypothesize that the English "mascara" is borrowed from the Italian word *maschera* (a jester's mask). (Incidentally, the word "mask" itself, which derives from the Latin *masca* (witch, specter), is also believed to relate to the Arabic مسخرہ.)

For another example, consider the following. Note that the Urdu word is rare.

| English (via Italian *materasso*) | | Urdu | | Arabic |
|---|---|---|---|---|
| mattress | (place of deposit) | مَطرَح | ← | مطرح |

Because English borrows terms at different times, through multiple languages, and from different traditions, in some cases multiple English words are derived from a single Arabic root. For example:

| English | Urdu | | Arabic |
|---|---|---|---|
| cipher, zero | (zero) صِفر | ← | (zero) صِفر |

The following English cognates and their Arabic etymon are said to derive from the Sanskrit word कृमिज *kṛimi-ja* (born of a worm). It refers to a red scale insect used as a source of red dye.

| English | Urdu | | Arabic |
|---|---|---|---|
| crimson, carmine, kermes | (a red insect) قرمز | ← | قِرمِز |

The Arabic root شَرِب (to drink) is the source of numerous English and Urdu cognates.

| English | Urdu | | | Arabic |
|---|---|---|---|---|
| syrup (via Turkish) | (wine) | شراب | ← | (to drink) شرب |
| sherbet, sorbet (via Persian or Turkish) | (sherbet, punch) | شربت | ← | |
| shrub (a kind of cocktail) | (drinking) | شُرب | ← | |

*E. Practice recognizing cognates. Read the following Urdu words borrowed or derived from Arabic aloud. Then guess their English cognates.*

| | | | | |
|---|---|---|---|---|
| ۱۔ کباب | ۲۔ حُقّہ | ۳۔ قِسمت | ۴۔ مدرسہ | ۵۔ زَعفران |
| ۶۔ وزیر | ۷۔ شیخ | ۸۔ تعریف | ۹۔ حَرَم | ۱۰۔ سُلطان |

*F. The relationship between some English-Urdu cognates of Arabic origin is not intuitive. Here follows a matching exercise comprising words whose relationship may not appear obvious at first. Look up the English words in a dictionary such as the* New Oxford American Dictionary *or the* Oxford English Dictionary *to learn more about their histories. English glosses of the Urdu words whose meanings are not close to their English relatives are given in parentheses. Note that the etymology of some words is contested or uncertain.*

| | | | |
|---|---|---|---|
| carat | ا | ___ | ۱۔ قالب (cast, mold) |
| safflower | ب | ___ | ۲۔ موسم (season) |
| lute, oud | پ | ___ | ۳۔ قبّہ (niche, vault) |
| coffee | ت | ___ | ۴۔ عود (a type of wood) |
| caliph | ٹ | ___ | ۵۔ قیراط |
| caliber | ث | ___ | ۶۔ اصفر (yellow) |
| alcove | ج | ___ | ۷۔ غربال (sieve) |
| garble | چ | ___ | ۸۔ خلیفہ |
| monsoon | ح | ___ | ۹۔ قہوہ |

*G. Match the Urdu and English cognates borrowed from Arabic.*

| | | | |
|---|---|---|---|
| hakim | ا | ___ | ۱۔ مِنار / مینار |
| camphor | ب | ___ | ۲۔ ترجمان |
| muezzin | پ | ___ | ۳۔ قاضی |
| (El) Cid | ت | ___ | ۴۔ جرّہ |
| jar | ٹ | ___ | ۵۔ کافور |
| minaret | ث | ___ | ۶۔ حکیم |
| cadi | ج | ___ | ۷۔ سید |
| dragoman | چ | ___ | ۸۔ مؤذن |

## 1.5 English-Urdu Cognates—Persian

Both English and Urdu have long histories of borrowing from Persian. The following word first appeared in written Urdu and English around the same time (c. 1600).

| English | Urdu | | Persian |
|---|---|---|---|
| caravan | کاروان | ← | کاروان |

The Persian word literally means "moving (روان) work (کار)."

The related English word "caravansary" is built of two words with cognates in Urdu:

| | | | |
|---|---|---|---|
| (serai; traveler's lodge) | سرائے | (caravan) | کاروان |

The word سرائے offers an especially interesting opportunity to explore the complex, rich histories of linguistic borrowing in Urdu and English. English borrowed the word in "seraglio" from Italian, which had itself borrowed it from Turkish. سرائے is also the etymon of the first part of the English name for the city of Sarajevo, which is borrowed from the Turkish. English also borrowed the word "serai" from Turkish, which had borrowed it from Persian. Thus the word appears in three forms in English, each of which is borrowed from a different linguistic tradition at a different time:

| English | Urdu | | Persian |
|---|---|---|---|
| seraglio, Sarajevo, serai | سرائے | ← | سرائے |

English also borrows the following word from Turkish, which had borrowed it from Persian. Urdu likewise borrows it from Persian. The Persian word is itself derived from Proto-Indo-European and therefore has a cognate cousin in Sanskrit.

| English (via Turkish) | Urdu | | Persian |
|---|---|---|---|
| jackal | شغال | ← | شغال |

The following words, though Persian in origin, were borrowed into English via Urdu:

| English | | Urdu | | Persian |
|---|---|---|---|---|
| baft (a kind of course fabric) | ← | (texture; tissue; vein) بافت | ← | (woven) بافت |
| pyjamas, pajamas | ← | پاجامہ | ← | پا جامہ |

The second example is a helpful word to remember, since it contains two Persian words پا (foot, leg) and جامہ (clothing), both of which frequently occur in Persianate Urdu vocabulary.

The following word traveled from Persian through Turkish to Italian before being borrowed into English. Urdu borrowed it directly from Persian. According to lexicographers, it first appeared in written English in the fourteenth century. It seems to have appeared in written Urdu in the fifteenth:

| English | Urdu | | Persian |
|---|---|---|---|
| bazaar | بازار | ← | بازار |

The etymologies of many borrowings from Persian are well documented, but some are not. For example, the following English word is believed to come from the Persian etymon of the Urdu, but the etymology is uncertain:

| English | Urdu | | Persian |
|---|---|---|---|
| calabash | خربوزہ | ← | خربوزہ |

Philology is an inexact science involving some amount of estimation and guesswork. The etymologies of words are often contested and philologists' theories as to their origins frequently change. For example, the English word "pagoda," which entered English via Portuguese, was once thought to derive from the Persian word بتکدہ (idol-house), but philologists now believe it to be derived from Tamil or Sanskrit.

Philological claims about the origins of a word can also be misleading. The following example, قند and "candy," nicely illustrates the complexities involved in identifying the origins of a word. The English word is borrowed from Arabic via French, but the Arabic is ultimately borrowed from a Persian word whose origins lie in Proto-Indo-European. The Persian word is therefore cognate with a Sanskrit word related to the Urdu word کھنڈ (piece, part). This means that the Prakritic-Sanskrit کھنڈ and Perso-Arabic قند are related.

| English | | French | | Arabic |
|---|---|---|---|---|
| candy | ← | sucre candi | ← | قند |

| Urdu | | Persian |
|---|---|---|
| (a type of sweet; sugarcane syrup) قندی (sugar) قند | ← | قند |

| Urdu | Sanskrit | Proto-Indo-European |
|---|---|---|
| کھنڈ | کھنڈ | ← |

*A. Match the Urdu and English cognates of Persian origin. Look up the Urdu words in a dictionary and note any meanings that differ from the English.*

| | | | |
|---|---|---|---|
| scimitar | ا | ____ | ۱۔ فرنگ |
| dervish | ب | ____ | ۲۔ کوشک |

| English | | | Urdu |
|---|---|---|---|
| kiosk | پ | ____ | ۳۔ مشک |
| cummerbund | ت | ____ | ۴۔ تاج |
| taj | ٹ | ____ | ۵۔ کمر بند |
| chinar | ث | ____ | ۶۔ چادر |
| carboy | ج | ____ | ۷۔ درویش |
| Frank, French, (linga) franca | چ | ____ | ۸۔ چنار |
| musk | ح | ____ | ۹۔ شمشیر |
| chador | خ | ____ | ۱۰۔ قرابہ |

The semantic relationship between many English words and their Persian etymons is often quite fascinating. For example, the Persian word دُلبند is not only the etymon of the English word "turban," but also the etymon of the word "tulip" (the flower so named for its resemblance to the shape of the headdress). Both entered English through French from Turkish.

| English | Urdu | | Persian |
|---|---|---|---|
| tulip; turban | (turban) دُلبند | ← | دُلبند |

Just as Arabic and Persian gave شاہ مات to Urdu and "checkmate" to English, so too Persian gives Arabic another important term in chess, which is then borrowed into Urdu and English. Note the many meanings of the word in Urdu:

| English | Urdu | | Persian |
|---|---|---|---|
| rook | (face; direction; rook) رُخ | ← | رُخ |

The Urdu and English cognates derived from the Persian word گُلاب have fascinating etymologies and meanings. The word comprises two parts, گُل (rose) and آب (water), and, not surprisingly, means "rosewater" in Persian. It is believed that the word traveled from Persian into Arabic, then into medieval Latin to French, and finally into English as "julep." Urdu seems to have borrowed the word from Persian directly.

| English | Urdu | | Persian |
|---|---|---|---|
| julep | (rose , rosewater) گلاب | ← | (rosewater) گلاب |

The following Persian phrase is a common Urdu idiom and has a specialized meaning in English:

| English | Urdu | | Persian |
|---|---|---|---|
| seersucker | (idiom. blended; intimate) شیر و شکر | ← | (lit. milk and sugar) شِیر و شَکَر |

The English word marzipan may come from the word مرتبان, which is also the source of the English the name of an earthen jar characteristic of the city of Martaban (Mottama today). Philologists do not know if مرتبان is an Arabic or Persian word.

| English | | Urdu | | Persian (?) |
|---|---|---|---|---|
| marzipan, Martaban | (jar) | مرتبان | ← | مرتبان / مرطبان |

The English word "orange" and its Urdu cognates نارنگ and نارنج properly belong in a section on English and Urdu cognates ultimately derived from Dravidian languages. But since the English word is borrowed from Persian via Arabic and the Urdu words are borrowed from Persian, it is not inappropriate to include them here. The Persian and Urdu انار (pomegranate), which is cognate with نارنگ etc. are also listed here.

| Urdu | | Persian |
|---|---|---|
| (orange) نارنگ / نارنج | ← | نارنگ |
| (pomegranate) انار | ← | انار |

| English (via French) | | Arabic | | Persian |
|---|---|---|---|---|
| orange | ← | نارنج | ← | نارنگ |

*B. Match the following English and Urdu cognates. Then look up the English words in an etymological dictionary to learn more about their fascinating and complicated histories.*

| | | | |
|---|---|---|---|
| diwan/dewan | ا | ____ | ۱۔ یاسمین |
| jasmine | ب | ____ | ۲۔ دیوان |
| borax | پ | ____ | ۳۔ لاجورد |
| lazuli, azure | ت | ____ | ۴۔ بورق |

The *Oxford English Dictionary* asks us to compare the etymon of jasmine and یاسمین with Greek vocabulary found in the writings of the first-century physician Dioscorides, whose work influenced discussions of medicine and healing in Latin and Arabic. In the next section, we shall examine the shared and divergent histories of borrowing from Latin and Greek traditions into English and Urdu.

## 1.6 English-Urdu Cognates—Latin and Greek

Both English and Urdu inherit long legacies of engagement with classical Greek and Latin thought. Indeed, the post-classical Latin tradition through which most English writers have engaged the classical world was itself mediated by the Arabic and Persian traditions of engagement with Greek and Latin, and it is from these Arabic and Persian traditions that Urdu inherits much of its philosophical, medical, astronomical, and other scientific vocabulary. This is often overlooked by scholars who neglect the significant role that Arabic intellectual culture played in animating European interest in classical thought during the Renaissance.

Greek philosophy provides an excellent example of the shared history of English and Urdu. Urdu inherits a great deal of Greek vocabulary related to philosophy and medicine from Arabic and Persian. English inherits most of its Greek vocabulary through Latin (some of which Latin is borrowed from Arabic) and Latinate languages like French.

Read the following pairs of names of figures from Greek antiquity as they are used in Urdu and English.

| | |
|---|---|
| Plato | اَفلاطون |
| Socrates | سُقراط |
| Aristotle | اَرَسطو |
| Alexander | سِکَندَر |

*A. Match the English and Urdu names of classical Greek scientists, philosophers, and statesmen.*

| | | | |
|---|---|---|---|
| Hippocrates | ا | ____ | ۱۔ جالینوس |
| Euclid | ب | ____ | ۲۔ دقیانوس |
| Galen | پ | ____ | ۳۔ بقراط |
| Pythagorus | ت | ____ | ۴۔ دیموقراطیس |
| Archimedes | ٹ | ____ | ۵۔ اقلیدس |
| Ptolemy | ث | ____ | ۶۔ فیثاغورس / فیثاغورث |
| Decius | ج | ____ | ۷۔ بطلیموس |
| Democritus | چ | ____ | ۸۔ ارشمیدس |

The names of some classical figures carry idiomatic meanings in Urdu. For example:

| | | | |
|---|---|---|---|
| (stubbornness; arrogance; ostentation) | افلاطونی | ← | افلاطون |
| (an arrogant, pretentious, or domineering person) | اَفلاطُون کا بچّہ | | |
| (an arrogant, pretentious, or domineering person) | افلاطون کا سالا | | |
| (fortunate) | مقدر کا سکندر | ← | سکندر |
| (fortunate) | سکندر نصیب | | |

(fortunate; formidable) سکندر صَولَت

(brave) سکندر نژاد

(fortunate) سکندر طالع

(old-fashioned, conservative; antiquated) دقیانوسی ← دَقیانُوس

*B. The following matching exercise reviews many of the Greek and Latin cognates found in Urdu and English. Match the English and Urdu, then look up the Urdu words in a dictionary to learn more about their meanings and uses.*

| | | | |
|---|---|---|---|
| ecclesial | ا | ____ | ۱۔ فِردَوس |
| mile | ب | ____ | ۲۔ پِستَہ |
| ocean | پ | ____ | ۳۔ کِلیسیا |
| music | ت | ____ | ۴۔ فَلسَفہ |
| carat | ٹ | ____ | ۵۔ قانون (law) |
| paradise | ث | ____ | ۶۔ قِرطاس (paper) |
| marble | ج | ____ | ۷۔ دُلفِین |
| climate, clime | چ | ____ | ۸۔ قَلَمون |
| dolphin | ح | ____ | ۹۔ طِلِسم |
| philosophy | خ | ____ | ۱۰۔ قِیراط |
| pistachio | د | ____ | ۱۱۔ قَیصَر |
| canon | ذ | ____ | ۱۲۔ قامُوس |
| evangelical, Evangel (the Gospel) | ڈ | ____ | ۱۳۔ اِنجِیل |
| stable | ر | ____ | ۱۴۔ اِسطبل، اصطبل |
| caesar / kaiser | ز | ____ | ۱۵۔ اِقلِیم |
| talisman | ڑ | ____ | ۱۶۔ موسیقی |
| naphtha | ژ | ____ | ۱۷۔ مَرمَر |
| chameleon | س | ____ | ۱۸۔ نَفت |
| chart | ش | ____ | ۱۹۔ مِیل |

## Vocabulary from Greek Physiology and Medicine

The etymology of the name given to the Greek medicinal traditions in Urdu (یونانی طب) hints at the composite and hybrid history of the tradition. The word یونانی [yūnānī] (Greek) derives from the Greek and is cognate with the English word "Ionian," while the word طب [ṭibb] (medicine) comes from Arabic, and is the root of a cluster of Urdu words related to medicine and medicinal practice. Greek medicine remains a vibrant and popular aspect of discourses about health and healing in Urdu (and in South Asia general), in which it coexists with, interacts with, and complements allopathic and Ayurvedic traditions.

*C. Match the Urdu and English cognates related to physiology.*

| | | | |
|---|---|---|---|
| chyle | ا | ____ | ۱۔ قَوَلَنج |
| melancholy | ب | ____ | ۲۔ تِریاق |
| chyme | پ | ____ | ۳۔ کَیلُوس |
| basilic (vein) | ت | ____ | ۴۔ باسَلِیق |
| cephalic (vein) | ٹ | ____ | ۵۔ کَیمُوس |
| theriac | ث | ____ | ۶۔ قِیفال |
| colic, colon | ج | ____ | ۷۔ ماخُولیا |

One of the ways in which Greek / یونانی medicine treats illness is by the use of herbs. It is not surprising, therefore, that Urdu and English share a large number of cognates related to botany and biology that derive from Greek.

*D. Match the following cognates, all of which share a common Greek ancestor.*

| | | | |
|---|---|---|---|
| cannabis | ا | ____ | ۱۔ لادن |
| squill | ب | ____ | ۲۔ لُبان (frankincense) |
| organ | پ | ____ | ۳۔ اِسقیل |
| scammony | ت | ____ | ۴۔ مصطگی |
| labdanum | ٹ | ____ | ۵۔ نَرگِس |
| agaric | ث | ____ | ۶۔ اغاریقون |
| euphorbium | ج | ____ | ۸۔ اِسفُنج |
| gentian | چ | ____ | ۹۔ قِنَّب |
| olibanum | ح | ____ | ۱۰۔ ارغنون |
| absynthium | خ | ____ | ۱۱۔ سقمونیہ |
| acacia | د | ____ | ۱۲۔ اَفسَنتِین |
| narcissus | ذ | ____ | ۱۳۔ جَنطیانا |
| mastic | ڈ | ____ | ۱۴۔ فَرِفیون |
| sponge | ر | ____ | ۱۵۔ اَقاقِیا |
| sagapenum | ز | ____ | ۱۶۔ سکبینج |

Keep in mind that یونانی / Greek terminology in Urdu, as in English, is technical and used chiefly by specialists and most such words are rare. For example, the Urdu cognate of the English word cumin, which is Semitic in origin, is found in Greek, Latin, Hebrew, and Arabic, but is not the commonly used word for cumin in Urdu.

| English | Urdu Arabic-Ionian term (technical) | Urdu (common) |
|---|---|---|
| cumin | کَمُّون | زیرہ |

English and Urdu also share a large number of cognates related to physics and metaphysics that come from Greek. The following word, which is central to Aristotle's philosophy, was borrowed into Arabic and entered Urdu through works in the Arabic rational sciences, such as logic.

hyle (matter) ← ہیّولی / ہیولا

*E. Match the cognates from Greek related to the physical sciences and philosophy.*

| | | | |
|---|---|---|---|
| astrolabe | ا | ____ | ۱۔ اِسطُقسِات |
| magnet | ب | ____ | ۲۔ انبِیق |
| ether | پ | ____ | ۳۔ جُغرافیہ |
| nous | ت | ____ | ۴۔ کیمیا |
| alembic | ٹ | ____ | ۵۔ فانوس (candle glass) |
| geography | ث | ____ | ۶۔ اسطرلاب |
| stoichiometry | ج | ____ | ۸۔ مِقناطِیس |
| pharos | چ | ____ | ۹۔ اثیر |
| chemistry | ح | ____ | ۱۰۔ نُس |

Although the words in this section have been grouped into the fields of medicine, physics, and philosophy for pedagogical purposes, it is important to keep in mind that such divisions among fields of learning are not necessarily reflected in the traditions themselves. The Greek medicinal / یونانی طب tradition in Urdu, for example, is a holistic one. For that reason, medical manuals in this tradition often draw from psychology, ethics, physics, and religious mysticism.

## 1.7 English-Urdu Cognates—Turkish

Both English and Urdu borrow vocabulary from Turkish. In the case of English, Turkish not only loaned its own vocabulary, but was also a means through which Latin borrowed a significant amount of vocabulary from Arabic and Persian. Turkish was also an important language at the Timurid and Ottoman courts, both of which played important role in the development of Persian literature and language. It also played an important role at the Mughal court. The founder of the Mughal Empire, Ẓahīr ud-Dīn Bābar (d. 1530), wrote his autobiography in Chaghatai Turkish. The Mughal statesman ʿAbd ur-Raḥīm Ḳhān-e Ḳhānān (d. 1627) wrote Chaghatai poetry. In the late-Mughal, early-colonial period, Inshā Allāh Ḳhān Inshā (d. 1818), who is chiefly known for his Urdu poetry, the first grammar in Urdu, *Daryā-e Laṭāfat*, and an early work of Modern Hindi romance, *Rānī Ketkī kī Kahānī*, also kept a diary in Chaghatai Turkish (later translated into Urdu and published as *Inshā kā Turkī Roznāmchah* [Inshā's Turkish diary]). The long history of Turkish in South Asia, and the long history of interaction between Turkish and Persian, helps to explain why a considerable number of Turkish words have been borrowed into Urdu.

The most outstanding example of an English-Urdu cognate of Turkish origin is the word "Urdu" itself, which is a Turkish word meaning "camp." According to one theory, the name of the Urdu language is a shortened form of a longer phrase, زبانِ اردوے معلّٰی [zabān-e Urdū-e muʿallā] (the language of the [royal] camp [surrounding the Red Fort in Delhi]), which was shortened to زبانِ اردو, meaning, "the language of (the) Urdu (royal camp)," and, finally shortened to "Urdu" following a Persian convention; for example, زبانِ فارسی (The Language of Persian) is shortened to فارسی (Persian). The word was borrowed into English in the sixteenth century as "horde," when it was associated with the Tartars.

| English | Urdu | | Turkish |
|---|---|---|---|
| horde | اردو | ← | اردو |

Turkish also played a role in the development of European languages and English spellings (and sometimes senses) hint at the fact that words of Persian origin entered English through Turkish and other Mediterranean languages. For example, the form of the word tulip in various European languages suggests that the Persian word دلبند was borrowed through the Turkish. Likewise, the spelling of jackal suggests that it was borrowed from the Turkish چقال rather than from its Persian cousin, شغال. Conversely, Urdu borrows it from Persian. Other examples of spellings suggestive of Turkish origins include kismet and minaret. English word meze or mezze (appetizer) is borrowed from Turkish (perhaps via Greek), but ultimately derives from the Persian word مزه (taste, flavor). Urdu borrows the word from Persian as مزه and retains its meanings.

| English | | Turkish | | Persian |
|---|---|---|---|---|
| meze or mezze | ← | مزه | ← | مزه |

| Urdu | | Persian |
|---|---|---|
| مزه | ← | مزه |

Another example is the name of a popular Greek dish. This time, the etymon is an Arabic word derived from the root سقی (to give water). Urdu borrows or derives a handful of words from the root.

| English | ← | Greek | ← | Turkish | ← | Arabic |
|---|---|---|---|---|---|---|
| moussaka | | | | | | (given water) مسقی |
| | | | | Urdu | ← | (to give water) سقی |
| | | (wine steward) ساقی | | (water-bearer) سقّا | | |
| | | | | (female wine steward) ساقن | | |

Another food name shows the complexities of relationships between English and Urdu:

| | | Urdu | | Arabic |
|---|---|---|---|---|
| | | (a bite of food, morsel, mouthful) لُقمہ | ← | (to bite) لقم |
| English | | Turkish | | |
| lokum (Turkish delight) | ← | (Turkish delight) لقم | ← | |
| Lokma (bite-sized fried dessert) | ← | لقمہ | | |

Another food-related borrowing is the following, which is used in Persian and Urdu to describe various dishes. In Turkish, it refers to cooked meat.

| English | Urdu | | Turkish |
|---|---|---|---|
| korma | قورمہ | ← | قاوُرمہ |

The first element in the following English and Urdu words is oda /اُتا, which means "room" in Turkish.

| English | Urdu | | Turkish |
|---|---|---|---|
| odalisque | (tutor) اتالیق | ← | (tutor, guardian) اتالیق |
| | (room) اتاق | ← | (room) اوطہ |

## Turkish Names and Titles

Many Turkish titles are found in the surnames of Urdu-speakers; for example, the title خان in the name of the nineteenth-century reformer سید احمد خان (Syed Ahmad Khan). Many are borrowed into Urdu through Persian. English also borrows words from Turkish names. "Ottoman" (as in the Ottoman dynasty, as well as the popular piece of furniture) is derived from the Arabic proper name عثمان (Uṡmān), from which the dynasty took its name.

ottoman/Ottoman ⟵ عثمان [Uṡmān]

*A. Match the Turkish titles as they are written in English and Urdu. (Note: ک is pronounced "ey" in some borrowings from Turkish.)*

| | | |
|---|---|---|
| ا۔ آغا | ____ | Khan ا |
| ۲۔ آفندی | ____ | Effendi ب |
| ۳۔ خان | ____ | Agha پ |
| ۴۔ پاشا | ____ | Bey, Beg ت |
| ۵۔ بک / بیگ | ____ | Pasha ٹ |

## 1.8 English-Urdu Cognates—Proto-Indo-European

Proto-Indo-European is the name that philologists and linguists give to a postulated yet historically unrecorded language from which Indo-European languages such as English, Latin, Persian, Sanskrit, and Urdu are said to derive.

The following words, which share an origin in Proto-Indo-European, exemplify the kinds of cognate relationships that exist among Urdu and English words:

| English | Urdu |
|---|---|
| can (to be able to) / know / cognize / gnosis / ignore | (to know) جاننا / (knowledge) گیان |

Note the layers of interrelationship and the parallel histories. Urdu borrows the word گیان from Sanskrit, just as English borrows "gnosis" from Latin. The Prakritic جاننا (to know), while related to گیان through their shared Proto-Indo-European root, is of a different register and carries a slightly different sense. In the same way, the English words "can" and "know," although related to the Latin *gnoscere* (to get to know) owing to their shared Proto-Indo-European root, are also of different registers and carry different senses and meanings. Compare with the Latinate "gnosis" (mystical knowledge) and "agnostic" (lit. not knowing). The verb "can" in English was once idiomatically used in the sense of "to know" or "to know how (to do something)." Indeed, the idiom "that I can of," meaning, "that I know of," was idiomatic in English as late as the nineteenth century. This sense is retained in its English relatives, including "canny," "uncanny," and "cunning."

Many English and Urdu words are cognate not only with each other, but also with words in other Indo-European languages such as Germanic languages, Latin (thence French, Italian, Spanish, etc.), Persian, and Sanskrit. For example, the Germanic English words "nave" and "navel," and their Latinate English relative "umbilical," all derive from Greek and are cognate with the Indic-Urdu نابھ (navel) and the Persianate-Urdu ناف (navel).

Another interesting example is the connection between the Proto-Indo-European root of the following English words and their Urdu cognates, some of which are listed here. The English words variously relate to English (yoke) and related English words borrowed from Greek (e.g. zygote) and Latin (e.g. juncture, conjugate), including ones borrowed through French (e.g. join, joint, rejoinder).

| | Urdu | English |
|---|---|---|
| (yoga) | یوگ / جوگ | yoke, **zyg**ote, join, **junc**ture, con**jug**ate |
| (yogi) | یوگی / جوگی | yoga, yogi (borrowed from Sanskrit) |
| (pair) | جگ | |
| (pair, duo) | جُگل | |
| (duet [in music]) | جگلبندی | |
| (to arrange) | جُگانا | |

Many Indo-European cognates in English and Urdu are easily recognized because they have retained similar meanings even with thousands of years of borrowing and use. Note that, in these sections, the Urdu words may have been borrowed from Persian, Prakrit, Sanskrit, or other Indo-European languages.

| English | | Urdu |
|---|---|---|
| lip | (lip) | لب |
| path | (path) | پتھ |
| new | (new) | نو |
| love | (desire; greed) | لوبھ |
| mouse | (mouse) | موش |
| thirst | (to yearn for) ترسنا (thirst) | تشنہ |
| father, paternal, padre | (father) | پدر / پتا |
| mother, maternal | (mother) | مادر / ماتا |
| daughter | (daughter) | دختر |
| brother | (brother) | برادر |

As in the examples above, the semantic connection between the following cognates is clear.

| English | | Urdu |
|---|---|---|
| deity, divine, demon, devil | (god; demon, monster) | دیوتا / دیو |

The semantic relationship between other Urdu and English cognates is less obvious. Consider the following. Note that these examples, like others in this section, demonstrate not only the relationship between English and Urdu, but also the relationship among Urdu and other Indo-European languages, such as Persian, Prakrit, and Sanskrit. In the first example, we see that the Sanskrit چھایا, its Prakritic descendants and derivatives چھاؤں and پرچھائیں, and its Persian cousin سایہ are all distant relatives of the English "shine" and its derivative "shimmer."

| English | | Urdu |
|---|---|---|
| shine, shimmer | (shadow, reflection) | چھایا / چھاؤں / پرچھائیں / سایہ |
| be | (the earth, land, site; to be) | بھومی / بھوم / بوم / ہونا |
| safe, save, salvage, salvation | (all, every) | سب / ہر |

The somewhat vague phonological and semantic relationship between safe, save, etc., and سب / ہر is clarified by comparing these terms with their Sanskrit cognate, सर्व [sarva] (all, every; whole, entire). The Latin and Middle French etymons of the English ("salvus" and "sauf," respectively) carry the sense of wholeness or completion, connoting intactness and thus the modern sense of "free from harm." This is one of many Sanskrit-Persian pairs in which we find the s-h variation; for example, compare Sanskrit सुनर [sunar(a)] (good man) and Persian ہنر [hunar] (excellence, skill). The phonetic variations between the Urdu سب and the Sanskrit sarv(a) are typical; we will discuss them in greater detail in the unit on Sanskrit and Prakrit. Although sunar is not an Urdu word, its elements, the prefix su- (good) and the noun nar (man) are found in everyday Urdu words; for example, سُناڑی (clever; a clever man) سُڈول (well-shaped, handsome) and نر ناری (males and females).

Study the following list of common Urdu verbs and their English cognates.

| English | | Urdu |
|---|---|---|
| thin | (to stretch, pull) | تننا / تاننا |
| cult | (to move) | چلنا |
| to rout (cry out) | (to cry) | رونا |
| was | (to settle, remain) | بسنا |

The Urdu word پڑوس (neighborhood) is built of two words with Proto-Indo-European roots. The first part of the word پڑ is related to the Sanskrit प्रति [prati-] (against), which is thought by some to be related to the Proto-Indo-European root from which the English "price," "precious," and "prize" are derived. The second element, is related to the Sanskrit root वस् [vas-] (to dwell, live; be, exist), from which comes the everyday Urdu verb بَسنا (to settle), and is cognate with the English word "was."

| English | | Urdu |
|---|---|---|
| price; was | (neighborhood) | پڑوس |

*A. Match the Urdu and English cognates whose roots lie in Proto-Indo-European. The meanings of Urdu words whose semantic relationship to the English is not immediately apparent have been given in parentheses.*

| | | | |
|---|---|---|---|
| me | ا | ____ | ۱۔ کاو (digging) |
| ask | ب | ____ | ۲۔ نیل (indigo) نیلا (blue) |
| reign, regal | پ | ____ | ۳۔ مے (wine) مدھو (honey) |
| lilac | ت | ____ | ۴۔ اِچھّا (desire) |
| decimal | ٹ | ____ | ۵۔ دانت |
| mead | ث | ____ | ۶۔ راج / راجا |
| dental, tooth | ج | ____ | ۸۔ دس |
| comma | چ | ____ | ۹۔ انتر (difference) |
| other | ح | ____ | ۱۰۔ میں |

Because Old Persian and Sanskrit are closely related, many Persian words in Urdu resemble their Sanskrit relatives. For this reason, Sanskrit is an effective third point of comparison that helps to illuminate the phonetic and semantic connections between and among English and Urdu cognates.

| English | Urdu (from Persian) | Sanskrit |
|---|---|---|
| long | دراز | (to stretch) drāgh |

The following is another good example of the many words descendent from a single root in Proto-Indo-European are found in Urdu and English. Once again, Sanskrit provides a useful point for comparison

| English | | Urdu | | Sanskrit |
|---|---|---|---|---|
| voice | (sound) | آواز | (a word, sound) | vāch (from vach) |
| | (sound) | بانگ | | |
| | (to prattle) | بکنا | | |

Here are a few more examples of the way the relationshiops between Urdu and English cognates are illuminated by Sanskrit.

| | English | | Urdu |
|---|---|---|---|
| (cf. Sanskrit *asma-* [base of first person plural; us]) | us | (our) | ہمارا |
| (cf. Sanskrit *kati* [how many]) | quota | (several) | کئی |

*B. Use the* Oxford English Dictionary *and Platts' Urdu dictionary to find the Urdu and Sanskrit cognates of the following English words.*

1. other 2. come 3. hand 4. month 5. light

The following English and Urdu cognates show just how many Urdu words may be related to one English word (or more). Perhaps even more fascinating is the fact that of the three Urdu words, گوشت comes from Persian, گائے is a Hindi-Urdu word proper, and گو is a term that is common to Persian, Sanskrit, Prakrit, and Urdu:

| English | Urdu |
|---|---|
| cow | (cow) گو (cow) گائے (meat) گوشت |

Here is another interesting food-related cognate:

| English | Urdu |
|---|---|
| sweet, suave | (flavor) سواد |

*C. Use the* Oxford English Dictionary *and Platts' Urdu dictionary to find connections between the following English words and their Urdu cognates.*

1. lemon 2. widow 3. free 4. mist 5. video, visual, wit

## 1.9 English-Urdu Cognates—Prakrit and Sanskrit

We have already seen that the roots of a large number of Urdu and English cognates lie in Proto-Indo-European and are sometimes also cognate with words in Sanskrit. In this section, we shall set these relationships aside and discuss only the shared vocabulary that English and Urdu have borrowed directly from Sanskrit or Prakrit.

English has borrowed some of these words from Sanskrit via Urdu, Hindi, Punjabi, and other South Asian languages.

| Sanskrit | | Urdu | | English |
|---|---|---|---|---|
| (lord of the world) | جگن ناتھ | (Jagan Nath [deity]) | جگن ناتھ | juggernaut |
| (weighty; teacher) | گُرو | (teacher) | گُرو | guru |

By the way, guru گُرو (weighty) is also cognate with the English words "grave," "gravitas," and "gravity."

The following words were borrowed directly into English from Sanskrit and into Urdu either from Sanskrit or Prakrit. Note that in Prakrit, "j" often takes the place of Sanskrit's "y." Since much of this vocabulary was borrowed into Urdu before the movement for Sanskritization began in the nineteenth century, Urdu often retains the Prakritic pronunciations and spellings. Conversely, English often borrows directly from Sanskrit. Note that English words retain the fully vocalized "a" ending associated with Sanskrit pronunciation and transliteration.

| English | Urdu | Sanskrit | |
|---|---|---|---|
| raga | راگ | [rāga] | راگ |

The popularity of yoga has resulted in a large number of borrowings from Sanskrit into English. Many of these Sanskrit words are related to Urdu words.

| English | Urdu | Sanskrit |
|---|---|---|
| yogi, yoga | یوگ / یوگی جوگی / جوگ | یوگ |

As we noted above, this word is also related to the English "yoke," "juncture," and other words related to the concept of joining. The Sanskrit یوگ covers a wide semantic range (joining, union, contact; fitness, propriety; devotional seeking). The Urdu (Prakritic) جوگ covers a similarly wide semantic range, from "union" and "the (auspicious) alignment of stars" to "yogic practice."

Students familiar with the names of various poses (آسن) in yoga will discover that many of them contain words that are borrowed into Urdu, either in their entirety or as parts of words.

| English | Urdu Cognate(s) | | Yoga Term | |
|---|---|---|---|---|
| Asana | (lion-seat; throne) | سنگھاسن | (pose) | آسن |
| Balasana | (darling, child) | بال | (child's pose) | بالاسن |
| Dandasana | (staff, stick) | ڈنڈا | (staff pose) | ڈنڈاسن |
| Halasana | (plow) | ہل | (plow pose) | ہلاسن |

| | | | | |
|---|---|---|---|---|
| Padmasana | (lotus) | پدما | (lotus pose) | پدماسن |
| Virasana | (hero, warrior) | ویر / بیر | (hero pose) | ویراسن |
| Virabhadrasana | (virtuous) بھدر (hero) | ویر / بیر | (warrior pose) | ویربھدراسن |

Other yogic vocabulary is found in Urdu in the form of cognates. The following chart surveys some common examples.

| English | Urdu Cognates | | | Yoga Term |
|---|---|---|---|---|
| Ardhachandrasana | (moon) چاند ، چندر | (half) آدھا | (half moon pose) | اردھا چندراسن |
| Chaturanga | (body, limb) انگ | (four) چار | (four-limb staff) | چتر انگ |
| Ashtanga | (body, limb) انگ | (eight) آٹھ | (eight-part pose) | اشٹانگ |
| Surya Namaskar | (greetings) نمسکار | (sun) سورج | (sun salutation) | سوریا نمسکار |
| Adho Mukha Svanasana | (dog) سگ (face) مکھ | (downward) اوندھا | (downward dog) | ادھو مکھ سوناسن |

Many words that philologists trace to Sanskrit entered English and Urdu circuitously and thus offer evidence of the rich histories of linguistic cross-pollination and lexical borrowing that characterize both languages. In the following case, the English word has come through medieval Latin, but its spelling suggests that it entered English and Urdu through Arabic, either by direct borrowing or through another language. Ultimately, however, both words are believed to derive from the Sanskrit word چندن (sandalwood).

| English | Urdu |
|---|---|
| sandal(wood) | صندل |

*A. Match the Urdu and English cognates borrowed from Sanskrit. Find the Urdu words in a dictionary. Then use English and Urdu dictionaries to compare their meanings.*

| | | | | |
|---|---|---|---|---|
| maya | ا | ___ | شانتی | ۱۔ |
| dharma | ب | ___ | منتر | ۲۔ |
| shakti | پ | ___ | مایا | ۳۔ |
| avatar | ت | ___ | کرم | ۴۔ |
| ashram | ٹ | ___ | دھرم | ۵۔ |
| Aryan | ث | ___ | اوتار | ۶۔ |
| chakra | ج | ___ | آشرم | ۷۔ |
| mantra | چ | ___ | آریہ | ۸۔ |
| karma | ح | ___ | شکتی | ۹۔ |
| shanti | خ | ___ | چکر | ۱۰۔ |

## 1.10 English-Urdu Cognates—East-Asian Languages

Sanskrit and other South Asian languages have played an important role in literary and religious discourse in East, Southeast, South, Central, and West Asia across a range of languages. This cosmopolitanism has unsurprisingly resulted in the borrowing of Sanskrit words into Chinese, Japanese, and other East- and Southeast Asian languages.

One example of this complex web of borrowing is the English name of the most widely spoken dialect of Chinese, "Mandarin," which English borrows not from Chinese but from Portuguese, which probably borrowed the Sanskrit-origin word منتری [mantrī] (consul or councilor to a king) from Hindi-Urdu, Malay, or another South or Southeast Asian language. In any case, it appears that this exonym was used by Portuguese traders to refer to the language of the consuls who had come to courts in South and Southeast Asia.

| English | Urdu |
|---|---|
| Mandarin | منتری |

Similarly, the word "China" does not enter Latin through East Asian languages, but apparently through Sanskrit. The Sanskrit word (chīna) has been known from the time of the Sanskrit epics; that is, around the time of the Common Era. Its derivatives are used in English, Urdu, Persian, and many other Indo-European languages.

| English | Urdu |
|---|---|
| China | چین |

The importance of Sanskritic languages to religious traditions in East Asia, especially Buddhism, has led to the borrowing of many Sanskrit words into Japanese and Chinese through languages like Pali. The name "Buddhism" itself comes from a Pali-Sanskrit word meaning "aware," "knowing," or "enlightened." Its Urdu cousins relatives include بُدھ (learned man; the Buddha); بدھی (intelligence, wisdom); بُدّھو (a fool); as well as derivative words such as سمجھنا (to understand) from سم (together, complete) and بدھ (understanding).

| English | | Urdu | Sanskrit |
|---|---|---|---|
| Buddha | (learned man) | بدھ | بدھ |
| | (wisdom, intelligence) | بُدھی | |
| | (a fool) | بُدّھو | |

The English words "tea" and "chai" are both related to the Urdu word چائے, and all three ultimately derive from the same Chinese root pronounced differently in Mandarin and Amoyese (Xiamenese) dialects.

| English | Urdu | [through other languages] | Mandarin Chinese |
|---|---|---|---|
| chai | چائے | ⟵ | ch'a |

| English | [through other languages] | Amoyese (Xiamenese) Chinese |
|---|---|---|
| tea | ⟵ | te |

The word "zen" and its etymon دھیان [dhyān] (focus; meditation) beautifully exemplify the interconnectedness and interdependence of world languages, of which English and Urdu are two important ones. By comparing Platts' Urdu dictionary, Monier-Williams' Sanskrit dictionary, the *Oxford English Dictionary*, and the relevant entry in the *Encyclopaedia of Islam, Second Edition*, we learn that the word دھیان is related to the Sanskrit root دھیے [dhyai] [ध्यै] (thought, reflection, meditation). This Sanskrit root is almost certainly related to another Sanskrit root دھی [dhī] [धी] (intellect, understanding, thought). Some philologists think that the Arabic word دِین (religion, among a wide range of other meanings) is not a Semitic word, but an Indo-European one related to the latter Sanskrit root (دھی) [dhī]. If this is true, then it means that the three words, *dhyān*, "zen," and *dīn*, which are used to refer to three of the most important concepts in world religious traditions (Hinduism, Buddhism, and Islam) are related and share a long, interrelated and interdepedent history.

| English (from Japanese) | Urdu (from Arabic, Persian) | Urdu (from Sanskrit) |
|---|---|---|
| zen | (religion) دِین | (meditation) دھیان |

*A. Match the Urdu and English cognates related to Buddhism. Note that all the words come from Sanskrit and are also used in non-Buddhist contexts. Look up unfamiliar vocabulary in a dictionary and compare the meanings of the English and Urdu words.*

| | | | |
|---|---|---|---|
| zen | ا | ___ | ۱۔ دھیان |
| nirvana | ب | ___ | ۲۔ ستوپ |
| stupa | پ | ___ | ۳۔ تَنتر |
| sangha | ت | ___ | ۴۔ سَنگھ |
| mandala | ٹ | ___ | ۵۔ نِروَان |
| Tantra | ث | ___ | ۶۔ منڈل |

## 1.11 Cognates, Connections, and Conclusions

The historical processes of linguistic borrowing are complex and defy reduction to geographical, national, political, religious or other types of borders and boundaries. In this unit, we have seen that English and Urdu are linked by shared engagements with Arabic, Chinese, Dravidian languages, French, German, Greek, Japanese, Latin, Malay, Persian, Portuguese, Prakrit, Proto Indo-European, Sanskrit, and Spanish across time. By studying the ways in which this richly intertwined history of cultural and linguistic exchange has shaped the lexica of English and Urdu, we can begin to appreciate the interconnectedness and interdependence of the languages as part of broader processes of movement and exchange in history. As we move into the following units, which once again divide our subject into distinct linguistic categories ("The Arabic Element"; "The Persian Element"; "The Hindi Element"; "The Prakrit-Sanskrit Element"), we must bear in mind that these distinctions, while productive, threaten to mask the interconnectedness, interdependence, and occasional ambiguities between and among these languages. We must resist the temptation to reify languages by treating them as essentially and concretely disparate.

As a final illustration of the interconnected histories of Urdu and English, consider the English word "ginger," which English borrows from Latin through French, and its Urdu cognate, زنجبیل [zanjabīl], which Urdu borrows from Arabic. (As we have seen in the case of other medical vocabulary, زنجبیل [zanjabīl] is used in medical texts, but is not the everyday word for ginger in Urdu. That is اَدرَک [adrak].) Philologists disagree about the origins of زنجبیل, but it seems to have been borrowed into Indo-European languages from a Southeast Asian language through a Dravidian one. From the Dravidian it seems to have entered Prakrit through Sanskrit. Dravidian also seems to have given it to Pali, whence it traveled through Greek into Latin and eventually into English. Naturally, its form in all these languages changed as it was borrowed. During its many journeys, it also entered Arabic and is found in a verse of the Quran (76:17) to describe a drink to be given and enjoyed in Paradise.

ویسقون فیہا کاسا کان مزاجہا زنجبیلا

(And they will be given to drink therein a cup mixed with *zanjabīl*.)

# UNIT 2

# THE ARABIC ELEMENT

Urdu borrows a great deal from Arabic, from orthographic traditions through words and idiomatic expressions to genres of literature. Knowing a bit about Arabic morphology will help you acquire a large vocabulary relatively quickly.

Before beginning this unit, readers should be familiar with the following twenty words. Not only are they some of the most common Arabic words in Urdu, but they and their linguistic relatives are repeated throughout this unit.

| | | | | | | | |
|---|---|---|---|---|---|---|---|
| (country) | ملک | (known) | معلوم | (sight) | نظر | (often) | اکثر |
| (effect) | اثر | (state) | حالت | (remaining) | باقی | (government) | حکومت |
| (type) | قسم | (nation) | قوم | (love) | محبت | (form, face) | صورت |
| (clear) | ظاہر | (right) | حق | (action) | عمل | (special) | خاص |
| (site) | مقام | (present) | موجود | (near) | قریب | (related) | متعلق |

## 2.1 Recognizing Arabic Words in Urdu

The first step in applying one's knowledge of Arabic morphology to Urdu vocabulary acquisition is to learn to recognize Arabic words in Urdu. With a bit of practice, you will easily recognize when a word is of Arabic origin. The simplest way to do so is to learn to recognize letters that mark Arabic origin. As a rule, all words with the following letters come from Arabic:

ث ح ذ ص ض ط ظ ع

In the case of ذ, the only exception is a small number of Persian words.

گذشتہ گذشت گذار گذارش پذیر پذیرا پذیرائی پذیرہ

The letter ق is also often good evidence that a word comes from Arabic, but occasionally appears in words not borrowed from Arabic, too. It is worth noting that compound words may include an Arabic word or particle as one of its elements without being Arabic itself. For example, صورت (form, face) is an Arabic word, but the compound خوبصورت (beautiful) is not.

Equally helpful in identifying Arabic words is to keep in mind that if a word contains any of the following letters, it has *not* been borrowed from Arabic (Arabic lacks them):

پ ٹ چ ڈ ڑ ژ گ ھ(aspiration)

**Note on ھ (aspiration).** Arabic lacks the Indic distinction between aspirated and unaspirated consonants, and therefore the ھ of aspiration is not found in Arabic words. Note that some styles of Urdu writing (especially those used before the twentieth century) use ھ and ہ interchangeably.

Another piece of evidence that a word is Arabic in origin is that it contains other signs of Arabic origin (e.g. the triliteral root pattern). These will be studied closely in subsequent sections.

*A. Identifying Arabic words. Read the following words and write an* ع *next to all the Arabic words that show tell tale signs of their Arabic origin. Write an x next to those words which cannot be borrowed from Arabic. Finally, look up any remaining words in an Urdu dictionary to learn more about their origins.*

صرف　پیدا　حالت　محبت　عمل　سلطنت　متعلق

معلوم　گھر　پڑنا　قوم　یعنی　صبح　طور

حاصل　چھوڑنا　شروع　حال　ضرورت　لڑکی　ڈالنا

آنکھ　حکومت　نکلنا　خاص　اکثر　عورت　اٹھانا

صاحب　کبھی　صورت　جگہ　ظاہر　گذشتہ　پیسہ

*B. Finding etymologies in a dictionary. In some cases, it will not be immediately apparent that a word comes from Arabic. Find out whether the following words are Arabic in origin by looking them up in an Urdu dictionary. Mark the Arabic words with* ع*.*

خبر　شہر　شاخ　درد　جہان　زمانہ　نہایت

*C. Exceptions. There are rare exceptions to the general guidelines outlined here. Read the following words, which are not Arabic in origin. Look them up in a dictionary to learn about their etymology.*

طوطا　طوطی　گذشتہ　گذارش

## 2.2 Arabic Roots

Nouns in Arabic typically have three root letters to which vowels and consonants are infixed, prefixed, and suffixed to derive words that are conceptually related. The root letters are typically related to a root verb with a range of meanings. Study the following chart, which surveys Urdu words derived from the Arabic دَخَل (to enter).

دَخل (entrance; access; power; intrusion)

دُخُول (entrance; penetration)

دَخِیل (admitted; included)

داخِل (entering; entered; registered; included)

داخِلہ (admission; registration document; a receipt of payment/income)

مَدخُول (entered; registered)

مَدخَل (site of entrance; income; mouthpiece of a telephone receiver)

مَداخِل (income)

مُداخلت (interference; interruption)

اِدخال (insertion; introduction; penetration)

تَداخُل (interference [of light]; sets of divisible integers; indigestion caused by overeating; performing noontime and afternoon prayers at the same time; commixture, intermixture)

Note that each of these words contains all the letters of the root (د خ ل) in the same order. This is the key to recognizing that Arabic words are related. That is, Arabic words are morphologically (and therefore semantically) related only if they share **the same root letters in the same order**.

Recognizing that a word comes from Arabic and, more importantly, recognizing relationships among Arabic words of the same root and how various patterns affect meaning, is the key to developing a large and nuanced Arabic vocabulary in Urdu.

*A. Match the words on the right with the words on the left that share the same Arabic root.*

۱۔ فرق ____ ا تفریق

۲۔ نظر ____ ب تصویر

۳۔ علم ____ پ معمول

۴۔ غیر ____ ت بعید

۵۔ بعد ____ ٹ اوقات

۶۔ عمل ____ ث انتظار

۷۔ ملک ____ ج تغیر

۸۔ وقت ____ چ معلوم

۹۔ خبر ____ ح مالک

۱۰۔ صورت ____ خ اخبار

## Recognizing Arabic Roots

Since Arabic words are formed by prefixing, infixing, and suffixing vowels and consonants to root letters, the easiest way to recognize the root is to gain familiarity with the standard paradigms of affixation. Such paradigms are the main focus of this unit. Even if you do not know the paradigms yet, a few basic rules will help you to distinguish root letters from other kinds of letters in Arabic words.

The most commonly affixed letters to the root are و ا ت م and ی. As a general rule, if a word that you recognize to be Arabic contains one or more of these letters **in addition** to three other letters, you can safely assume that the three other letters are the root letters. Another helpful point to keep in mind is the fact that م is often prefixed but neither infixed nor suffixed to derive nouns, adjectives, or adverbs in Arabic. Likewise, و is never prefixed. Hence, when م appears in medial or final positions and و in initial position, they are almost certainly root letters. Otherwise, they are likely derivational affixes.

For example, in the following word, we find م and و in addition to three letters, one of which (ص) marks the word as Arabic. If we remove the م and و (here highlighted with an underline) we are left with three letters. These are the three letters of the root.

مصروف ← م ص ر و ف ← ص ر ف

In the following example, we see three recognizable root letters and two instances of the letter ا, which is among the most common affixes. Thus, ignoring the ا, we are left with the root.

اطفال ← ا ط ف ا ل ← ط ف ل

Removing the two common derivational affixes from the following word, we are once again left with the root.

تعریف ← ت ع ر ی ف ← ع ر ف

Consider the following pair of words.

عالم　　　　معلوم

If we were to remove all the commonly affixed letters, we would be left with only two root letters (ع and ل) in both words. But we know that this is not sufficient and that م is never suffixed as part of a pattern. Which letters do we retain? Finding the answer depends on our ability to recognize the most likely roots and our familiarity with this common Arabic root and the patterns (or forms or paradigms) into which it has been set. Knowing both, we can easily deduce that the three letters that appear in the same order in both words are ع ل م. We might also have reasoned to this conclusion if we recognized either of the patterns. We learned just now that ص ر ف are the root letters in مصروف. We can then assume that the prefixed م and the infixed و are the affixed letters in the current pattern, too. Removing them from the present word, we are left with ع ل م (علم), which are indeed the root letters. Indeed, the root علم means "to know" and is among the most common Arabic roots in Urdu.

عالم معلوم ← ع ل م

Here are a few more Arabic words with the roots extracted. The underlined letters to the left of the arrows are the affixed and infixed vowels and consonants. Note that the roots are written as three separate letters for illustrative purposes here, but are typically connected in grammar books and dictionaries (thus, عرف rather than ع ر ف).

اعتراف ← اِ ع تِ ر ا ف ← ع ر ف

محفل ← مِ ح ف ل ← ح ف ل

مفتاح ← مِ ف ت ِا ح ← ف ت ح

تدریس ← تِ د ر ی س ← د ر س

حقائق ← ح ق ا ئِ ق ← ح ق ق

These guidelines are generally effective, but it is important to note that the five common affixes may in some cases be root letters. The key to knowing which letters are affixes and which are root letters is to recognize two elements: (1) commonly used roots; (2) commonly used derivational patterns. The following sections will train you to recognize both and to understand how the interaction between roots and patterns creates or affects meaning. Knowing how roots relate to patterns to create meaning, and recognizing the relationships among words of the same root or pattern, is the key to building a large vocabulary quickly and to understanding the nuances of Arabic word meanings in Urdu.

*B. Write the three root letters of the following words.*

۱۔ مغلوب ۲۔ قابل ۳۔ معبود ۴۔ مکتوب ۵۔ ناظر ۶۔ عالم ۷۔ مختلف ۸۔ بعید ۹۔ انتظار ۱۰۔ حکومت

۱۱۔ شروع ۱۲۔ صورت ۱۳۔ ضرورت ۱۴۔ متعلق ۱۵۔ مبارک ۱۶۔ مشہور ۱۷۔ حدیث ۱۸۔ اسلام ۱۹۔ عمارت ۲۰۔ منظور

*Review Exercise. Arabic roots matching exercise. Match the words on the left with the related words on the right. Remember that in order for two words in Arabic to be related, they must have the same root letters in the same order.*

۱۔ عبادت ____ ا مصلحت

۲۔ بعد ____ ب تعلیم

۳۔ خیال ____ پ مبارک

۴۔ سفر ____ ت مسافر

| | | | |
|---|---|---|---|
| ۵۔ برکت | ____ | ٹ | تخیل |
| ۶۔ حاصل | ____ | ث | اظہار |
| ۷۔ شروع | ____ | ج | تحصیل |
| ۸۔ صلح | ____ | چ | بعید |
| ۹۔ علم | ____ | ح | معبود |
| ۱۰۔ ظاہر | ____ | خ | شریعت |

## 2.3 Irregular Patterns of Triliteral Roots

Arabic words whose three root letters are consonants are considered regular. In the following sections, we shall also examine words whose root letters are not regular (that is, not all consonants) and the derived nouns of which are therefore considered irregular. These concepts will be clarified through repeated examples in subsequent lessons. Here follows a general introduction.

### Geminate (Doubled) Root Letters

Many Urdu nouns of Arabic origin have doubled root letters. In some cases, not all three root letters appear in the word. For example, the Form I (root) word حق (truth; right; God) appears to have only two root letters, but it actually contains three (ح ق ق). This is because there is no short vowel between the two ق letters and therefore the second is not written. Roots in which two letters are the same are called geminate.

### Mutable Root Letters

As we have seen, most Arabic words are built on three root letters. When one of these letters is a vowel (e.g. و or ی) or hamza (ء), the otherwise regular patterns of noun derivation are affected. This is because these letters are mutable and typically assimilate the short vowels that precede them. Grammarians of Arabic distinguish four basic kinds of such roots.

1. **Assimilated** are those whose first root letter is و or ی. In Urdu, nouns derived from assimiliated verbs typically begin with the letter و [v]. They include:

   وزن ولد وقف وجہ وقوع یاس

2. **Hollow** are those in which the middle letter of the root is و or ی. Urdu nouns derived from hollow verbs can have و, ی, or ا as their middle letter.

   غور طور خوف غیر قید حال

3. **Defective** are those in which the final letter is و or ی. Nouns derived from defective verbs may end in any vowel, but their basic form most often ends in ا [ā].

   عطا دعا دعویٰ دعوت وفا خفا

4. **Hamzated** are those in which a root letter is hamzah. Urdu typically drops the hamza and simply retains the alif ا [a].

اثر امن امر اہل الم اصل

Some roots are mixed. For example, the root (and its related verbal noun) ولی (friend; saint) is both assimilated (initial v) and defective (final ī). Similarly, رائے / رأی (opinion) is both hamzated (middle letter) and defective (final ī, e).

The following sections will review the many ways in which geminate, assimilated, hollow, defective, and hamzated nouns interact with the standard patterns of noun derivation in Arabic. This information may seem overwhelming at first, but with a bit of practice it will become second nature. Indeed, the deviations from the irregular patterns are themselves quite predictable and thus, in a sense, regular. Once you have grown accustomed to the patterns, many of them will hardly seem like deviations from regular noun patterns at all.

*A. Recognizing relationships among irregular nouns. Match the irregular nouns on the right to the those on the left which share the same root. Note that the vowels in weak roots may change.*

| | | | |
|---|---|---|---|
| ۱۔ دعا | ___ | ا | اختفا |
| ۲۔ خفا | ___ | ب | مبنی |
| ۳۔ رضا | ___ | پ | مرضی |
| ۴۔ غذا | ___ | ت | استدعا |
| ۵۔ بِنا | ___ | ٹ | تغذیہ |

## 2.4 Paradigms for Arabic Nouns

Arabic grammarians use a paradigm that corresponds with the typical three-letter root of Arabic words in order to facilitate generalized and easy representation of the underlying structure of words. The paradigm uses the letter ف to represent the first letter of a root word, ع to represent the second, and ل to represent the third. Like the words that they represent, the paradigms also include affixed vowels and consonants. This unit will use these paradigms to refer to the structure of derived nouns. It is therefore important to understand how the paradigms represent patterns of derived nouns. Read the words in the following chart and the paradigm to the left of the arrow.

| | | | | |
|---|---|---|---|---|
| عالِم | غالِب | ناظِر | ← | فاعِل |
| مطلوب | منظور | معلوم | ← | مفعول |
| کِتاب | حِساب | مِثال | ← | فِعال |
| تقریب | تفریق | تصویر | ← | تفعیل |

Notice that the paradigms to the left of the arrows share exactly the same prefixed, infixed, and suffixed vowels and consonants as the words on the right. For example, in the first row, the words to the right of the arrow all have ا infixed between the first and second root letters and a short ِ [i] between the second and third. Substituting ف ع and ل for the three root letters in each word, we produce the pattern فاعِل. This pattern is used to refer to all Urdu words in this form. As the pattern forming the active participle of the basic form of the noun, it imparts an agentive sense (compare with -er, -ing) to the root.

The same system is modified to represent irregular nouns. Thus, the geminate (doubled) root is represented as فلّ:

حقّ   حلّ   شکّ   ←   فلّ

Other irregular roots are represented by substitutions for the mutable letter.

قول   خوف   قوم   ←   فول

قائل   خائف   قائم   ←   فائل

خلا   بقا   فنا   ←   فعا

*A. Recognizing paradigms. Match the words on the right with the appropriate paradigm on the left.*

| | | | |
|---|---|---|---|
| ۱۔ تحریر | ________ | ا | فاعِل |
| ۲۔ عالِم | ________ | ب | مفعول |
| ۳۔ مالِک | ________ | پ | تفعیل |
| ۴۔ تعلیم | ________ | | |
| ۵۔ مصروف | ________ | | |
| ۶۔ قابِل | ________ | | |
| ۷۔ ظالِم | ________ | | |
| ۸۔ موجود | ________ | | |
| ۹۔ صاحِب | ________ | | |
| ۱۰۔ معلوم | ________ | | |

*B. Classifying by paradigms. Write two Urdu words that fall under the following paradigms. Your examples may be drawn from the aforegoing discussion or your own reading.*

| | | |
|---|---|---|
| ۱۔ فاعِل | ________ | ________ |
| ۲۔ مفعول | ________ | ________ |
| ۳۔ تفعیل | ________ | ________ |

*C. Producing paradigms. Next to each of the following words, write the appropriate paradigm. Use the paradigms discussed in this unit to guide you. The first three have been done for you.*

| | | | | | |
|---|---|---|---|---|---|
| ۱۔ ثابِت | <u>فاعِل</u> | ۶۔ تفصیل | ___________ | ۱۱۔ نازل | ___________ |
| ۲۔ مَشہور | <u>مَفعُول</u> | ۷۔ لازِم | ___________ | ۱۲۔ حاکم | ___________ |
| ۳۔ تَسلیم | <u>تَفعِیل</u> | ۸۔ محفوظ | ___________ | ۱۳۔ ظالم | ___________ |
| ۴۔ منظور | ___________ | ۹۔ تدبیر | ___________ | ۱۴۔ مخلوق | ___________ |
| ۵۔ قابض | ___________ | ۱۰۔ ساحِل | ___________ | ۱۵۔ تقریب | ___________ |

## 2.4.I The Pronunciation of Arabic Letters in Urdu

Urdu follows its own set of rules for the pronunciation of Arabic letters, most of which should be familiar to readers. However, the letters ع (ʿain) and ح (baṛī he) present specific problems of pronunciation and it is therefore worthwhile to spend some time examining their pronunciation in detail. Unless noted, the pronounciations in this section correspond to those in everyday use. Similarly, specialized pronunciations of the letter ain ع as a glottal stop (as is sometimes done to indicate its prosodic weight) or as a pharyngeal fricative (as it is pronounced in Arabic and by Urdu speakers who wish to Arabicize Urdu) are not discussed. Neither reflects what is considered standard Urdu pronunciation.

### The Pronounciation of ع (ʿAin)

This letter appears in four positions: initial, medial, and final.

### Initial Position

The pronunciation of ع in initial position is the same as ا in the same position. That is, it simply carries an appropriate vowel. It can have seven pronunciations in this position: ā, au, ī, ai, a, u, i. Consider the following. Transliterations reflect Urdu pronunciation.

| | | | | | | | |
|---|---|---|---|---|---|---|---|
| ۱۔ عارف | [ārif] | ۲۔ عَورت | [aurat] | ۳۔ عِید | [īd] | ۴۔ عَین | [ain] |
| ۵۔ عَدالت | [adālat] | ۶۔ عُرف | [urf] | ۷۔ عِبادت | [ibādat] | | |

### Medial Position

In the medial position, the pronunciation of ʿain depends upon the vowels that come immedately before and after it.

If ʿain is preceded by a short vowel and no vowel immediately succeeds it, it extends the vowel according to the rules of ain extension [a becomes ā; u becomes o; i becomes e].

| | | | | | |
|---|---|---|---|---|---|
| ۱۔ بَعد | [bād] | ۲۔ رُعب | [rob] | ۳۔ نِعمت | [nemat] |
| ۴۔ لَعنت | [lānat] | ۵۔ بُعد | [bod] | ۶۔ مِعیار | [meyār] |

If ʿain is preceded by ا [ā] or َ [a] and succeeded by ا [ā] or َ [a], it is often not pronounced. Instead, the combination of vowels is pronounced as a long ā.

۱۔ مَعاش [māsh] ۲۔ سَعادت [sādat] ۳۔ اِشاعَت [ishāt] ۴۔ ساعَت [samāt]

۵۔ اربَعَہ [arbā] ۶۔ تَعَلُّق [tālluq] ۷۔ تعجب [tājjub]

If ʿain is preceded by a short u or long ū and followed by a short a or long ā, it is elided.

۔ شُعاع [shuā] ۔ شروعات [shurūāt] ۔ مُعَمّا [muammā]

When ʿain is preceded by a short i or long ī and followed by a short a or long ā, it is either elided or pronounced as a y.

۱۔ رِعایت [ri(y)āyat] ۲۔ اِستعِارہ [isti(y)ārā] ۳۔ استیعاب [istī(y)āb]

۴۔ طبیعَت [tabī(y)at] ۵۔ بَیعَت [bai(y)at]

When ʿain is preceded by a short a or long ā and followed by short i or long ī, it is elided.

۱۔ شاعِر [shāir] ۲۔ رباعی [rubāī]

When ʿain is preceded by short or long i and followed by long ī, it is sometimes pronounced "y."

۱۔ طبیعی [tabīyī] بے طالعی [betāliyī]

When ʿain is not preceded by a vowel (that is, there is sukūn on the preceding letter), but is followed by a vowel, it is elided in everyday speech.

۱۔ اِنعام [inām] ۲۔ طلعت [talat] ۳۔ صنعت [sanat]

However, in the recitation of poetry and in speech which seeks to mimic prosodic meter, the preceding consonant may be doubled. Some speakers may also pronounce the ʿain as a glottal stop.

۱۔ اِنعام [innām] ۲۔ طلعت [tallat] ۳۔ صنعت [sannat]

## Final Position

The pronunciation of ع in final position depends on the vowel that precedes it. If long, the ع has no pronunciation. If short, it extends the vowel according to ain extension rules (a becomes ā; i becomes e; u becomes o). If no vowel precedes it, it is pronounced ā (e.g. شَمع [shamā] or جَمع [jamā]).

۱۔ وداع [vidā] ۲۔ شروع [shurū] ۳۔ نوع [nau] ۴۔ بدیع [badī]

۵۔ موقَع [mauqā] ۶۔ توقُّع [tavaqqo] ۷۔ قاطع [qāte] ۸۔ منَع [manā]

Note that in some cases, idiomatic use takes precedence over formal rules of vowelization. For example, the following words should be pronounced according to the rules given here, but they are in fact typically pronounced as shown in brackets.

۱۔ جامِع [jāmā] ۲۔ ضائع [zāyā] ۳۔ شائع [shāyā]

## ʿAin in Iẓāfat Constructions

In general, the pronunciation of ʿain does not change when it is part of iẓāfat [-e] (the Persian genitive; "of") compounds. But when a word ending in an ع is the first component in an iẓāfat construction and there is no vowel immediately preceding ع, then ع is dropped and the preceding, unvocalized consonant is doubled.

۱۔ شَمع [shamā] محفل [mehfil] شمعِ محفل [shamm-e mehfil]

۲۔ قطع [qatā] تعلّق [tālluq] قطعِ تعلق [qatt-e tālluq]

*A. Practice pronouncing ع by reading the following words.*

عادت عام عَون عَوذ عُود عُور عِیدی عِیسیٰ عَین عَیش

عَدل عَلامت عُذر عُموم عِوَض عِنایت

لَعل بَعض ضُعف زُعم اِعزاز استِعمال اجتماع ممنوع وسیع طَبع منُع

اطاعت جماعت تَعَصُّب مِصرَعَہ

اردوئے مُعَلّیٰ دُعا مَجمُوعَہ مَصنُوعات

بَعید داعی مُدَّعی اَعِزَّہ

اَسعَد بِدعَت

وَضعِ حمل رَفعِ حاجت

## The Pronunciation of ح and ہ and Surrounding Vowels

In Urdu, the pronunciation of the letter ح [ḥ] is identical to the pronunciation of ہ [h] in all cases except when ہ is pronounced as a vowel at the end of words (such as تازہ [tāzā]). Like ہ, ح affects the pronunciation of the vowels around it. The rules governing the pronunciation of both, the similarities and differences between them, and the ways in which both letters affect the pronunciation of the vowels around them are surveyed here. Transliterations reflect pronunciation rather than strict transliteration.

## Initial Position

In this position, both letters are identically pronounced as "h" in all cases regardless of the vowels around them.

حول [haul] ہول [haul]

## Medial Position

In this position, both letters are pronounced as a breathy "h." When preceded by a short vowel but not succeeded by a vowel, both letters change the pronunciation of the vowel as follows: a becomes e (similar to e in "set"), i becomes e, and u becomes o. Note that, in this case, short a and short i are indistinguishable.

بَحر [behr] مَہر [mehr] مِحراب [mehrāb] بِہتر [behtar]

مُحتاط [mohtāt] مُہرہ [mohrā]

When preceded and succeeded by short vowels, the same rules of change to the short vowels often apply.

سَحَر [seher] اَہَم [ehem]

When preceded or succeeded by a long vowel, ح and ہ do not affect the sound of the vowel.

روحانی [rūhānī] ابراہیم [ibrāhīm] راحت [rāhat] ساحل [sāhil] سہولت [sahūlat]

## Final Position

At the end of a word, the rules governing the pronunciation of ح and ہ differ in some cases. Unlike ہ, ح is always pronounced "h." If preceded by a short vowel, the vowel's pronunciation will change. In the case of final-position ح, the rules for short vowels preceding an unvoweled ح change slightly (a may remain a; i becomes e; u becomes o). The rules for ہ (as h) are slightly irregular (a becomes e, but sometimes remains a; i becomes e; u becomes o).

اصلاح [islāh] روح [rūh] مدیح [madīh]

اَفصَح [afsah] تفرُّح [tafarroh] سوانح [savāneh]

کلاہ [kulāh] مکروہ [makrūh] تنبیہ [tanbīh]

تَہ [teh] توجُّہ [tavajjoh] دِہ [deh]

When ح and ہ follow an unvoweled consonant at the end of a word, they are standardly pronounced as "h". When they follow consonants that are sometimes aspirated in Urdu, their pronunciation may closely resemble aspiration.

صبح [subh] شرح [sharh]

Alternatively, some speakers suffix a short or long a to ح and ہ. The resulting pronunciation of h closely resembles (and sometimes is) aspiration.

صبح [subhā] شرح [sharhā] طرح [tarhā]

Other speakers infix a short a between the unvoweled consonant and the ح or ہ.

صبح [subah] شرح [sharah] طرح [tarah]

In some cases, this pronunciation is now considered standard:

طرح [tarah]

In rare cases, the infixed vowel mirrors the initial vowel.

صبح [subuh]

However, when such words appear with Persian iẓāfat or conjunctive constructions (and, more generally, Persian phrases), they retain their basic pronunciation without any affixed vowels.

صبحِ آزادی [subhe āzādī] صبح و شام [subh-o-shām] صبح بخیر [subh bakhair]

Regardless of their position in a word, when preceded by a vowelless consonant that can be aspirated in Urdu (ب ت ج د ک), ح and ہ sometimes take on an aspirated quality. This is not considered standard, but is prevalent.

سبحان اللہ [subhān allah]

*B. Practice the pronunciation of ح and ہ by reading the following words.*

قَدْح جَرْح شارِح صالِح فتح شَرح محل پہر

## Predicting the Pronunciation of Ambiguous Letters: ح ع ہ و ی.

Knowing a bit about the way that words are formed in Arabic will often remove ambiguities in pronunciation. In the case of و and ی, some amount of ambiguity is removed simply by recognizing that these letters appear in an Arabic word. Because Arabic lacks o and e in long vowels, the letters و and ی, when long vowels in Arabic words, are almost always pronounced either as au or ū and ai or ī, respectively, and only in rare and exceptional cases as o or e. Arabic paradigms remove further ambiguities. For example, the vowel patterns in the paradigms مَفعل [maf'al or maf'il] and مَفعُول [maf'ūl], which are two of the most common in Urdu, tell us exactly how any ambiguous or mutable letters or diacritics should be pronounced. Consider the following.

مَوقِف [mauqif] مَوقُوف [mauqūf]

Here, learning to recognize the underlying patterns removes any doubt about how the vowel is to be pronounced, since the infixed short vowel َ [thus **au**] and long vowel و [**ū**] in مَوقُوف [m**au**q**ū**f] are regular, as is the short infixed vowel َ in the first syllable of مَوقِف [hence, m**au**qif].

*C. Practice pronouncing و in the following words, all of which fall under the paradigms مَفعل or مَفعُول.*

| | | | | | |
|---|---|---|---|---|---|
| موقَع | مولِد | معرِفَت | معبَد | محفِل | محشر |
| موجود | مولود | معلوم | معبود | محمود | محصول |

## 2.5 The Arabic Noun

In the following sections, we shall learn how Arabic morphology works in Urdu. We shall see that, although quite involved, the rules by which words are formed and derived are highly regular and therefore predictable. Learning these rules will allow us not only to learn a large number of related words quickly, but also to predict accurately the meaning of unfamiliar vocabulary on the basis of familiar root meanings, related words, and patterns of derivation. To begin, we shall survey a series of Arabic noun patterns and their associated active and passive participles. We shall use the same terminology as Arabic grammarians as we survey the basic (Form I) and derived forms (Form II-X; skipping IX, which is rarely used in Urdu) of the Arabic noun. Grammarians typically refer to these patterns as verbal nouns and their related participles. To avoid confusion and complication, we shall follow this tradition. But it is well to keep in mind that these so-called nouns can be used as nouns, adjectives, or adverbs in Urdu. Indeed, in Arabic, the distinction between nouns and adjectives is typically one of use, not of form. The difference is made clear only by the way that the word is used in a sentence. In some cases, the same is true in Urdu.

## 2.6 Basic (Form I) Verbal Nouns

In this section, we shall survey the many forms of the basic (Form I) form of the Arabic noun. Unlike the derived Forms II-X, the basic form (Form I) of an Arabic verbal noun can fall under a very large number of patterns. Read the following chart, which groups words based on shared patterns of affixed vowels and consonants. The paradigm has been given above each group.

| فَعْل | فَعَل | فُعْل | فِعْل | فُعْلان | فَعْلان | فِعْلان |
|---|---|---|---|---|---|---|
| وَقْت | عَمَل | عُمْر | عِلْم | نُقصان | مَیدان | اِنسان |
| بَعْد | شَرَف | مُلْک | صِرف | طوفان | شَیطان | عِرفان |

| فُعُول | فُعُولَت | فَعُولَہ | فِعال | فَعال |
|---|---|---|---|---|
| ضُرُور | حُکُومَت | عَجُوبَہ | کِتاب | جَواب |
| شُرُوع | ضُرُورَت | | خِلاف | خَیال |

| فِعالَت | فَعالَت | فَعالَہ | فِعالَہ |
|---|---|---|---|
| کِتابَت | مَہارت | خَزانَہ | عِلاوَہ |
| رِیاسَت | جَماعَت | خَرابَہ | عِلاقَہ |

| فَعلَت | فُعلَت | فِعلَت | فَعلَہ | فُعلَہ | فِعلَہ |
|---|---|---|---|---|---|
| عَورَت | صُورَت | قِیمَت | جَذبَہ | جُملَہ | قِلعَہ |
| طاقَت | قُدرَت | مِحنَت | عَرصَہ | عُہدَہ | قِطعَہ |

Arabic grammarians typically group nouns into paradigms according to the position of consonant and vowel affixation, ignoring the particular quality of the affixed vowels. Thus, because عُمْر ['umr] and وَقْت [vaqt] both have a short vowel between the first and second letter of the root and no vowel between root letters two and three, most Arabic grammarians consider them to be members of the same paradigm (فعل). By contrast, because وَقْت [vaqt] and عَمَل ['amal] do not share the same pattern of affixation (in عَمَل, an additional short vowel is infixed between the second and third letters of the root), they are not considered instances of the same pattern of Form I nouns. One might also contrast them in terms of their metrical weight (vaqt is long-short; amal is short-long). In sum, the pattern of Form I nouns is generally defined by the placement of infixed vowels, not by their quality (a, i, u).

Most Arabic roots have more than one Form I noun. This allows for the different shades of meaning that attach to the root to be expressed in different words. For example:

شرف (honor) شرافت (nobility)

حکم (fiat, rule, order) حِکمت (wisdom) حُکومت (government, governance)

*A. Practice grouping words according to noun patterns. Read the following numbered words. Then read the list of words that follows. Next to each numberless word, write the number of the word which shares the same pattern. The first has been done for you.*

| | | | | | | |
|---|---|---|---|---|---|---|
| ۱۔ عُمر | ۲۔ شِعر | ۳۔ صَبر | ۴۔ سَفَر | ۵۔ حُضُور | ۶۔ مِزاج | ۷۔ شَراب |
| لُطف ۱ | قُصور | مِثال | فِکر | خَبَر | جَبْر | خَراب |
| نِثار | ثَواب | حُضور | قَبْر | ذِکر | عُرف | صَدَف |

*B. Match the basic (Form I) nouns which share the same root.*

| | | | |
|---|---|---|---|
| ۱۔ حال | ____ | ا | قسمت |
| ۲۔ قسم | ____ | ب | جماعت |
| ۳۔ جمع | ____ | پ | عمران |
| ۴۔ ضرر | ____ | ت | ضرورت |
| ۵۔ عمارت | ____ | ٹ | حالت |

## Vocabulary Concepts for Form I Nouns

Although there is a large number of patterns that may be used to form Form I (root) Arabic verbal nouns, they can be grouped into categories corresponding to certain formal features corresponding to certain semantic ones. Study the following chart.

| | | | | |
|---|---|---|---|---|
| فَعْل | فَعْلَہ / فَعْلَت | فَعْلَی | فَعَال | فَعُول |
| فِعْل | فَعَلَہ / فَعَلَت | فَعْلَی | فِعَال | فُعُول |
| فُعْل | فَعِلَہ / فَعِلَت | فُعْلَی | فُعَال | فَعُولَہ / فَعُولَت |
| فَعَل | فِعْلَہ / فِعْلَت | فَعلان | فَعَالَہ / فَعَالَت | فُعُولَہ / فُعُولَت |
| فَعِل | فُعْلَہ / فُعْلَت | فِعْلان | فِعَالَہ / فِعَالَت | |
| فُعَل | | فُعْلان | فُعَالَہ / فُعَالَت | |

First, note that the words in the various categories are similar in terms of metrical weight. This is determined by the placement of short and long vowels. Thus, فَعْل [fa'l] (pronounced fāl in Urdu), فُعْل [fu'l] (pronounced fol in Urdu), and فِعْل [fu'l] (pronounced fel in Urdu) all scan as long-short, whereas فَعَل [fa'al], فَعِل [fa'il], and فُعَل [fu'al], are all short-long, and so on. Long feet or syllables are identified by the combination of consonant-short vowel-consonant-(no vowel) (e.g **fa'** in fa'l) or consonant-long vowel (e.g. **'ū** in fu'ūl). Short feet or syllables are identified by a consonant lacking a vowel (e.g. **l** in fa'l) or a consonant-short vowel followed by a another voweled consonant (e.g. **fu** in fu'ūl). Arabic prosody identifies flexible feet, too, but what is important to understand for what follows is that words whose underlying syllabic patterns are the same often share a semantic relationship to their root concepts and their meaning is thus to some extent predictable.

Because these patterns bear on the meaning of Arabic words in Urdu, it is important to be familiar with them. The following lessons survey forms of the Form I noun.

The basic Form I verbal noun, that is, the one which conveys the basic sense of the action of the verb, will typically fall under one of three paradigms: فَعْل, فعول , or فَعَل. Other Form I verbal noun patterns often, but not always, impart specific senses to the meaning of the root. The important point to observe is how the words in each pattern relate to words in other patterns from the same root and how each pattern affects the sense of different roots. Here follows an overview.

1. فَعْل is the verbal noun from a certain class of transitive Arabic verbs; for example, those which take an object (e.g. to take, to give). Thus, فَہْم (understanding) and صَرْف (passing) are both nouns that have an an active or transitive sense (that is, the act of understanding and the act of passing suggest that there is an object which is understood or passed). The transitivity or activeness of these verbs has implications for the sense of derived verbal nouns and adjectives in Urdu. We will examine this in subsequent sections.
2. فُعُول is a verbal noun associated with a certain class of intransitive verbs, meaning those that do not take an object (e.g. to be faulty). Thus, many Urdu words in this pattern carry a passive or intransitive sense; for example, قصور (fault) and حضور (presence). Once again, the passivity of these roots has implications for the sense of derived nouns.
3. فَعَل is the verbal noun from a certain class of intransitive verbs. Thus, words like شَرَف (honor; being high born) and خَبَر (information) often have a passive or intransitive sense, though they may be combined with verbs in Urdu that give them an active one; for example, خبر دینا (to inform).
4. The Noun of Severity فَعَلان, فِعْلان, and فُعْلان. Nouns in this pattern typically convey a sense of severity or intensity. The following chart relates the verb to the nouns of severity.

| | | | | |
|---|---|---|---|---|
| (flood; typhoon) | طوفان | ← | (to surround, go round) | طوف |
| (deprivation, famine) | فُقدان | ← | (to be missing to lose); | فقد |
| (sin, transgression) | عِصیان | ← | (to disobey) | عصی |

*C. Given the meaning of the root concept (root verb) on the right, guess the meaning of the word on the left.*

| | | | | | | | |
|---|---|---|---|---|---|---|---|
| نِسیان | ← | (to forget) | ۲۔ نسی | نُقصان | ← | (to lose) | ۱۔ نقص |
| عِرفان | ← | (to know) | ۴۔ عرف | کُفران | ← | (to disbelieve) | ۳۔ کفر |
| | | | | طُغیان | ← | (to exceed limits) | ۵۔ طغی |

5. The Noun of Office, Profession, or Trade فِعالَت or فَعالَت. The pattern فِعالَت or فَعالَت often forms nouns related to a position, office, profession, or trade related to an agentive noun derived from the root. As such they are often best defined as "the office, position, profession, occupation, craft, or art of" the office associated with the agentive noun.

| | | | | |
|---|---|---|---|---|
| (the profession of a copyist; writing) | کِتابت | ← | (a copyist, scribe) | کاتب |
| (apostleship, messengerhood) | رِسالت | ← | (apostle, messenger) | رسول |

These nouns may also convey the identity or abstract quality associated with a person or profession. Their meaning is often close to that of a related agentive noun and best defined as "the quality associated with (Form I agentive noun)." For this reason, the meaning imparted by this pattern is often analogous to the English -ship or -ity. Consider the following.

| | | | | | | |
|---|---|---|---|---|---|---|
| (nobility) | شَرافت | ← | (noble) | شریف | (honor) | شرف |
| (guardianship, protection) | حِفاظت | ← | (guardian) | حافظ | (guarding) | حفظ |

*D. Given the form and meaning of the agentive nouns on the right, generate the related noun of office, profession, trade, or quality and guess its meaning. Assume that the short vowel in the initial syllable of the noun of office, etc. is ِ [i] unless otherwise indicated in brackets.*

| | | | |
|---|---|---|---|
| (merchant) | ۲۔ تاجر | (manufacturer, industrialist) | ۱۔ صنّاع |
| (consul, ambassador) | ۴۔ سفیر | (organizer; master of ceremonies) | ۳۔ ناظم |
| (caliph, successor) | ۶۔ خلیفہ | (minister) | ۵۔ وزیر |
| (physician) | ۸۔ طبیب | (prince, gossssvernor; wealthy) | ۷۔ امیر |
| [a] (president; presiding figure) | ۱۰۔ صدر | (leader; imam) | ۹۔ امام |

6. The Nominal Diminutive. One way in which Arabic forms the diminutive is by the pattern فُعَیل. This form is mostly encountered in personal names in Urdu, in which it conveys a sense of affection. Consider the following:

| | | | | | |
|---|---|---|---|---|---|
| | | (little dog; puppy) | کُلَیب | ← | (dog) | کلب |
| (little servant of God) | عبیداللہ | (little servant) | عبید | ← | (servant) | عبد |

*E. Form the Nominal Diminutive from the following and give the meaning of the resulting name.*

| | | | | | |
|---|---|---|---|---|---|
| (soldier) | ۳۔ جُند | (beautiful) | ۲۔ حَسَن | (child) | ۱۔ طِفل |

7. The Suffixes of Diminution or Instance ہ and ت. These suffixes, both of which are derived from the Arabic letter ۃ, are often used to nominalize or instantiate the root concept. In Urdu, they often indicate a relative noun or adjective of adverb.

| | | | | |
|---|---|---|---|---|
| ضرور | (necessary) | ← | ضرورت | (necessity) |
| خراب | (ruined, spoiled) | ← | خرابہ | (wasteland) |

They may also form relative nouns from other nouns. In such cases, the relative noun is typically either instantiative or technical. By instantiative is meant that the noun typically conveys a concrete sense if the basic noun is abstract (compare the English abstract "writing" with the concrete "a writing").

| | | | | |
|---|---|---|---|---|
| ضرب | (striking; a strike) | ← | ضربت | (a strike) |
| شجر | (a tree) | ← | شجرہ | (a family tree) |

They sometimes impart a sense of diminution.

| | | | | |
|---|---|---|---|---|
| بلد | (country, area) | ← | بلدہ | (city, town) |

The pattern فعلہ in particular often carries the sense of a small piece.

| | | | | |
|---|---|---|---|---|
| فَرَق | (to divide) | ← | فِرقَہ | (sect) |

*F. Given the meaning of the word on the right, choose the most likely meaning of the noun on the left. The root concept in number two is written as an infinitive verb (to ...), whereas in all other cases the Urdu words that convey the basic root concept are glossed.*

| | | | | | | |
|---|---|---|---|---|---|---|
| ١۔ قَطَعَ | (cut) | ← | قِطعہ | (bandage) | (scissors) | (fragment) |
| ٢۔ لَقَمَ | (to swallow) | ← | لُقمہ | (morsel, bite) | (throat) | (chewing) |
| ٣۔ قرض | (loaning money) | ← | قرضہ | (bank) | (money) | (loan) |
| ٤۔ خطر | (peril) | ← | خطرہ | (danger) | (daredevil) | (cut) |
| ٥۔ شرب | (to drink) | ← | شربت | (cup) | (fountain) | (a kind of drink) |
| ٦۔ فرح | (joy) | ← | فرحت | (laughter) | (playground) | (joy) |
| ٧۔ لعن | (cursing) | ← | لعنت | (a curse) | (praise) | (shortcoming) |
| ٨۔ نقش | (impression, imprint) | ← | نقشہ | (printer) | (chart, map) | (impressive) |

8. Nouns of Illness. Words indicating illness are often formed using the pattern فُعال.

| | | | |
|---|---|---|---|
| زکم | (to catch a cold) | زُکام | (a cold) |
| طِحام | (the spleen) | طُحام | (spleen disease) |

*G. Write the corresopnding Form I noun of illness and guess its meaning.*

۱۔ بخر (to cause vapor)

9. Nouns of State فُعُولت / فُعُولہ. Nouns in these patterns either nominalize or convey the stative, abstract sense of nouns in the فعل form. Note that these nouns and the nouns of office, occupation, or quality (فعالت / فعالہ) both convey a sense of abstraction and are both of the same metrical weight (short-long-long).

| | | | | | |
|---|---|---|---|---|---|
| حکم | (a ruling, fiat) | | ← | حکومت | (governance [state of rule]; government) |
| عقب | (rear, end; following) | عُقبیٰ (end, next world) | ← | عقوبت | (punishment) |
| عجب | (strange, wonderful, marvelous) | | ← | عجوبہ | (a wonder [of the world]) |

*H. Form nouns of state from the following nouns and adjectives (all end in ت), then guess their meaning.*

| | | | |
|---|---|---|---|
| ۱۔ صعب | (difficult, refractory) | ۲۔ عطف | (inclination, kindness) |
| ۳۔ برد | (cold [noun]) | ۴۔ سہل | (easy, convenient) |
| ۵۔ اُمّ | (mother) | ۶۔ خصم | (adversary, antagonist) |
| ۷۔ عفص | (gall) | ۸۔رُطب | (humid) رَطب (greenery) |

10. The Instrumental Noun. The pattern فِعال is remarkably productive. One of its many uses is to form instrumental Form I nouns, that is, nouns indicating the means by which the action of the root is undertaken, performed, or accomplished.

| | | | | |
|---|---|---|---|---|
| رکوب | (riding or mounting) | ← | رکاب | (stirrup) |
| جمع | (gathering, coming together; amassing) | ← | جِماع | (sexual intercourse) |

Sometimes, the suffix of diminution or instance is affixed.

| | | | | |
|---|---|---|---|---|
| رسول | (messenger) | ← | رِسالہ | (journal; tract, treatise) |

*I. Form the instrumental noun related to the following root concepts and give its meaning.*

| | | | |
|---|---|---|---|
| ۱۔ حَسب | (computing, counting; on account of) | ۲۔ حَجب | (intervening, preventing; secluding) |
| ۳۔ بسط | (spreading; extension) | ۴۔ ربط | (tying, binding; connection) |
| ۵۔ کتب | (writing) | | |

## 2.6.1 Form I Active and Passive Participles

We have learned that Arabic words typically include three root letters, and that vowels and consonants are prefixed, infixed, and suffixed to these letters to form conceptually related words. In this section, we shall learn how active and passive participles are formed from the basic form (Form I) of the Arabic verb. We shall also learn how the patterns of formation affect meaning.

### The Form I Active Participle (فاعِل)

Active participles denote the performer of an action. In English, they are typically formed by suffixing -er (e.g. performer). The Arabic Form I active participle is formed by infixing ا [ā] between the first and second letters of the root and ِ [i] between the second and third. Active participles can be nouns or adjectives (or both). They are thus often best defined as "the performer or agent of the root" or "possessed of the quality of the root." Hence, an عالم (scholar; [lit. "knower"]) is someone who possesses علم (knowledge), a ناظر (viewer, reader) is someone who performs the act of نظر (seeing), and something that is واقع (located) is possessed of the quality of وقوع (occurrence) at a particular place.

| | | | | |
|---|---|---|---|---|
| عِلم | (knowledge) | ← | عالِم | (lit. "knower"; scholar) |
| نَظر | (glance, sight) | ← | ناظِر | (viewer; reader) |
| وقوع | (occurrence) | ← | واقع | (occurring, located) |

Note that, in the last instance, the form of the verbal noun وقوع (occurrence) tells us that it carries a passive or intransitive sense (see 2 above). Consequently, its active participle واقع (occurrent, located) is an adjective. Indeed, most active participles corresponding to verbal nouns in the passive pattern فعول form are adjectives.

| | | | | |
|---|---|---|---|---|
| قبول | (acceptance) | ← | قابل | (acceptable, worthy) |
| دخول | (entrance) | ← | داخل | (entered) |
| عبور | (crossing; mastery) | ← | عابر | (crossing, passing; a passenger) |
| طلوع | (rising) | ← | طالع | (rising, appearing; a star; destiny) |

Adjectival active participles are sometimes nominalized with the suffix of instance ہ.

| | | | | |
|---|---|---|---|---|
| (an occurrence) | واقعہ | ← | (occurrent, located) | واقع |

## Irregular Forms

In the case of hollow verbal nouns (those whose middle letter is a vowel), the medial letter of the root (ع in our paradigm فاعل) is replaced with hamzah:

| | | | | |
|---|---|---|---|---|
| (idiom. believing; believer; lit. sayer; saying) | قائل | ← | (saying) | قوَل |
| (inclined) | مائل | ← | (inclination) | میَل |

Active participles of nouns derived from defective roots (those whose final letter is a vowel) end in ی. This may not seem intuitive at first, but if one understands that the infixed vowel ِ (i) of the paradigm فاعل is effectively elongated to replace the root letter with the long vowel ی, the change is logical and predictable. (Note: Arabic scholars may recognize this form as the definite state of the active participle; for example, الباقی).)

| | | | | |
|---|---|---|---|---|
| (remaining) | باقی | ← | (permanence) | بقا |
| (excessive) | غالی | ← | (excess) | غلو |
| (supporter, defender) | حامی | ← | (support, defense) | حمایت |

Sometimes, roots of this kind omit the ی, though grammarians explain this with reference to the fact that the final root letter is in fact ء, not و or ی. Urdu rarely represents ء as the final root letter.

| | | | | |
|---|---|---|---|---|
| (clean) | صاف | ← | (cleanliness) | صفا |

Geminate roots, that is, those whose second and third letters are identical, also take a special form. The ا [ā] is infixed, but the ِ [i] is dropped, and the geminate letter remains doubled.

| | | | | |
|---|---|---|---|---|
| (special; elite) | خاص | ← | (particularity) | خصوصیت |
| (general, common; public) | عام | ← | (generally) | عموماً |

*A. Recognizing the Form I active participle. Read the following list of Arabic words. Pay close attention to long and short vowels. Place a check mark next to the basic form (Form I) active participles. Note that not all words are active participles.*

| | | | | | |
|---|---|---|---|---|---|
| طاقَت | واقع | مالِک | علوم | شامِل | عالِم |
| مناسِب | اجازت | داخِل | حالَت | شمار | ظالِم |
| راضی | اسلام | قابِل | علاقہ | اعظم | تمام |

*B. Form the active participles corresponding to the following Form I nouns. Use the synonyms given in parentheses to estimate their meanings.*

| | | | |
|---|---|---|---|
| ۱۔ عشق (love) | ۲۔ علم (knowledge) | ۳۔ عمل (action) | ۴۔ طلب (seeking) |
| ۵۔ مِلک (possession) | ۶۔ ظلم (tyranny) | ۷۔ عبادت (worship) | ۸۔ حکومت (governance) |
| ۹۔ شمول (inclusion) | ۱۰۔ ظہور (appearance) | ۱۱۔ حصول (obtainment) | ۱۲۔ حضور (presence) |
| ۱۳۔ خوف (fear) | ۱۴۔ قیام (standing) | ۱۵۔ بنا (basis) | ۱۶۔ فنا (annihilation) |
| ۱۷۔ خلا (empty space) | ۱۸۔ کفایت (sufficiency) | ۱۹۔ رضا (will) | ۲۰۔ حرارت (heat, temperature) |

## The Form I Passive Participle (مَفعُول)

Passive participles denote the past tense of an action or someone or something that has received or been affected by an action. English typically forms the passive participle by suffixing -ed, -t, or -en (or -n) (e.g. performed, kept, eaten, known), and in other ways for irregular verbs. Arabic forms the passive participle of Form I nouns by prefixing مَ [ma] to the first letter of the root and infixing و [ū] between the second and third letters. Read the following pairs aloud.

| | | | | |
|---|---|---|---|---|
| (known) | مَعلوم | ← | (knowledge) | عِلم |
| (renowned, famed) | مشہور | ← | (renown, fame) | شُہرَت |
| (accepted) | مقبول | ← | (acceptance) | قبول |

### Irregular Forms

Hollow roots whose middle letter is و follow the paradigm (مَفُول). Note the ا in the following verbal noun.

| | | | | |
|---|---|---|---|---|
| (reproached, reproachable) | ملوم | ← | (reproach) | ملامت |

Roots whose middle letter is ی follow the paradigm (مَفِیل).

| | | | | |
|---|---|---|---|---|
| (increased; augmentation) | مزید | ← | (increase) | زید |
| (sold) | مبیع | ← | (sale) | بَیع |

Roots whose final letter is و follow the paradigm (مَفعُو)

| | | | |
|---|---|---|---|
| (invited) مدعو | ← | (invitation) دَعوَت |

Roots whose final letter is ی follow the paradigm (مَفعِی). Remember that the Form I verbal nouns of these roots typically end in ا [ā] in Urdu.

| | | | |
|---|---|---|---|
| (pleasure, will, choice; that which is willed, chosen) | مرضی | ← | (contentment; will) رضا |
| (the guided; the Mahdi) | مہدی | ← | (guidance) ہدایت |

The passive participle can be nominalized (changed from an adjective to a noun) by suffixing ہ.

منصوب (established; planned, contrived) ← منصوبہ (plan; contrivance)

*C. Read the following list of words and write a checkmark next to each Form I passive participle. Not all the words are passive participles.*

مذکور شروع قوم موجود ضرورت قانون معبود

مقام مضمون منظور وصول مشورہ دستور محصول

*D. Form the passive participle of the following verbal nouns and use the synonym given in parentheses to estimate its meaning.*

۱۔ عشق (love) ۲۔ علم (knowledge) ۳۔ عمل (action) ۴۔ طلب (seeking)

۵۔ مِلک (posession) ۶۔ ظلم (tyranny) ۷۔ عبادت (worship) ۸۔ حکومت (governance)

۹۔ شمول (inclusion) ۱۰۔ حصول (obtaining) ۱۱۔ رجوع (inclination) ۱۲۔ وجود (existence)

۱۳۔ خوف (fear) ۱۴۔ زید (increase) ۱۵۔ بنا (basis) ۱۶۔ خفیہ (hidden)

۱۷۔ ہدایت (direction) ۱۸۔ دعوت (invitation) ۱۹۔ رضا (will) ۲۰۔ غمّ (grief)

*E. Form the passive participle corresponding to the active participles.*

۱۔ ضابط ۲۔ غالب ۳۔ لازم ۴۔ ناظم ۵۔ وارث ۶۔ وافق ۷۔ عاقل ۸۔ عارف ۹۔ جانّ ۱۰۔ ہادی

*F. Form the passive participle from the following roots. Then nominalize them using the ہ of instance and give the meaning of the resulting noun.*

۱۔ فرض (supposing) ۲۔ جمع (collecting) ۳۔ طلب (seeking) ۴۔ قول (speech, saying)

## 2.6.2 Form I Agentive, Intensive-Occupational, and Comparative-Superlative Nouns

### The Agentive Noun فَعِیل (faʿīl)

This important paradigm is ubiquitous in Urdu. When used to form a personal noun, it has a very similar sense to that of the Form I active participle فاعل (-er). The difference is that while the active participle connotes the performer or enactor of the root, the فعیل pattern connotes the person who either is endowed with the quality of the root or enacts it by intrinsic nature, assimilation, character, or passive reception. Thus, an ادیب (man of letters, scholar; refined gentleman) is someone in whose character is found a capacity for اَدَب (etiquette; literature); a حکیم (philosopher, physician, sage) is someone in whose character

حِکمت (wisdom, philosophy) is found; and a قتیل (the slain) is someone who has passively received قتل (killing).

| | | | | |
|---|---|---|---|---|
| (man of letters, scholar; refined gentleman) | ادیب | ← | (literature; etiquette) | اَدَب |
| (philosopher, physician, sage) | حَکیم | ← | (wisdom, philosophy) | حِکمت |
| (murder victim; the slain) | قتیل | ← | (killing) | قتل |

This form may also imply constant and complete embodiment or enaction of the root concept. This helps to explain why verbs or root concepts with a stative, abstract, or inherent sense typically take فعیل, while those with an active, concrete, or non-essential sense take فاعل. For example, عالِم (intellectual, scholar; lit. "knower") is someone who possesses عِلم (knowledge), whereas علیم (the all-knowing, omniscient; God) is someone who possesses knowledge in his very nature.

| | | | | |
|---|---|---|---|---|
| (intellectual, scholar) | عالِم | ← | (knowledge) | عِلم |
| (the all-knowing, omniscient; God) | علیم | | | |

Sometimes, the two forms are used to distinguish the agent of one Form I noun from that of another. In such cases, too, the فَعیل paradigm retains its connotation of intrinsicness, assimilation, embodiment, completeness, or constancy. For example:

| | | | | |
|---|---|---|---|---|
| (ruler; commander) | حاکم | ← | (order; command) | حکم |
| (philosopher, sage; physician) | حکیم | ← | (philosophy, wisdom) | حِکمت |

Many words in this paradigm are used as adjectives:

| | | | | |
|---|---|---|---|---|
| (pleasant, fine) | لطیف | ← | (pleasure, fineness) | لطف |
| (close) | قریب | ← | (closeness) | قربت |

Some may be treated as both:

| | | | | |
|---|---|---|---|---|
| (commander, admiral; wealthy, rich; "the wealthy") | امیر | ← | (command) | امر |

Relative nouns are formed by suffixing ت / ہ (Arabic ة):

| | | | | |
|---|---|---|---|---|
| (way [e.g. method]) | طریقہ | ← | (way [e.g. the way of the Prophet]) | طریق |

*A. Read the following list of words and mark the agentive nouns (فعیل) with a check.*

مالِک حقیقت سلوک کمال نظیر ذریعہ سلیقہ کریم عظیم سلطان رفیق فرق

*B. Form the agentive nouns (فعیل) corresponding to the Form I nouns and give their meanings. The parts of speech of the resulting words are given in parentheses.*

| | | | | | |
|---|---|---|---|---|---|
| ۱۔ غربت | ( poverty) | (n./adj.) | ۲۔ وزارت | (ministry) | (adj.) |
| ۳۔ ادب | (literature) | (n.) | ۴۔ شرافت | (nobility) | (n./adj.) |
| ۵۔ عجوبہ | (wonder) | (adj.) | ۶۔ حُسن | (beauty) | (adj.) |
| ۷۔ قدامت | (antiquity) | (adj.) | ۸۔ شرکت | (inclusion) | (adj.) |
| ۹۔ جمال | (beauty) | (adj.) | ۱۰۔ صحّت | (soundness, health) | (adj.) |

## The Intensive or Occupational Noun فعّال

Words in this pattern may be treated as either adjectives or nouns in Urdu (and sometimes both). When intensive, the resulting word is best defined either as "intensely or extremely possessed of the quality of the root" or "someone who embodies the quality of the root intensely." When occupational, it is best defined as "someone whose occupation or profession is to perform the root." Thus, someone intensely possessed of فیض (benefit, bounty; grace) is فیّاض (beneficent), and someone whose occupation is to do the work of حجامت (a barber's work) is a حجّام (barber).

فیض (benefit, bounty) ⟵ فیاض (beneficent)

حجامت (a barber's work) ⟵ حجام (barber)

The diminutive suffix is occasionally used to distinguish senses.

علم (knowledge) ⟵ علام (all-knowing; God) علامہ (a very learned scholar)

The difference between the active participle and the intensive noun is illustrated by the following pair. Note that the active participle merely refers to an agent of the root concept (someone who performs or is possessed of it), whereas the intensive refers to someone who performs it to an intense or extreme extent.

کذب (lying, a lie) ⟵ کاذب (a liar) کذّاب (an inveterate liar)

*C. Read the following words and underline the intensive or occupational nouns.*

جبّار حکّام حاکم زکام کتاب رتاز خبّاز عیّاش ضرّاب قصّاب

*D. Form the intensive or occupational noun from the following Form I verbal nouns and give its meaning.*

| | | | | | | | |
|---|---|---|---|---|---|---|---|
| ۱۔ صید | (hunting) | ۲۔ عِطر | (perfume) | ۳۔ نقل | (copy) | ۴۔ ظلم | (tyranny) |
| ۵۔ سیاحت | (travel) | ۶۔ عیش | (life, pleasure) | ۷۔ غدر | (mutiny) | ۸۔ صنعت | (manufacturing) |

## The Elative or Comparative-Superlative أفعل

This form is derived by prefixing ا [a] to the first root letter and infixing َ [a] between the second and third. It generates comparative and superlative adjectives and nouns comparable to English words ending in -er and -est. In Urdu (as in Arabic) context alone tells us whether the words are used in a comparative or superlative sense. Consider the following:

| | | | | |
|---|---|---|---|---|
| کبیر | (great) | ← | اکبر | (greater; greatest) |
| صغیر | (small) | ← | اصغر | (smaller; smallest) |

The feminine form of the comparative-superlative is فُعلیٰ. It is most often encountered in fixed phrases and technical terms.

| | | | | |
|---|---|---|---|---|
| کبیر | (great) | ← | کُبریٰ | (the major term of a syllogism) |
| صغیر | (small) | ← | صُغریٰ | (the minor term of a syllogism) |

## Irregular Forms

Hollow roots whose middle letter is ی take the following form, which is similar to the feminine form above.

| | | | | |
|---|---|---|---|---|
| طیّب | (fine) | ← | طوبیٰ | (finer, finest) |

Defective verbs (those ending in و or ی) follow the pattern افعیٰ in most cases. This is the masculine form in Arabic.

| | | | | | |
|---|---|---|---|---|---|
| علی | (high, over) | | ← | اعلیٰ | (higher, highest) |
| دنی | (low, near) | (rarely used in Urdu) | ← | ادنیٰ | (lowest) |

The Arabic feminine form of defective verbs is فعیا.

| | | | | |
|---|---|---|---|---|
| ادنیٰ | (lowest) | ← | دُنیا | (lit. lowest; idiom. the world) |

Geminate roots follow the pattern افلّ.

| | | | | | |
|---|---|---|---|---|---|
| حق | (right, truth) | حقیقت | (reality) | ← | احق | (truest; most deserving) |

*E. Read the following words and underline the comparative-superlative nouns.*

اصغر اصلاح اظہر اسلوب اقبال اعلم

*F. Form the comparative-superlatives from the nouns and give their meanings. Use the form* افعل.

| | | | | | | | |
|---|---|---|---|---|---|---|---|
| ۱۔ فصیح | (eloquent) | ۲۔ ظاہر | (clear, evident) | ۳۔ عظیم | (great) | ۴۔ شریف | (noble) |
| ۵۔ طویل | (long) | ۶۔ قدس | (holiness) | ۷۔ جاہل | (ignorant) | ۸۔ سعید | (fortunate) |
| ۹۔ قلّت | (scarcity) | ۱۰۔ کثرت | (multitude; plenty) | ۱۱۔ حبیب | (beloved) | ۱۲۔ شدید | (intense) |

## 2.7 A Note on ة in Urdu

In Arabic, the letter ة (tā marbūṭah) is pronounced either ت [t] or ہ [a] depending on its position in a phrase. In Urdu, this letter is rarely used. Instead, when Arabic words ending in ة are used in Urdu, the ة is replaced with either ت or ہ. Consider the following examples.

| Arabic | | Urdu |
|---|---|---|
| عبادة | ← | عبادت |
| ارادة | ← | ارادہ |

Sometimes, a single word ending in ة in Arabic is borrowed as two words in Urdu. In such cases, the Urdu words often have different, though related, senses. For example:

جلوَت (public; appearance; company; crowd) جلوَہ (manifestation; splendor)

The letter ة (and therefore the Urdu letters ہ and ت), as a suffix, is often used to form relative nouns. These may have a diminutive, nominative, or instantive function.

| | | | | |
|---|---|---|---|---|
| خراب | (ruined) | ← | خرابہ / خرابت | (ruin, devastation; a ruined area) |
| قسم | (part, piece; type) | ← | قِسمت | (fate, kismet) |

The following sections will discuss the many applications of this concept in greater detail.

*A. Suffix the indicated letter derived from ة and give the meaning of the resulting instantiative term.*

**ہ**

۱۔ دقیق (minute [adj.]) ۲۔ واقع (occurrent, located)

**ت**

۱۔ حال (circumstance) ۲۔ ضرور (certain, certainly)

## 2.8 Nouns of Place and Instrument

Arabic nouns of place and instrument are built from the root form (Form I) of the verb.

## Nouns of Place (اسمِ ظرف)

Nouns of place are formed according to the following paradigms.

مَفعَل / مَفعِل　　　　مَفعَلَہ / مَفعِلَہ　　　　مَفعَلَت / مَفعِلَت

Note that in all nouns of place, مَ [ma] is prefixed to the first root letter. The short َ [a] infixed between م and the first letter of the root distinguishes the noun of place from the noun of instrument and most participles, which begin with مِ [mi-] and مُ [mu] (in almost all cases), respectively. In addition, a short vowel (either َ [a] or ِ [i]) is infixed between the second and third letters of the root. The letters ت [-at] or ہ [ā] (both translations of the Arabic letter ة) may also be suffixed in some nouns of place.

Urdu grammarians (following Arabic ones) refer to these words as اسمِ ظرف (lit. nouns of container) because, as the term suggests, this pattern indicates the location, space, or time where or when the root is performed or occurs. They are best defined as such. For example, a مَدرَسہ (madrasa) is the place where درس (lesson, instruction) (from the root د ر س meaning to study) takes place. Likewise, a مجلِس (assembly) is where a جلسہ (session) (from the root ج ل س meaning to sit) occurs.

| | | | | |
|---|---|---|---|---|
| (school; madrasa) | مَدرَسہ | ← | (lesson) | درس |
| (assembly) | مَجلِس | ← | (session) | جلسہ |
| (the object of one's intention; purpose) | مَقصَد | ← | (intention; purpose) | قصد |

Note the difference in sense between the words in the last pair. Both can correctly be translated as "purpose" in English. The first, قصد, being the verbal noun, refers to the purpose or intention that one has or forms in one's mind to do something. Hence, میں نے سفر کا قصد کیا۔ (I formed the intention of traveling.). By contrast, one's مقصد is the thing or occasion for which one has formed the intention or purpose, that is, one's purpose or goal. Hence, سفر کرنا میرا مقصد تھا۔ (To travel was my purpose.).

### Irregular Forms

In nouns of place built on geminate roots, the two identical root letters remain doubled and the infixed vowel is shifted. Note that Urdu speakers typically pronounce the last-mentioned noun of place as مُحِبَّت.

| | | | | |
|---|---|---|---|---|
| (a doctor's office) | مَطَب | ← | (medicine) | طِب |
| (a place of refuge) | مَفَر | ← | (fleeing; flight) | فرار |
| (love) | مَحَبَّت | ← | (love) | حُب |

Hollow roots take the form مفال, to which ہ or ت may be added.

| | | | | |
|---|---|---|---|---|
| (station; site, place) | مقام | ← | (standing, remaining) | قیام |
| (reproach; disgrace) | ملامت | ← | (meanness, vileness) | لوم |

Occasionally, a word which, in Arabic, has ء (hamza) as a medial letter, will appear to be a hollow root in Urdu. In such cases, the hamza will be written in the noun of place. For example, the word سوال (question), which is written and pronounced سؤال in Arabic, yields the following noun of place.

(issue; point in question) مسئلہ ← (question) سوال

Defective roots end in kharā zabar or alif maqṣūrah (ىٰ).

(battlefied) مغزیٰ ← (righteous war) غزا

*A. Read the following words and place a check mark next to the nouns of place. Then indicate the three root letters as they appear in the noun of place.*

مُقیم مَذاق مُفلِس مَحفِل مَنزِل مُسلِم مَغرِب مَشرِق مُوجِد مُجَدِّد مَسئَلہ مَشرَب

*B. Given the meanings of the words on the right, choose the synonym that best fits the noun of place on the left.*

۱۔ اخذ (deriving, taking) ← ماخذ (finance) (source) (theft)

۲۔ ذوق (taste) ← مذاق (fork) (sensibility) (smell)

۳۔ سجدہ (prostration) ← مسجد (forehead) (carpet) (mosque)

۴۔ شعلہ (flame) ← مشعل (lantern) (heat) (firewood)

۵۔ وقوف (standing; wisdom) ← مَوقِف (language) (school) (stance, position)

*C. Form nouns of place from the following Form I nouns according to the given pattern and give their meaning.*

**مَفعَل**

۱۔ وقوع (occurrence) ۲۔ جمع (gathering)

۳۔ عبادت (worship) ۴۔ عیش (living)

**مَفعِل**

۵۔ غروب (sinking [of the sun]) ۶۔شرق (rising [of the sun])

۷۔نزول (descent, alightment) ۸۔ ولادت (birth)

**مَفعَلہ**

۹۔ سوال (question) ۱۰۔ حکم (ruling, order, judgment)

۱۱۔قبر (grave) ۱۲۔ رتبہ (rank)

**مَفعُلت**

| | | | |
|---|---|---|---|
| ۱۳۔ ملک | (region, reign) | ۱۴۔ کرم | (kindness) |
| ۱۵۔ ذِلّت | (disgrace) | ۱۶۔ خوف | (fear) |

**مَفعِلت**

| | | | |
|---|---|---|---|
| ۱۷۔ غفر | (forgiveness) | ۱۸۔ عرف | (knowledge) |
| ۱۹۔ عُذر | (apology) | ۲۰۔ عیش | (life, living) |

## Nouns of Instrument (اسم آلہ)

Nouns of instrument are formed according to the following paradigms.

مِفعَل مِفعَلَہ مِفعال

Note that in all nouns of instrument, مِ [mi] is prefixed to the first root letter. This short vowel ِ [i] is extremely important, since it distinguishes nouns of instrument from other verbal nouns (e.g. the noun of place) and most participles. Consider the following homographic nouns of place and instrument built on the root طبخ (to cook). (Note that they are rare in Urdu and used here for the sake of demonstration.) The only difference between them is the short vowel.

| | | | |
|---|---|---|---|
| مَطبخ | (kitchen) | مِطبخ | (cooking utensil) |

As their name implies, nouns of instrument are the means by which the root concept is enacted or occurs. For example, مِفتاح (key) is the instrument or means by which فتح (opening) occurs; a مِسطَر (ruler) is the instrument by which a سَطَر (line) is formed; and a مِقدار (measurement, amount) is the means by which the قدر (value; extent) of something is gauged.

| | | | | |
|---|---|---|---|---|
| فتح | (opening) | ← | مِفتاح | (key) |
| سطر | (line) | ← | مِسطَر | (ruler) |
| قدر | (value) | ← | مِقدار | (measurement, amount) |

## Irregular Forms

The initial vowel of assimilated verbs (those whose first letter is a vowel) assimilate the short ِ [i] and their first root letter changes to ی.

| | | | | |
|---|---|---|---|---|
| وزن | (weight) | ← | میزان | (scale) |

*D. Read the following list of Arabic nouns, some of which are nouns of place and instrument. Mark all nouns of place (اسم ظرف) with ظ and all nouns of instrument (اسم آلہ) with آ.*

مَوقعہ مُبارَک مَذہَب مُمکِن مَنزِل مُلازِم ملاقات مستشرق مسند مِصداق مِضراب مِقراض

مُسلِم مخلوق مِزاج مُخالفت امداد مَشوَرَہ مُشکِل مَطلب محلّہ

*E. Form nouns of instrument from the following Form I words according to the given pattern and give their meaning.*

**مِفعال**

| | | | |
|---|---|---|---|
| ۱۔ضرب | (striking, stroking [an instrument]) | ۲۔عمارت | (building) |
| ۳۔ورثہ | (inheritance) | ۴۔ قیاس | (estimate, syllabus) |
| ۵۔صدق | (truth, verity) | ۶۔ رائے | (view) |

**مِفعَل**

۷۔صیقل (polish)

**مِفعَلہ**

۸۔شرب (drink)

*Review Exercise. Guessing meaning. Based on the meaning of the word on the right, guess the meaning of the related words on the left.*

| | | | | | |
|---|---|---|---|---|---|
| ۱۔ عبادت | (worship) | عابد | معبود | مَعبَد | |
| ۲۔ حکم | (ruling; command) | حاکم | محکوم | محکمہ | |
| ۳۔ نظر | (sight, seeing) | ناظر | منظور | مَنظر | مِنظار |
| ۴۔ قتل | (killing, murder) | قاتل | مقتول | مقتل | |
| ۵۔ کتابت | (writing) | کاتب | مکتوب | مکتب | |

## 2.9 Personal Gender and Arabic Nouns

Urdu does not follow the Arabic rules for gender except in the case of persons. In Arabic, the feminine gender is marked by the letter ة. When used as a marker of feminine personal gender, this letter is rendered as ہ in Urdu. Consider the following examples:

| | | | |
|---|---|---|---|
| والد | (father) | والدہ | (mother) |
| حسین | (beautiful) | حسینہ | (a beautiful woman) |

This suffix is not used exclusively with Arabic words in Urdu. For example, it is used to make the feminine form of the following word, which is built from an Arabic word and Indic-Persian agentive suffix.

اداکار (actor) ← اداکارہ (actress)

When such nouns are pluralized using the standard Urdu suffixes for unmarked feminine nouns in the nominative and oblique cases (یں and وں), the ہ changes to ا.

| | | | | |
|---|---|---|---|---|
| خادمہ | (female servant) | ← | خادمائیں | (female servants) |
| اداکارہ | (actress) | ← | اداکاراؤں کے ساتھ | (with actresses) |

*A. Underline the personal nouns that show feminine gender. Note that ہ may appear at the end of words which are not personal nouns. In such cases, the words are not necessarily feminine.*

| | | | | | | |
|---|---|---|---|---|---|---|
| عالم | عالمہ | مُصنّفہ | مقابلہ | مُصوّرہ | رقّاصہ | مطرب |
| مطربہ | ملکہ | مصنف | شاعر | خالو | خالہ | معشوقہ |

*B. Write the corresponding feminine form of the following words. Then give their meanings.*

۱۔ صاحب (lord, sir) ۲۔ محترم (esteemed) ۳۔ شاعر (poet) ۴۔ محبوب (beloved) ۵۔ مَلِک (king)

*C. Gender and names. Here follows a list of Urdu women writers. Underline the names in which the Arabic marker of feminine personal gender is found.*

| | | | |
|---|---|---|---|
| شبنم شکیل | رابعہ پنہاں | زاہدہ زیدی | جمیلہ نشاط |
| ادا جعفری | ریحانہ روحی | رشید جہاں | واجدہ تبسم |
| عشرت آفرین | صفیہ اختر | قرۃ العین حیدر | جیلانی بانو |
| عارفہ شہزاد | ساجدہ زیدی | بانو قدسیہ | الطاف فاطمہ |
| منصورہ احمد | شاہدہ حسن | رضیہ بٹ | جمیلہ ہاشمی |
| نسیم سید | تنویر انجم | عصمت چغتائی | فہمیدہ ریاض |
| پروین شاکر | زاہدہ حنا | کشور ناہید | |

## 2.10 Form II Verbal Nouns تفعیل تفعِلت تفعِلہ تفعال

These occur in three paradigms. The most common by far is تَفعِیل. This paradigm prefixes تَ [ta] to the first letter of the root and infixes ی [ī] between the second and third letters of the root. Less common is تفعِلہ or تفعِلت. The least common is تِفعال or تَفعال.

Form II verbal nouns are factitive, that is, they impart senses of causation, intensification, iteration (repetition), or declaration (considering someone or something to be something or a certain way) to the root concept from which they are derived. For this reason, they may impart factitive or transitive senses to intransitive or stative ones; or causative senses to active ones. They may also form verbal nouns from words that are not, in Arabic, verbal roots; for example, تنویر (illumination) from the noun نور (light).

In less theoretical terms, the meaning of Form II verbal nouns is best defined in most cases as causing, imparting, or enacting the Form I (root) meaning. For example, with regard to the Form I (root) noun علم (knowledge), the Form II verbal noun تعلیم means "causing or imparting knowledge"; thus, "education."

| | | | | |
|---|---|---|---|---|
| (imparting knowledge; education) | تعلیم | ← | (knowledge) | علم |

Likewise, the Form II noun of the Form I noun خوف (fear) gives the sense of "causing, imparting fear (to someone)"; thus, terrorization.

| | | | | |
|---|---|---|---|---|
| (terrorization) | تخویف | ← | (fear) | خوف |

Note that a single English word may sometimes be used to translate both the Form I and Form II nouns if the English word carries both a stative and an active sense. For example, the Form I (root) noun عمارت (building) refers to the concrete, actual building (walls, doors, and so on), while the Form II noun تعمیر is best defined as causing or bringing about a building; that is, "(the act of) building."

| | | | | |
|---|---|---|---|---|
| ([the act of] building; construction) | تعمیر | ← | (a building) | عمارت |

The following chart reviews the most common forms of the Form II verbal nouns. Pay close attention to the ways in which the Form II verbal noun relates to the meaning of the Form I noun.

| | | | | |
|---|---|---|---|---|
| ([the act of] building; construction) | تعمیر | ← | (a building) | عمارت |
| (enaction) | تعمیل | ← | (action) | عمل |
| | | | | |
| (remembrance; making mention) | تذکرہ | ← | (memory; mention) | ذکر |
| (empowerment, encouragement) | تقویّت | ← | (power) | قوت |
| | | | | |
| (showing likeness; resemblance) | تمثال | ← | (likeness) | مثال |
| (explanation) | تبیان | ← | (clear description) | بیان |

Note that تفعلہ/تفعِلت is the preferred paradigm for verbs whose third root letter is a long vowel (e.g. و). For example, the root خلو (to be empty), whence خلا (empty space) and خالی (empty) yields تخلیہ (evacuation; clearing); ربو (to grow up) yields تربیت (upbringing, training).

## A Note on Pronunciation

In Urdu, the pronunciation of words in the تَفعِلہ / تَفعِلت paradigm does not necessarily follow what is considered standard according to the rules of Arabic. Indeed, the following word is pronounced variously as shown:

tajurbā tajarbā tajrabā tajribā (experience) تجربہ

*A. Recognizing Form II verbal nouns. Read the following list of words and mark the Form II verbal nouns.*

| | | | | | |
|---|---|---|---|---|---|
| تجربہ | تنظیم | تحصیل | حرام | تقسیم | تحریر |
| قریب | اتفاق | تشریف | تجزیہ | تغزل | تسلیم |
| تعلیم | تحقیق | سفید | تقریب | حلیم | تارک |
| طریقہ | تزکیہ | تفرقہ | تلازم | تغزّل | تَجزِیہ |

*B. Predicting meanings. Underline the most likely English synonym of the Form II verbal nouns on the left based on the the meaning of basic form (Form I) nouns on the right.*

| | | | | | | |
|---|---|---|---|---|---|---|
| (depiction) | (thought) | (difference) | تصویر | ⟵ | (form; face) | ۱۔ صورت |
| (modification) | (arrangement) | (disagreement) | ترتیب | ⟵ | (rank, station) | ۲۔ رتبہ |
| (expansion) | (bonus) | (approximation) | تقریب | ⟵ | (nearness) | ۳۔ قُربت |
| (research) | (testimony) | (exaggeration) | تحقیق | ⟵ | (truth) | ۴۔ حقیقت |
| (falsification) | (investigation) | (assertion) | تصدیق | ⟵ | (verity) | ۵۔ صدق |

*C. Create Form II verbal nouns from the following nouns using the given paradigm and give their meanings.*

تفعیل

| | | | | | |
|---|---|---|---|---|---|
| (understanding) | ۳۔ فہم | (ruined) | ۲۔ خراب | (instruction, lesson) | ۱۔ دَرس |
| (knowledge) | ۶۔ علم | (etiquette) | ۵۔ ادب | (gain, acquisition) | ۳۔ حصول |
| (share, portion; type) | ۸۔ قسم | (motion) | ۸۔ حرکت | (breadth) | ۷۔ وُسعَت |

تفعلت

(powerful) ۱۔ قوی

## 2.10.1 Form II Active and Passive Participles

The active (مُفَعِّل) and passive (مُفَعَّل) participles of Form II verbal nouns follow a predictable pattern. To form the Form II participles, مُ [mu] is prefixed to the first letter of the root in both the active and passive participles, ِ [i] is infixed between the second and third root letters of the active participle, and َ [a] is infixed between the second and third root letters of the passive participle. We shall see that this pattern is repeated with all active and passive participles forms II-X. What distinguishes Form II participles is that the second letter of the root is doubled with ّ (tashdīd). The active participle imparts a sense similar to the English agentive suffix -er (and its variants) and the passive imparts one similar to the passive suffix -ed (and its variants). In theory, both participles may be used as nouns or adjectives. In practice, each is typically used as one or the other. Study the following chart:

| Passive Participle | Active Participle | Verbal Noun | |
|---|---|---|---|
| مُفَعَّل | مُفَعِّل | تفعیل | II |

Consider the following example:

(civilized, cultured) مُہذَّب (refiner, civilizer) مُہذِّب ← (refinement, culture, civility) تہذیب

Note that the participles are the same for the rare forms of the Form II verbal noun. Thus:

(rememberer) مُذکِّر ← (remembrance; mention) تذکرہ

### Irregular Form II Active and Passive Participles

Roots that end in a vowel take the forms مُفَعِّی [mufa‘‘ī] (active) and مُفَعّیٰ [mufa‘‘ā] (passive). The following chart shows the Form II verbal noun and active and passive participles for the root verb ربو (to foster):

(preserved; [fruit] preserves) مربّیٰ (fosterer, patron) مربّی (training; fostering) تربیت

*A. Mark the Form II active and passive participles with an a and p, respectively. Note that not all the words are Form II participles.*

مَحفِل مُطابِق مُسلِم مُکمَّل مُحاسِب

مُنَوَّر مُفید مَرتبہ مَجلِس مُقدَّس

*B. Write the active participles of the following verbal nouns and estimate their meanings.*

(instruction) ۳۔ تدریس (education) ۲۔ تعلیم (writing) ۱۔ تصنیف

(strengthening, empowering) ۶۔ تقویت (research) ۵۔ تحقیق (renewal) ۴۔ تجدید

*C. Write the passive participles of the following verbal nouns and estimate their meanings.*

| | | | | | |
|---|---|---|---|---|---|
| ۱۔ تصویر | (illustration) | ۲۔ تسلیم | (acceptance) | ۳۔ تدریس | (instruction) |
| ۴۔ تکمیل | (completion) | ۵۔ تنظیم | (organization) | ۶۔ تقویت | (strengthening, empowering) |

*D. Write the verbal nouns corresponding to the following active and passive participles and give their meanings. Use the paradigm* تفعیل

| | | | | | |
|---|---|---|---|---|---|
| ۱۔ مفکّر | (thinker, intellectual) | ۲۔ مُقلِّد | (follower; imitator) | ۳۔ مُعلِّم | (teacher, educator) |
| ۴۔ مُشرَّف | (ennobled, honored) | ۵۔ مُعظَّم | (honored) | ۶۔ مُشکَّل | (formed, fashioned) |

*Review Exercise. Given the meaning of the word on the right, estimate the meaning of the words on the left.*

صحت (soundness, correctness) ← ۱۔ صحیح ۲۔ تصحیح ۳۔ مُصحِّح

## 2.11 Form III Verbal Nouns

The most common paradigm of the Form III noun in Urdu is مفاعلت / مفاعلہ. In the standard dictionary pronunciation of words of this form, مُ [mu] is prefixed, ا [ā] is infixed between the first and second root letter, َ [a] is infixed between the second and third root letters, and either ہ or ت is suffixed to the final root letter. Study the following chart.

| | | | | |
|---|---|---|---|---|
| عمل | (action) | ← | مُعاملہ | (affair, business, deal, dealing) |
| قبل | (before, front) | ← | مقابلہ | (confrontation; comparison) |
| خلِاف | (opposite) | ← | مخالفت | (opposition, dissent) |

The Form III noun suggsts reciprocity or mutual involvement in enacting the root concept. It is often best defined as "two (or more) parties enacting the root to each other," "one person enacting the root vis-à-vis something or someone else," or "enacting the root vis-à-vis two (or more) parties."

For example, the Form III noun معاملہ refers to two (and perhaps more) parties enacting some kind of action (عمل) to each other; hence, "business, dealing, affair." Likewise, مقابلہ denotes a situation in which to two (or more) parties or entities stand or are placed or made to stand before or in front of (قبل) each other either for the purpose of competition or comparison, hence "confrontation" or "comparison." Further, مخالفت is the condition in which one party stands opposite or opposed to (خلاف) another, often in a state of in mutual opposition, hence "opposition."

A comparison can also be made between the Arabic paradigm مفاعلہ / مفاعلت and the Latin prefix con- (and its variants), which similarly implies reciprocity or mutuality.

| | | |
|---|---|---|
| confrontation | ← | front, before |
| مقابلہ | ← | قبل |

You will have noticed that Form III nouns end in either ہ or ت. The reason for this is that, in Arabic, Form III nouns end in ة, and, in Arabic, this letter is pronounced either as ہ [a] or ت [t] depending on context. Since Urdu (following Persian) does not use ة except in rare cases, it uses either ہ [a] or ت [t]. Sometimes, Urdu derives two words from what are, in Arabic, only one, by using both letters. These words often have similar meanings in Urdu. For example:

(less common) (business dealings) معاملت    (affair, matter; business) معاملہ

## Pronunciation of Form III

In standard Arabic, the pronunciation of Form III nouns is مُفاعَلَت / مُفاعَلَہ. In Urdu, the pronunciation of short vowels in this form is flexible. Dictionaries will generally suggest pronunciation according to the standard Arabic paradigm. However, Urdu speakers often pronounce Form III nouns according to the following paradigm and one can argue that it, too, should be considered standard in Urdu.

[mufāilat]    مُفاعِلت / [mufāilā]    مُفاعِلہ

For example:

[muḳhālifat]    مخالفت

In idiomatic use, the pronunciation of Form III words becomes even more flexible. Often, the short vowel [a/i] between the second and third root letter is dropped.

[mufālat]    مفاعلت / [mufālā]    مفاعلہ

[muqāblā]    مقابلہ

When the initial root letter is ع , the short u suffixed to م is often dropped. A good example of this is the word معاملہ, which is pronounced along the following spectrum:

| | | | | | |
|---|---|---|---|---|---|
| māmlā | muāmlā | muāmilā | muāmalā | ← | معاملہ |

Another common variation is to substitute ´ [a] for the ʼ [u] infixed between the prefix م and the first root letter:

| | | | | | |
|---|---|---|---|---|---|
| mavāznā | mavāzinā | muvāzinā | muvāzanā | ← | موازنہ |

## Irregular Forms

Defective roots (those ending in و or ی) (often ا in the verbal noun) take the form مُفاعات.

| | | | | |
|---|---|---|---|---|
| (encounter; visit) | مُلاقات | ← | (meeting; face) | لقا |
| (compensation; retalliation) | مکافات | ← | (sufficiency) | کفایت |

Hollow roots (those whose middle letter is و or ی) substitute ء or ی for the vowel. Thus, مفائلہ or مفائلت, مفایلہ or مفایلت

| | | | |
|---|---|---|---|
| (difficulty, problem) | مضائقہ | ← | (straits, hardship) ضیق |

## Rare Form III Pattern

A second, less common pattern used for Form III is فِعال. Here are two examples.

| | | | | |
|---|---|---|---|---|
| (struggle; jihad) | جِہاد | ← | (exertion, endeavor) | جہد |
| (contention) | جِدال | ← | (fighting) | جدل |

*A. Read the following words and underline the Form III verbal nouns.*

| | | | | | | |
|---|---|---|---|---|---|---|
| مراعات | وِصال | میدان | مذاکرہ | مشاعرہ | مضمون | ملازمت |
| مراسلہ | مندرجہ | ملاقات | مطابقت | مسافر | ملاحظہ | محامد |

*B. Write the Form III nouns related to the Form I nouns on the right using the paradigm مفاعلہ. Then choose the best synonym.*

| | | | | | |
|---|---|---|---|---|---|
| (spectacles) | (perspective) | (examination) | _____ | ← | (eye) ۱۔ عین |
| (observation) | (debate) | (inspection) | _____ | ← | (viewpoint, theory) ۲۔ نظریہ |
| (trial) | (disobedience) | (declaration) | _____ | ← | (ruling, order) ۳۔ حکم |
| (confession) | (denial) | (claim) | _____ | ← | (demand) ۴۔ طلب |
| (consideration) | (friendship) | (neglect) | _____ | ← | (regard) ۵۔ لحاظ |

*C. Write the Form III nouns corresponding to the following Form I nouns using the given paradigm and estimate their meaning.*

مفاعلہ

| | | | | | |
|---|---|---|---|---|---|
| (a book, writing) | ۳۔ کتاب | (poem, poetry) | ۲۔ شعر | (speech) | ۱۔ کلام |

مفاعلت

| | | | | | |
|---|---|---|---|---|---|
| (resemblance) | ۳۔ شباہت | (safety) | ۲۔ حفاظت | (understanding) | ۱۔ فہم |

فِعال

(union) ۱۔ وصل

## 2.11.1 Form III Participles

The active (مُفاعِل) and passive (مُفاعَل) participles of Form III nouns remove the ت / ہ ending of the verbal noun and follow the predictable vowel patterns of infixing ِ [i] between the second and third root letters to form the active participle and َ [a] between them to form the passive participle.

| Passive Participle | Active Participle | | Verbal Noun |
|---|---|---|---|
| مُفاعَل | مُفاعِل | ← | مُفاعلہ / مفاعلت |

For example:

| | | | | | | |
|---|---|---|---|---|---|---|
| (addressee) | مُخاطَب | (addresser) | مُخاطِب | ← | (address) | مخاطبت |

Note that the active participles are the same for the rare forms of the Form III noun. Thus:

| | | | | |
|---|---|---|---|---|
| (struggler, mujahid) | مجاہِد | ← | (struggle, jihad) | جِہاد |

### Irregular Form III Active and Passive Participles

Defective roots (those whose final letter is و or ی) take the special forms مُفاعِی (active) and مُفاعیٰ (passive) in Form III.

| | | | |
|---|---|---|---|
| (a person whom one meets) | ملاقی | (encounter, meeting) | ملاقات |

Geminate roots have identical forms for the active (مُفال) and passive (مُفال) participles. These are rare.

*A. Mark the Form III active and passive participles with a and p, respectively.*

مدخل    مُطابِق    مُسلِم    موافِق    مُحاسِب

مصور    مبین    مَجالِس    مجلس    مَساجِد

*B. Write the active participle of the following Form III verbal nouns. Then give their meanings. Since participles can be adjectives or nouns (or both), the part of speech of the resulting participle has been given in parentheses.*

| | | | | | |
|---|---|---|---|---|---|
| ۱۔ ملازمت | (employment) | (n.) | ۲۔ مناسبت | (appropriateness) | (adj.) |
| ۳۔ موافقت | (agreeability) | (adj.) | ۴۔ محافظت | (protection) | (n.) |
| ۵۔ مساوات | (equality) | (adj.) | ۶۔ مناظرہ | (debate) | (n.) |

*C. Write the passive participle of the following Form III verbal noun and give its meaning.*

۱۔ مبارکت (auspiciousness, blessedness)

*D. Write the verbal noun corresponding to the following participles using the given paradigm and estimate its meaning.*

مفاعلہ

۱۔ مراقِب (meditator) ۲۔ معالِج (doctor, "treater") ۳۔ مشاہَد (observed; observed phenomenon)

## 2.12 Form IV Verbal Nouns

Form IV nouns follow the pattern اِفعال, in which اِ [i] is prefixed to the first letter of the root and, in standard cases, ا [ā] is infixed between the second and third. Most nouns in this pattern are masculine.

Form IV pattern imparts a sense of activation, emphasis, or implementation to the root and is thus often best defined as "causing, applying, activating, instantiating, emphasizing, or implementing the root." In many cases, the Form IV noun imparts a sense similar to the Latinate prefixes ad- (to, toward) and in- or en- (in, into, toward). For example, the Form IV noun اِظہار may be defined as "causing the appearance (ظُہور) (of something)," thus, "expression." Likewise, اِمداد may be defined as "implementing or instantiating help (مَدَد); thus, "(rendering) assistance."

| | | | | |
|---|---|---|---|---|
| ظہور | (appearance) | ← | اِظہار | (expression, demonstration) |
| مَدَد | (help) | ← | اِمداد | (assistance) |

### Irregular Forms

Roots whose first letter is a vowel take the form اِیعال, since the ِ is assimilated.

| | | | | |
|---|---|---|---|---|
| اَمن | (safety, security) | ← | ایمان | (belief, faith; integrity) |
| وجود | (existence) | ← | ایجاد | (creation, invention) |

Roots whose middle letter is a vowel take the form اِفالہ or اِفالت. (In Arabic, the form is اِفالة.)

| | | | | |
|---|---|---|---|---|
| (permission, allowance) | اجازت | ← | (justification) | جواز |
| (enclosing; an enclosure; boundary) | احاطہ | ← | (an enclosure; a court) | حیطہ |

Defective roots (those whose final letter is و or ی) also take a special form, following the paradigm اِفعا / اِفعاء. Remember that verbal nouns derived from defective roots often end in ا.

| | | | | | | |
|---|---|---|---|---|---|---|
| (implementation) | اجرا | ← | (current) | جاری | ← | جری |

## Distinguishing Form IV from Form II

Since both Form II تفعیل and Form IV افعال paradigms suggest the implementation or activation of the root, it is important to distinguish between their senses. Whereas Form II typically conveys implementation, enaction, or application of the root concept, Form IV typically conveys a stronger sense of causation, outward-directed performance, or projection. For example, while تعلیم (education) suggests the transmission of knowledge (عِلم), اعلام (notice, announcement) suggests the outward projection of it. Consider the following minimal pairs.

| | | | | | |
|---|---|---|---|---|---|
| (notification) | اعلام | (education, instruction) | تعلیم | (knowledge) | عِلم |
| (favor; beneficence) | احسان | (approbation; praise) | تحسین | (fineness, goodness) | حُسن |
| (permission) | اجازت | (suggestion; resolution) | تجویز | (justification) | جَواز |

*A. Read the following words aloud and underline the Form IV nouns. Pay close attention to the pronunciation of the initial vowel.*

| | | | | | | |
|---|---|---|---|---|---|---|
| اِحساس | اِنتظار | اِیمان | امید | اَفکار | اِنکار | اَخبار |
| آداب | اِرشاد | اَخلاق | اِجلاس | اصلی | اَولاد | اِنصاف |
| | | | | | اَصناف | اِجابت |

*B. Produce the Form IV verbal noun from the Form I nouns on the right. Then choose the best meaning.*

| | | | | | | |
|---|---|---|---|---|---|---|
| (rejection) | (invitation) | (assembly) | _____ | ← | (session) | ۱۔ جَلسہ |
| (assistance) | (ignorance) | (welfare) | _____ | ← | (help) | ۲۔ مَدَد |
| (acknowledgment) | (resistance) | (award) | _____ | ← | (gift) | ۳۔ نِعمت |
| (facilitation) | (law) | (affirmation) | _____ | ← | (necessity) | ۴۔ وجوب |
| (collaboration) | (fairness) | (collection) | _____ | ← | (half) | ۵۔ نِصف |

*C. Derive the Form IV nouns from the Form I (root) words and give their meanings.*

| | | | | | |
|---|---|---|---|---|---|
| ۱۔ صلح | (peace, well-being) | ۲۔ بدل | (change) | ۳۔ قدم | (step) |
| ۴۔ تمام | (all, complete) | ۵۔ خروج | (exit, exodus) | ۶۔ عزّت | (honor) |

*D. Form the irregular Form IV verbal nouns corresponding to the following Form I nouns and participles. Then give their meanings. In the case of hollow verbs, use the suffix indicated.*

| | | | | | |
|---|---|---|---|---|---|
| ۱۔ جواب | (response) | (use ت) | ۲۔ قیام | (residence, stay) | (use ت) |
| ۳۔ فائدہ | (benefit) | (use ہ) | ۴۔ بقا | (permanence) | |
| ۵۔ حیات | (life) | | ۶۔ اثر | (effect) | |

## 2.12.1 Form IV Participles مُفعِل and مُفعَل

The Form IV active (مُفعِل) [mufʿil] and passive (مُفعَل) [mufʿal] participles follow predictable patterns: مُ [mu] is prefixed; ِ [i] and َ [a] are infixed between the second and third letters of the root in the active and passive participles, respectively. The mute letter sukūn (no vowel) is infixed between the first and second letters of the root. Like other participles, Form IV participles may be adjectives or nouns and sometimes both.

| Verbal Noun | | Active Participle | Passive Participle |
|---|---|---|---|
| اِفعال | ← | مُفعِل | مُفعَل |

Consider the following example:

اِثبات (positing; establishment; proof) ← مُثبِت (positive) مُثبَت (proven)

**Irregular Form IV Active and Passive Participles**

Hollow roots (those whose middle letter is و or ی) take the forms مُفِیل (active) and مُفال (passive).

افادہ (utility; benefit) مُفید (beneficial; useful) مفاد (profit, benefit)

Defective roots (those whose final letter is و or ی) take the forms مُفعِی and مُفعَی or مُفعا.

ابقا (perpetuation, preservation) ← مُبقی (perpetuator, preserver)

Geminate roots also have a special form for active (مُفِلّ) and passive (مُفَلّ) participles.

احقاق (establishing truth or justice) ← مُحِق (one who establishes truth or justice)

اضرار (causing harm) ← مُضِر (harmful)

Note that Form IV participles (مفعِل / مفعَل) are orthographically indistinguishable from Form II participles (مفعّل / مفعِّل) without diacritical markings. This creates ambiguity which context and prior knowledge alone can resolve. The following chart surveys the Form II and IV verbal nouns and corresponding active and passive participles of the root سلم. Note that the participles are indistinguishable without diacritics.

| | | | | |
|---|---|---|---|---|
| II | تسلیم | ← | مُسَلِّم | مُسَلَّم |
| IV | اسلام | ← | مُسْلِم | مُسْلَم |

Form II and IV participles are also indistinguishable from the مفعل form of the nouns of place and instrument. You will recall that these nouns are characterized by ◌َ [a] and ◌ِ [i] infixed between م and the first letter of the root. Therefore, there are six possible vocalizations (and their associated meanings) of words in the مفعل form. Prior knowledge and context typically resolve issues of ambiguity. When they do not, editors and copyists typically add diacritics.

*A. Recognizing active and passive participles. Mark the Form IV active and passive participles with a and p, respectively. Note that not all words are Form IV participles.*

مُقبِل　مُطابِق　مُسلِم　مصنّف　محاسِب　مَسلک　مَفرَق　مُجیب　مُرید　مُفید

مُراد　مُفید　مَرتبہ　مُمکِن　مُقدّس　مفکّر　مُہذّب　مَظہر　مَغرِب

*B. Write the active participles of the following Form IV verbal nouns and give their meanings.*

۱۔اشکال (difficulty)　۲۔امکان (possibility)　۳۔ارادت (discipleship; devotion)

۴۔انکار (denial)　۵۔ابطال (nullification)　۶۔اسلام (Islam)

۷۔انعام (award)　۸۔ احسان (favor, kindess)　۹۔اقامت (residence, stay)

*C. Write the passive participles of the following verbal nouns in the spaces provided.*

۱۔ابہام (ambiguity)　۲۔ابطال (nullification)　۳۔ارادہ (intention)

۴۔ادامہ (continuance, permanence)　۵۔ارسال (sending)

*D. Form the Form IV verbal noun corresponding to the participle. Then give its meaning.*

۱۔ ملزَم ([the] accused)　۲۔ مُخبِر (informant)　۳۔ مخلص (sincere)

۴۔ مُنصِف (just; a just person)　۵۔مفتی (mufti)　۶۔ محیط (encompassing) (use ہ)

*Review Exercise. Use the meaning given for the word to the right of the arrow to estimate the meanings of the words to the left of it.*

عمل (action) ← عامل　معمول　مَعمل　تعمیل　مُعمِل　معاملہ　اعمال　مُعمَل

*Review of Form I-IV Nouns and Participles. Review the following Arabic noun forms, all of which have been covered in this and the preceding sections.*

| Passive Participle | Active Participle | Verbal Noun(s) | |
|---|---|---|---|
| مَفعُول | فاعِل | فعل فعول فعال | I |
| | | مَفعَل / مَفعَلہ / مَفعَلت | Place |
| | | مِفعَل / مِفعال | Instrument |
| | | فعیل | Agency |
| | | فعّال | Intensity |
| | | افعل / فعلی | Comp. Super. |
| مُفعَّل | مُفعِّل | تَفعِیل | II |
| | | تَفعِلت / تَفعِلہ | |
| | | تَفعال / تِفعال | |
| مُفاعل | مُفاعِل | مُفاعلہ / مفاعلت | III |
| | | فِعال | |
| مُفعَل | مُفعِل | اِفعال | IV |

*Review Exercise. Write five Urdu words that fall under each of the following Arabic paradigms. Your examples can be drawn from words in these units or from outside readings.*

| | | | | | |
|---|---|---|---|---|---|
| ________ | ________ | ________ | ________ | ________ | مَفعل / مَفعلہ / مَفعَلت |
| ________ | ________ | ________ | ________ | ________ | مِفعَل / مِفعلہ / مِفعال |
| ________ | ________ | ________ | ________ | ________ | فاعل |
| ________ | ________ | ________ | ________ | ________ | مفعول |
| ________ | ________ | ________ | ________ | ________ | تفعیل |
| ________ | ________ | ________ | ________ | ________ | مفعِّل |
| ________ | ________ | ________ | ________ | ________ | مفعَّل |
| ________ | ________ | ________ | ________ | ________ | مفاعلہ |
| ________ | ________ | ________ | ________ | ________ | مفاعلت |
| ________ | ________ | ________ | ________ | ________ | مفاعِل |
| ________ | ________ | ________ | ________ | ________ | مُفاعل |
| ________ | ________ | ________ | ________ | ________ | اِفعال |
| ________ | ________ | ________ | ________ | ________ | مُفعِل |
| ________ | ________ | ________ | ________ | ________ | مُفعَل |

## 2.13 Form V Verbal Nouns تفعّل

The Form V verbal noun is formed by prefixing تَ [ta] to the root, infixing َ [a] between the first and second letters of the root, doubling [ّ] the second letter of the root, and infixing ُ [u] between the second and third root letters. Most nouns in this pattern are masculine.

Form V performs two main functions. It can be the reflexive form of Form II (تفعیل/تفعلہ), which means that it denotes the effect or resulting state of performing the action of Form II, especially to oneself. The resulting noun is thus often stative and abstract. In such cases, the best defition of a Form V noun is perhaps "the state resulting from the Form II noun" or "the abstract condition of the Form II noun."

(imagination) تَصَوُّر ← (making an image; an image) تصویر ← (an image) صورت

Here, تَصَوُّر (imagination) is the condition which results from depicting (تصویر) an image (صورت) (especially to oneself). Here are two other ways to translate the relationship between these words using somewhat analogous vocabulary in English:

(formation [abstract]) تَصَوُّر ← (a formation; the act of forming) تصویر ← (form) صورت

(depiction [abstract]) تَصَوُّر ← (a depiction; the act of depicting) تصویر ← (picture) صورت

Form V can also be used to form abstract nouns from Form I (root) words. In such cases, the best definition of a Form V noun is perhaps "the quality of the Form I noun." In this way, the Form V pattern is similar to the Latin suffixes -ity or -ation; the Greek -ism; or the English -ness. Consider the following examples.

(civilization) تمدُّن ← (city; Medina) مدینہ

("ghazal-ness"; lyricism) تغزل ← (ghazal; lyric) غزل

### Irregular Forms

Verbal nouns built from defective roots (those whose final letters are و or ی) take the form تَفَعِّی.

(relief; satisfaction of mind) تشفّی ← (recovery, remedy) شفا

(luminosity) تجلّی ← (illumination; beholding; purification) تجلیہ ← (manifestation) جلوہ

Defective roots in this paradigm sometimes differ in spelling and pronunciation from standard Arabic and instead share their form and pronunciation with the Persian form of the nouns, from which Urdu likely borrowed them.

(desire) تمنّا ← (wish, desire) مُنیَت

(friendship; sainthood; closeness to God) توَلّی ← (friend; saint) وَلی

*A. Practice pronouncing Form V words by reading the following out loud.*

تعلّق تصور توجہ تعجب توقع تبسم

*B. Produce the Form V relative to the Form I or Form II words below and give their meanings.*

| | | | | | |
|---|---|---|---|---|---|
| ۱۔ تقویت | (strengthening) | ۲۔ تبدیل | (change, exchange) | ۳۔ تحریک | (movement, motion) |
| ۴۔ تجدید | (renewal) | ۵۔ تفریح | (entertainment, fun) | ۶۔ تقریب | (drawing close; approximation) |
| ۷۔ تعلیم | (education) | ۸۔ صدقہ | (donation; sacrifice) | ۹۔ حیرت | (surprise, wonder) |
| ۱۰۔ رحم | (mercy) | ۱۱۔ صوفی | (Sufi) | ۱۲۔ شیعہ | (Shia) |
| ۱۳۔ برکت | (blessing) | ۱۴۔ عجب | (wonder, wondrous) | ۱۵۔ عدد | (number) |

## 2.13.1 Form V Participles

The active (مُتَفَعِّل) and passive (مُتَفَعَّل) participles of Form V verbal nouns follow patterns similar to other participles. As with all Form II-X participles, مُ [mu] is prefixed. In this case, the تَ [ta] of the verbal noun is retained, as is the infixed َ [a] between the first and second root letters. The second root letter remains doubled, but the ُ [u] of the verbal noun is replaced with ِ [i] or َ [a] to mark the active and passive participle, respectively. The tell tale signs of a Form V participle are the pair مُتَ preceding three Arabic root letters, the second of which is doubled.

The following examples illustrate the difference between Form V active and passive participles. Note that the Form V verbal noun typically carries a passive sense, so passive participles of this form are rare.

| | | | |
|---|---|---|---|
| تَصَوُّر (imagination) | ← | مُتَصَوِّر (imagining, imaginative) | مُتَصَوَّر (imagined) |
| تغیر (alteration) | ← | متغیِر (changing, alterative) | متغیَر (altered) |

The abstract and reflexive nature of the Form V noun is such that the active participle is often a relative adjective rather than an agentive noun. As such, in general, Form V active participles are typically best defined as "possessed of the quality of the Form V noun." Thus, someone who is متاسف (regretful) is possessed of تاسف (regret).

تاسف (regret, sorrow) ← متاسف (regretful, sorrowful)

Some Form V active participles are indeed active nouns. For example, a متغزل [mutaghazzil] (lyric poet) is so named for possessing of the kind of lyricism (ghazalness) (تغزل) associated with lyric (ghazal) poetry (غزل).

تغزل (lyricism) ← متغزل (a ghazal-writing or lyrical poet)

### Irregular Forms

Roots whose final letter is و or ی have special forms of active (مُتَفَعِّی) and passive (مُتَفَعَّیٰ) participles.

| | | | | | | |
|---|---|---|---|---|---|---|
| (desired) | مُتمنّیٰ | (desirous) | متمنی | ⟵ | (desire) | تمنا |
| | | (manifest; illuminated) | متجلّی | ⟵ | (manifestation; illumination) | تجلی |

*C. Underline the Form V active and passive participles. Not all words are Form V participles.*

متاثر　　متناسب　　متفرِق　　متبرک　　مطول　　متغیر　　متابعت

*D. Write the active participles of the Form V nouns and give their meanings.*

۱۔ تاثر (impression)　　۲۔ توجہ (attention)　　۳۔ توقع (expectation)

۴۔ تعلق (relationship)　　۵۔ تحیر (astonishment)　　۶۔ تسلی (consolation, satisfaction)

*E. Write the Form V verbal nouns related to the following active participles and guess their meanings.*

۱۔ متبسِّم (smiling)　　۳۔ متخیل (imagined)　　۴۔ متعدد (numerous)

## 2.14 Form VI Verbal Nouns تفاعل

Form VI verbal nouns are formed by prefixing تَ [ta] to the root, infixing ا [ā] between the first and second root letters, and infixing ُ [u] between the second and third root letters.

Form VI conveys two meanings. First, it may be the reflexive or reciprocal form of Form III (مفاعلت / مفاعلہ). As such, words in this pattern typically convey an abstraction of Form III or the state or condition which results from performing the Form III noun. Likewise, whereas Form III typically implies that either two parties, or a specified or countable number of parties, are involved in an action, Form VI may imply that more than two parties, or an unspecified number of parties, are involved. Sometimes, the differences between them are quite subtle. The most general definition of Form VI nouns as the reflexive or reciprocal noun of Form III is "the state associated with or resulting from the Form III noun." A less common, but still important, definition is "the state resulting from a multiplicity or uncountable number of parties performing Form III." For example, the Form VI noun تشابہ (similitude) is the abstract state associated with the mutual similiarity or resemblance (مشابہت) between or among people or things. Similarly, تقابل (comparison, encounter) is the abstract state associated with making a comparison or engaging in confrontation (مقابلہ). Whereas مقابلہ typically refers to a comparison between two things, تقابل refers to the abstract process or method of comparison. A تقابلی جائزہ is a comparative study, which necessarily involves the comparison (مقابلہ) of things.

Consider the following:

| | | | | |
|---|---|---|---|---|
| مشابہت | (resemblance) | ← | تشابہ | (similitude) |
| مقابلہ | (confrontation; comparison) | ← | تقابل | (comparison; encounter) |
| مطابقت | (conformity; congruity) | ← | تطابُق | ([state of] conformity; congruity) |

Second, the Form VI noun may imply the affectation or pretense of Form I nouns. In this case, the best definition of a Form VI noun is, "affecting, pretending (to be or have), or feigning Form I." Consider the following:

| | | | | |
|---|---|---|---|---|
| جَہالَت | (ignorance) | ← | تجاہُل | (feigned ignorance) |
| مرض | (illness) | ← | تمارُض | (feigning illness) |

## Irregular Forms

Roots whose final letter is و or ی follow the pattern (تفاعی) in standard Arabic and Urdu.

| | | | | |
|---|---|---|---|---|
| ملاقات | (encounter, meeting) | ← | تلاقی | (reunion) |

The pronunciation of the final vowel in this noun can vary in Urdu, as it does in Persian:

| | | | | |
|---|---|---|---|---|
| قضیہ | (proposition; disputation; case; action) | ← | تقاضا | (demand) |

Geminate roots take the form تفالّ.

| | | | | |
|---|---|---|---|---|
| ضِدّ | (contrariness; obstinacy) | ← | تضاد | (contradiction) |

*A. Indicate the Form VI nouns with a check mark.*

| | | | | | | |
|---|---|---|---|---|---|---|
| تواضع | تاثر | تماثل | تنزل | تنازل | تناسب | تمثیل |
| تماشا | تجزیہ | تلافی | تساوی | تبدیلی | تمکین | مساوات |

*B. Form the Form VI verbal noun from the Form I and Form III nouns. Then give their meanings.*

| | | | |
|---|---|---|---|
| ا۔ غفلت | (negligence, ignorance) | ۲۔ سہل | (ease) |
| ۳۔ فخر | (pride) | ۴۔ مناسبت | (relationship; appropriateness) |
| ۵۔ مطابقت | (accordance) | ۶۔ مساوات | (equality) |
| ۷۔ موافقت | (agreement) | ۸۔ منازعت | (quarrel, hostility) |

## 2.14.1 Form VI Active and Passive Participles

Form VI participles are represented by the paradigms مُتَفاعِل (active) and مُتَفاعَل (passive). They are formed by prefixing مُ [mu], retaining the intial ت of the verbal noun, and replacing the ُ [u] of the verbal noun with ِ [i] or َ [a] to indicate the active and passive participle, respectively. Because the Form VI noun is reflexive and therefore carries a passive sense, passive participles in this form are rare. Like the active participles of Form V, the active participles of Form VI nouns are typically adjectives and are best defined as "possessed of the quality of the Form VI noun." Consider the following active participles.

| | | | | |
|---|---|---|---|---|
| (act. part.) (similitudinous; equivocal) | مُتَشابِہ | ← | (similitude) | تشابہ |
| (pass. part.) (introduced; acquainted) | مُتَعارَف | ← | (introduction; acquaintance) | تعارف |

### Irregular Forms

The Form VI active (مُتَفاعی) and passive (مُتَفاعیٰ) participles of defective roots (those whose third root letter is و or ی) have special forms.

| | | | | |
|---|---|---|---|---|
| (equal) | مُتَساوِی | ← | (state of equality) | تساوی |
| (demanding [e.g. of payment]) | مُتَقاضی | ← | (demand [of payment]) | تقاضا |

Geminate roots have identical active (مُتَفالّ) and passive (مُتَفالّ) participles in Form VI.

| | | | | |
|---|---|---|---|---|
| (contradictory, opposite) | مُتَضاد | ← | (contradiction; the opposite) | تضاد |

*C. Mark the Form VI participles.*

متناسب　　مطابق　　متطابق　　متعارف　　متاثر　　متناہی　　متفرق

*D. Given the meaning of the word on the right, estimate the meaning of the active participles to the left of the arrows.*

| | | | |
|---|---|---|---|
| مُتَغافِل | ← | (purposeful neglect; avoidance) | ۱۔ تغافل |
| مُتَساہِل | ← | (carelessness) | ۲۔ تساہل |
| مُتَوازِن | ← | (balance, equal measurement) | ۳۔ توازن |
| مُتَناسِب | ← | (proportion, proportionality) | ۴۔ تناسب |
| مُتَطابِق | ← | (accordance; concordance) | ۵۔ تطابق |

*E. Form the active participle of the Form VI nouns. Then give their meanings.*

| | | | | | |
|---|---|---|---|---|---|
| (buffeting [of waves]) | ۳۔ تلاطم | (hospitality) | ۲۔ تواضع | (excess) | ۱۔ تجاوز |
| (synonymy) | ۶۔ ترادف | (recompense) | ۵۔ تلافی | (agreement) | ۴۔ توافق |
| (introduction, familiarity) | ۹۔ تعارف | (continuity) | ۸۔ تواتر | (comparison) | ۷۔ تقابل |

*Review Exercise. Reflexive meanings. Use the meaning of the root word on the right to estimate the meanings of the words on the left.*

| | | | | | | | | | | |
|---|---|---|---|---|---|---|---|---|---|---|
| ________ | متاثر | ← | ________ | تاثُّر | ← | ________ | تاثیر | ← | (effect) | ۱۔ اثر |
| ________ | متصوّر | ← | ________ | تصور | ← | ________ | تصویر | ← | (image) | ۲۔ صورت |
| ________ | متخیّل | ← | ________ | تخیل | ← | ________ | تخییل | ← | (idea) | ۳۔ خیال |
| ________ | متفرق | ← | ________ | تفرق | ← | ________ | تفریق | ← | (difference) | ۴۔ فرق |
| ________ | متنافر | ← | ________ | تنافر | ← | ________ | منافرت | ← | (dislike) | ۵۔ نفرت |
| ________ | متداخل | ← | ________ | تداخل | ← | ________ | مداخلت | ← | (entry) | ۶۔ دخل |
| ________ | تماثل | ← | ________ | تماثُل | ← | ________ | مُماثلت | ← | (likeness) | ۷۔ مثال |
| ________ | متعامل | ← | ________ | تعامل | ← | ________ | معاملہ | ← | (action) | ۸۔ عمل |

## 2.15 Form VII Verbal Nouns اِنفِعال

The Form VII verbal noun is formed by prefixing اِن to the root, infixing ِ [i] between the first and second root letters, and infixing ا [ā] between the second and third root letters. Most (some would say all) nouns in this pattern are masculine.

Form VII is the passive form of the root. It typically conveys the sense of the abstraction of the root concept. Hence, it is perhaps best defined as "the state or condition resulting from the performance of Form I."

(insertion, being inserted; enrollment) اِندِراج ← (folding up; insertion) درج

(disclosure; discovery) اِنکِشاف ← (opening; explanation; revelation) کشف

### Irregular Forms

Roots that end in و or ی have a special form (اِنفِعا / اِنفِعاء).

([state of] evacuation) انخلا ← (space; emptiness; vacuum) خلا

Roots whose middle letter is و or ی have a special form (اِنفِیال).

(obedience, compliance) انقیاد ← (confinement; rule) قید

*A. Underline the Form VII verbal nouns.*

استعمال انقلاب اختیار انتظار انحصار افتخار انکسار

*B. The relationship between the root and the Form VII noun is surveyed in the following examples, some of which are not intuitive. Given the definition of the Form I (root) noun on the right, underline the most appropriate synonym of the Form VII noun on the left.*

| | | | | | | |
|---|---|---|---|---|---|---|
| (irrelevance) | (relationship) | (dependence) | انحصار | ← | (restriction) | ۱۔ حصر |
| (acceptance) | (repulsion) | (decline) | اندفاع | ← | (repelling) | ۲۔ دفع |
| (activity) | (modification) | (revolution) | انقلاب | ← | (turning, overturning) | ۳۔ قلب |
| (indifference) | (care) | (humility) | انکسار | ← | (breaking) | ۴۔ کسر |
| (joyfulness) | (straits) | (pain) | انبساط | ← | (joy) | ۶۔ بسط |

*C. For each Form I word, give the corresponding Form VII noun and guess its meaning.*

| | | | | | |
|---|---|---|---|---|---|
| (reflection; contrary) | ۳۔ عکس | (trivial) | ۲۔ خفیف | (stamp, imprint) | ۱۔ طبع |
| (barrier, obstruction) | ۶۔ سَدّ | (repelling) | ۵۔ دفع | (control) | ۴۔ ضبط |
| | | (type, division) | ۸۔ قسم | (cut) | ۷۔ قطع |

## 2.15.1 Form VII Active and Passive Participles

The active (مُنفعِل) and passive (مُنفعَل) participles follow predictable rules: مُ is prefixed, ن is retained, and ِ or َ is infixed between the second and third root letters to indicate the active and passive participles, respectively. Because Form VII nouns are by definition passive, the passive participle is rare and the active participle typically carries an adjectival sense best defined as "possessed of the qualities of the Form VII noun."

| | | | |
|---|---|---|---|
| (enrolled; inserted) | مُندرِج or مُندرَج | ← | (folding up; insertion) اِندِراج |
| (disclosed, discovered) | مُنکشِف | ← | (disclosure, discovery) اِنکِشاف |

### Irregular Forms

Roots whose middle letters are و or ی have a special, identical form in the active (مُنفال) and passive (مُنفال) participles.

| | | |
|---|---|---|
| (obedient) منقاد | ← | (obedience) انقیاد |

Roots whose final letters are و or ی take special forms in the active (مُنفعِی) and passive (مُبفَعیٰ) participles.

| | | |
|---|---|---|
| (extirpated; complete) منقضی | ← | (extirpation; completion) انقضا |

Geminate roots take special forms in the active (مُنفَلّ) and passive (مُنفِلّ) participles.

(degraded, decayed) مُنحط ← (degradation, decay) انحطاط

*A. Write the active participles of the following Form VII verbal nouns and guess their meanings.*

| | | | | | |
|---|---|---|---|---|---|
| ۱۔ اندراج | (registration) | ۲۔ انکشاف | (revelation, disclosure) | ۳۔ انعکاس | (reflection) |
| ۴۔ انبساط | (joyousness) | ۵۔ انقلاب | (revolution, change) | | |

## 2.16 Form VIII Verbal Nouns اِفتِعال

Form VIII nouns are formed by prefixing اِ [i] to the root, infixing تِ [ti] between the first and second letters of the root, and infixing ا [ā] between the second and third letters of the root.

Form VIII is the reflexive of the root. It may also impart a passive sense to a root whose sense is active. Sometimes, it carries a sense nearly identical to the root. It is perhaps best defined as "the state resulting from or associated with the performance of the root concept." Hence, Form VIII nouns are comparable to English words ending in -ation, -ance, and -ity.

For example, اختلاف (difference) is the state resulting from acting or being against (خِلاف) someone or something. Likewise, انتظار (expectation; waiting) is the state of looking (نظر) for or forward to someone or something.

خِلاف (against, opposing) ← اختلاف (difference)

نظر (sight) ← انتظار (expectation; waiting)

### Irregular Forms

Roots whose first letter is ء (written as ا in root nouns in Urdu) take the form (اِیتِعال) in which the root letter assimilates the initial اِ [i]. Such words are rare.

الفت (affection, intimacy) ← اِیتلاف (familiarity, intimacy)

Roots whose first letter is و or ی take the form (اِتّعال). That is, the و is assimilated to the infixed ت.

وحدت (oneness) واحد (one, sole) ← اِتّحاد (unity)

Roots whose middle letter is و or ی take the form (اِفتِیال).

خیر (good; happiness) ← اختیار (free will; authority, autonomy; selection)

شوق (interest, passion) ← اشتیاق (eagerness)

Roots whose final letter is و or ی take the form (اِفْتِعا / اِفْتِعاء)

| | | | | |
|---|---|---|---|---|
| (end; the utmost point) | انتہا | ← | (extremely) | نہایت |

## Assimilation in Form VIII

The spelling and pronunciation of the inflixed ت of the Form VIII paradigm changes according to the letter that immediately precedes it (the first of the three root letters). The following chart surveys the changes.

| | | | | | |
|---|---|---|---|---|---|
| | | تّ | ← | ت + | ت |
| | (obedience) | اِتّباع | ← | (following) | تبع |
| | | دّ | ← | ت + | د |
| | (claim) | اِدّعا | ← | (a claim) | دعوی |
| | | دّ | ← | ت + | ذ |
| (rare) | (mentioning; recalling) | اِدّکار | ← | (mention) | ذکر |
| | | زد | ← | ت + | ز |
| | (crowd, throng) | ازدحام | ← | (trouble) | زحمت |
| | | صط | ← | ت + | ص |
| | (technical term; phraseology) | اصطلاح | ← | (rectitude) | صلاح |
| | | ضط | ← | ت + | ض |
| | (agitation, restlessness) | اضطراب | ← | (beating) | ضرب |
| | | طّ | ← | ت + | ط |
| | (announcement; information) | اِطّلاع | ← | (appearance) | طلوع |
| | | ظّ | ← | ت + | ظ |
| (rare) | (suffering tyranny) | اِظّلام | ← | (tyranny) | ظلم |

*A. Underline the Form VIII verbal nouns.*

انسان　امتحان　اختلاف　اصلی　انتقال　انتخاب　الزام

اعتراض　ابتداء　اغراض　استقلال　اعتراف　اشتعال　انتقام

اضطرار　استطرلاب

*B. Write the Form VIII nouns related to the Form I words and give their meanings.*

۱۔ جماعت (group) ۲۔ محنت (toil, work) ۳۔ خلط (mixture)

۴۔عقیدہ (a belief) ۵۔ ختم (end, finish) ۶۔ منع (forbidden)

۷۔ عدل (justice, balance) ۸۔ نِقمت (punishment)

*C. Give the Form VIII verbal nouns of the following irregular Form I verbal nouns and estimate their meanings.*

۱۔ ضرر (harm) ۲۔ زوجہ / زوج (husband/wife) ۳۔ وہم (suspicion)

۴۔ وصل (union) ۵۔ وفق (agreement)

*D. Given the definition of the word on the right, underline the most appropriate synonym of the Form VIII noun on the left. Use a dictionary to help resolve any issues.*

| | | | | | |
|---|---|---|---|---|---|
| ۱۔ شرکت | (participation) | ← اشتراک | (compositeness) | (contract) | (signature) |
| ۲۔ نقل | (transference) | ← انتقال | (death) | (resignation) | (fax) |
| ۳۔ ضرب | (strike, blow) | ← اضطراب | (agitation) | (hammer) | (wound) |
| ۴۔ عرض | (petition, statement) | ← اعتراض | (silence) | (record) | (objection) |
| ۵۔ شعلہ | (flame) | ← اشتعال | (fire) | (fuel) | (incitation) |

## 2.16.1 Form VIII Active (مُفتَعِل) and Passive (مُفتَعَل) Participles

The active and passive participles are formed according ot predictable patterns. Note that because this form often carries a passive sense, the passive participle is rare.

اِختِلاف (difference) ← مُختَلِف (different)

انتظار (expectation, waiting) ← مُنتظِر (one expecting) مُنتظَر (expected, awaited)

### Irregular Forms

Roots whose first letter is و or ی retain the assimilated ت in the active (مُتَّعِل) and passive (مُتَّعَل) participles.

اتفاق (agreement) ← مُتَّفِق (in agreement)

Roots whose middle letter is و or ی take special forms of the active (مُفتار) and passive (مُفتار) participles. Note that they are indentical.

اختیار (choice, will; authority) ← مختار (invested with authority) مختار (selected)

Roots ending in و and ی have special forms of active (مُفتَعی) and passive (مفتعا / مُفتَعیٰ) participles.

(finisher; one who has perfected a skill) مُنتہی ← (end) انتہا

(finished; conclusion) مُنتہا

Geminate roots have special forms of the active (مُفتَلّ) and passive (مُفتَل) participles.

(perturbed, despairing) مضطر ← (despair) اضطرار

*E. Underline the Form VIII participles.*

مختلف منتقل مستقبل معتقد منتخب مزلم منعکس

*F. Write the active participle of the Form VIII verbal noun and give its meaning.*

۱۔ اختلاف (difference) ۲۔ اعتقاد (belief) ۳۔ ابتدا (beginning)

۴۔ اعتراض (objection) ۵۔ انتقال (lit. transference; idiom. death)

۶۔ انتظام (arrangement) ۷۔ اعتراف (acknowledgment)

## 2.17 Form X Verbal Nouns اِستِفعال

The Form X verbal noun is formed by prefixing اِستِ [isti], infixing ْ [no vowel] between the first and second letter of the root, and infixing ا [ā] between the second and third.

Form X conveys a number of meanings. Perhaps most frequently, it denotes an attempt to perform the root (Form I). Thus, it is best defined as "attempting, requesting, or desiring to enact the root concept." It can also be declarative, in which case it is best defined as "regarding or considering something to be possessed of the quality of the root." It can also be a reflexive form of Form IV (اِفعال), in which case it is best defined as "the state associated with or resulting from performing Form IV."

For example, استعمال (use) is a attempt to put (something) into action (عمل). Likewise, استحصال (exploitation) is an attempt to acquire (حصول; حاصل) something for unfair selfish advantage. استحسان (praising, approving; regarding as favorable) can be defined as "regarding something to be possessed of beauty or fineness (حُسن)" or the "state associated with or resulting from showing favor (اِحسان) to someone." استحقاق (entitlement, rightfulness) may be defined as "the state resulting from the acknowledgment or affirmation of a right (احقاق)" or "regarding (someone) as being possessed of a right (حق)."

۱۔ عمل (deed) ← استعمال (putting to use; application; use)

۲۔ حصول (acquisition) ← استحصال (exploitation)

۳۔ حُسن (beauty) اِحسان (favor) ← استحسان (praise; approval; regarding as favorable)

۴۔ حق (a right) احقاق (acknowledging a right) ← استحقاق (entitlement, rightfulness)

## Irregular Forms

Roots whose first letter is و or ی follow the paradigm (استیعال).

| | | | |
|---|---|---|---|
| (extirpation, eradication) استیصال | ← | (root; principle) اصل | |

Hollow roots (whose middle letter is و or ی) follow the paradigm (استفالہ/استفالت)

| | | | | | |
|---|---|---|---|---|---|
| (availing of something; deriving benefit) | استفادہ | ← | (utility) افادہ | (benefit, use) | فائدہ |
| (repose) | استراحت | ← | | (rest) | راحت |

Roots whose final letter is و or ی take the paradigm (اِستِفعا/اِستِفعاء) and sometimes (اسیفعیٰ)

| | | | | |
|---|---|---|---|---|
| (exception) | استثنا | ← | (second) | ثانی |
| (resignation) | استعفا | ← | (pardon) | عفو |
| (supplication) | استدعا | ← | (prayer) | دعا |

*A. Underline the Form X verbal nouns.*

| | | | | | | |
|---|---|---|---|---|---|---|
| استقبال | استحکام | استجازت | اسپتال | اسناد | استقلال | استعمال |
| استدعاء | استعارہ | استھان | اُستوار | استدلال | اصطلاح | استاد |

*B. Derive the Form X nouns from the following Form I words (nouns and participles) and give their meanings. For nouns derived from hollow roots, use ت unless otherwise indicated.*

| | | | | | |
|---|---|---|---|---|---|
| (present) | ۳۔ حاضر | (understanding) | ۲۔ فہم | (fixity, settlement) | ۱۔ قرار |
| (service, employment) | ۶۔ خدمت | (rationale) | ۵۔ جواز | (response, answer) | ۴۔ جواب |
| (use ہ) (benefit) | ۹۔ فائدہ | (rest) | ۸۔ راحت | (external) | ۷۔ خارِج |

*C. Given the meaning of the word on the right, guess the meaning of the Form X noun on the left.*

| | | | | | | |
|---|---|---|---|---|---|---|
| (source) | (case) | (reasoning) | استدلال | ← | (evidence) | ۱۔ دلیل |
| (desire) | (supplication) | (God) | استدعا | ← | (prayer) | ۲۔ دُعا |
| (welcome) | (confrontation) | (inquiry) | استقبال | ← | (before) | ۳۔ قَبل |
| (charity) | (donation) | (augury) | استخارہ | ← | (good) | ۴۔ خَیر |
| (excuse) | (resignation) | (anger) | استعفا | ← | (pardon) | ۵۔ عَفو |

## 2.17.1 Form X Active and Passive Participles

The active (مُستَفعِل) and passive (مُستَفعَل) participles of Form X nouns follow predictable patterns. مُ is prefixed to the root; the تِ of the verbal noun is replaced by تَ in the participle, the ا of the verbal noun is dropped and replaced with ِ [i] َ [a] in the active (-er) and passive (-ed) participles, respectively.

(used) مُستَعمَل ← (use) استعمال

## Irregular Forms

Roots whose medial letters are و or ی take special forms of the active (مُستَفِیل) and passive (مُستَفال) participles.

(benefitted) مستفاد (advantageous) مستفید ← (taking advantage) استفادہ

Roots whose final letter is و or ی take special forms of the active (مُستَفعِی) and passive (مُستَفعیٰ) participles.

(resigner) مستعفی ← (resignation) استعفا

Geminate roots have special forms of the active (مستفِل) or passive (مستفَل) participles.

(entitled) مستحق ← (entitlement) استحقاق

As always, one should bear in mind that the meaning of participles may be idiomatic.

(the future) مستقبل ← (welcome; reception) استقبال ← (before; in front of) قبل

*A. Underline the Form X participles.*

مستعمل مصیبت مسلم مستحکم مستقبل مستحسن مستانہ

*B. Derive the Form X passive participle from the Form X noun and give its meaning.*

| | | | |
|---|---|---|---|
| ۱۔استحضار | (summoning; recalling [to mind]) | ۲۔ استحکام | (stability, durability) |
| ۳۔ استعمار | (colonization) | ۴۔ استغراق | (immersion) |
| ۵۔ استعمال | (use) | ۶۔ استخراج | (derivation) |
| ۷۔ استجابت | (answering [of prayer]) | ۸۔ استحباب | (favor, belovedness) |

*C. Read the following Form X active participles, then give the corresponding Form X verbal noun and its meaning.*

| | | | | | |
|---|---|---|---|---|---|
| ۱۔ مستوجب | (deserving) | ۲۔ مستقیم | (erect; upright) (use ت) | ۳۔ مستقل | (permanent; independent) |
| ۴۔ مستقرّ | (settled, fixed) | ۵۔مستعِدّ | (capable, prepared) | ۶۔ مستشرق | (orientalist) |
| ۷۔ مستعمِر | (colonizer) | | | | |

*Review Exercise. Match the nouns on the right with their participles.*

| | | | |
|---|---|---|---|
| ۱۔ استحکام | ___ | ا | منقلب |
| ۲۔ استغراق | ___ | ب | مستحکم |
| ۳۔ انتقال | ___ | پ | مستحسن |
| ۴۔ استحسان | ___ | ت | مختصر |
| ۵۔ اِنکسار | ___ | ٹ | منکسر |
| ۶۔ استفادہ | ___ | ث | منتقل |
| ۷۔ انقلاب | ___ | ج | مستفید |
| ۹۔ اختصار | ___ | چ | مستغرق |
| ۱۰۔ استقلال | ___ | خ | مستقل |

## 2.18 Quadriliteral Roots, Nouns, and Participles Forms I, II, and IV

In the preceding lessons, we have studied Arabic's triliteral root system, which produces most of the Arabic vocabulary used in Urdu. In addition to these triliteral roots, Urdu also contains a number of Arabic words built on four root letters, here called quadriliteral. The derived noun forms and related participles of quadriliteral roots closely resemble the triliteral ones.

### Quadriliteral Form I Nouns and Participles فعلل فعللت فعللہ فعلال

Unlike triliteral Form I nouns, quadriliteral nouns in Arabic are limited to a small number of paradigms. Many of these words are Arabicized borrowings from other languages.

Two common paradigms are فعلل and فعللہ / فعللت. A rarer pattern is فعلال. Note that many of these nouns include redoubled syllables. Here follow examples:

| | | | | | | | |
|---|---|---|---|---|---|---|---|
| بُلبُل | (nightingale) | غُرغُر | (growling) | ہُدہُد | (hoopoe) | | |
| بُرقع | (burka) | | | | | | |
| سِلسِلہ | (series, chain) | وَسوَسہ | (evil suggestion) | قہقہہ | (laughter) | زَلزَلہ | (earthquake) |
| شیطنت | (devilry) | تَرجُمہ | (translation) | ہندسہ | (geometry) | فَلسَفہ | (philosophy) |
| بُرہان | (argument) | شیطان | (satan) | | | | |

Occasionally, a word built on a triliteral root will be relexicalized as a quadriliteral noun. Consider the following:

سَلَطَ (to hold power over, govern) ⟵ سُلطان (sultan, ruler) ⟵ سَلطنت (sultanate)

Here, the Form I triliteral noun of intensity, سُلطان (sultan) has been used as the basis of the relative quadriliteral noun سَلطَنت (sultanate), wherein the ن of the suffix in the former is treated as a root letter in the latter.

## Quadriliteral Form I Active (مُفَعْلِل) and Passive (مُفَعْلَل) Participles

These are regular and predictable. مُ [mu] is prefixed to the root, َ [a] is infixed between the first and second root letters, no vowel between root letters two and three, and ِ [i] or َ [a] is infixed between the third and fourth root letters to form the active and passive participles, respectively.

(geometer) مُہَندِس ← (geometry) ہَندسہ

(continuous) مُسَلسَل ← (series, chain) سِلسِلہ

*A. Underline the quadriliteral nouns.*

| ہندسہ | مذہب | طوفان | تحریر | تجزیہ | محفل | وسوسہ |
|---|---|---|---|---|---|---|
| قمقمہ | قریب | علوم | مصنف | فلسفہ | اکبر | محلہ |

*B. Form the indicated participle of the quadriliteral noun, and estimate its meaning.*

| | | |
|---|---|---|
| (passive) | (argument; reason) | ۱۔ بُرہان |
| (active) | (translation) | ۲۔ ترجمہ |
| (active) | (mad prattle; evil suggestion) | ۳۔ وسوسہ |
| (passive) | (burqa) | ۴۔ برقع |

## Quadriliteral Form II Nouns and Participles

The quadriliteral Form II verbal noun تَفَعلُل is formed by prefixing تَ [ta] to the root and infixing ُ [u] between the penultimate (third) and final (fourth) root letters. It is the intransitive and reflexive counterpart to quadriliteral Form I nouns and is best defined as "the state or quality resulting from or associated with the quadriliteral Form I noun." All nouns in the quadriliteral Form II pattern are gramatically masculine in Urdu.

For example, تَسَلسُل (sequentiality, continuity) is the quality associated with a sequence (سلسلہ).

(sequentiality, continuity) تَسَلسُل ← (series, sequence) سلسلہ

The active (مُتَفَعلِل) and passive (مُتَفَعلَل) participles are predictable. مُ [mu] is prefixed, the vowel pattern is retained, except that ِ [i] and َ [a] replace ُ [u] in the active and passive participles, respectively. Note that because the quadriliteral Form II noun is already reflexive or passive, the passive participle is rare.

(sequential, continuous) مُتَسَلسِل ← (sequentiality) تَسَلسُل

The quadriliteral Form II pattern is sometimes used to form abstract nouns from quadriliteral nouns that are themselves formed from triliteral roots. In the following example, the noun of place مَرکَز (center) has been treated as a quadriliteral noun, and an abstract noun derived from it:

(centered) متمرکز ← (centrality) تمرکز ← (center) مرکز

They may also be used to form abstract nouns from names and borrowings that can be interpreted as having four root letters.

(acting like or becoming Kashmiri) تکشمر ← (Kashmir) کشمیر

*C. Underline the Form II quadriliteral nouns.*

تذکرہ تسلسل تجربہ تقریر تزلزل تقابل

*D. Form the Form II quadriliteral noun and estimate its meaning.*

ا۔ زلزلہ (quake, shaking)

*E. Write the active participle of the Form II noun.*

ا۔ تزلزل

### Quadriliteral Form IV Nouns and Participles

Form III quadriliteral nouns are extremely rare and therefore not covered here. Form IV is also extremely rare. It involves doubling the final letter of the quadriliteral root and infixing alif. The only frequently occurring quadrilateral Form IV noun in Urdu (along with its active participle) is written here for the sake of example.

(at rest, at ease; satisfied, confident) مطمئن ← (quiet, rest; satisfaction, confidence) اطمینان

## 2.19 Arabic Plurals in Urdu

Urdu speakers and writers regularly use Arabic patterns of pluralization, so it is helpful to have at least passing familiarity with them when encountering new vocabulary. Arabic pluralizes nouns in many different ways. Although it will take some time to familiarize yourself with all the variations, there are some recurring patterns which can be learned quickly and facilitate the rapid acquisition of new vocabulary.

## 2.20 Arabic Plural Suffixes

### The Personal Plural Suffix ین [-īn]

Personal nouns of masculine, mixed, or unspecified gender are often pluralized by suffixing ین [-īn]. For example:

مُصَنِّف (writer) ← مُصَنِّفِین (writers)

*A. Underline the personal nouns pluralized with the Arabic plural suffix.*

منتظمین محرکین خبریں حاضرین سامعین شوقین عمارتیں

*B. Use the Arabic personal plural suffix to pluralize the following Arabic personal nouns and give their meanings.*

۱۔ محقق (researcher) ۲۔ مؤرخ (historian) ۳۔ مخاطب (addresser) ۴۔ مخالف (opponent)
۵۔ ناظر (viewer)

### The Dual Personal Suffix ین [-ain]

This suffix generates pairs. In Urdu, such pairs are often either conventional (e.g. parents) or carry poetical, literary, metaphysical, or exaggerative senses.

والِد (father) والِدہ (mother) ← والدَین (parents)

کَون (world) ← کونَین (the two worlds; this world and the next)

Note that the personal plural and the dual are homographs, not homophones.

*C. Write and pronounce the dual of the following nouns. Guess the meaning of each word and the context in which it might be used. Check your guesses in an Urdu dictionary.*

۱۔ بحر (sea) ← ________

۲۔ جانب (side) ← ________

۳۔ ضد (contrary) ← ________

۴۔ طرف (side) ← ________

۵۔ مشرق (east) ← ________

### The Plural Suffix ات [-āt]

The suffix ات [-āt] is among the most common Arabic pluralizing suffixes used in Urdu. In Arabic, one of the most common ways in which ات is used is as the plural suffix of nouns that end in ة (U: ہ / ت). This is because, in Arabic, ة marks feminine nouns and ات is the feminine plural suffix. This explains why ات is used in Urdu to pluralize Arabic feminine personal nouns. ات also can be used to form the plural of all Form II-X verbal nouns. Sometimes, Urdu uses ات to pluralize nouns of Arabic origin that are not pluralized with ات in Arabic. Note that, in Urdu, when a word ends in ہ or ت, and these letters are, in terms of etymology, substitutions for ة, the ہ or ت is dropped. Consider the following:

| | | | | | |
|---|---|---|---|---|---|
| I | شاعرہ | (female poet) | ← | شاعرات | (female poets) |
| I | صِفت | (attribute) | ← | صفات | (attributes) |
| I | سوال | (question) | ← | سوالات | (questions) |
| II | تصویر | (image) | ← | تصویرات | (images) |
| III | مقابلہ | (confrontation) | ← | مقابلات | (confrontations) |
| IV | اِشکال | (difficulty) | ← | اِشکالات | (difficulties) |
| V | تصوُّر | (imagination) | ← | تصوُّرات | (imaginations) |
| VI | تقابُل | (encounter) | ← | تقابُلات | (encounters) |
| VII | اختلاف | (difference) | ← | اختلافات | (differences) |
| VIII | انقلاب | (revolution) | ← | انقلابات | (revolutions) |
| X | استعمال | (use) | ← | استعمالات | (uses) |

An exception to the general rule that ات pluralizes feminine personal nouns is the following:

| | | | | |
|---|---|---|---|---|
| حضرت | (gentleman) | ← | حضرات | (gentlemen) |

This may be explained by the fact that, in Arabic, the word حضرة (presence) is feminine, but is used to mean "gentleman" in special constructions.

*D. Mark the plural nouns with a ج.*

اثرات حالت مقامات سلطنت حضرات اختیارات تاثیرات

تصنیفات ریاست حیات کثرت ملاقات اختلافات ہمت

*E. Pluralize the following nouns using ات.*

۱۔والدہ ۲۔مصنّف ۳۔ تحقیق ۴۔ تجربہ ۵۔ حرکت ۶۔ واقعہ ۷۔ معاملہ ۸۔ اِظہار ۹۔ تعلق

## 2.21 Arabic Broken Plurals

Many Arabic nouns are pluralized by what Arabic grammarians call "broken plurals." Instead of suffixation (e.g. ات or ین), these plurals are formed by infixation (in some cases, along with prefixation and suffixation), thereby "breaking" the singular form of the noun.

### 2.21.1 Broken Plurals of Form I Nouns

#### The Paradigm اَفعال

Among the most common broken-plural paradigms for Form I nouns is اَفعال. This broken plural form is typically used with the most basic pattern (فعل). Other Form I nouns have different broken plural patterns or do not use broken plurals at all. In this paradigm, ا [a] is prefixed to the root and ا [ā] is infixed between the first and second root letters. Note that this paradigm is distinguished from Form IV verbal nouns (اِفعال) by its initial اَ [a].

| | | | |
|---|---|---|---|
| فعل | ← | اَفعال | |
| عَمَل (action) | ← | اَعمال | (actions) |
| وَقت (time) | ← | اَوقات | (timings; schedule) |

In the case of many "hollow" nouns whose middle letter is ا [ā], the و of their verbal root appears in the broken plural.

| | | |
|---|---|---|
| حال | ← | احوال |
| مال | ← | اموال |

In the case of words whose first letter is ا, the prefixed ا combines to form an initial آ.

| | | |
|---|---|---|
| اثر | ← | آثار |

In some cases, broken plurals are used in a singular sense and can therefore be re-pluralized.

خبر (news) ← اخبار (newspaper) ← اخبارات (newspapers)

*A. Pluralize the following nouns using the pattern اَفعال.*

۱۔سبب ۲۔لفظ ۳۔ شعر ۴۔ سند ۵۔ طرف ۶۔ باب ۷۔ افق ۸۔ فکر ۹۔ وقف ۱۰۔ نور

*B. Give the singular form of the following plurals.*

۱۔ اوزان ۲۔اغراض ۳۔ آلام ۴۔ آداب ۵۔ اقوام ۶۔ ادوار ۷۔اوصاف ۸۔ اسرار

## The Paradigm فُعُول

This paradigm is also found in singular forms; for example, شروع (beginning). But one of its main uses is to form broken plurals of Form I nouns.

| | | | | |
|---|---|---|---|---|
| فعل | | ← | فُعُول | |
| عِلم | (knowledge) | ← | عُلُوم | (sciences) |
| امر | (matter) | ← | اُمور | (matters) |

Plurals formed with this pattern can be repluralized:

وجہ (aspect; reason) ← وجوہ (aspects; reasons) ← وجوہات (aspects; reasons)

*C. Pluralize the following nouns using the pattern فُعُول.*

۱۔ نجم ۲۔ عیب ۳۔ رسم ۴۔ سطر ۵۔ صدر

*D. Write the singular forms of the following plural nouns.*

۱۔نفوس ۲۔ نقوش ۳۔ حروف ۴۔ ملوک (kings) ۵۔اصول

## Broken Plurals of Geminate Form I Nouns

Geminate Form I nouns are typically pluralized as فُلُول. Those with ہ or ت suffixed are pluralized as فلَل (the initial vowel remains the same). Consider the following:

| | | | | |
|---|---|---|---|---|
| فل | | ← | فلول | |
| حق | (right) | ← | حُقوق | (rights) |
| خط | (letter) | ← | خُطوط | (letters) |
| فلّہ / فلّت | | ← | فلَل | |
| قِصّہ | (story) | ← | قِصَص | (stories) |
| اُمّت | (a people) | ← | اُمَم | (peoples) |

Note that some geminate nouns take افعال as their broken plural form:

| | | | | |
|---|---|---|---|---|
| سِرّ | (mystery) | ← | اسرار | (mysteries) |
| حبیب | (beloved) | ← | احباب | (loved ones, friends) |

*E. Give the plural form of the following nouns using either* فعول *or* فعَل*.*

۱۔حد ۲۔ فن ۳۔ خط ۴۔ ذِمّہ ۵۔عِلَّت

*F. Give the singular form of the following nouns.*

۱۔شقوق ۲۔ شکوک ۳۔ صفوف ۴۔ظنون ۵۔حِصَص

## The Pattern فعائل

This pattern is quite flexible and is applied to a number of forms. It almost always applies to non-humans. It is most often applied to a set of nouns whose metrical weight is similar: فعالت / فعالہ / فعال / فعیلت/ فعیلہ / فعیل. The only difference in the metrical weight of these patterns is in the case of the third metrical foot (short-long-[flexible, long, or short]).

فعال / فعالہ / فعالت

شمال (north) ← شمائل (northern regions)

رسالہ (treatise) ← رسائل (treatises)

فعیل/ فعیلہ / فعیلت

دلیل (proof, evidence) ← دلائل (proofs, evidences; arguments)

بدیعہ (rarity; rhetorical device) ← بدائع (rarities; rhetorical devices)

فضیلت (virtue, excellence) ← فضائل (virtues, excellent qualities)

The same pattern is applied to words in these patterns built from geminate roots (as فلائل).

حقیقت (reality, truth) ← حقائق (realities, truths)

Note that when nouns in this pattern can refer either to humans or non-humans, the non-human noun is typically pluralized using this form. The human noun is typically pluralized differently.

غریب (strange; poor [person]) ← غرائب (strange things) غُربا (the poor)

In rare cases, the pattern may be applied to the following Form I noun:

فعل

مَلَک (angel) ← ملائک (angels)

*G. Pluralize the following words using the* فعائل *paradigm.*

۱۔خزانہ ۲۔ ذخیرہ ۳۔ دقیقہ ۴۔ صحیفہ ۵۔ صناعت ۶۔ ضمیر ۷۔ طبیعت ۸۔ نصیحت ۹۔ عقیدہ

۱۰۔ غریب ۱۱۔ فریضہ ۱۲۔ فضیلت ۱۳۔ قصیدہ ۱۴۔ لطیفہ ۱۵۔ نتیجہ ۱۶۔ عجیب ۱۷۔ عجوبہ ۱۸۔ وظیفہ

## Rare Broken Plural Patterns

A large number of rare broken plural patterns are used. The following chart surveys them.

| | فَعَلہ | | | فُعَل | |
|---|---|---|---|---|---|
| طلبہ | ← | طالب | جُمَل | ← | جملہ |
| | **فُعلان / فِعلان** | | | **فُعُل** | |
| بلُدان | ← | بلد | کتب | ← | کتاب |
| صِبیان | ← | صبی | مدن | ← | مدینہ |
| | | | رسل | ← | رسول |
| | | | طرق | ← | طریقہ |
| اَفعِلاء | ← | فعیل | | **فِعال** | |
| اقرباء | ← | قریب | بِلاد | ← | بلَد |
| اصدقاء | ← | صِدّیق | رِجال | ← | رَجُل |
| | **اَفاعِیل** | | | **اَفاعِل** | |
| اقالیم | ← | اقلیم | اقارب | ← | قریب |
| اسالیب | ← | اُسلوب | | | |
| | | | اَحادیث | ← | حدیث |
| | **اَفعِلہ** | | | **فِعَل** | |
| ادویہ | ← | دوا | صُوَر | ← | صورت |
| امثلہ | ← | مثال | حِکَم | ← | حِکمت |
| فواعیل | ← | فاعول | | **فعالی** | |
| قوانین | ← | قانون | اراضی | ← | ارض |
| خواتین | ← | خاتون | اہالی | ← | اہل |

The following patterns, while rare, are entirely regular. Form I nouns referring to humans and nouns ending in ی take the plural اَفعیاء/ اَفعیا. Nouns of the paradigm فعیت / فعیہ, which are built on defective roots (those whose final letter is a vowel), take the plural form فَعایا.

| | افعیا | | | فعایا | |
|---|---|---|---|---|---|
| اقویا | ← | قوی | قضایا | ← | قضیہ |
| انبیا | ← | نبی | وصایا | ← | وصیت |

*H. Write the plural form of the following nouns.*

۱۔ بقیہ ۲۔ ہدیہ ۳۔ رعیت ۴۔ غنی ۵۔ ولی ۶۔ جاسوس

*I. Pluralize the following nouns using the* فِعال *paradigm.*

۱۔ رقبہ ۲۔ خصلت ۳۔ جبل

## 2.21.2 Broken Plurals of Form I Participles

The Form I active participle (فاعل) can be pluralized in any number of ways. When it refers to a person, it is most commonly pluralized in one of the following two ways:

| | | | | |
|---|---|---|---|---|
| | فُعّال | ← | | فاعِل |
| (merchants) | تجّار | ← | (merchant) | تاجر |
| (heretics) | کفّار | ← | (heretic) | کافر |
| | فُعَلاء / فُعَلا | ← | | فاعِل |
| (intellectuals, scholars) | عُلَماء | ← | (intellectual; scholar) | عالِم |

Rarely, such human participles are pluralized using the following paradigm.

| | | | | |
|---|---|---|---|---|
| | فَعَلَہ | ← | | فاعِل |
| (students) | طَلَبَہ | ← | (student) | طالب |

Non-human Form I active paticiples فاعل / فاعلہ / فاعلت are pluralized with the paradigm فَواعِل. Note that this paradigm is occasionally applied to human active participles, too.

| | | | | |
|---|---|---|---|---|
| | فَواعِل | ← | | فاعِل |
| (sides; environs) | جوانب | ← | (side; part) | جانب |
| (followers; dependents) | توابع | ← | (follower; dependent) | تابع |
| | فَواعِل | ← | | فاعِلہ / فاعِلت |
| (rules, regulations) | قواعد | ← | (rule, regulation) | قاعدہ |
| (benefits, profits) | فوائد | ← | (benefit, profit) | فائدہ |

Geminate active participles sometimes take the following form.

| | | | | |
|---|---|---|---|---|
| | فَوال | ← | | فال |
| (private attendants; elites) | خواص | ← | (private; elite) | خاص |

Note that human active participles marked by the feminine gender (فاعِلہ) are pluralized with the feminine suffix ات.

| | | | | |
|---|---|---|---|---|
| (intellectuals [f.]) | عالمات | ⟵ | (intellectual [f.]) | عالمہ |

*A. Pluralize the following Form I active participles using the paradigm فُعَلا or فُعَلاء. Note that all participles refer to humans.*

۱۔ کامل ۲۔ عاقل ۳۔ عارف ۴۔ وارث ۴۔ جاہل ۵۔ صالح

*B. Pluralize the following Form I active participles using the paradigm فَواعِل.*

۱۔مانع ۲۔ لازم ۳۔ ضابطہ ۴۔ قافلہ ۵۔ دائرہ ۶۔ زائدہ

*C. Give the singular active participle of the following plurals.*

۱۔عُبّاد ۲۔ حُجّاب ۳۔ حُجّاج ۳۔ عوام ۴۔ فُضَلا ۵۔ شُعَرا

## Broken Plurals of Form I Passive Participles (مفعول)

Form I passive participles are often pluralized by the paradigm مفاعیل [mafā'īl].

| | | | | |
|---|---|---|---|---|
| (essays; subjects; contents) | مَضامِین | ⟵ | (essay; subject; content) | مضمون |
| (famous people) | مشاہیر | ⟵ | (famous) | مشہور |

When the first root letter is a vowel, it becomes و and the plural paradigm is مواعیل.

| | | | | |
|---|---|---|---|---|
| (victuals) | مواکیل | ⟵ | (victual) | ماکول |

*D. Give the broken plural of the following passive participles.*

۱۔ ملعون ۲۔ مکتوب ۳۔ مجذوب ۴۔ مفہوم

*E. Give the singular form of the following plural passive participles.*

۱۔ مطالیب ۲۔ مخادیم ۳۔ مغافیر ۴۔ معاشیق

## 2.21.3 Broken Plurals of the Agentive Noun فعیل

When the Form I agentive noun (فعیل) refers to a human being, it is typically pluralized according to the following pattern. Note that this is the same pattern used to pluralize some active participles that refer to humans.

| | | | | |
|---|---|---|---|---|
| فعیل | | ← | فُعَلاء / فُعَلا | |
| امیر | (wealthy) | ← | امراء | (wealthy people) |
| غریب | (poor) | ← | غرباء | (poor people) |

Non-human agentive nouns, as well as the feminine or diminutive form of the agentive (فعیلت / فعیلہ) are most often pluralized using the paradigm فَعائِل. Note that this is the same paradigm used to pluralize non-human active participles.

| | | | | |
|---|---|---|---|---|
| دلیل | (evidence, proof) | ← | دلائل | (proofs, evidences) |
| حقیقت | (fact, reality) | ← | حقائق | (facts, realities) |
| ذریعہ | (a means) | ← | ذرائع | (means) |

The pattern فِعال is used to pluralize adjectives in this pattern. Such adjectives can be nominalized.

| | | | | |
|---|---|---|---|---|
| عظیم | (great) | ← | عِظام | (great) |
| کبیر | (great) | ← | کِبار | (great) |

*A. Pluralize the following human agentive nouns using the فُعَلاء / فُعَلا pattern.*

۱۔ ادیب (littérateur) ۲۔ حکیم (philosopher) ۳۔ ضعیف (weak, elderly) ۴۔ رفیق (colleague, comrade)
۵۔ فصیح (eloquent) ۶۔ شریف (noble) ۷۔ فقیر (poor; fakir) ۸۔ قدیم (old, ancient)
۹۔ وزیر (minister) ۱۰۔ خلیفہ (successor, caliph)

*B. Pluralize the following non-human agentive nouns.*

۱۔ ذخیرہ (treasure, store) ۲۔ جزیرہ (island) ۳۔ لطیفہ (joke, pleasantry)
۴۔ قصیدہ (ode) ۵۔ دقیقہ (subtlety, minute point)

### Broken Plurals of Human Geminate Agentive Nouns

Such nouns follow two predictable and similar patterns. The first is more common.

| | | | | |
|---|---|---|---|---|
| فلیل | | ← | اَفِلّہ | |
| عزیز | (dear one, relative) | ← | اَعِزّہ | (dear ones, relatives) |
| فلیل | | ← | اَفِلّاء | |
| طبیب | (physician) | ← | اطباء | (physicians) |

*C. Give the plural form of the following agentive nouns using the pattern افلہ.*

| | | | |
|---|---|---|---|
| ۱۔ حبیب | (beloved) | ۲۔ امام | (imam, leader) |

## 2.21.4 Broken Plurals of Comparative-Superlatives

When treated as nouns, comparative and superlative nouns are pluralized according to the following patterns.

افعل ← افاعل

اکبر ← اکابر

What is in Arabic the feminine form of the comparative is sometimes used in Urdu, especially in compounds. It can also be pluralized.

فعلی ← فُعَل (rare)

کُبریٰ ← کُبَر (rare)

The masculine and feminine comparatives and superlatives of defective roots take special forms.

افعیٰ ← افاعی

اعلیٰ ← اعالی

فعیا ← فُعی

علیا ← عُلی

*A. Pluralize the following comparative and superlative nouns or adjectives.*

| | | | | | |
|---|---|---|---|---|---|
| ۱۔ اصغر | ([the] smallest) | ۲۔ امجد | ([the] most glorious) | ۳۔ اقصیٰ | ([the] remote; extreme) |

## 2.21.5 Broken Plurals of Quadriliteral Form I Nouns

These are pluralized using the following paradigms. Note similarities with the patterns for pluralizing non-human active participles and comparative-superlative nouns as well as with the patterns for the Form 1 passive participle. Once again, ا [ā] is infixed at the end of the first syllable, thus rendering the first syllable short and creating a long second syllable.

فعلل / فعللہ ← فَعالِل

دفتر ← دفاتر

سلسلہ ← سلاسل

فعلال ← فعالیل

سلطان ← سلاطین

برہان ← براہین

*A. Form the broken plural of the following nouns.*

۱۔ زُخرُف (embellishment) ۲۔ زلزلہ (earthquake) ۳۔ ترجمہ (translation) ۴۔ شیطان (satan)

## 2.21.6 Broken Plurals of Nouns of Place and Instrument

Nouns of place (مَفعَل مَفعَلہ مَفعَلت) and instrument (مِفعَل مِفعَلہ مِفعَلت مِفعال) are pluralized by the following broken plural patterns. Note the similarity of this pattern with the patterns used with the Form I active participle, comparative-superlative nouns, and quadriliteral nouns.

| | | | |
|---|---|---|---|
| مفعل / مفعلہ / مفعلت | | ← | مَفاعِل |
| مَسجِد | (mosque) | ← | مساجد |
| مَدرَسہ | (school) | ← | مدارس |
| مَعرِفَت | (science; gnosis) | ← | معارف |
| مِسطَر | (ruler) | ← | مساطر |

Nouns of instrument in the مِفعال pattern change to the broken plural مَفاعِیل. Note the sameness of this pattern and the pattern that is used to pluralize the Form I passive participles.

| | | |
|---|---|---|
| مِفعال | ← | مَفاعِیل |
| مفتاح (key) | ← | مفاتیح |
| میزان (scale) | ← | موازین |

*A. Give the broken plurals of the following nouns of place and give their plural meanings.*

۱۔ منظر (scene) ۲۔ مقصد (purpose) ۳۔ مطبع (press) ۴۔ مرکز (center)

۵۔ محفل (gathering) ۶۔ مجلس (assembly) ۷۔ مذہب (religion) ۸۔ منزل (floor; destination)

۹۔ موقع (occasion) ۱۰۔ مرتبہ (rank, office) ۱۱۔ مرحلہ (stage) ۱۲۔ محکمہ (bureau)

۱۳۔ مقبرہ (gravesite) ۱۴۔ مرحمت (kindness) ۱۵۔ منزلت (station) ۱۶۔ مصیبت (trouble)

*B. Give the broken plurals of the following nouns of instrument.*

۱۔ مِسمار (stake, nail) ۲۔ مقدار (quantity) ۳۔ مِنبر (pulpit) ۴۔ مِنطقہ (girdle, belt)

## 2.21.7 Broken Plurals of Form II Nouns

Form II nouns (تفعلہ/تفعیل) may be pluralized according to the following paradigms.

تفعیل ← تفاعیل

تصویر ← تصاویر

تحریر ← تحاریر

If the first root letter is ا, و is infixed.

تاریخ ← تواریخ

The less common Form II noun uses the following paradigm.

تفعلہ / تفعلت ← تفاعِل

تجربہ ← تجارب

*A. Form the broken plurals of the following Form II nouns.*

۱۔ تحریک (movement) ۲۔ تفصیل (detail) ۳۔ تقریر (speech)

۴۔ تکلیف (trouble) ۵۔ تجویز (strategy; resolution)

*B. Give the singular form of the following plural nouns.*

۶۔ تصانیف (writings) ۷۔ تقاریب (gatherings) ۸۔ تدابیر (strategies, remedies)

۹۔ تراکیب (recipies) ۱۰۔ تفاسیر (exegeses)

## 2.21.8 Metric Weight and Broken Plurals

Certain broken plural patterns are used with nouns of a similar or identical metrical or prosodic weight. This means that by recognizing the metrical weight of Urdu words, one can often guess (or recall) which broken plural form they will take. For example, words whose weight comprises two long and one short feet take a broken plural pattern which infixes ا after the first full metrical foot and ی at the place of the second long foot.

سلطان ← سلاطین

تاریخ ← تواریخ

By long is meant either a syllable beginning with a long vowel, a consonant followed by a long vowel (e.g. فا) or the combination of a consonant, a short vowel, and another consonant not followed by a vowel (e.g. فَغ). By short is meant a consonant followed by a short vowel or a consonant without a vowel. Thus, the weight of سُلطان is سُل (long), طا (long), ن (short) and, similarly, that of تاریخ is تا (long) ری (long) خ (short). Although these words are derived from different patterns (سلطان is a Form I noun and تاریخ is a Form II verbal noun), their metrical or prosodic weight is the same.

To represent metrical weight, Urdu prosodists use paradigms built on the root letters ف ع ل. For example, long-long-short is represented as مفعول [maf (long) + ū (long) + l (short)]. Note that these prosodic paradigms differ from the morphological paradigms discussed above. That is, when using prosodic paradigms, we are not talking about the use of فعل as substitutes for root letters. Instead, these prosodic patterns are paradigms for words that share a metrical weight (in this case, long-long-short). All the following words differ in terms of morphology and derivation, but all are of the same metrical weight. Accordingly, they are represented using the same metrical pattern مفعول. Thus, their broken plurals all share the same metrical weight and form.

| | | |
|---|---|---|
| مفاعیل | ← | مفعول |
| تصاویر | ← | تصویر |
| قوانین | ← | قانون |
| مضامین | ← | مضمون |
| مفاتیح | ← | مفتاح |
| سلاطین | ← | سلطان |

The following chart dissects the words above to reveal the metrical feet and vowel patterns of the paradigm in parallel with the metrical feet and vowel patterns of the vocabulary words. Note the regularity of the voweling to the left of the arrows. The uniform metrical weight of the singular words to the right of the arrows (short-short-long) is matched by a highly regular pattern of vowel infixation and metrical weight in the broken plural: initial letter + short a (short) ; second letter + ā (long); third letter plus ī (long); final letter (short). Study the following.

| | | | | | | | |
|---|---|---|---|---|---|---|---|
| ل | عی | فا | مَ | ← | ل | عو | مف |
| ر | وی | صا | تَ | ← | ر | وی | تَص |
| ن | نی | وا | قَ | ← | ن | نو | قا |
| ن | می | ضا | مَ | ← | ن | مو | مَض |
| ح | تی | فا | مَ | ← | ح | تا | مِف |
| ن | طی | لا | سَ | ← | ن | طا | سُل |

A similar pattern emerges for words whose metrical weight is either two long feet (long-long) or one long, one short, and one long (or flexible) foot (long-short-long/short). Prosodists categorize these words under the paradigms فَعْلُن (فع long, لن long) and فاعِلن (فا long عِ short لن long). Singular word forms that fall under this category are comparative-superlative nouns (اَفعَل), nouns of place and instrument (مِفعِل /مَفعلت / مَفعله /مَفعل), quadriliteral nouns (فعلل / فعلله), the rare Form II verbal noun form (تَفعِله), and Form I active participles (فاعل / فاعله / فاعلت). In all cases, the broken plural is formed by infixing ا at the second syllable and a short ِ [i] (rather than a long ی [ī]) in the final long foot. The result is the paradigm فَعالِن. Note that, in the case of the Form I active participles, و must be infixed in order to support the infixed ā and maintain the metrical weight (thus, فواعل). Study the following chart and note the regularity of the vowel patterns in the plural forms:

| فعلن / فاعلن | | فعالِن | فَ | عا | لِن |
|---|---|---|---|---|---|
| اکبر | ← | اکابر | ا | کا | بِر |
| مسجد | ← | مساجد | مَ | سا | جِد |
| مقبره | ← | مقابر | مَ | قا | بِر |
| سلسله | ← | سلاسل | سَ | لا | سِل |
| ترجمه | ← | تراجم | تَ | را | جِم |
| تجربه | ← | تجارب | تَ | جا | رِب |
| قاعده | ← | قواعد | قَ | وا | عِد |

*A. Group each of the following nouns into one of the **metrical** paradigms according to its prosodic weight. Then give the broken plural and the meaning. Broken plural paradigms are given in parentheses.*

۱۔ مفعول (مفاعیل) ۲۔ فعلن (فعالِن) ۳۔ فاعلن (فعالِن)

۱۔ ضابطہ (principle, rule) ۲۔ رابطہ (connection) ۳۔ مظلوم (oppressed) ۴۔ مضمون (essay)

۵۔ تصدیق (confirmation) ۶۔ تحریر (writing, text) ۷۔ خاتون (lady)

۸۔ اعظم (greatest) ۹۔ افضل (most excellent)

۱۰۔ مضمار (training field) ۱۱۔ مضراب (plectrum)

۱۲۔ دفتر (office) ۱۳۔ مسجد (mosque) ۱۴۔ مسئلہ (issue)

*Review Exercise. Give the broken plural of the following singular nouns using the indicated paradigm.*

افعال

۱۔ شخص ۲۔ مثل ۳۔ سبب ۴۔ قول ۵۔ حکم ۶۔ رکن ۷۔ ولد ۸۔ عمل

فُعُول

۹۔ قلب ۱۰۔ علم ۱۱۔ نفس ۱۲۔ شک ۱۳۔ حد

فُعَلاء

| | | | |
|---|---|---|---|
| ۱۴۔ حکیم | ۱۵۔ فقیر | ۱۶۔ قدیم | ۱۷۔ ادیب |

فعائل

| | | | | | |
|---|---|---|---|---|---|
| ۱۸۔ قبیلہ | ۱۹۔ جزیرہ | ۲۰۔ عقیدہ | ۲۱۔ مصیبت | ۲۲۔ لطیفہ | ۲۳۔ حقیقت |

فُعَلاء

| | | | |
|---|---|---|---|
| ۲۴۔ عالم | ۲۵۔ شاعر | ۲۶۔ عاقل | ۲۷۔ فاضل |

فواعد

| | | | | |
|---|---|---|---|---|
| ۲۸۔ عامل | ۲۹۔ جانب | ۳۰۔لازمہ | ۳۱۔ فائدہ | ۳۲۔ قاعدہ |

مفاعیل

| | |
|---|---|
| ۳۳۔ مکتوب | ۳۴۔ مفہوم |

مفاعِل

| | | | | | | |
|---|---|---|---|---|---|---|
| ۳۵۔ مجلس | ۳۶۔ محفل | ۳۷۔ منظر | ۳۸۔ مقبرہ | ۳۹۔ مدرسہ | ۴۰۔ مسئلہ | ۴۱۔ مذہب |

تفاعیل

| | | | | |
|---|---|---|---|---|
| ۴۲۔ تحریر | ۴۳۔ تقریب | ۴۴۔ تنظیم | ۴۵۔ تفصیل | ۴۶۔ تقریر |

## 2.22 Plurals and Adjectives in Arabic

Following a rule of Arabic grammar, Urdu often suffixes ہ to Arabic adjectives that modify plural nouns. This is most commonly done to adjectives in Arabic and Persian iẓāfat (genitive) constructions. Consider the following:

| | | | | | | |
|---|---|---|---|---|---|---|
| علم | (science) | جدید | (modern) | ← | علومِ جدیدہ | (modern sciences) |
| اثر | (trace, relic) | قدیم | (ancient) | ← | آثارِ قدیمہ | (ancient monuments; archaeology) |

The same change is made to many Arabic adjectives when in the attributive position, regardless of the number of the noun.

| | | | | | | |
|---|---|---|---|---|---|---|
| موجود | (present) | دور | (era) | ← | موجودہ دور | (present age) |
| موجود | (present) | حالات | (conditions) | ← | موجودہ حالات | (present conditions) |

*A. Use iẓāfat and ہ to combine the following plural nouns with the adjectives to form Urdu phrases.*

| | | | |
|---|---|---|---|
| ۱۔ حالات | (circumstances) | حاضر | (present) |
| ۲۔ اوصاف | (qualities) | مذکور | (mentioned) |
| ۳۔ اصول | (principles) | معلوم | (known) |
| ۴۔ فنون | (arts) | لطیف | (fine) |

## 2.23 Arabic Nouns and Urdu Gender

Several aspects of Arabic morphology produce predictable patterns of gender in Urdu. Here follows a summary of the most common ones.

### The Letter ة and Marked Genders of Arabic Nouns in Urdu

In Arabic, the letter ة is pronounced "a" or "t" depending on how it is used. In Urdu, this letter is not typically retained. Instead, like Persian, Urdu renders ة as either ہ [a] or ت [t]. Consider the following pairs of words.

(Urdu Form III) معاملت معاملہ ⟵ (Arabic Form III) معاملة

(Urdu Form IV) افادت افادہ ⟵ (Arabic Form IV) افادة

Although both words to the left of the arrow are in fact the same word in Arabic, in Urdu they are different words with different (but similar) meanings.

Nearly all Urdu nouns ending in ہ in which ہ translates the Arabic ة are masculine. Exceptions are rare; they include, for example, the feminine دفعہ (time, occasion). Similarly, nearly all Urdu nouns ending in ت in which ت translates the Arabic ة are feminine. Once again, exceptions are rare; an example of one is the masculine شربت (sherbet). It is therefore possible, with minimal information, to predict the gender of many Arabic words in Urdu. Thus, in the example above, معاملہ and افادہ are predictably masculine and معاملت and افادت are predictably feminine.

The letter ة is never one of the root letters in an Arabic word. Thus, if an Urdu word ending in ہ or ت contains the root letters and affixational patterns characteristic of Arabic words in addition to the ہ or ت , then it is safe to assume that the ہ or ت translates the Arabic ة. The gender of such Urdu words should be considered "marked" and predictable.

Let's use this knowledge to reason to the gender of an Urdu noun together. Suppose that we do not know the gender of the Urdu word حکومت (government). The letter ح tells us that this word comes from Arabic. The familiar pattern of فعولت indicates that the triliteral root is حکم. Because ت is not one of the root letters, we can assume that it must be a translation of ة. This is a marked feminine noun.

Similarly, consider the word ذریعہ. The letters ذ and ع mark this as an Arabic word. The agentive noun pattern فعیلہ suggests that the triliteral root is ذ ر ع. We can now recognize that ہ is a translation of ة and that ذریعہ is masculine.

Now consider the case of ثبوت. The letter ث marks the word as Arabic. The paradigm فُعُول suggests that the root letters are ث ب ت. Thus, the letter ت is one of the three root letters, and not a translation of ة. Therefore, the gender of this word is unmarked. (It happens to be masculine.)

*A. Indicate all marked feminine nouns with "f" and all marked masculine nouns with "m." Mark all unmarked nouns with "u."*

| | | | | | |
|---|---|---|---|---|---|
| وقت | دِقّت | حکومت | حالت | صورت | حال |
| طرح | خدشہ | سلطنت | حِصّہ | وجہ | واقعہ |
| سلسلہ | واسطہ | فیصلہ | موت | حقیقت | نظر |
| بیان | تحت | فائدہ | نتیجہ | جماعت | علاقہ |
| سمت | علم | عمارت | معاملہ | قلعہ | روایت |
| نسبت | طریقہ | قیمت | عمل | ارادہ | صوت |

## Form II Verbal Nouns of the Pattern تفعیل

With only one exception (تعویذ), all nouns of the pattern تفعیل are feminine in Urdu. Use the following words in a phrase or sentence that reflects their feminine gender.

| | | | | | |
|---|---|---|---|---|---|
| ۱۔ تحریک | (movement, motion) | ۲۔ تجویز | (proposal) | ۳۔ تصویر | (image) |
| ۴۔ تقریر | (speech) | ۵۔ تحریر | (writing) | ۶۔ تحقیق | (research) |

## Defective Form I Verbal Nouns Ending in ا [ā]

With very few exceptions (e.g. سما), Form I nouns ending in ا [ā] derived from a defective verbal root (one which ends in a vowel) are feminine in Urdu.

*B. Here follows a list of nouns ending in ا [ā]. Not all of them are Arabic or feminine. Mark the Form I feminine verbal nouns ending in ا [ā]. Use a dictionary to help resolve ambiguity. Then use three of the words in a sentence that reflects their gender.*

| | | | | | | |
|---|---|---|---|---|---|---|
| عطا | گھٹا | جوا | دعا | وفا | رسّا | خفا |
| دنیا | لوہا | غذا | غزا | بِنا | رضا | سونا |
| بقا | گلا | فنا | صدا | صبا | صہبا | شفا |
| سزا | بلا | جزا | | | | |

## 2.24 The Adverbializing Suffix اً [-an]

This suffix, called تنوین [tanvīn] ("nūnization") is used to form adverbs in Urdu (compare with the English suffix -ly). Note that in case a word ends in ہ, the ہ may be dropped before tanvīn is suffixed.

| | | | | |
|---|---|---|---|---|
| تقریب | (approximation; gathering) | ← | تقریباً | (approximately) |
| تخمینہ | (conjecture, guess; hypothesis) | ← | تخمیناً | (at a guess; nearly; hypothetically) |

This suffix is also applied to words that are not Arabic in origin.

| | | | | |
|---|---|---|---|---|
| (by estimation; roughly) | اندازاً | ← | (guess) | اندازه |

If an Arabic word ends in a hamza which is not typicaly written in Urdu, the hamza is written and tanvīn is superscript.

| | | | | |
|---|---|---|---|---|
| (initially) | ابتداءً | ← | (beginning) | ابتدا |

In words ending in ہ in which ہ is a translation of ة, the ہ is typically changed to ت. Rarely, the ہ is written as ة and the two lines of tanvīn are superscript.

| | | | | | |
|---|---|---|---|---|---|
| (particularly) | (rare) خاصةً | or | خاصتاً | ← | (particularity) خاصہ |

*A. Adverbialize the following nouns using tanvīn and give their meanings.*

| | | | | | | | |
|---|---|---|---|---|---|---|---|
| (compelled) | ۴۔ مجبور | (certainty) | ۳۔ یقین | (chance, happening) | ۲۔ اتفاق | (near) | ۱۔ قریب |
| (principle, basis) | ۹۔ اصل | (second) | ۷۔ ثانی | (practice, action) | ۶۔ عمل | (habit) | ۵۔ عادت |
| | | | | | | (one time) | ۱۰۔ دفعہ |

## 2.25 The Nominal Suffix یت [-iyat/-iyyat]

Arabic uses the suffix يّة [iyya] to form nouns from adjectives or to form abstract nouns from concrete nouns. Urdu replaces ة either with ہ or ت , and thus uses یہ or یت. The latter form (یت) is much more common and is generally considered the standard way in which Urdu uses this suffix to form abstract nouns. Urdu speakers typically pronounce this without the doubling of ی , thus, یت [-iyat]. Note that Urdu freely uses the suffix with words that are not of Arabic origin (e.g. the Persian word خر below). Recall that, like all other Urdu nouns derived from Arabic words ending in ة , all words of this kind which end in یت are feminine and all those which end in یہ are masculine. Consider the following examples.

| | | | | |
|---|---|---|---|---|
| (importance) | اہمیت | ← | (important) | اہم |
| (humanity) | انسانیت | ← | (human) | انسان |
| (asininity, stupidity) | خریت | ← | (ass, donkey) | خر |
| (generalization) | کلیہ | ← | (all, entire) | کل |

Note that in the case of کلیہ, some would argue that this is actually not an example of the present suffix, but rather an adjectival suffix implying that the word has been extracted from an Arabic phrase in which it is used as a modifier; for example, جملہ کلیہ (a general or universal sentence).

If a word ends in ی, the ی is dropped:

| | | | | |
|---|---|---|---|---|
| (strangeness, foreignness) | اجنبیت | ← | (stranger, foreigner) | اجنبی |

All nouns ending in the nominal suffix can be pluralized with the marked feminine plural ات [āt].

| | | | | |
|---|---|---|---|---|
| (personalities) | شخصیات | ← | (personality) | شخصیت |

*A. Read the following words aloud and underline those which include the Arabic nominal suffix.*

ذہنیت　بَیت　بقیہ　اجنبیت　خاصیت　خریت　شکریہ

حیثیت　تربیت　خیریت　شخصیت　کیفیت　نیت　حمایت

*B. Given the meaning of the word on the right, choose the most appropriate English synonym for the word on the left.*

| | | | | | | |
|---|---|---|---|---|---|---|
| (thought) | (mentality) | (intelligence) | ذہنیت | ← | (mind) | ۱۔ ذہن |
| (merit) | (specialty) | (refinement) | خاصیت | ← | (special) | ۲۔ خاص |
| (good deed) | (superiority) | (well-being) | خیریت | ← | (good) | ۳۔ خیر |
| (nativity) | (nationality) | (people) | قومیت | ← | (nation) | ۴۔ قوم |
| (importance) | (cost) | (ability) | قابلیت | ← | (able) | ۵۔ قابل |

*C. Read the following Urdu words and their English synonyms. Form the abstract noun of each word and guess its meaning.*

۱۔ آدمی (man[kind])　۲۔ واقف (familiar)　۳۔ مظلوم (tyrannized)　۴۔ اکثر (most)　۵۔ اقل (least)

## 2.26 Suffixes of Completeness and Fields of Knowledge: ات [-āt] and یات [-iyāt]

The plural suffixes ات [-āt] and یات [-iyāt] in addition to denoting simple plurality, are often used in Urdu to denote either the complete collection of something or a field of knowledge or academic discipline.

| | | | | |
|---|---|---|---|---|
| (the complete works [of a poet or a writer]) | کلیات | ← | (the whole) | کلیت |
| (physics) | طبیعیات | ← | (natural, physical) | طبیعی |

| | | | | |
|---|---|---|---|---|
| الٰہی | (divine) | ← | الٰہیات | (theology; divinity studies) |
| عمرانی | (societal) | ← | عمرانیات | (sociology) |

*A. Read the following words aloud and underline those which include the Arabic suffix of completeness.*

ملاقات  باقیات  ریاضیات  منقولات  لسانیات  معاشیات  بات

*B. Given the meaning of the word on the right, choose the most appropriate English synonym for the word on the left.*

| | | | | | | |
|---|---|---|---|---|---|---|
| ۱۔ ضروری | (necessary) | ← | ضروریات | (money) | (necessities) | (importance) |
| ۲۔ مادیت | (materiality) | ← | مادیات | (motion) | (energy) | (material objects) |
| ۳۔ معدنی | (mineral) | ← | معدنیات | (rocks) | (gems) | (mineralogy) |
| ۴۔ باقی | (remainder) | ← | باقیات | (dividend) | (all remaining items) | (plurals) |
| ۵۔ معقول | (rational) | ← | معقولات | (principles) | (intelligent ideas) | (the rational sciences) |

*C. Read the following Urdu words and their English synonyms. Then use the plural form of the abstract suffix to form a related academic discipline and write the name of the discipline.*

| | | | | | |
|---|---|---|---|---|---|
| ۱۔ لسانی | (linguistic) | ۲۔ ریاضی | (math) | ۳۔ ما بعدالطبعی | (metaphysical) |
| ۴۔ معاشی | (economic) | ۵۔ انسانی | (human) | | |

*Review Exercise. You now have all the tools you need to make informed guesses about the meanings of nearly all Urdu words of Arabic origin. Review the aforegoing lessons as you study the following chart. All the paradigms and permutations should be familiar to you.*

| | | | | | | | |
|---|---|---|---|---|---|---|---|
| حکم | (order) | اَحکام | (orders) | | | | |
| حِکمت | (wisdom, philosophy) | حِکَم | (wisdoms, philosophies, sciences) | | | | |
| حِکمیات | (philosophical sciences) | | | | | | |
| حکومت | (government; governance) | | | | | | |
| احکم | (strongest; firmest; stablest) | | | | | | |
| محکَمہ | (court of law; tribunal; state office) | محاکم | (courts, tribunals; state offices) | | | | |
| حکیم | (physician; philosopher) | حُکَماء | (physicians, philosophers) | | | | |
| حاکم | (ruler) | حاکِمین | (rulers) | حُکّام | (rulers) | حُکّامی | (of, by, related to rulers) |
| حاکمہ | (ruler [f.]) | حاکمات | (rulers [f.]) | | | | |
| محکوم | (ruled [adj.]; the ruled [n.]) | محکومین | (the ruled [pl.]) | | | | |

| | | | | | |
|---|---|---|---|---|---|
| تحکیم | (ruling; authority) | تحکیمات | (rulings) | | |
| مُحاکمہ | (arbitration) | محاکمات | (arbitrations) | مُحاکِم | (arbitrator) |
| اِحکام | (strengthening; a kind of pillar) | مُحکِم | (strengthener) | مُحکَم | (strengthened) |
| تحکّم | (the authority to rule; sovereignty) | متحکِّم | (sovereign) | | |
| تحاکم | (the authority to arbitrate) | متحاکم | (one endowed with authority to arbitrate) | | |
| اِستحکام | (firmnesss, stability; ratification) | مستحکم | (stable; firm) | | |

*D. Keeping in mind the patterns discussed in the preceding lessons, read the following words aloud. Then, based on the meaning of the root word, guess the meanings of the derived words in each section. Be sure to check your guesses in an Urdu dictionary.*

۱۔ عَمَل (action; practice; deed)

| | | | | | |
|---|---|---|---|---|---|
| | | اَعمال | ________ | | |
| عملاً | ________ | | | | |
| مَعمَل | ________ | | | | |
| عامِل | ________ | معمول | ________ | | |
| تعمیل | ________ | مُعَمِّل | ________ | مُعَمَّل | ________ |
| معاملہ | ________ | | | | |
| اِعمال | ________ | مُعمِل | ________ | مُعمَل | ________ |
| استعمال | ________ | مُستَعمَل | ________ | | |

۲۔ ولادت (birth)

| | | | | | | | |
|---|---|---|---|---|---|---|---|
| ولد | ________ | اولاد | ________ | | | | |
| والد | ________ | والدہ | ________ | والدَین | ________ | مولود | ________ |
| مَولِد | ________ | میلاد | ________ | | | | |
| تولید | ________ | | | | | | |
| تَوَلُّد | ________ | مُتَوَلِّد | ________ | | | | |
| توالُد | ________ | | | | | | |

## 2.27 Arabic in Urdu: An Overview

Arabic has played a unique and important role in the intellectual history of South Asia in general, and Urdu in particular, for centuries. From philosophers and Islamic scholars in small towns to secretaries and poets at the Mughal court, and from candidates for British-colonial administrative service to students at twenty-first-century madrasas, Arabic has been an indispensable component of the rational, literary, and religious training of scholars from a wide range of regional, linguistic, and even religious backgrounds. A sound training in Arabic is as essential to the appreciation of the celebrated *Gulistān*, an influential work of Persian wisdom literature, as it is to the study of the Quran.

Given the history and legacy of Arabic in South Asia, it is hardly surprising that Urdu borrows not only a great deal of vocabulary, but also a number of phrases and maxims from the language. This section presents an overview of the essential components of Arabic grammar that appear in Urdu. Naturally, a complete study of Arabic grammar and morphology is beyond the scope of this book. Still, it is hoped that the information and exercises provided here will assist students when encountering the large number of Arabic phrases, maxims, and quotations used in Urdu, and that they will inspire students to pursue further studies of Arabic.

## A Note on Orthography and Pronunciation

Urdu tends to follow the spelling conventions of Arabic, but Arabic phrases, when quoted in Urdu literature, are often written in the Naskh script rather than Nastaliq. This style sets Arabic phrases apart from Urdu in texts, making it easier to recognize Arabic as such. The following chart reviews the Arabic alphabet in Naskh.

ا آ

ب ت ث

ج ح خ

د ذ

ر ز

س ش

ص ض

ط ظ

ع غ

ف ق ك

ل م ن

ھ / ه و ي ء

Note the following: Arabic does not distinguish between the pronunciations of ہ and ھ (the two were interchangeable in Urdu, too, until standardization in the twentieth century); ک in the final position is often written as Naskh; and that in Modern Arabic, ہ/ھ precedes و in alphabetical order, whereas in Urdu (and Persian) و precedes ہ. The last-mentioned is useful to note in case students would like to look up words in an Arabic dictionary.

Arabic also has a number of phonemes that are not found in Urdu. According to the rules of classical Arabic, the letters ز ذ ض ظ have distinct pronunciations, whereas in Urdu they are homophones. The same is true of ت and ط, and س and ص. The letter ع in Arabic has a distinct pronunciation (linguists call this a pharyngeal fricative). Some Urdu speakers have learned, through the study of Arabic, to produce this sound. Others approximate it through the use of a glottal stop. But most simply follow standard Urdu pronunciation when reading Arabic texts aloud. Similarly, the letter ح in classical Arabic is distinct from ہ. Urdu speakers rarely make the distinction, whether incorporating an Arabic phrase or aphorism into their language, quoting classical Arabic poetry, or reciting the Quran. The reality is that, like all languages that cross linguistic regions, the pronunciation of Arabic, too, varies according to the regional languages of the people who speak or recite it.

*A. Practice Naskh and your Urdu pronunciation of Arabic phrases by reading the following Urdu idioms and phrases aloud.*

الفقرُ فخري　　مِنها　　سلام عليك　　لِهاذا　　كُن فَيَكُون

## 2.28 The Definite Article ال [al-] (the)

This section introduces the rules for pronouncing the Arabic definite article ال [al-] in Urdu. The Arabic definite article is ubiquitous in Urdu. You will find it in personal names, book titles, and common phrases. It has also been borrowed into English, mainly through Latin:

| | | |
|---|---|---|
| **al**chemy | ← | الکیمیا |
| **al**gebra | ← | الجبر |
| **al**cohol | ← | الکحل |

In Arabic and Urdu, the pronunciation of ال [al-] (the) changes according to the letter that immediately follows it. To teach the pronunciation of ال as a prefix, grammarians of Arabic divide the letters of the Arabic alphabet into two groups: قمری [qamarī] (moon) letters; and شمسی [shamsī] (sun) letters. Read the following chart, which reviews the letters in each category.

قمری: ا ب ج ح خ ع غ ف ق ک م و ہ ی

شمسی: ت ث د ذ ر ز س ش ص ض ط ظ ل ن

When ال precedes the letters of the قمری group at the beginning of a phrase, it is pronounced exactly how it is written [al].

| | |
|---|---|
| [al-qamar] | القمر |
| [al-kīmiyā] | الکیمیا |

*A. Read the following aloud.*

| | | | | | |
|---|---|---|---|---|---|
| القمر | الباسط | الخبیر | الغرض | الماجد | الغیاث |
| الکیمیا | الجبرا | الغزالی | القصہ | الواجب | |
| الباری | الحاصل | الامان | الکتاب | الحق | |

When ال precedes a شمسی letter, ل is assimilated and the letter that immediately follows it is doubled. Read the following aloud.

| | | |
|---|---|---|
| الشمس | [ash-shams] | (the sun) |
| السلام | [as-salām] | ([the] peace) |
| النور | [an-nūr] | ([the] light) |

When ال precedes ل, it is redoubled as itself [al-l . . .]. When it is followed by the Arabic word لہ (god), it has a special spelling.

اللہ [al-lāh] (Allah; lit. the lord or god)

Note that doubling occurs only when ال is the definite article (the). There are many Urdu words of Arabic origin in which the letters ال precede شمسی letters, but because ال is not the definite article in those cases, the letters are pronounced as one would otherwise expect. For example, التجا [iltijā], التزام [iltizām], الطاف [altāf], and so on. It is almost always easy to tell that ال is the definite article, since the word that follows it will exibit standard features of Arabic words (e.g. three root letters and a recognizable paradigm).

*B. Read the following words aloud. In all cases, ال is the definite article.*

| | | | | | | |
|---|---|---|---|---|---|---|
| الداعی | الراقم | الشہید | الرؤف | السمیع | الصبوح | اللیل |
| الرحمٰن | الشکور | اللطیف | النبی | | | |

## The Pronunciation of ال in Genitive Constructions

In Urdu, when ال appears between two nouns (as in compound names), it performs a genitive function. That is, it asserts a relationship of possession or composition (compare with English "of [the]"). In terms of pronunciation, ا is effectively suffixed to the preceding word and pronounced اُ [u]. Here follow two examples.

| | |
|---|---|
| عبد الباسط | [Abd ul-Bāsit] |
| زیب النسا | [Zeb un-Nisā] |

Note that there is no space between the pronunciation of ا [u] and the end of the preceding word. The first name above is not pronounced Abd (pause) ul-bāsit, but rather Abdulbāsit (as one word); in terms of pronunciation, ا [u] has effectively been suffixed to the preceding letter.

Now consider the pronunciation of زیب النسا. The name is built of three components: زیب [zeb] (ornament); ال [al-] (the); نسا [nisā] (women). Since this is a genitive construction, ال [al-] becomes اُل [ul] and is, in terms of pronunciation, effectively suffixed to زیب [zeb], becoming زیب ال [zebul-]. Then follows نسا [nisā]. But because نسا begins with a شمسی letter, ل is assimilated and ن is doubled; thus, النسا [unnisā]. Putting it all together, it becomes زیب النسا [Zebunnisā].

In ال constructions, Urdu occasionally retains the Arabic letter ة. It is a convention in Arabic that when ة is followed by ال , it is pronounced ت [t]. Typically, Urdu replaces ة with ت in such constructions.

فضیلة النساء [Fazīlat un-Nisā] or فضیلت النساء [Fazīlat un-Nisā] (more typical)

*C. Read the following personal names, which Urdu borrows from Arabic.*

عبد اللہ　　عبد الماجد　　شان الحق　　مہر النساء　　عبد الرؤف　　شریف النساء

*D. Read the following Arabic names of Urdu books. Pay close attention to the position and pronunciation of the definite article and the pronunciation of the succeeding letter.*

| | | | | | |
|---|---|---|---|---|---|
| آثار الصنادید | سیرۃ النبی [سیرت النبی] | شعر الہند | نور اللغات | مناظر المصائب | تفسیر القرآن |
| المامون | مفتاح المنطق | سیرت الفاروق | احکام القرآن | کاشف الحقائق | ترجمان القرآن |
| الفاروق | مصباح الکلام | سحر البیان | مصباح اللغات | مرآۃ الحکما | شعر العجم |

## ال and Genitive Constructions

ال is used to join two words together to form phrases which can be divided into two kinds: adjective-noun and noun-noun.

In adjective-noun phrases, ال simply acts to tie the adjective to the noun. The resulting phrase is typically adjectival, but may be nominalized.

| | | | | | |
|---|---|---|---|---|---|
| کثیر | (many) | المعنی | (the meaning) | ← کثیر المعنی | (multivalent) |
| آخر | (last) | الذکر | ([the] mention) | ← آخر الذکر | ([the] last-mentioned) |

*E. Read the following Arabic phrases commonly used in Urdu and give their meanings. Use the word bank below to help you.*

| | | | | |
|---|---|---|---|---|
| ۱۔اشرف المخلوقات | ۲۔سریع الفہم | ۳۔ عظیم المرتبت | ۴۔ کثیر اللسان | ۵۔عزیز القدر |
| ۶۔دائم المرض | ۷۔رائج الوقت | ۸۸۔عدیم الفرصت | ۹۔غریب الوطن | ۱۰۔ عظیم الشان |

| | | | | | | | |
|---|---|---|---|---|---|---|---|
| اشرف | (noblest) | مخلوقات | (created beings) | سریع | (fast) | فہم | (understanding) |
| عظیم | (great) | مرتبت | (rank) | کثیر | (many) | لسان | (language) |
| عزیز | (dear) | قدر | (value) | دائم | (eternal) | مرض | (illness) |
| رائج | (current) | وقت | (time) | عدیم | (absent) | فرصت | (free time) |
| غریب | (away) | وطن | (homeland) | عظیم | (great) | شان | (eminence) |

In noun-noun phrases, ال is never prefixed to the first word in the compound and is usually best translated as "of the." The phrase as a whole is considered definite and is therefore often translated into English beginning with "The ..."

| | | | | | |
|---|---|---|---|---|---|
| نور | (light) | حق | (truth; God) | ← نور الحق | (The light of truth/God) |
| وقار | (honor) | ملک | (country) | ← وقار الملک | (The dignity of the country) |
| شعر | (poetry) | ہند | (India) | ← شعر الہند | (The poetry of India) |

*F. Read the following Arabic phrases used in Urdu and write their meaning. The vocabulary has been given in a word bank to assist you.*

۱۔رسول اللہ ۲۔امیر المومنین ۳۔ حُب الوطن ۴۔ یوم الحشر ۵۔نفس الامر

۶۔دار الحکومت ۷۔راقم الحروف ۸۔دستور العمل ۹۔دار الشفا ۱۰۔ملکِ الشّعرا

| | | | | | | | |
|---|---|---|---|---|---|---|---|
| رسول | (messenger) | لہ | (god, lord) | امیر | (commander) | مومن | (believer) |
| حب | (love) | وطن | (homeland) | یوم | (day) | حشر | (doomsday) |
| نفس | (essence) | امر | (matter) | دار | (house, seat) | حکومت | (government) |
| راقم | (writer) | حروف | (letters) | دستور | (rule) | عمل | (action) |
| دار | (house) | شفا | (health) | مَلِک | (king) | شعرا | (poets) |

*G. Read the following names of Urdu books and translate their meanings into English. Refer to the word bank when needed.*

۱۔شعر الہند ۲۔کاشف الحقائق ۳۔ نور اللغات ۴۔ مفتاح المنطق ۵۔ترجمان القرآن

۶۔ شعر العجم ۷۔مرآۃ الحکما ۸۔ مناظر المصائب ۹۔ سیرت النبی ۱۰۔دستور الفصاحت

| | | | | | | | |
|---|---|---|---|---|---|---|---|
| شعر | (poem) | ہند | (India) | کاشف | (revealer) | حقائق | (truths) |
| نور | (light) | لغات | (languages, words) | مفتاح | (key) | منطق | (logic) |
| ترجمان | (house) | قرآن | (health) | شعر | (king) | عجم | (poets) |
| مرآت | (mirror) | حکما | (philosophers) | مناظِر | (scenes) | مصائب | (afflictions) |
| سیرت | (character) | نبی | (prophet) | دستور | (rule) | فصاحت | (eloquence) |

## 2.29 Arabic Prepositions

Many Urdu words and phrases include Arabic pronouns and prepositions. It is therefore useful to be familiar with them. The following chart reviews the most common Arabic prepositions. Those consisting of a single letter are in prepositional prefixes attached to the word which they modify. Those comprising multiple letters are written separately.

| | | | |
|---|---|---|---|
| بِ | (by, with; in, at) | كَ | (like) |
| لِ | (to; for) | وَ | (by [for making vows, swearing by]) |
| علٰی | (upon; on) | مِن | (from; than [in comparisons]) |
| اِلٰی | (to; at) | عَن | (about; from; on) |
| فوق | (above, over) | فی | (in) |
| حتّٰی | (as far as, until) | | |

Arabic prepositions are often found in Urdu phrases. Read the following aloud.

| | | | |
|---|---|---|---|
| لہٰذا | (therefore) | منہا | (lit. from it; deducted, subtracted) |
| مِن و عَن | (lit. from and about; as it is or was; circumstantially; to the very letter) | | |

Note on pronunciation. When prepositional prefixes ending in a vowel precede ال, the ا [a] is assimilated to the vowel quality of the prefix. Thus, in the first example below, بِ [bi] (by, with) + ال [al-] becomes بِال [bil-] (by the). When long vowels precede ال, the long vowel is shortened. Thus, فی [fī] (in) + ال [al-] is pronounced فی ال [fil-] (in the). Read the following examples.

| | | | |
|---|---|---|---|
| بِ + ال + کُل (total) | ⟵ | بالکل | [bilkul] (totally) |
| فی + ال + فور (haste) | ⟵ | فی الفور | [filfaur] (quickly, immediately) |
| نعوذ + بِ + للہ (God) | ⟵ | نعوذ باللہ | [naūzbillāh] (we seek refuge in God) |

When لِ (for, by) is prefixed to ال, the ا is not written:

| | | |
|---|---|---|
| للہ | [lillāh] | (for God['s sake]) |

Note that many phrases resulting from the combination of a preposition and definite article with a noun carry an adverbial sense.

| | | | | |
|---|---|---|---|---|
| فی + ال + حقیقت | (reality) | ⟵ | فی الحقیقت | (in reality; really) [filhaqīqat] |
| علٰی + ال + تدریج | (gradation) | ⟵ | علی التدریج | (gradually) [alat-tadrīj] |

*A. Read the following Urdu phrases aloud. All of them include Arabic prepositions, though not all of the phrases are borrowed from Arabic.*

من ابتدا　　من اللہ　　من قبل　　بالفرض　　بالواسطہ　　علی العموم　　علیحدہ

فی گھنٹا　　فی الوقت　　فی الحال　　فی الواقع　　فی الاصل　　واللہ　　حتی المکان

کالعدم

*B. Given the meaning of the word on the right, predict the meaning of the phrase on the left. Check your answers in an Urdu dictionary.*

| | | | | |
|---|---|---|---|---|
| ۱۔ علم | (knowledge) | ← | حتی العلم | ________________ |
| ۲۔ امکان | (possibility) | ← | حتی الامکان | ________________ |
| ۳۔ فرض | (supposing) | ← | بالفرض | ________________ |
| ۴۔ واسطہ | (intermediary) | ← | بالواسطہ | ________________ |
| ۵۔ حال | (the present) | ← | فی الحال | ________________ |
| ۶۔ واقع | (reality) | ← | فی الواقع | ________________ |
| ۷۔ عموم | (generality) | ← | علی العموم | ________________ |
| ۸۔ ابتدا | (beginning) | ← | من ابتدا | ________________ |
| ۹۔ قبل | (before) | ← | من قبل | ________________ |
| ۱۰۔ عدم | (non-existence) | ← | کالعدم | ________________ |

*C. Use the list of prepositions above to form five prepositional phrases with the following and give their meanings. Two examples have been given.*

۱۔ الشمس (the sun)　　۲۔ الہند (India)

۱۔ کالشمس [kash-shams] (like the sun)

۲۔ من الشمس [min ash-shams] (from/than the sun)

*D. Read the following expression, which appears at the beginning of each chapter of the Quran and is commonly said at the beginning of undertakings. Then parse it and translate it literally. Use the word bank to help you.*

بسم اللہ الرحمٰن الرحیم

ب (in)　　اسم (name)　　اللہ (God)　　رحمٰن (merciful)　　رحیم (compassionate)

## 2.30 Arabic Pronouns in Urdu

Arabic pronouns are often encountered when Urdu speakers and writers quote Arabic phrases. The pronouns can be divided into three forms corresponding to their function. As subjects, they take their independent form. As objects and possessives, they take the form of suffixes. The following chart reviews the three forms.

| Possessive | | Object | | Subject | | |
|---|---|---|---|---|---|---|
| (my) | ی | (me) | نی | (I) | انا | 1st-person sing. |
| (our) | نا | (us) | نا | (we) | نَحنُ | 1st-person pl. |
| (your) | کَ | (you) | کَ | (you (s.m.)) | انتَ | 2nd-person sing. masc. |
| (your) | کِ | (you) | کِ | (you (s.f.)) | انتِ | 2nd-person sing. fem. |
| (your) | کُما | (you) | کُما | (you (two)) | انتما | 2nd-person dual |
| (your) | کُم | (you) | کُم | (you (pl.m.)) | اَنتُم | 2nd-person pl. masc. |
| (your) | کُنّ | (you) | کُنّ | (you (pl. fem.)) | انتنّ | 2nd-person pl. fem. |
| (his) | ہٗ | (him) | ہٗ | (he) | ہوَ | 3rd-person sing. masc. |
| (her) | ہا | (her) | ہا | (she) | ہیَ | 3rd-person sing. fem. |
| (their) | ہما | (them) | ہما | (they (two)) | ہُما | 3rd-person dual |
| (their) | ہُم | (them) | ہُم | (they (m.)) | ہُم | 3rd-person pl. masc. |
| (their) | ہُنّ | (them) | ہُنّ | (they (f.)) | ہُنّ | 3rd-person pl. fem. |

| | | |
|---|---|---|
| [hāżā/hāżihi] | ہٰذا (m) /ہٰذہٖ (f) | this |
| [żālika/tilka] | ذٰلک (m) / تلک(f) | that |
| [hażāni/hatāni] | ہٰذان / (m) ہتان (f) | these/those (dual) |
| [hā'ulā] | ہٰؤلاء | these |
| [ūlā'ika] | اولائک | those |

Note that the vowel pattern of the suffixes changes when they are the objects of prepositions. Thus, in the third person singular, ہ [hu] changes to [hi] in some cases. Thus علیہ (upon him) is pronounced [alaihi]. We will discuss this in detail later.

The personal pronouns and pronominal suffixes are found in a large number of phrases and idioms used in Urdu. Read the following aloud:

| | |
|---|---|
| السلام علیکم | (peace be upon **you** [pl./s. formal]) |
| سلام علیک | (peace be upon **you** [s. informal]) |

| | |
|---|---|
| السلام علیکم و رحمت اللہ و برکاتہ | (peace be upon **you** [pl./formal] and the mercy of God and **his** blessings) |
| علیہ السلام / علیہا السلام / علیہم السلام | (peace be upon **him/her/them**) |
| صلی اللہ علیہ و سلم | (may God bless **him** and grant [him] peace) |
| صلی اللہ علیہ و آلِہٖ و سلم | (may God bless **him** and **his** family and grant [them] peace) |
| قدس اللہ سِرّہٗ | (may God sanctify **his** secret [or grave or inner self]) |
| رَضِیَ اللہ عنہٗ / عنہا / عنہم | (may God be pleased with **him/her/them**) |
| رَحمَۃُ اللہِ علیہ | (God's mercy be upon **him**) |
| یا الٰہی | (O **my** God!) |
| مرحومی | (**my** [dearly] departed [friend]) |
| انا | (ego) |
| سبحانی | (Glory be to **me**!) (a phrase attributed to the Sufi Bayazid Bastami) |

*A. Read the following phrases. The first is a common greeting; the second is its response. Break them into their constituent parts, including articles, prepositions, nouns, and pronouns. Then translate them literally into English.*

السلام علیکم ____________ ____________

و علیکم السلام ____________ ____________

*B. Change the phrase* علیہ السلام *(upon him be peace) for the following pronouns: you (m. singular and plural); her; them (3rd-person masculine).*

*C. Use the chart of possessive suffixes to form the possessive of the following nouns for the following persons: I, we, you (s.m.), you (s.f.), you (pl. m.), he, she, they (pl. m.).*

۱۔ حبیب (beloved) ۲۔ ربّ (lord, god)

*D. The following stanza by Mir Anis demonstrates the use of the Arabic pronominal suffix in Urdu. It is found as the object of the imperative* اَدرِک *(See! or Recognize!). Read the stanza aloud and underline the pronominal suffix. Also note the use of other Arabic forms.*

اے مددگار و معین الضعفا ادرکنی — اے خبرگیر گروہ غربا ادرکنی
پاؤں لغزش میں ہے اے دست خدا ادرکنی — ہاتھ باندھے ہوں میں اے عقدہ کشا ادرکنی
دیجئے حر کو سندنار سے آزادی کی — آئیے جلد خبر لیجئے فریادی کی

*E. Use the chart of pronominal suffixes to form phrases with the singular imperative* اَدرِک *(Recognize!) corresponding to the following English pronouns: me, us, him, her, them (masculine).*

## 2.30.1 Arabic Interrogative Pronouns and Pronominal Phrases

In literary and scientific registers of Urdu, especially in philosophy, logic, and theology, a considerable number of technical terms borrowed from Arabic are built on a combination of participles, prepositions, and pronouns. Consider the following set of terms regularly encountered in discussions of hadith (reports of the sayings of the Prophet).

([the person] reported to) مروی عنہ (reported) مروی (reporter) راوی

Here is a set with ties to legalistic contexts. The compound literally means "claimed upon him."

(a defendant) مدعیٰ علیہ (claimed; claim) مدعیٰ (claimant) مدعی

*A. Given the meaning of the words on the right, estimate the meaning of the word on the left.*

______________ مکتوب الیہ (written; a letter) مکتوب (writer) ۱۔ کاتب

______________ مختلف فیہ (different) ۲۔ مختلف

Here follow some of the Arabic interrogative pronouns that are regularly encountered in Urdu.

| | | | | | |
|---|---|---|---|---|---|
| لِماذا | why | | مَن | who |
| کَم | how much | | ما | what |
| کَیف | how | اَین | حیث | where |
| | | متیٰ | حین | when |

Many of these interrogative pronouns are found in common Urdu words and phrases.

(capacity; wherewithal; status) حیثیت

(quantity) کمّیت

(quality, mood) کیفیت

(quiddity; essence [lit. "what-it-is-ness"]) ماہیت

The interrogative pronouns often double as relative pronouns in Arabic, just as the English word "what" may signify a question ("What did you do?") or be used in relative clauses (I know what you did). Consider the following.

(What God wills.) ما شاء اللہ

*B. Read the following Urdu words and phrases aloud. Then estimate their meanings.*

لہٰذا　　مِنہا　　معتمد علیہ　　مفروق منہ

*C. Review the meaning of the pronouns on the right, then choose the best meaning from those on the left.*

| | | | |
|---|---|---|---|
| ۱۔ معتمد علیہ | (enemy) | (customary) | (reliable supporter) |
| ۲۔ لہٰذا | (thus) | (additionally) | (forthcoming) |
| ۳۔ منہا | (subtraction) | (lowliness) | (extremely) |
| ۴۔ منتقل علیہ | (transferee) | (transferer) | (transference) |
| ۵۔ مکتوب الیہ | (a letter) | (addressee) | (addresser) |

*D. Read the following words and phrases aloud. Use an Urdu dictionary to help you guess and learn their meanings.*

مابعد　　مابعدالطبیعیات　　مابقا　　مابین　　مابین السطور

ماتحت　　ماتقدّم　　ماتقرّر　　ماجرا　　ماحصل

ماحضر　　ماحول　　ماشاءاللہ　　ماسعیٰ　　ماسلف

مافوق　　مافوق الانسان　　مافوق الفطرت　　مافوق البیان　　مافوق البشر

مافیہا　　دنیا و مافیہا　　ماقبل الذکر　　کیف و کم

## 2.31 Arabic Syntax and Common Arabic Phrases in Urdu

Urdu speakers of all backgrounds regularly use Arabic phrases in speech and writing. Some, but by no means all, such phrases are tied to Islamic traditions, in which Arabic, as the language of the Quran and much of the Islamic textual and scholarly tradition, plays a central role. It is hardly surprising, therefore, that Urdu borrows many Arabic phrases related to God or tied to Islamic thinking. These phrases, while certainly Islamic, are not used exclusively by the Muslim community. They are part of a shared and pluralist ecumene of linguistic, literary, and religious interaction in which Islam plays an important role.

The following phrase, which opens the first sūra of the Quran, is commonly spoken in response to inquiries after well-being.

اَلحمدُ للہ　　(Praise [is/be] for/to God)

Note that the ُ [u] suffixed to الحمد is regularly found in Arabic phrases. This is because the rules of Arabic syntax require that the subject of Arabic sentences be marked by ُ [u] (the nominative case). Note that there is no correlative of "be" in the phrase above. This is because the present and subjunctive tenses of the verb "to be" (is/are) are typically implied rather than stated in Arabic. In most copular sentences (i.e. "x is y"), the subject and predicate alone are stated (i.e. "x y"). The verb is implied. You now have all the information required to understand the meaning of this statement:

| (God) | اللہ | (for, to) | لِ | ([the] praise [is]) | الحمدُ |
|---|---|---|---|---|---|

Now consider the following phrase, which is commonly spoken after taking the name of major religious figures, such as Prophets.

(peace be upon him) [alaihis-salām] علیہ السلام

The pronominal suffix ہ attached to the pronoun علیٰ (upon) yields علیہ "upon him." Note that here, instead of ُ, we have the suffix ِ [i] [alaihis-salām]. This is because the rules of Arabic syntax require nouns and pronouns modified by most prepositions to be marked by ِ [i] (the genitive case).

*A. Read the Arabic phrase on the right. Then select the best translation.*

۱۔ دنیا و مافیہا
- (The world and everything in it.) [ ]
- (What does the world have in it?) [ ]
- (The world without anything.) [ ]

۲۔ فی زماننا
- (On time.) [ ]
- (In our time.) [ ]
- (In his time.) [ ]

۳۔ کالشمس فی نصف النہار
- (Half the day, half the sun.) [ ]
- (Like the day, so the sun.) [ ]
- (Like the sun at midday.) [ ]

۴۔ کالنقش فی الحجَر
- (Like a stone impression.) [ ]
- (Like an impression in stone.) [ ]
- (Like a stone in an impression.) [ ]

۵۔ اظہر من الشمس
- (The brightest sun.) [ ]
- (Hotter than the sun.) [ ]
- (More apparent than the sun.) [ ]

| | | | |
|---|---|---|---|
| (God's mercy be upon him.) | [ ] | رَحمتُ اللہ علیہ | ۶۔ |
| (God's will be done.) | [ ] | | |
| (God's mercy be upon us.) | [ ] | | |
| (Half for me, half for you.) | [ ] | نِصف لی و نِصف لک | ۷۔ |
| (Half way, half done.) | [ ] | | |
| (Half the time, half the price.) | [ ] | | |
| (Light to light.) | [ ] | نور علیٰ نور | ۸۔ |
| (Light upon light.) | [ ] | | |
| (Light from light.) | [ ] | | |
| (From this perspective.) | [ ] | علیٰ ہذا القیاس | ۹۔ |
| (Over the top.) | [ ] | | |
| ([Based] on this reasoning.) | [ ] | | |

## 2.32 Arabic Verbs and Syntax in Urdu

Urdu borrows a large number of Arabic proverbs and maxims from religious literature (such as the Quran), as well as from literary traditions in philosophy, poetry, linguistics, ethics, and mathematics. In order to understand many of these maxims and proverbs, it is necessary to know some basic information about Arabic sentence structure and verbs. Both are cursorily reviewed here.

### The Verb "To Be" in the Present Tense

In simple, present-tense statements, Arabic does not typically use a verb for "to be." Examples of this fact are found in the common phrases الحمد للہ (Praise (be/is) to/for God!) and اللہ اکبر (God (is) the greatest). Read the following sentence, which is a hadith of the Prophet often quoted in Urdu to indicate that the moral value of an action lies in its intention. Note that there is no verb for "to be" in the phrase.

| | | |
|---|---|---|
| (Actions [are] in intentions) | [al-āmālu bin-niyyāt(i)] | الاعمال بالنیات |

This sentence comprises two parts: the subject الاعمال ([the] actions) and the predicate بالنیات (in [the] intentions). In Arabic, the present-tense conjugation of the verb "to be" (the "are" in our English translation) in this kind of sentence is not expressly stated. Instead, it is implied by the juxtaposition of the subject and predicate.

Here is another example.

(The command [is] above [the] etiquette.) [al-amru fauqal-adab(i)] الامر فوق الادب

Note that the subject الامر (the command) is immediately followed by the predicate فوق الادب (above [the] etiquette), and that the verb "to be" (is) is not written, but implied. The sense of this aphorism is that duty takes precedent over etiquette, meaning that if one has been given an order, one should perform it even if it violates social protocol.

## Arabic Cases

The above examples demonstrate a number of important points about Arabic cases. Arabic nouns and adjectives have three cases. In each case, the words are marked by one of three short vowels. The nominative marker ُ or ٌ [u or un] is suffixed to the subjects of sentences. The accusative َ or ً [a or an] is suffixed to objects of verbs (or subjects after the conjunctive ان). The genitive ِ or ٍ [i or in] is suffixed after a preposition or secondary elements in genitive ("of") constructions and prepositional phrases.

Recall the common sayings:

[al-hamd**u** lillāh] الحمد لله

[alaih**i** s-salām] علیہ السلام

In the first example, u marks the subject (praise). In the second, because the 3rd-person masculine pronoun (هُ) [hu] is the object of the preposition علیٰ (upon), the vowel "u" changes to "i."

## Arabic Verb Tenses

Many Arabic proverbs and maxims commonly used in Urdu, as well as some everyday idioms, involve verbs in the present and past tenses. The following chart reviews the paradigms of Arabic verbs in the present (indicative) (is, does, etc.), past (perfective) (was, did, etc.), and imperative (be!, do!, etc.) tenses of Form I verbs.

| Imperative | Past | Present | |
|---|---|---|---|
| | فعلتُ | افعلُ | 1st-singular (I) |
| | فعلنا | نفعلُ | 1st-plural (we) |
| افعل | فعلتَ | تفعلُ | 2nd-singular-m (you, m) |
| افعلی | فعلتِ | تفعلِین | 2nd-singular-f (you, f) |
| افعلا | فعلتُما | تفعلانِ | 2nd-dual-m |
| افعلا | فعلتُما | تفعلانِ | 2nd-dual-f |
| افعلوا | فعلتُم | تفعلُون | 2nd-plural-m |
| افعلن | فعلتنَّ | تفعلنَ | 2nd-plural-f |

| | | |
|---|---|---|
| فعلَ | يفعل | 3rd-singular-m (he) |
| فعلَت | تفعل | 3rd-singular-f (she) |
| فعلا | يفعلانِ | 3rd-dual-m |
| فعلتا | تفعلانِ | 3rd-dual-f |
| فعلوا | يفعلُون | 3rd-plural-m |
| فعلن | يفعلن | 3rd-plural-f |

The ending in وا is pronounced ū (the alif is elided). Here is the verb درک (to see, perceive) in the second-person masculine tenses (singular and plural)

| | | | | | |
|---|---|---|---|---|---|
| (See!) (s. m.) | ادرک | (you [s. m.] saw) | درکتَ | (you [s. m.] see) | تدرکُ |
| (See!) (pl. m.) | ادرکوا | (you [pl. m.] saw) | درکتم | (you [pl. m.] see) | تدرکون |

The same pattern is followed for verbs of Forms II-X preserving recognizable patterns of infixation and suffixation. Here is an example using the Form VIII (verbal noun اعتبار).

| | | | | | |
|---|---|---|---|---|---|
| (Take heed!) (s. m.) | اعتبر | (you [s.m.] took heed) | اعتبرت | (you [s.m.] take heed) | تعتبر |
| (Take heed!) (pl. m.) | اعتبروا | (you [pl.m.] took heed) | اعتبرتم | (you [pl.m.] take heed) | تعتبرون |

The following everyday word may help you remember the form of the third-person present-tense singular verb. It is derived from the verb عنیٰ (to have in mind; to mean) and is related to the noun of palace معنیٰ (meaning).

(that is; lit. "it means") یعنی

The past tense may also carry an optative sense.

(may his prosperity last) دامَ اقبالہ

*A. Using the chart as a model, conjugate the following verbs in the present and past tenses for the following pronouns: I; we; you (m, f singular); you (m plural); he, she (singular); they (m plural). Then conjugate the second-person masculine imperatives (singular and plural).*

نظر عمل

## Negative Phrases with لا and ما. Abstract Compounds

The negative particle لا is often used to negate verbs in the present tense. Here is an example of an everyday Urdu idiom that includes لا in this sense:

(lit. it doesn't mean; idiom. meaningless) لایعنی

لا is also frequently used as the first component in negative Urdu compounds.

| | |
|---|---|
| (lit. without response; speechless; without equal, exceptional) | لا جواب |
| (lit. without religion; irreligious, impious) | لا دین |
| (with no doubt; undoubtedly) | بِلا شبہہ |

Urdu may form abstract nouns from these phrases by suffixing ی.

| | |
|---|---|
| ("lack of response"; speechlessness; unequalledness) | لا جوابی |
| (religiouslessness; irreligiousness) | لا دینی |

*B. Given the meaning of the verbal noun on the right, guess the meaning of the phrase on the left.*

| | | | |
|---|---|---|---|
| ________________ | لایعنی | (meaning) | ۱۔ معنی |
| ________________ | لایزال | (decline, decay) | ۲۔ زوال |
| ________________ | لایعلم | (knowledge) | ۳۔ علم |
| ________________ | لایموت | (death) | ۴۔ موت |
| ________________ | لاأبالی | (mind, care; circumstances) | ۵۔ بال |

*C. Negate the following words using لا and give the resulting meaning.*

۱۔ مذہب ۲۔ مکان ۳۔ ولد ۴۔ ثانی ۵۔ حاصل ۶۔ حل ۷۔ علاج ۸۔ زوال

## 2.33 Arabic Proverbs and Maxims in Urdu

Arabic aphorisms, proverbs, maxims, and quotations can be found across a range of discursive contexts in Urdu, from the poetry of Muhammad Iqbal through idioms associated with philosophy and history to religious speeches and conversations in literary gatherings. One reason that Arabic remains central to the training of Urdu scholars is its long history in South Asia as a language of the rational sciences. Even through the colonial period, Arabic works on literature, logic, philosophy, and theology were used as textbooks to train scholars and bureaucrats in the methods and techniques of clear thinking. This legacy has continued into the twenty-first century, although the shape and context of Arabic studies has changed considerably. In Arabic academies, which are mainly associated with Islamic Studies, emphasis has become increasingly placed on hadith and Quranic sciences and less on logic, speculative theology, and literature.

The preceding lessons have given you most of the tools you need to make sense of the aphorisms, idioms, and phrases that you will encounter in Urdu. Let us now turn to applying our knowledge of Arabic word forms and the basics of Arabic grammar to the study of some Arabic phrases that you are likely to encounter.

The following qaul (قول) attributed to the Prophet is an integral part of qavvālī (قوالی) performance in South Asia. It also demonstrates the importance of knowing basic forms of the Arabic verb. Here, the verb کان (to be) appears in the first-person perfective tense, in which its medial vowel is shortened. Note the verb ending.

[man kuntu maulā(hu) fa-hāzā Ali-un maulā(hu)] من کنت مولا فہذا علی مولا

(Whosoever's lord I was [=am], indeed Ali is [his] lord.)

The following phrase is likewise an integral part of Sufi discourse.

(God is he.) [Allāh hu] اللہ ہو

The following phrase appears in the Quran in reference to God's creation of the universe and is often repeated when referring to God's power.

(Be! So it is.) [kun fayakūn] کُن فیکُون

The following verse of the Quran (59:2) is invoked to encourage others to learn a moral lesson from what they have observed.

(So take heed, O possessors of eyes!) [fātabirū yā ūli l-absār] فاعتَبِرُوا یا اولی الابصار

Here is the same phrase, broken into its constituent parts and literally translated:

([of] the eyes) الابصار (possessors) اولی (O) یا (take heed! [pl.]) اعتَبِرُوا (and so) ف

See if you can parse the following expression, which is spoken when the meaning of something is unclear.

(The meaning is in the inside [=mind] of the poet) [al-mānī fī batni sh-shāir] المَعنِی فِی بطنِ الشاعِر

*A. Read the following verses of the Quran, quotations from hadith traditions, proverbs, and maxims. Then use your knowledge of Arabic to mark the best translation.*

۱۔فَضَّلنا بَعضَہُم علٰی بَعض
(Quran 2:253)

(We favored some of them over others.) [ ]

(And they favored some of us more than others.) [ ]

(And we favored all of them.) [ ]

۲۔ الاشیاء تُعرَف باضدادہا

(Things are known by their opposites.) [ ]

(She knows the opposite of everything.) [ ]

(Her opposites know everything.) [ ]

۳۔ الانتظار اشدّ من الموت

(Death is more intense than waiting.) [ ]

(Waiting is more intense than death.) [ ]

(Waiting is as intense as death.) [ ]

۴۔ السعی منّی و الاِتمام من اللہ

(Effort and completion are from me.) [ ]

(Effort is from me and completion is from God.) [ ]

(Effort and completion are from God.) [ ]

۵۔ السکوت کالاقرار

(Silence is not acceptance.) [ ]

(Silence is like acceptance.) [ ]

(I accept your silence.) [ ]

۶۔الناس علی دین ملوکہم

(The people [walk] upon the religion of their kings.) [ ]

(Your people [walk] upon the path of your kings.) [ ]

([We] people [walk] upon the path of our kings) [ ]

۷۔ مات المفتی مات الفتویٰ

(The mufti killed the fatwa.) [ ]

(The mufti and his fatwa never die.) [ ]

(When the mufti dies, the fatwa dies.) [ ]

۸۔ ما شاء اللہ

(What God wills!) [ ]

(What does God will?) [ ]

(God wills what?) [ ]

۹۔ مُوتوا قبلَ ان تَمُوتوا

(I died before I died.) [ ]

(He will die before he dies.) [ ]

(Die before you die.) [ ]

۱۰۔ سید القوم خادمهم

(The leader of the community has servants.) [ ]

(The leader of the community is their servant.) [ ]

(The leader of the community is our servant.) [ ]

*B. Read the Arabic hadith, proverbs, and sayings on the right, then select the best translation.*

۱۔ الفقرُ فخرِی

(Proud poverty.) [ ]

(The poor are proud.) [ ]

(Poverty is my pride.) [ ]

۲۔ ذکرُ العَیشِ نِصفُ العَیش

(The mention of pleasure is half the pleasure.) [ ]

(Mention pleasure in the first half of pleasure.) [ ]

(The mention of pleasure causes suffering.) [ ]

۳۔ لا حول و لا قوت الا باللّٰہ

(There is no power and there is no strength except in God.) [ ]

(There is no rest and there is no happiness except in God.) [ ]

(There is no space and there is no time except in God.) [ ]

۴۔ ہذا من فضل ربی

(This is my graceful lord.) [ ]

(My lord is full of grace.) [ ]

(This is from the grace of my lord.) [ ]

۵۔ النَّحو فی الکَلام کالملح فی الطعام

(Grammar in speech is like salt in food.) [ ]

(Grammar in speech is like salty food.) [ ]

(Grammar in speech is like food without salt.) [ ]

The following formulaic expression is often found at the conclusion of Arabic texts. (As a final exercise, see if you can parse it and translate it into English.)

واللّٰہُ اَعلَم

## 2.34 Suggestions for Further Study

Arabic vocabulary permeates Urdu, from newspapers to popular film songs, and students who wish to continue developing facility with Arabic vocabulary in Urdu should have no trouble finding sources. Any works by the following authors will contain large amounts of Arabic words, phrases, and passages. The following books are suggested as starting points for further study. Nażīr Aḥmad *Ibn ul-Vaqt*. (first printed 1888); Alṭāf Ḥusain Ḥālī, *Muqaddamah-e Shi'r o Shā'irī*; Shiblī Nu'mānī, *Safarnāmah-e Rūm o Miṣr o Shām* (Agra: Mufīd-e 'Ām, 1894); Sayyid Sulaimān Nadvī, *Sīrat al-Nabī* (second volume and after); Ashraf 'Alī Thānavī, *Bavādir un-Navādir.*

# UNIT 3

# THE HINDI ELEMENT

This unit reviews the ways in which Urdu forms nouns and adjectives. In particular, it surveys the most common prefixes and suffixes that Urdu uses to affect the meaning of common words. It also reviews the most common ways in which Urdu derives nouns and adjectives from verbs.

The key words for this unit are given in the section on Hindi-Urdu verbs.

## 3.1 Recognizing Indic and Hindi Words

Indic words are those which belong to the family of languages including Sanskrit, Prakrit, and modern Indian languages like Hindi-Urdu, Panjabi, and Gujarati. In general, they exhibit a handful of tell tale signs that distinguish them from Arabic, Persian, and other sources of Urdu vocabulary. Since this book uses "Urdu" as an umbrella term that includes all the vocabulary in the language, this unit uses "Hindi" to distinguish the vernacular Indic vocabulary in Urdu from Arabic, Persian, Sanskrit, and other registers.

Two markers of Indic vocabulary are retroflex consonants (ٹ ڈ ڑ) and the distinction of consonants (and therefore meaning) by aspiration (ھ). Of these, ڑ is exclusive to the vernaculars, which means that any word that contains it belongs to what is here called the Hindi element. The other two retroflexes are also found in Sanskrit (the classical Indic language) and are therefore not necessarily indicators of Indic vernacular vocabulary. Note that borrowings from English and other European languages are an exception to this rule, since Urdu typically borrows the English t and d as ٹ and ڈ. This is not, however, a problem for English-language students, since they can usually recognize English borrowings as such. As for aspiration, Arabic, Persian, English, and other languages contain aspirated consonants, but they do not distinguish meaning by aspiration alone, and aspiration in those languages is thus never indicated in writing. Hence there is no equivalent of the distinction between the Indic پھل (fruit) and پل (moment) in any of these languages.

As a rule, any word in which the retroflex consonants or the ھ of aspiration is found in Urdu is likely an Indic word, with the exception of words borrowed from English in which retroflex consonants are also found, and, as mentioned, a word is certainly Hindi (Indic vernacular) if it contains ڑ. However, mere presence of retroflex or aspirated letters or phonemes is therefore not sufficient to distinguish the vernacular Hindi element from, for example, the classical Sanskritic one. For that, we must rely on our understanding of verbal forms and the word patterns to distinguish Indic vernacular (Hindi) vocabulary from Sanskritic vocabulary.

One way to reason to discern a word's Indic origin is by process of elimination. If the word contains any letters that are exclusive to Arabic (ث ح ذ ص ض ط ظ ع), it is, with very few exceptions, not an Indic word. Likewise, words containing Persian phonemes that are not classically considered Indic (خ ز ژ غ ف ق) are, in general, not Indic in origin.

Differences between spoken or vernacular Indic languages like Urdu and the classical Indic language, Sanskrit, help to distinguish what is here called the Hindi Element from the Sanskrit element discussed in more detail in Unit 5. For example, Hindi-Urdu, like other vernaculars, prefers consonant-vowel pairs to clusters of consonants, especially at the beginning of words. Sanskrit prefers clusters. Compare the Sanskrit word کرشن [kr̤iṣhṇa (typically transliterated as kṛṣṇa)] with the Hindi کشن [kishan]. Note that this is the reason that Urdu prefixes اِ [i] to English borrowings that begin, like other Germanic languages, with a consonant pair or cluster. Compare the English **st**udent with the Urdu اِسٹوڈنٹ [**is**ṭūḍinṭ].

However, two points must be kept in mind as we draw distinctions among Indic, Persian, Semitic, and other language groups. First, because Sanskrit and Persian are closely related (as they are to Latin and other Indo-European languages such as English), the category "Indic" does not mean that a word so categorized is not *related* to a Persian one. On the contrary, the differences among related Hindi, Persian, and Sanskrit words are often minor, e.g. the Hindi-register Indic word سوکھا (dry) is obviously related both to the Sanskrit شُشک (dry) and to the Persian خشک (dry). Sometimes, there is no difference at all, e.g. the Hindi کار (work), the Persian کار (work), and the Sansrit کار (work). The Latinate word "Indic" points to the branch of the Indo-European family tree in which a word has spent most its life, not to its having sprung up from separate roots.

Second, the phonemes that are said to distinguish Indic languages from Persian and others do not, in practice, always do so. What have been identified here as Persian phonemes have been used by speakers of Indic languages for centuries. Although it can be useful to use them to distinguish a classical Indic language such as Sanskrit from classical Persian, it can be misleading to apply the same logic to identify words in a modern language like Hindi-Urdu as Indic versus Persian. To do so would be to assume that Sanskrit phonetics define what counts as Indic and to ignore the centuries of borrowing, exchange, adoption, adaptation, and change among Indic, Persian, and other regional languages that include these phonemes. In Urdu, for example, the word چٹخارا (the slapping sound made by the palate when chewing; the taste in one's mouth) exhibits both Indic (ٹ) and Persian (خ) phonemes. So does the word غُنڈا (gangster; bully). This suggests that the classical Indic-Persian paradigms do not consistently determine word origins in modern Indic languages in all cases.

*A. Read the following words and mark the words that are certainly Indic, those that are Hindi, and those that are likely or certainly neither.*

| | | | | | | | |
|---|---|---|---|---|---|---|---|
| بار | بھاڑ | باڑھ | بہار | پہاڑ | دانت | ڈانٹ | چاپ |
| چٹاخ | سراخ | خزانہ | پٹاخا | دار | دھار | برابر | بڑبڑانا |
| تِنکا | تُرِن | کُشار | کھارا | کُشُدرُک | چھُٹکا | گُرِہ | گھَر |
| زاغ | کاگ | خیال | کھیل | زبان | جیبھ | زار | جار |

## 3.2 Nouns of Place

Urdu typically forms nouns of place by suffixation. Here follows an overview.

### The Suffixes ال [-āl] and الا or الہ [ālā]

These suffixes and their Sanskrit relative الے [-ālay] are used to indicate the place or space where something lives, occurs, or is found. The Sanskrit suffix is typically seen in Sanskritic registers of Urdu.

| | | | | |
|---|---|---|---|---|
| سسر / ساس | (father- and mother-in-law) | ← | سسرال | (in-laws' household) |
| نانا / نانی | (maternal grandparents) | ← | ننیال | (maternal grandparents' household) |
| پستک | (book) | ← | پستکالے | (library) |

*A. Use the given suffix to form the noun of place and give its meaning.*

۱۔ دادا / دادی (paternal grandparents) -ال

۲۔ دیو (god) -الا

۳۔ شو (Shiva) -الا

۴۔ ہِم (snow) -الہ

*B. Read the following idiom and choose the best translation.*

۱۔ سسرال کا کتا (a shrewd businessman) (a freeloading son-in-law) (a lost son-in-law)

### The Suffix گھر [ghar]

Perhaps the most easily recognizable suffix of place is گھر (home, house), which forms everyday nouns of place.

| | | | | | | |
|---|---|---|---|---|---|---|
| ڈاک | (mail) | گھر | (home, house) | ← | ڈاک گھر | (post office) |
| چڑیا | (bird) | گھر | (home, house) | ← | چڑیا گھر | (zoo) |

*C. Using the suffix گھر, form nouns of place from the following nouns and give the meaning of the resulting noun.*

| | | | | | |
|---|---|---|---|---|---|
| ۱۔ عجائب | (wonders, curiosities) | ۲۔ گھنٹا | (hour) | ۳۔ نیلام | (auction) |
| ۴۔ ناچ | (dancing) | ۵۔ ہتھیار | (weapon) | | |

## The Suffix پُور

Related to a Sanskrit word meaning "castle" or "fortified city," the suffix پُور is used ubiquitously in Urdu to mark a city of any kind. For example:

| | |
|---|---|
| رام پور | Rampur |
| بہاول پور | Bahawalpur |

*D. Match the cities on the right with their English spellings. Locate each city on a map and mark its country, region, and district. Note that some of these names may be given to multiple cities across South Asia. Others may refer both to cities as well as districts. Be sure to note this where appropriate.*

| | | |
|---|---|---|
| ۱۔ جے پور | ___ | Gurdaspur ا |
| ۲۔ ناگ پور | ___ | Jaipur ب |
| ۳۔ کان پور | ___ | Firozpur پ |
| ۴۔ جبل پور | ___ | Fatehpur ت |
| ۵۔ مظفر پور | ___ | Jabalpur ٹ |
| ۶۔ خیر پور | ___ | Afzalpur ث |
| ۷۔ افضل پور | ___ | Khairpur ج |
| ۸۔ فیروزپور | ___ | Nagpur چ |
| ۹۔ فتح پور | ___ | Muzaffarpur ح |
| ۱۰۔ گرداس پور | ___ | Kanpur خ |

*E. Use a map to find cities named فتح پور and write the name of the counties in which they are located. Note that city names can have more than one spelling in English. For example:*

| | | |
|---|---|---|
| میر پور | Meerpur | Mirpur |

## The Suffix نگر

Borrowed from Sanskrit and meaning "town," نگر is commonly used to refer to municipalities, townships, and even districts or neighborhoods within a city. The most famous city bearing this name is perhaps سری نگر (Srinagar) in Kashmir.

*F. Match the following towns and cities. Use a map to find in which states, districts, and cities the foregoing names are found.*

| | | |
|---|---|---|
| Ramnagar ا | ___ | ۱۔ کشی نگر |
| Kushinagar ب | ___ | ۲۔ مظفر نگر |
| Daulat Nagar پ | ___ | ۳۔ رام نگر |
| Bahawalnagar ت | ___ | ۴۔ دولت نگر |
| Biratnagar ٹ | ___ | ۵۔ احمد نگر |
| Ahmadnagar ث | ___ | ۶۔ بِراٹ نگر |
| Muzaffarnagar ج | ___ | ۷۔ بہاول نگر |

## The Suffix گڑھ

The suffix گڑھ, meaning fort, is also commonly used in place names.

*G. Match the following names. Then find the towns and cities on a map.*

| | | |
|---|---|---|
| Aligarh ا | ___ | ۱۔ چنڈی گڑھ |
| Chandigarh ب | ___ | ۲۔ علی گڑھ |
| Muzaffargarh پ | ___ | ۳۔ چھتّیس گڑھ |
| Shakkargarh ت | ___ | ۴ مظفر گڑھ |
| Chattisgarh ٹ | ___ | ۵۔ شکر گڑھ |

The foregoing suffixes are the most common, but are not the only Hindi markers of place in Urdu. Read the following chart, which surveys suffixes typically found in place names.

| | | | |
|---|---|---|---|
| (square, market; pass, intersection) | چوک | (village) | گاؤں |
| (place; quarter, ward) | واڑا | (quarter, ward) | ٹولا |
| (village, hamlet [esp. used in the Deccan]) | پلی | (village [from Persian]) | دِہ / دیہ |
| (fort, castle) | کوٹ | (quarter; hamlet) | پاڑا |
| (corner) | کونا | (area; enclosure) | باڑہ / باڑا |
| (marketplace, storehouse) | گنج | (village) | گرام |
| (section) | کھنڈ | (descent to a tank or river) | گھاٹ |

*H. Using a map of South Asia, locate two place names in which each of the following suffixes is used. Typical romanizations of the names are given in brackets.*

| | | | | | |
|---|---|---|---|---|---|
| [ala] | ۳۔ الا | [palli, pally] | ۲۔ پلی | [gaon] | ۱۔ گاؤں |
| [ganj] | ۶۔ گنج | [bara] | ۵۔ باڑہ / باڑا | [kot] | ۴۔ کوٹ |

## 3.3 Verbal Nouns

Like English, Urdu derives a substantial number of nouns, adjectives, and adverbs from verbs. By studying the many patterns of noun derivation in Urdu, you will quickly acquire a large, nuanced vocabulary. For example, just as English derives the noun "meeting" (which it then uses in both general and specific senses) from the verb "to meet," so too Urdu derives میل (friendship) and مِلَن (meeting; harmony), inter alia, from the verb مِلنا (to meet; to get). The following sections examine the large number of ways in which Urdu derives verbal nouns. Read the following list, which reviews Urdu words related to the verb مِلنا (to meet; to find; to receive).

| | |
|---|---|
| (to meet; to find; to receive; to get; meeting; finding; receiving; getting) | مِلنا |
| (to introduce; to mix; to give; introducing, mixing, giving) | مِلانا |
| (to have meet; to cause to be given; having introduced) | مِلوانا |
| (concord, friendship harmony; meeting; sexual intercourse; reconciliation) | مِلاپ |
| (sociable, friendly; companion) | مِلاپی |
| (comparison; adjustment; reconciliation) | مِلان |
| (mixture; comparison) | مِلانی |
| (mixture) | مِلاؤ |
| (mixture; combination; meeting) | مِلاوا |
| (mixture; adulteration; mutual affection; relations; conspiracy) | مِلاوٹ |
| (company; friendship) | مِلّت |
| (meeting, encountering; harmony) | مِلَن |
| (kind; faithful; a friend; an associate) | مِلَنی |
| (sociable; affable; a social or affable person) | مِلَنیا |
| (sociable; affable) | مِلنسار |
| (sociableness; affability) | مِلنساری |
| (a gift made to the bride; wedding reception; welcome; visit) | مِلنی |
| (adulteration, contamination) | مِلَونی |
| (friendship; society; connection; unity) | میل |
| (large gathering; festival) | میلا/میلہ |
| (a close friend) | میل ملاپی |
| (irrelevant; stranger recluse; incoherent) | اَنمِل / اَن مِل |
| (unrelated; incoherent; unsuitable) | اَن میل / اَن میل |

This list demonstrates several important facts about verbal nouns in Hindi-Urdu. First, like other Indo-European languages, they are typically formed by suffixation and prefixation. Second, in some cases, derivation involves changes to the quality of internal vowels by elongation. Third, the paradigms for derivation are very large in number. Fourth, different patterns may produce words with very similar if not identicals meanings. Often, the differences in sense and connotation among them (if any) are intelligible only by reference to use, idiom, and context. The following sections examine their structure and meaning in detail.

## 3.4 Infinitives and Verbal Nouns

The following section surveys the patterns of verbal nouns, adjectives, and adverbs derived from Hindi-Urdu verbs Urdu. Before moving on, review the following verbs, which are among the most common. Recall that all Hindi-Urdu infinitives comprise two parts: a verb stem and the infinitive suffix نا. All infinitives double as verbal nouns (gerunds) similar to the English "doing" from "to do." For example, ملنا means both "to meet" and "meeting"; ملانا means both "to introduce" and "introducing"; and ملوانا means both "to have (someone) introduced" and "having (someone) introduced." This shoud be born in mind as we progress through this section.

| | | | |
|---|---|---|---|
| (to speak) بولنا | (to join) جوڑنا | (to prepare, make) بنانا | (to meet; to get) ملنا |
| (to share, divide) بانٹنا | (to climb) چڑھنا | (to desire) چاہنا | (to strike) مارنا |
| (to eat) کھانا | (to be missed) چھوٹنا | (to apply, affix, strike) لگنا | (to come) آنا |
| (to shine, glimmer) چمکنا | (to cut) کاٹنا | (to settle, finish) چکنا | (to see) دیکھنا |
| | (to understand) سمجھنا | (to be) ہونا | (to sow) بونا |
| | (to let go) چھوڑنا | (to save) بچانا | (to fill) بھرنا |
| | (to advance, increase) بڑھنا | (to move) چلنا | (to earn) کمانا |

*A. Remove the infinitive suffix from the following verbs to yield the verb stem.*

۱۔ ملنا ۲۔ بننا ۳۔ بولنا ۴۔ آنا ۵۔ لگنا ۶۔ کھانا ۷۔ دیکھنا ۸۔ ہونا ۹۔ سمجھنا ۱۰۔ چلنا

### Derivation of Causative or Factitive Verbs

The suffixation of ا [ā] to the verb stem or the elongation of a vowel in the verb stem are two common ways in which Hindi forms transitive verbs from intransitive ones or causative verbs from transitive ones. Causative verbs formed in this way typically imply that the agent of causation (e.g, the person who has people meet) and the performer of the action (e.g., the person who introduces them) are the same. For example, ملانا refers to a person causing others to meet ملنا by introducing them to each other.

By contrast, the suffixation of وا [vā] to the verb stem implies that the agent of the causation is not involved in carrying out the action, but rather has the action of the verb carried out by others. For example, ملوانا refers to a person causing someone to be introduced or causing people to meet (ملنا) by means of a third party. To illustrate this difference in English, this book uses the rough-and-ready distinction between "to make" for ا [ā] causal verbs and "to have (someone or something)" for وا [vā] third-party causal ones. Consider the following:

(to introduce [make meet]) مِلانا (to meet; to get; to find) مِلنا

(to have [someone] introduced; to cause someone to make meet) مِلوانا

(to have [something] made) بنوانا (to make [something] made) بَنانا (to be made) بَننا

*B. Form the transitive-causal (ا) and third-party causal (وا) verbs from the following and give their meanings.*

| | | | | | |
|---|---|---|---|---|---|
| (to be filled) | ۳۔ بھرنا | (to ascend, climb) | ۲۔ چڑھنا | (to be attached) | ۱۔ لگنا |
| (to move) | ۶۔ چلنا | (to be saved) | ۵۔ بچنا | (to understand) | ۴۔ سمجھنا |
| (to read, study) | ۸۔ پڑھنا | (to do) | ۸۔ کرنا | (to grow, develop) | ۷۔ بڑھنا |

## Vowel Changes in Transitive-Intransitive Verb Pairs

Some pairs of intransitive and transitive verbs show regular patterns of vowel lengthening and shortening in the first syllable of the verb stem. Short vowels are often indications of intransitivity and long ones of transitivity. This is not universally true, of course. There is a large number of intransitive Urdu verbs with long vowels in the stem (بھولنا, ڈوبنا and so on). But the distinction between short and long vowels is nevertheless generally helpful. Consider the following regular changes to short vowels that form transitive verbs.

| | Transitive | | | Intransitive |
|---|---|---|---|---|
| [ā] | آ | ← | [a] | اَ |
| (to cut) | کاٹنا | ← | (to be cut) | کٹنا |
| [o, ū] | او | ← | [u] | اُ |
| (to open [something]) | کھولنا | ← | (to [be] open) | کھُلنا |
| (to suck) | چُوسنا | ← | (to be sucked) | چُسنا |
| [ī, e, ai] | ای اے | ← | [i] | اِ |
| (to show [something]) | دیکھنا | ← | (show, appear) | دِکھنا |
| [ī or ai] (to draw) | کھینچنا | ← | (be drawn) | کھِنچنا |

*C. From the following intransitive verbs, form the transitive counterpart by lengthening the vowel in the first syllable of the stem. Then give the meaning of the transitive verb.*

| | | | | | | | |
|---|---|---|---|---|---|---|---|
| ۱۔ کٹنا | (to be cut) | | ۲۔ مَرنا | (to die; be struck) | | ۳۔ کُھدنا | (to be dug) (use o) |
| ۴۔ جُڑنا | (to be joined) | (use o) | ۵۔ مُڑنا | (to be turned) | (use o) | ۶۔ پِٹنا | (to be beaten) (use ī) |
| ۷۔ چِھدنا | (to be pierced) | (use e) | ۸۔ پِھرنا | (to turn) | (use e) | | |

The suffixation of the causative marker ا [ā] to the verb stem typically causes any long vowels in the first syllable of the stem to be shortened. The only exception to this rule is the long vowel [au], which does not change. The same shortened form is sustained when the third-party causal suffix وا is suffixed to the stem. The following chart surveys the changes to long vowels in the first syllable of intransitive verbs.

| Stem | | Causative | | Third-Party Causal |
|---|---|---|---|---|
| اے / ای [ī, e, ai] | ← | اِ [i] | | |
| بیٹھنا (to sit) | ← | بِٹھانا (to seat, set) | ← | بِٹھوانا (to cause to be seated) |
| دیکھنا (to see) | ← | دِکھانا (to show) | ← | دِکھوانا (to cause to show) |
| بیتنا (to pass) | ← | بِتانا (to pass [something]) | ← | بِتوانا (to cause to be passed) |
| او [o, ū] | ← | اُ [u] | | |
| کھولنا (to open) | ← | کُھلانا (to make open) | ← | کُھلوانا (to have opened) |
| گھومنا (to go around) | ← | گُھمانا (to take around) | ← | گُھموانا (to cause to rotate) |
| آ [ā] | ← | اَ [a] | | |
| کاٹنا (to cut) | ← | کَٹانا (to make someone cut) | ← | کَٹوانا (to have cut) |
| اَو [au] | ← | اَو [au] | | |
| کھولنا (to boil) | ← | کھولانا (to make boil) | ← | کھولوانا (to cause to boil) |

*D. Derive both causative forms of the following verbs by suffixing ا and وا to the verb stem and changing vowel lengths where appropriate. Then give the meanings of the resulting verbs.*

| | | | | | |
|---|---|---|---|---|---|
| ۱۔ کھینچنا | (to draw, drag) | ۲۔ چھیڑنا | (to tease) | ۳۔ پھینکنا | (to toss, throw [away]) |
| ۴۔ جیتنا | (to win) | ۵۔ بولنا | (to speak) | ۶۔ چھوڑنا | (to leave, let go) |
| ۷۔ رُوکنا | (to stop) | ۸۔ پھولنا | (to swell, blossom) | ۹۔ جاگنا | (to wake up) |
| ۱۰۔ بھاگنا | (to flee, run away) | ۱۱۔ ہارنا | (to lose) | ۱۲۔ ناچنا | (to dance) |

### The Infix ل [l] in Verb Stems Ending in a Vowel

If a verb stem ends in a long vowel, then its causative form shortens the vowel and infixes ل between the shortened vowel and the causative marker ا. In such cases, the aforementioned rules of vowel-shortening apply except in rare cases such as کھانا (to eat), which becomes کِھلانا (to serve, feed).

| | | | | | |
|---|---|---|---|---|---|
| (to have [someone] lulled to sleep) | سُلوانا | (to lull to sleep) | سُلانا | (to sleep) | سونا |

*E. Form the causative and third-party causative of the following verbs and give their meanings.*

| | | | | | |
|---|---|---|---|---|---|
| (to wash) | ۳۔ دھونا | (to cry) | ۲۔ رونا | (to give) | ۱۔ دینا |
| (to drink) | ۶۔ پینا | (to live) | ۵۔ جینا | (to sew) | ۴۔ سینا |

### Consonant Changes in Transitive-Intransitive Verb Pairs

A handful of verbs display a regular shift in consonants from transitive to intransitive verbs. A typical change to the consonant at the end of the verb stem is ٹ [ṭ] in the intransitive to ڑ [ṛ] in the transitive. Such changes are usually accompanied either by a lengthening of the vowel as discussed above or a change in its quality. A typical change in vowel quality is وٹ [ūṭ] in the intransitive to وڑ [oṛ] in the transitive.

| | Transitive | | | Intransitive |
|---|---|---|---|---|
| | ڑ | ← | | ٹ |
| (to break [something]) | توڑنا | ← | (to break) | ٹُوٹنا |

*F. From the intransitive verb, derive the transitive by changing the vowel in the stem and changing the final consonant. Then form the causative and third-party causative, too. Give the meanings of all derivations.*

| | | | | | |
|---|---|---|---|---|---|
| (to be torn) | ۳۔ پھٹنا | (to burst) | ۲۔ پھُوٹنا | (to be let go, set free) | ۱۔ چھُوٹنا |

## 3.5 The Verb Stem as a Noun

The simplest way in which Urdu derives nouns from verbs is by using the verb stem as a verbal noun. The verb stem is produced simply by dropping the infinitive marker نا. Such stems typically carry a sense very close to the verb, but are instantiative, that is, they name the object or action associated with the verb. Thus, if سمجھنا means to understand or the act of understanding, سمجھ (understanding, comprehension, though, view) is understanding itself; if مارنا is the act of striking, مار is the strike, and so on.

| | | | | |
|---|---|---|---|---|
| (understanding) | سمجھ | ← | (to understand) | سمجھنا |
| (a strike, hit, blow) | مار | ← | (to hit) | مارنا |
| (shine, sparkle) | چمک | ← | (to shine) | چمکنا |

Note that in some cases the noun precedes the verb historically.

| | | | | |
|---|---|---|---|---|
| (to purchase) | خریدنا | ← | (purchase; cost) | خرید |

*A. Write the stems of the following verbal nouns and give their meanings.*

| | | | | | |
|---|---|---|---|---|---|
| (to pass) | ۳۔ گزرنا | (to miss) | ۲۔ چھوٹنا | (to pillage) | ۱۔ لوٹنا |
| (to identify) | ۶۔ پہچاننا | (to inquire) | ۵۔ پوچھنا | (to reach) | ۴۔ پہنچنا |
| (to fear) | ۹۔ ڈرنا | (to stop, hinder) | ۸۔ روکنا | (to ask for) | ۷۔ مانگنا |
| | | | | (to play) | ۱۰۔ کھیلنا |

## 3.6 Verb Stems and the Suffix ن [-an]

Many verbal nouns are formed by suffixing ن to the stem (or, put another way, by removing ا from the infinitive form of the verb). The resulting nouns are usually abstract and refer to the action of the verb.

| | | | | |
|---|---|---|---|---|
| (living) | رہن | ← | (to live, stay) | رہنا |
| (burning) | جلن | ← | (to burn) | جلنا |

Some verbal nouns of this pattern are found only (or nearly only) in pairs that are fixed idioms. The cumulative sense of these compounds is often greater than the sum of their parts.

| | | | | |
|---|---|---|---|---|
| (food and drink) | کھان پان | ← | (to eat and to drink) | کھانا پینا |
| (culture, lifestyle) | رہن سہن | ← | (to live and to make do) | رہنا سہنا |

*A. Give the verbal noun of the following verbs by suffixing ن to the root. Estimate its meaning.*

| | | | | | |
|---|---|---|---|---|---|
| ۱۔ دینا | (to give) | ۲۔ لینا | (to take) | ۳۔ چلنا | (to move) |
| ۴۔ ملنا | (to meet) | ۵۔ اترنا | (to descend) | ۶۔ سوجنا | (to swell) |
| ۷۔ تھکنا | (to tire) | ۸۔ اتارنا | (to remove) | ۹۔ تڑپنا | (to writhe) |
| ۱۰۔ جلنا | (to burn, be jealous) | | | | |

## 3.7 Verb Stems and the Suffix ت [-at, -t]

Another typical way that Urdu forms verbal nouns is by means of the suffix ت [-at (or -t in case the root ends in a vowel)] to the verb stem. These nouns are etymologically related to the Urdu participle ending in تا تی تے, which are related to the Sanskrit آپتی आप्ति [āpti] (attained, acquired). Hence, they often connote the state or object associated with the attainment, acquisition, or completion of the action of the verb. For example, چاہت (desire, love) from چاہنا (to desire; desiring) is the state in which a person has become desirous of or fallen in love with someone or something.

چاہنا (to desire, love) ← چاہت (desire, love)

In some cases, the verbal noun may reflect archaic forms of the verb. Compare the following with لگنا.

لاگنا (archaic) (to be attached) ← لاگت (expense; value; cost)

In some cases, the final consonant in the stem is doubled.

مِلنا (to meet, associate) ← مِلَّت (sociability)

*A. Form verbal nouns from the following verbs by suffixing ت and give their meaning.*

| | | | | | |
|---|---|---|---|---|---|
| ۱۔ لکھنا | (to write) | ۲۔ سکنا | (to be able) | ۳۔ چلنا | (to be current) |
| ۴۔ چکنا | (to settle) | ۵۔ چھونا | (to touch, handle [and thus pollute]) | | |
| ۶۔ ماننا | (to acknowledge, to promise) | (shorten the vowel; double the final letter in the root) | | | |

## 3.8 Verb Stems and the Suffix ی [-ī]

Another simple way that Urdu forms verbal nouns is to suffix ی [ī] to the stem. These are often best defined as "the action of the verb." Thus ہنسی (laughter) is the action of laughing. Alternatively, they may indicate a concrete or abstract object associated with or possessed of the quality associated with the action of the verb. For example, چمکی (glitter, tinsel) is a concrete object characterized by shining (چمکنا).

| | | | | |
|---|---|---|---|---|
| (laughter) | ہنسی | ← | (to laugh) | ہنسنا |
| (glitter, tinsel) | چمکی | ← | (to shine) | چمکنا |

*A. Form verbal nouns from the following verbs by suffixing ی and give their meaning.*

| | | | | | |
|---|---|---|---|---|---|
| (to strike) | ۳۔ مارنا | (to pair, to join) | ۲۔ جوڑنا | (to speak) | ۱۔ بولنا |
| | | (to ensnare) | ۵۔ پھانسنا | (to make rounds, return) | ۴۔ پھیرنا |
| | | (shorten the vowel; double the ٹ) | | (to have a break from; to be free) | ۶۔ چھوٹنا |

## 3.9 Verb Stems and the Suffix ا [-ā]

Verbal nouns and adjectives are often formed by suffixing ا [ā] to the stem. These cover a wide semantic range, from the actions to objects associated with the verb. In most cases, the objects are those which receive or result from the action of the verb (as opposed to the instrument by which it occurs). Thus, a پھیرا (a round) is the action associated with someone who goes around (پھیرنا). Similarly, a میلا (festival, fair) is what results from a great deal of people meeting (ملنا).

| | | | | |
|---|---|---|---|---|
| (a round) | پھیرا | ← | (to make rounds, to go around) | پھیرنا |
| (festival, fair) | میلا | ← | (to meet) | ملنا |

*A. Form the verbal nouns using the suffix ا [ā], then choose the best meaning from those on the left.*

| | | | | | |
|---|---|---|---|---|---|
| (crowd) | (glue) | (pair) | _____ | (to join) | ۱۔ جوڑنا |
| (pushcart) | (fall) | (pressure) | _____ | (to push, shove) | ۲۔ ٹھیلنا |
| (knapsack) | (a strap) | (a nail) | _____ | (to swing, hang) | ۳۔ جھولنا |
| (farm) | (army) | (enclosure) | _____ | (to surround) | ۴۔ گھیرنا |

## 3.10 Verb Stems and the Suffix ائی [-āī]

Suffixed to the verb stem, this suffix typically suggests the quality, mood, or action of the verb. Long vowels in the first syllable of the verb stem will always be shortened according to the standard rules.

(writing) لکھائی ← (to write) لکھنا

When verb stems end in ا [ā], the ا is elided.

(earning(s); income) کمائی ← (to earn) کمانا

Note that the form of this suffix makes it difficult to know if the noun has been formed from intransitive or transitive verbs whose stems end in ا [ā]. In the case of the latter, it is similarly impossible to distinguish between nouns formed by the ائی [āʾī] suffix and those formed simply by suffixing ی [ī] to the verb stem. For example, the verbal noun کمائی may be formed either by suffixing ائی to the stem کما (and eliding the ا [ā]) or by suffixing ی to it. In the following case, too, it is unclear if the verbal noun has been formed from the intransitive or transitive verb, although Platts tells us that it has been formed from the latter (دکھانا) (to show).

(showing, appearance) دکھائی ← (to show, to cause to appear) دکھانا (to show, appear) دکھنا

Just as Urdu verbs carry many idiomatic senses, so verbal nouns often convey highly idiomatic meaning. This is true of nouns formed with the present suffix, too. For example:

(death, fate; occasion) آئی ← (to come) آنا

The ائی suffix may also suggest the cost or wages involved in performing an action or having that action performed. This is especially true of verbal nouns derived from causative forms involving labor or service. Consider the following:

(needlework; the cost of having something sewn) سلائی ← (to sew or have sewn) سلانا

(washing; the cost of having something washed) دھُلائی ← (to have washed) دھُلانا

*A. Form the verbal nouns of the following verbs using ائی [āʾī] and give their meanings. In all the cases in this exercise, the meaning is related to the quality, mood, or action of the verb. Remember to shorten the vowel in the first syllable where appropriate.*

۱۔ لڑنا (to fight) ۲۔ کھلانا (to feed) ۳۔ چڑھنا (to incline, increase)

۴۔ بھرنا (to fill) ۵۔ ابکنا (to vomit) ۶۔ پیسنا (to grind)

۷۔ بونا (to sow) ۸۔ سننا (to hear)

۹۔ چکانا (to settle, to clear [an account]) ۱۰۔ لکھنا (to write)

*B. Given the meaning of the verb on the right, estimate the meaning of the words on the left. All the derived nouns carry the sense of the cost or wages involved in performing an action or having that action performed.*

۱۔ تولنا (to weigh) ← تُلائی

۲۔ بننا (to make) ← بنوائی

| | | | |
|---|---|---|---|
| ۳۔ جوتنا | (to plough, till) | ← | جتائی |
| ۴۔ پیسنا | (to grind, mill) | ← | پسوائی |
| ۵۔ رکھنا | (to keep) | ← | رکھوائی |
| ۶۔ کھودنا | (to dig) | ← | کھدوائی |
| ۷۔ چھوڑنا | (to release) | ← | چھڑوائی |

## 3.11 The Active Participle

The active particle of the verb is formed by suffixing تا تی or تے to the verb stem. It may be nominalized to indicate the agent of the action. Compare with "the x-ing" (e.g. "the living" from "to live") in English. The most common are these formed from the singular masculine participle.

| | | | | |
|---|---|---|---|---|
| مرنا | (to die) | ← | مرتا | (the dying) |
| سونا | (to sleep) | ← | سوتا | (the sleeping) |

The feminine form of the active participle may also be used.

| | | | | |
|---|---|---|---|---|
| چلنا | (to move) | ← | چلتی | (that which moves; activity) |

Such verbal nouns are especially common in fixed phrases, such as aphorisms. Read the following.

| | | | |
|---|---|---|---|
| مرنا | ← | مرتا کیا نہ کرتا | (What wouldn't a dying person have done?) |
| چلنا | ← | چلتی کا نام گاڑی | (Whatever moves is named "car.") |

Although typically agentive, such nouns sometimes take on slightly different meanings:

| | | | | |
|---|---|---|---|---|
| پھرنا | (to return) | ← | پھرتا | (return; a response to a letter; commission) |

*A. Form the active participle of the following verbs and guess their meanings.*

۱۔ دیکھنا (to see) ۲۔ گرنا (to fall)

## 3.12 The Instrumental Suffixes وتی [-autī] and وتا [-autā]

These suffixes can also be suffixed to verb stems. The resulting word often carries an instrumental sense. Long vowels in the stem will typically be shortened.

| | | | | | |
|---|---|---|---|---|---|
| | (discount, reduction, cut) | کٹوتی | ← | (to be cut) | کٹنا |
| (archaic) | (ransom; money paid to be let go) | چھٹروتی | ← | (to release, drop) | چھوڑنا |

*A. Form the instrumental verbal nouns using the suffix indicated and give the meaning of the resulting word.*

| | | |
|---|---|---|
| (use وتا) | (to understand) | ۱۔ سمجھنا |
| | (to agree) | ۲۔ ماننا |
| | (to choose; to call out, to challenge) | ۳۔ چننا |
| (use وتا) | (to settle (a debt or stipulated amount)) | ۴۔ چکانا |

## 3.13 Verb Stems and the Suffix اؤ [-āo]

Verbal nouns are commonly formed by suffixing اؤ [āo] to verb stems. This suffix may be applied to causative verbs and typically involves some degree of abstraction from the sense of the verb. Note that if the verb stem ends in ا (as many causative verbs do), the ا is elided. Long vowels in the first syllable of the verb are usually shortened.

| | | | | |
|---|---|---|---|---|
| (tension) | کھنچاؤ | ← | (to pull) | کھینچنا |
| (encampment, halting-place) | پڑاؤ | ← | (to fall; to lie; to halt) | پڑنا |
| (attachment, interest, love) | لگاؤ | ← | (to be attached) | لگنا |

*A. Use the اؤ suffix to derive verbal nouns from the following verbs and give their meaning.*

| | | | | | |
|---|---|---|---|---|---|
| (to be at rest) | ۳۔ ٹھہرنا | (to be safe, saved) | ۲۔ بچنا | (to be sold) | ۱۔ بکنا |
| (to move, leave) | ۶۔ چلنا | (to climb, increase) | ۵۔ چڑھنا | (to fly) | ۴۔ اڑنا |
| (to use, handle, treat) | ۸۔ برتنا | | | (to be decorated; get along; turn out well) | ۷۔ بننا |
| (to entangle, confuse) | ۱۱۔ اُلجھانا | (to spread) | ۱۰۔ پھیلنا | (to grow, expand) | ۹۔ بڑھنا |

## 3.14 Verb Stems and the Agentive Suffixes و [-ū] or اؤ [-āū]

These suffixes form agentive adjectives (compare with English -ing). The adjectives are often nominalized (compare with -er).

| | | | | |
|---|---|---|---|---|
| (an earner; earning) | کماؤ | ← | (to earn) | کمانا |

In the following example, the suffix is applied to an archaic relative of the verb چلنا (to work; to move).

چالنا (to work, move) ← چالُو (working, running)

*A. Derive the agentive adjective from the following and give its meaning. Use اؤ [āū] in all cases unless otherwise indicated. Remember that the ا [a] ending of a verb stem is elided (e.g. کمانا to کماؤ).*

۱۔ اڑانا (to waste)
۲۔ جمانا (to make stick, adhere)
۳۔ برسانا (to cause to rain)
۴۔ بکنا (to be sold)
۵۔ چکانا (to settle; to pay [a debt])
۶۔ جلانا (to burn)
۷۔ پھُسلانا (to coax)
۸۔ کھانا (to consume, to eat)
۹۔ جاگنا (to awake, to be wakeful) (use و)
۱۰۔ جھاڑنا (to sweep) (use و)

## 3.15 Verb Stems and the Suffix اوا [-āvā]

This suffix is etymologically related to اؤ [-āo] and is similar to it in meaning. Most verbal nouns that involve this ending have a transitive sense; that is, they denote an action or idea that involves doing something to someone or something. Most of these nouns are abstract and general, but may be concretized to refer to specific events. Thus, چھلاوا is both the action associated with چھلنا (to deceive, to trick), thus, "deception" or "trickery," and the event itself, thus "a trick of the eyes."

دِکھانا (to show) ← دکھاوا (showiness, ostentation)

چھلنا (to deceive, trick) ← چھلاوا (a trick of the eyes; will-o'-the-wisp)

*A. Derive the verbal noun using the suffix اوا [āvā] and give its meaning.*

۱۔ پہنانا (to clothe)
۲۔ بڑھانا (to increase, encourage, promote)
۳۔ بلانا (to invite)
۴۔ چڑھانا (to offer; to gift)
۵۔ بھُلانا (to cause to forget, err)
۶۔ ملانا (to mix)
۷۔ ڈرانا (to cause to fear)
۸۔ بہکانا (to mislead)

## 3.16 Verb Stems and the Suffix اوٹ [-āvaṭ]

Like other suffixes in this section, this suffix conveys abstraction from the root.

بنانا (to make; to make up) ← بناوٹ (make; make-up; artifice)

*A. Derive the verbal nouns of the following verbs using the suffix اوٹ- and their meanings.*

| | | | |
|---|---|---|---|
| ۱۔ ملانا | (to mix, adultrate) | ۲۔ لگانا | (to attract) |
| ۳۔ لکھنا | (to write) | ۴۔ تھکانا | (to fatigue, exhaust) |
| ۵۔ رُکنا | (to be stopped, hindered) | ۶۔ پھیلنا | (to fill space, spread) |
| ۷۔ سجانا | (to decorate, adorn) | ۸۔ پھولنا | (to swell) |

## 3.17 Verb Stems and the Suffix اہٹ [-āhaṭ]

This suffix also conveys abstraction.

گھبرانا (to worry) ← گھبراہٹ (worry)

In some cases, the resulting noun is concretized. The meaning of such words can be quite idiomatic.

آنا (to come) ← آہٹ (footfall)

This is also the preferred abstract-nominal suffix for onomatopoeic verbs, which often involve doubling in the root.

ہِنہِنانا (to neigh) ← ہِنہِناہٹ (neigh, neighing)

*A. Derive the verbal nouns using اہٹ- and give their meanings.*

| | | | |
|---|---|---|---|
| ۱۔ چِلّانا | (to scream) | ۲۔ مسکرانا | (to smile) |
| ۳۔ چمکنا | (to shine) | ۴۔ کھُجلانا | (to itch) |
| ۵۔ بوکھلانا | (to become agitated, worried) | ۶۔ گھُلنا | (to melt, dissolve) |
| ۷۔ بھِنبھِنانا | (to buzz, hum) | ۸۔ پھڑپھڑانا | (to flutter) |
| ۹۔ پھُسپھُسانا | (to whisper, buzz) | ۱۰۔ بڑبڑانا | (to mutter, talk gibberish) |

## 3.18 Verb Stems and the Suffix واں [-vāṅ]

Verbal adjectives can also be formed by suffixing واں (sometimes spelled وان) to the verb.

کٹنا (to cut) ← کٹواں (cut; deducted; serrated; ledged)

*A. Given the meaning of the verbs on the right, guess the meaning of the nouns or adjectives on the left.*

۱۔ ڈھلنا (to slope, slant, incline decline) ۲۔ ملنا (to mix, meet)

۳۔ جوڑنا (to join, twin) ۴۔ لپیٹنا (to wrap)

## 3.19 Agentive Verbal Nouns with ہار- / ہارا- / کارا [-hār / -hārā / -kārā]

These suffixes, which are related to Sanskrit کار (कार) (work, do; doer), are suffixed the verb stem or to the verb stem plus ن. The literal meaning of these words is agentive (compare with English -er). However, they often take on quite idiomatic meanings. Many words formed with this suffix are considered archaic.

| | | | | |
|---|---|---|---|---|
| کھانا | (to eat) | کھانہارا | (eating, corrosive; eater) | (archaic) |
| ہونا | (to happen) | ہونہار | (promising, talented [said especially of a child]) | |
| چھوٹنا | (to escape, leave, be released) | چھٹکارا | (release) | |

*A. Read the verbal noun and write the verb from which it is derived. Look up the verbs in a dictionary and guess the meaning of the verbal noun.*

۱۔ جانہارا (archaic) ۲۔ رہنہار (archaic) ۳۔ سہارا ۴۔ جھجھکارا

## 3.20 Suffixes of Disapprobation and Humorous Censure

The following suffixes convey disapproval of the actions and the performers of the verb. It should be noted that such disapproval is often humorous and teasing.

### 3.20.1 The Habitual Agentive Suffix اکّڑ [-akkaṛ]

Among the most colorful agentive suffixes, اکّڑ [-akkaṛ] indicates the habitual performer of an action considered unfavorable or disgraceful, either in earnest or in jest. Note that suffixation requires shortening the long vowels in the initial syllable of the verb stem.

پادنا (to fart) ← پدکڑ (a farter; an inveterate farter)

*A. Use the suffix اکّڑ [-akkaṛ] to form the habitual agentive noun of the following verbs and guess their meanings.*

۱۔ گھومنا (to wander) ۲۔ بھولنا (to forget)

۳۔ پینا (to drink)

## 3.20.2 The Suffix و [-ū]

This suffix typically causes vowels in the stem to shorten and the final consonant to double.

(a farter) پدّو ← (to fart) پادنا

*A. Derive the negative or humorous verbal noun from the following and give the meaning.*

(to shit) ا۔ ہگنا

## 3.20.3 The Suffix وڑا [-oṛā]

This suffix typically forms agentive nouns and adjectives that express intensity. It typically causes long vowels in the verb stem to shorten.

(a farter) پدوڑا ← (to fart) پادنا

*A. Derive the verbal noun of negative emotion from the following and give its meaning.*

(to shit) ۲۔ ہگنا    (to piss) ا۔ موتنا

## 3.20.4 The Agentive Suffix الو [ālū]

This suffix forms nouns that, when used to refer to humans, often indicate disapproval of the performer of the action of the verb.

(quarrelsome) جھگڑالو ← (to fight, quarrel) جھگڑنا

*A. Use الو [ālū] to derive verbal nouns from the following verbs. Then guess their meanings. Check your guesses in an Urdu dictionary.*

(to be bashful) ۲۔ شرمانا    (to be afaid) ا۔ ڈرنا

(to blush, be ashamed) ۴۔ لجانا    (to be irritated, annoyed) ۳۔ چڑنا

## 3.21 Instrumental Nouns from Verbal Nouns

The suffix نی [-nī] is sometimes used to form instrumental nouns. The suffix ن may also be used in an instrumental sense.

(engagement) منگنی ← (to request) مانگنا

*A. Use the suffix نی to form instrumental nouns from the following verbs. Guess their meanings.*

۱۔ کھودنا (to dig)    ۲۔ کترنا (to cut)

## 3.22 Nominal and Adjectival Affixes

Like English, Urdu generates a great deal of vocabulary by prefixation and suffixation to nouns, pronouns, adjectives, and verb roots. Sometimes, such affixation results in slight changes to the form of the original word, such as the shortening of a long vowel. This section reviews some of the most common prefixes and suffixes used in Indic vernacular (Hindi) registers of Urdu. Most of these affixes are derived from Proto-Indo-European and therefore have cousins in Latin, Sanskrit, Persian, and other Indo-European languages. In some cases, they are borrowed directly from other Indic languages, such as Sanskrit and Prakrit.

Read the following prefixes aloud.

اَ (without; -less)    اَن (not; un-, dis-)    نِس / نِش / نِ / نِر (without, -less)

اَدھ (half)    اُن (less-one)

بھر (full)

سُ (good-; well-)    کُ (bad-; defective-)

### 3.22.1 The Negative Prefix ا [a-]

Like its Latinate English relative "a" (as in "asymmetrical"), this prefix negates the word that follows it and is usually best translated as "a-," "un-," or "-less."

تھاہ (bottom; depth)    اتھاہ (bottomless; fathomless)

لگنا (to attach, stick)    الگ (unattached, separate)

*A. Read the following adjectives, in which the negative prefix ا [a] is used.*

اپاہج (cripple; lazy; lit. without foot and hand)

اچانک (sudden; related to the verb jānnā [to know], thus "without foreknowledge")

اکھڑ (rude; uncouth)

*B. Form negative verbal nouns from the verb stems of the following verbs using the negative prefix ا.*

۱۔ناپنا (to measure)    ۲۔ تھکنا (to tire)    ۳۔ ٹوٹنا (to break)

۴۔ چھوتنا (to touch)    ۵۔مولنا (to price, to purchase) (noun is archaic)

## 3.22.2 The Negative Prefix ان [an]

Cognate with the English un-, the negative prefix ان [an] is among the most commonly used prefixes in Urdu. Like ا [a], to which it is related, ان [an] is often used with verb stems. It is related to the English "an-," "in-," and "un-," as in "unknown" and "anaerobic." Note that this prefix is typically written separately from the word that it negates.

| | | | |
|---|---|---|---|
| پڑھنا | (to read) | ان پڑھ | (illiterate) |

In Sanskrit, this prefix is only used to negate words which begin with a vowel. Although such words are certainly classifiable as Hindi-Urdu, we will deal with them in more detail in the unit on Sanskrit. Here are some Sanskrit words that use this prefix:

| | | | |
|---|---|---|---|
| ارتھ | (propriety; purpose) | ان ارتھ | (tyrannical; improper; meaningless) |
| انت | (end) | ان انت | (endless) |

This prefix is sometimes used along with the suffixes ا or ی to form adjectives.

| | | | |
|---|---|---|---|
| انوکھا | (uncommon, unique) | | (derived from a word related to Sanskrit ukt [speech]) |
| بونا | (to sow) | ان بویا | (unsown) |
| ہونا | (to be) | ان ہونی | (impossible [thing]) |
| سُننا | (to hear) | ان سُنی | (unheard, ignored [thing]) |

In the following case, the achaic participle ہوت has been negated to suggest the state of "not making it." The standard Urdu active participle ہوتا is also negated to form a term meaning extraordinary, strange, or rare.

| | | | | | |
|---|---|---|---|---|---|
| ہونا | (to be) | ان ہوت | (poverty) | ان ہوتا | (extraordinary, exceptional) |

*A. Form negative nouns and adjectives from the stems of the following verbs or from the given noun or adjective using اَن. Then estimate their meanings and check your guesses in a dictionary.*

| | | | |
|---|---|---|---|
| ۱۔ ملنا | (to meet, join) | ۲۔ بننا | (to be made, to get along) |
| ۳۔ جاننا | (to know) | ۴۔ مولنا | (to buy, to fix a price) |
| ۵۔ تھکنا | (to tire) | ۶۔ بولنا | (to speak) |
| ۷۔چِت | (thought, mind) | ۸۔ ہت | (friendship, love, affection) |

*B. Form the corresponding negative adjective by prefixing ان and suffixing ا. Then give its meaning.*

| | | | |
|---|---|---|---|
| ۱۔بھانا | (to be pleasing) | ۲۔بیاہ / بیاہنا | (marriage / to marry) |
| ۳۔ دیکھنا | (to see) | | |

## 3.22.3 The Negative Prefixes Related to نِس [nis]

This prefix and its related forms نِ [ni], نِر [nir], and نِش [nish], which are borrowed from Sanskrit, can create adjectives and nouns from nouns. Note that, in some cases, the form of the root noun may be altered.

| | | |
|---|---|---|
| ڈر (fear) | ← | نڈر (fearless) |
| کام (work, use) | ← | نکمّا (useless) |

*A. Use the indicated prefix to negate the given nouns and give the meaning of the resulting adjective.*

| | | |
|---|---|---|
| ۱۔ چِنت | (mind, thought) | نِ |
| ۲۔ لاج | (modesty) | نِر |
| ۳۔ بل | (power) | نِ |
| ۴۔ آس | (hope) | نِر |
| ۵۔ گُن | (quality) | نِر |

*B. Given the meaning of the nouns on the right, guess the meaning of the words on the left.*

| | | | |
|---|---|---|---|
| ۱۔ منہ | (mouth) | ← | نِمُہا |
| ۲۔ ہاتھ | (hand) | ← | نہتّھا / نہتّا |
| ۳۔ پُوت | (son) | ← | نپوتا |
| ۴۔ راج | (governance, rule) | ← | نراج |
| ۵۔ سنک | (fear) | ← | نِسنک |
| ۶۔ سکت | (ability, strength) | ← | نسک |

## 3.23 Prefixes of Quantity

The prefixes ادھ [adh] and آدھ [ādh] impart the sense of halfness or incompletion. This should not be surprising, since they are related to the word آدھا (half). But they can also suggest approximation. In general, ادھ [adh] is used with passive participles and adjectives, whereas آدھ [ādh] is used with measurements.

| | | | |
|---|---|---|---|
| کُھلنا | (to open) | ← | ادھ کھلا (half-opened) |
| گھنٹا | (hour) | ← | آدھ گھنٹا (half-hour; a while) |
| پاؤ | (pao [quarter]) | ← | آدھ پاؤ (an eighth of a pao) |

*A. Form adjectives beginning with ادھ using the past participle or adjective, then give the meanings.*

| | |
|---|---|
| ۱۔ بننا | (to be made) |
| ۲۔ کٹنا | (to cut) |
| ۳۔ مرنا | (to die) |
| ۴۔ جلنا | (to burn) |
| ۵۔ گلنا | (to melt, dissolve) |
| ۶۔ کہنا | (to say) |
| ۷۔ کچا | (raw) |
| ۸۔ پکا | (cooked) |

The prefix اُن [un] (less; one less than) is most commonly used in numbers.

(twenty-nine) اُنتیس ← (thirty) تیس

*B. Review the numbers 1–100. Note numbers beginning with اُن [un].*

## 3.24 The Prefix/Suffix بھر [bhar]

When used as a prefix, the word بھر [bhar] (full) can impart a sense of fullness, completion, or excess.

| | | | | |
|---|---|---|---|---|
| (chock-full; completely; extremely) | بھرپور | ← | (complete) | پورا |
| (excess; multitude) | بھرمار | ← | (to strike) | مارنا |

When used as a suffix with common nouns, it typically imparts a sense of fullness or completeness. When used with measurements, it can impart a sense of approximation.

| | | | | |
|---|---|---|---|---|
| (all day) | دن بھر | ← | (day) | دن |
| (a full mile; about a mile; a long way) | میل بھر | ← | (mile) | میل |

*A. Use the suffix بھر to form words and give their meanings.*

(moment) ۴۔ لمحہ (month) ۳۔ مہینہ (lifetime, age) ۲۔ عمر (stomach) ۱۔ پیٹ

(kilogram) ۵۔ کلو

## 3.25 Prefixes of Quality سُ [su-] and کُ [ku-/ka-]

These prefixes are only used with a small number of words in Urdu, but some of the words in which they appear are quite common. The prefix سُ [su] imparts a sense of goodness.

(shapely; attractive) سڈول ← (form, manner) ڈول

Not surprisingly, words that begin with this prefix, have a positive connotation:

(clean, pure) ستھرا

Linguists believe that سُ is related to the etymon of a prefix found in many Persian words. For example, the Persian word ہنر (skill) is believed to derive from from the Proto-Indo-European etymon of سُ (good) and the etymon of the Urdu نر (man, male).

*A. Given the meaning of the word on the right, estimate the meaning of the word on the left.*

| | | | |
|---|---|---|---|
| سبھاؤ | ← | (being; quality; temper) | ا۔ بھاؤ |
| سپوت | ← | (son) | ۲۔ پوت |
| سدھ | ← | (intellect; knowledge) | ۳۔ دھی |
| سگھڑ | ← | (to form) | ۴۔ گھڑنا |

The prefix کُ [ku; sometimes ka] (bad) is the counterpart of سُ.

| | | | |
|---|---|---|---|
| (ill-formed, ugly) | کڈول | ← | (form, shape; style) ڈول |

*B. Form nouns using the negative prefix of quality and give their meanings.*

| | | | | | |
|---|---|---|---|---|---|
| (son) | ۳۔ پُوت | (place) | ۲۔ ٹھور | (form, shape) | ا۔ ڈھب |

## 3.26 Suffixes

Like English, Urdu derives a great deal of vocabulary by means of suffixation. This section reviews the most common suffixes. It also discusses several less common yet significant ones.

## 3.27 Suffixes of Relation

Arguably the most common suffix of relation in Urdu is ی, which can show belonging, nationality, or other forms of relationship. If this suffix seems familiar, it is because it can be seen in a large number of words borrowed into English. It is also because it is found in other Indo-European languages, including Persian. Consider the following:

| | | | | |
|---|---|---|---|---|
| (Pakistani) | پاکستانی | ← | (Pakistan) | پاکستان |
| (Bengali) | بنگالی | ← | (Bengal) | بنگال |
| (Kashmiri) | کشمیری | ← | (Kashmir) | کشمیر |

In the nineteenth century, the following words carried the meanings shown in parentheses. Now, however, their meanings have been inverted, as Urdu has come to follow English.

Nineteenth century

| | | | | |
|---|---|---|---|---|
| (German) | جرمنی | ← | (Germany) | جرمن |

Twentieth century

| | | | | |
|---|---|---|---|---|
| (Germany) | جرمنی | ← | (German) | جرمن |

If a place name ends in a vowel, و is infixed between the final consonant and ی.

| | | | | |
|---|---|---|---|---|
| (of Delhi) | دہلوی | ← | (Delhi) | دہلی |

*A. Write the corresponding adjectives using the suffix ی.*

۱۔ ہندوستان ۲۔ لاہور ۳۔ گجرات ۴۔ حیدر آباد ۵۔ سندھ

## 3.28 Patronymic Suffixes جا [-jā] and ج [-aj]

These Sanskritic suffixes جا [jā] and ج [j] are not widely distributed in Urdu, but do appear in several everyday words. The former is found in two common terms of familial relation. The latter is most commonly encountered in Sanskrit loanwords. Study the following chart.

| | | | | |
|---|---|---|---|---|
| (brother's son) | بھتیجا | | (brother) | بھائی |
| (sister's son) | بھانجا | | (sister) | بہن |
| (mud-born; lotus) | پنکج | ← | (clay, soil, mud) | پنک |
| (water-born; lotus) | جلج | ← | (water) | جل |
| (water-born; lotus) | نیرج | ← | (water) | نیر |
| (love, Kamdev [born of the mind]) | منوج | ← | (mind) | منس |
| (child by a paramour) | جارج | ← | (lover, paramour) | جار |

## 3.29 Nominal Suffixes

This section surveys a number of Indic suffixes that are commonly used to form nouns (chiefly from adjectives, but occasionally from other nouns).

## 3.30 The Suffix ی [-ī] and ای [-āī]

This is used to form nouns (chiefly from adjectives, but also abstract nouns from concrete nouns).

| | | | | |
|---|---|---|---|---|
| (goodness) | اچھائی | ← | (good) | اچھا |
| (badness) | برائی | ← | (bad) | برا |

Note that in some cases the resulting nouns may take on specific or concrete meanings.

| | | | | |
|---|---|---|---|---|
| (a sweet, sweets; sweetness) | مٹھائی | ← | (sweet) | میٹھا |
| (a drink so named for its cooling effect) | ٹھنڈائی | ← | (cold) | ٹھنڈا |

The suffix ائی [-āī] is sometimes used to form abstract nouns of occupation or communal identity.

| | | | | |
|---|---|---|---|---|
| (the work of a pandit; learning, wisdom) | پنڈتائی | ← | (pandit) | پنڈت |

This suffix may also denote the cost of labor associated with objects, just as it does with verbal nouns.

| | | | | |
|---|---|---|---|---|
| (the cost of having skin cleaned or seasoned) | چمڑائی | ← | (leather) | چمڑا |

*A. Given the meaning of the noun on the right, guess the meaning of the noun on the left.*

| | | | |
|---|---|---|---|
| ٹھگائی | ← | (thug) | ۱۔ ٹھگ |
| نفرائی | ← | (laborer) | ۲۔ نفرا |
| چودھرائی | ← | (leader) | ۳۔ چودھری |

*B. Form abstract nouns from the following adjectives using ی [-ī] and give the meaning of the resulting words.*

| | | | | | | | |
|---|---|---|---|---|---|---|---|
| (high) | ۴۔ اونچا | (low) | ۳۔ نیچا | (tall) | ۲۔ لمبا | (wide) | ۱۔ چوڑا |
| (clean) | ۸۔ ستھرا | (true, sincere) | ۷۔ سچا | (big) | ۶۔ بڑا | (deep) | ۵۔ گہرا |

## 3.31 The Fractional Suffix ائی [-āī]

This suffix can be used to form fractions.

| | | | | |
|---|---|---|---|---|
| (third) | تہائی | ← | (three) | تین |

*A. Form the fractional noun and give its meaning.*

| | |
|---|---|
| (fourth) | ۱۔ چوتھا |

## 3.32 Abstract Nouns with پن / پا / پنا [-pan / -pā / -panā]

These suffixes are comparable to the English suffixes -ness, -ship, -ment, and (Latinate) -ion, etc. Note that in some cases, suffixation may affect pronunciation and spelling. All resulting nouns are masculine in Urdu.

| | | | | |
|---|---|---|---|---|
| (solitude, loneliness) | اکیلا پن | ← | (alone) | اکیلا |
| (boyhood, youth) | لڑکپن | ← | (boy) | لڑکا |
| (idiocy) | احمق پن | ← | (idiot) | احمق |

A note on use. When پن is suffixed to a marked adjective (one ending in ا), the adjective takes the oblique form (ے) when the noun is followed by a postposition.

| | | | | |
|---|---|---|---|---|
| (the pain of solitude) | اکیلے پن کا دکھ | ← | (solitude, loneliness) | اکیلا پن |

A related suffix is پا [pā]. This suffix requires that the long vowel in the first syllable of the root word be shortened.

| | | | |
|---|---|---|---|
| (old age; senility) | بُڑھاپا | (old man; senile) | بوڑھا |

A final variation of this suffix is the relatively rare پنا [panā].

| | | | |
|---|---|---|---|
| (meanness, wretchedness) | پاجی پنا | (mean, wretched) | پاجی |

Some words may be used with more than one of the suffixes discussed in this section. This may have to do with regional variation, idiom, or register. Here follows one example:

| | | | | | |
|---|---|---|---|---|---|
| (childhood; childishness) | بچپنا | (childhood) | بچپن | (child) | بچہ |

The example above demonstrates that although this is an Indic suffix, it can be used with non-Indic words such as the Persian بچہ (child).

*A. Use the suffix پن to form abstract nouns from the following adjectives. Then give their meanings.*

| | | | | | | | |
|---|---|---|---|---|---|---|---|
| (red) | ۴۔ لال | (simple) | ۳۔ سادہ | (crooked) | ۲۔ ٹیڑھا | (mad, crazy) | ۱۔ پاگل |
| (fair) | ۸۔ گورا | (stupid) | ۷۔ کمینہ | (yellow) | ۶۔ پیلا | (blue) | ۵۔ نیلا |
| (open; brash) | ۱۲۔ کھلا | (low) | ۱۱۔ نیچا | (full) | ۱۰۔ پورا | (small) | ۹۔ چھوٹا |
| (iron) | ۱۶۔ لوہا | (heavy) | ۱۵۔ بھاری | (light) | ۱۴۔ ہلکا | (old) | ۱۳۔ پرانا |
| (dry) | ۲۰۔ سوکھا | (wet) | ۱۹۔ گیلا | (blind) | ۱۸۔ اندھا | (new) | ۱۷۔ نیا |

*B. Use the suffix پا to form abstract nouns. Be sure to shorten long vowels in the initial syllable.*

| | | | |
|---|---|---|---|
| ۱۔ موٹا | (fat) | ۲۔ بڑا | (large) |
| ۳۔ چھوٹا | (small) | | |

*C. Form nouns from the following adjectives using پنا and guess the meaning of the resulting noun.*

| | | | | | |
|---|---|---|---|---|---|
| ۱۔ اناڑی | (clumsy; a fool) | ۲۔ مورکھ | (fool) | ۳۔ موذی | (pernicious) |

## 3.33 The Suffix ہٹ [-haṭ] or اہٹ [-āhaṭ]

We have already seen that these suffixes are used to form verbal nouns from verbs. It can also be used to nominalize adjectives.

| | | | |
|---|---|---|---|
| کڑوا | (bitter) | کڑواہٹ | (bitternes) |

As we have already seen, many nouns ending in اہٹ are verbal nouns, often onomatopoeic, formed from redoubled verb stems. Because verbs can easily be made from adjectives in Urdu, it is often impossible to know if the noun is derived from the verb or the adjective.

| | | | | | |
|---|---|---|---|---|---|
| پلپلا | (soft, overripe) | پلپلانا | (to soften) | پلپلاہٹ | (softness) |

*A. Form abstract nouns of the following words using the suffix ہٹ or اہٹ and give their meanings.*

| | | | | | | | |
|---|---|---|---|---|---|---|---|
| ۱۔ دھندلا | (hazy) | ۲۔ اودا | (brown) | ۳۔ نیلا | (blue) | ۳۔ گرم | (warm, hot) |

## 3.34 Abstract Nouns of Sensation and Desire with اس [-ās]

This suffix can be used either with nouns and adjectives or with verb stems. It usually colors the root word by imparting a sense of inclination or desire. Suffixation requires shortening the long vowel in the first syllable of the root word. Adjectives are formed by further suffixing ا [-ā].

| | | | |
|---|---|---|---|
| میٹھا | (sweet) | مِٹھاس | (sweetness) |
| نیند | (sleep) | نِنداس | (sleepiness) |
| پینا | (to drink) | پیاس | (thirst; desire to drink) |

*A. Form abstract nouns of sensation and desire from the following words and give their meaning. Use اس [-ās] in all cases and remember to shorten long vowels in the initial syllable of the root word where appropriate. Then form adjectives for nouns 2–4.*

| | | | |
|---|---|---|---|
| ۱۔ کھٹا | (sour) | ۲۔ رونا | (to cry) |
| ۳۔ ہگنا | (to shit) | ۴۔ موتنا | (to piss) |

## 3.35 Nouns of Odor with اند [-ānd]

This suffix, which is related to the Sanskrit گندھ [gandh] (smell), is used to denote a foul smell. The resulting nouns are always feminine. Consider the following pair of related words.

| | | | |
|---|---|---|---|
| (the smell of burnt flesh, hair, or bone) | چراند | (flesh, leather) | چمڑا |

*A. Given the meaning of the word on the right, guess the meaning of the noun on the left.*

| | | | |
|---|---|---|---|
| مچھراند | ← | (fish) | ۱۔ مچھلی |
| سڑاند | ← | (to spoil, rot) | ۲۔ سڑنا |

## 3.36 Instrumental Nouns

Hindi forms instrumental nouns in a variety of ways. Verbal nouns may be used in an instrumental sense. For example.

| | | | | |
|---|---|---|---|---|
| (the faculty of understanding) | سمجھ | ← | (to understand) | سمجھنا |
| (scissors, shears) | کترنی | ← | (to cut) | کترنا |

The suffixes وٹی [auṭī], وٹا [auṭā], and [autī], which are etymologically related to the Sanskrit پاتر [pātr] (vessel), are commonly used to form nouns of instrument or place. Note that long vowels in the initial syllable of the root word are shortened.

| | | | | |
|---|---|---|---|---|
| (a box or spoon for lime) | چُنَوٹی | ← | (lime; preparation chewed in pān) | چونا |
| (touchstone) | کسوٹی | ← | (to assay) | کَسنا |

*A. Given the meaning of the word on the right, estimate the meaning of the word on the left.*

| | | | |
|---|---|---|---|
| کجلوٹی | ← | (collyrium; eyeshadow) | ۱۔ کاجل |
| اگروٹا | ← | (incense, perfume) | ۲۔ اگر |

## 3.37 Agentive Suffixes Related to کار

A large number of Hindi suffixes related to the Sanskrit and Persian کار [kār(a)] (work; -er) are used to form agentive nouns and adjectives in Urdu. We have already surveyed some of these suffixes in the section on verbal nouns. They include the following:

| | | | | | | | |
|---|---|---|---|---|---|---|---|
| [-āṛiyā] | -اڑیا | [-āṛī] | -اڑی | [-āṛā] | -اڑا | [-āṛ] | -اڑ |
| [-āṛiyā] | - اریا | [-āṛī] | -اری | [-ārā] | -ارا | [-ār] | -ار |
| | | | | [-hāṛā] | -ہارا | [-hār] | -ہار |

Many of these words evolved over time in Prakrits before being borrowed into Urdu. This means that words ending in these suffixes are not necessarily formed directly by affixation to their cognate root. Instead, the cognate root and the derived agentive word may have changed simultaneously over time, thus leading to certain changes in form that are not regular across all instances of suffixation. Still, some patterns are regular, such as the shortening of long vowels in the initial syllable of the root word. Read the following examples aloud.

(blacksmith) لُہار / لوہار ← (iron) لوہا

(a palanquin-bearer) کَہار ← (shoulder) کندھا / کاندھا

(squirt-gun) پچکاری ← (to squeeze, press flat) پِچکنا

(running, race) دھپاڑ ← (rush, attack) دھاوا

*A. Given the meaning of the words on the right, guess the meaning of the words on the left.*

جواری ← (gambling) ۱۔ جُوا

گھسیارا ← (grass) ۲۔ گھاس

بھکاری ← (begging) ۳۔ بھیک

پجاری ← (prayer, worship) ۴۔ پوجا

سُنار ← (gold) ۵۔ سونا

گنوار ← (village) ۶۔ گاؤں

لکڑہارا ← (wood) ۷۔ لکڑی

کمہار ← (pottery) ۸۔ کُمبھ

کِھلاڑی ← (a game) ۹۔ کھیل

بٹوارا ← (to divide) ۱۰۔ بانٹنا

چمار ← (leather) ۱۱۔ چمڑا

دُہار ← (to milk) ۱۲۔ دوہانا

## The Colloquial Agentive یا [-iyā]

Suffixes formed with this agentive are characterized by a colloquial sense. Although we are discussing it as agentive here, the suffix, which is related to an oft-used Sanskrit relational suffix, has a wide semantic range.

(a jeweler; gem-setter) جڑیا ← (to attach or mount [gems]) جڑنا

(from Calcutta) کلکتیا ← (Calcutta) کلکتہ

*B. Given the meaning of the words on the right, guess the meaning of the words on the left.*

| | | | |
|---|---|---|---|
| ۱۔ طبلہ | (tabla) | ← | طبلیا |
| ۲۔ ستار | (sitar) | ← | ستاریا |
| ۳۔ سارنگی | (sarangi) | ← | سارنگیا |
| ۴۔ گانا | (to sing) | ← | گوّیا |

## Agentive Suffixes of Guardianship, Possession, or Relation

A similar set of suffixes is said to relate to the Sanskrit پال पाल: and the Urdu پالنا (to care for, keep, nuture). They include:

| | | | |
|---|---|---|---|
| والا | [vālā] | وال | [vāl] |
| روٹی | (bread) | روٹی والا | (bread-maker; bread-seller) |
| رکھنا | (to keep, guard) | رکھوالا | (guardian) |

*C. Given the meaning of the word on the right, guess the meaning of the word on the left.*

| | | | |
|---|---|---|---|
| ۱۔ کوٹھی | (storehouse, mercantile firm) | کوٹھی وال | ________ |
| ۲۔ پیسہ | (money) | پیسے والا | ________ |
| ۳۔ گھر | (home) | گھر والا | ________ |
| ۴۔ دہلی | (Delhi) | دہلی والا | ________ |
| ۶۔ گو | (cow) | گُوال | ________ |
| ۷۔ گھاٹ | (ghat, wharf) | گھٹوال | ________ |

## The Suffixes یرا [-era] یری [-erī]

These suffixes are related to کار and are essentially agentive, but carry a wider semantic range.

| | | | | | | |
|---|---|---|---|---|---|---|
| باس | (residence) | بسنا | (to reside) | ← | بسیرا | (place to stay) |

*D. Given the meaning of the noun on the right, estimate the meaning of the noun on the left.*

| | | | | | | | | |
|---|---|---|---|---|---|---|---|---|
| ۱۔سامپ | (snake) | ← | سپیرا | | ۲۔ لوٹ | (stealing, plunder) | ← | لٹیرا |

## The Suffixes ور [-or] ورا [-orā] وڑ [-oṛ/auṛ] وڑا [-oṛā/auṛā] ول [-ol] and ولا [-olā]

These suffixes and variations of them (note vowel changes in the examples below) are often used to form agentive nouns, though they may also be used to form non-agentive ones. Note that a number of suffixes with different etymons are written and spelled this way, which means that when we speak of these suffixes, we are in fact speaking of a number of homographic and homophonic particles with similar semantic ranges. We have already encountered some of these in the section on verbal nouns of disapprobation.

| | | | | |
|---|---|---|---|---|
| (runaway; deserter) | بھگوڑا | ← | (to run) | بھاگنا |
| (epicure, foodie) | چٹورا | ← | (relish) | چاٹ |
| (cheerful; facetious; a jester) | ہنسوڑ / ہنسوڑا | ← | (laughing) | ہنس |
| (a person with a thick head of hair) | جھنڈولا | ← | (bush; mop of hair) | جھنڈ |
| (jest; a pun) | چٹکلا | ← | (to jest, banter) | چٹکنا |

*E. Given the meaning of the noun on the right, estimate the meaning of the noun on the left.*

| | | | |
|---|---|---|---|
| متھورا | ← | (brow) | ماتھا |

## The Suffixes وا [vā] and و [ū]

Both suffixes have a wide semantic range. Often associated with local dialects of Urdu, they can indicate diminution, similarity, endearment, relation, or agency.

| | | | | |
|---|---|---|---|---|
| (servant, attendant) | ٹہلوا | ← | (going about; service) | ٹہل |
| (gluttonous; a glutton) | پیٹو | ← | (stomach) | پیٹ |

*F. Given the meaning of the noun on the right, estimate the meaning of the noun on the left.*

| | | | |
|---|---|---|---|
| خرچو | ← | (expenditure) | ۱۔ خرچ |
| پہروا | ← | (division of the day; a watch) | ۲۔ پہر |
| گانجو | ← | (ganja) | ۳۔ گانجا |

## The Suffixes ڑ [-aṛ], ڑا [-ṛā], and کڑ [-kaṛ]

These suffixes are related to the suffix of negative attitude or emotion used to derive verbal nouns. There is a handful of variations of the کڑ suffix, including voicing (گڑ) and doubling, especially when the root word ends in ک.

| | | | | |
|---|---|---|---|---|
| (a big deal; exaggeration) | بتنگڑ | ← | (matter; word) | بات |
| (starving, extremely hungry; very poor) | بھکّڑ | ← | (hunger) | بھوک |
| (lame; a cripple) | لنگڑا | ← | (lame) | لنگ |

*G. Given the meaning of the word on the right, guess the meaning of the word on the left.*

| | | | |
|---|---|---|---|
| بھنگڑ | ← | (bhang) | ۱۔ بھانگ |

## 3.38 Adjectival Suffixes

A group of suffixes related to the Sanskrit adjectival suffix ک [-ik] are common in Urdu. The suffix ی is among them.

(woolen) اُونی ← (wool) اون

(made of cotton thread) سُوتی ← (cotton thread) سوت

(made of muslin) ململی ← (muslin) ململ

### The Colloquial Adjectival Suffix یا [-iyā]

This suffix, also related to ک [-ik], has a wide semantic range which includes agency, relation, and diminution.

(great) بڑھیا ← (to increase) بڑھنا

(pained) دکھیا ← (pain) دکھ

*A. Form colloquial adjectives from the following words and guess their meanings.*

(juice; flavor; pleasure) ۲۔ رس    (decrease, loss [e.g. in quality]) ۱۔ گھٹ

### The Suffixes ـِیَل [-iyal], یار [-yār], ر [-ar], یالا [-yālā], یارا [-yārā], یال [-yāl]

These suffixes typically convey an adjectival sense. They also nicely demonstrate the frequent variation between ر and ل in Hindi-Urdu and other Indic languages.

(half-dead, moribund) مَریَل ← (to die) مرنا

(clayey; made of mud) مٹیالا ← (clay, soil) مٹی

*B. Given the meaning of the word on the right, guess the meaning of the word on the left.*

ہریالا ← (green, fresh) ۱۔ ہرا

دڑھیل ← (beard) ۲۔ داڑھی

دھتیل ← (habit, vice) ۳۔ دھت

مٹیار ← (mud, clay) ۴۔ مٹی

### The یلا [-īlā/-elā] Suffixes

Among the most common adjectivizing suffixes in Urdu are یلا [-īlā] and یلا [-elā]. Of these, یلا [-īlā] is the most common.

(colorful) رنگیلا ← (color) رنگ

*C. Form adjectives from the following nouns using the یلا [-īlā] suffix and give their meanings. Shorten any long vowels in the initial syllable of the root word.*

| | | | | | |
|---|---|---|---|---|---|
| (intoxication) | ۳۔ نشا | (grass) | ۲۔ گھاس | (shine, sparkle) | ا۔ چمک |
| (nectar, juice; beauty) | ۶۔ رس | (poison) | ۵۔ زہر | (point, tip) | ۴۔ نوک |

## The Relational Suffix ا [-ā]

This suffix forms marked masculine adjectives which can then be changed to reflect the gender of the nouns they modify.

| | | | | |
|---|---|---|---|---|
| (hungry) | بھوکا | ← | (hunger) | بھوک |
| (brackish) | کھارا | ← | (alkali; saltiness) | کھار |

*D. Form the relational adjective from the following words.*

| | | | |
|---|---|---|---|
| (dirt, filth) | ۲۔ مَیل | (love) | ا۔ پیار |

## The Suffix of Familial Relation یرا [-erā]

Note that this suffix typically requires the shortening of the vowel in the initial syllable.

| | | | | |
|---|---|---|---|---|
| (of the maternal uncle) | ممیرا | ← | (maternal uncle) | ماما |

These adjectives are used to specify familial relations.

| | |
|---|---|
| (a male cousin [literally, brother] by one's maternal uncle) | ممیرا بھائی |
| (a female cousin [literally, sister] by one's maternal uncle) | ممیری بہن |

*E. Form the relational adjective from the following words. Shorten long vowels in initial syllables where appropriate.*

| | | | | | |
|---|---|---|---|---|---|
| (paternal uncle) | ۳۔ چاچا | (maternal aunt) | ۲۔ خالہ | (maternal aunt) | ا۔ موسی |

## Other Adjectival Suffixes اون [-āvan] اونا [-āvnā] ونت [-vant] ونتی [-vantī] سار [-sār] لا [-lā] ہرا [-hrā] ہلا [-hlā]

Note that some of these are direct borrowings from Sanskrit. Study the following chart.

| | | | | | | |
|---|---|---|---|---|---|---|
| (beautiful) | سہاونا | (beautiful) | سُہاون | ← | (to be beautiful) | سہانا |
| | | (attractive) | لبھاونا | ← | (desire) | لوبھ |
| | | (meritorious) | گنونت | ← | (quality) | گن |
| | | (of good character) | شیلونت | ← | (good character) | شیل |
| | | (kind) | ملنسار | ← | (meeting, company) | ملن |

| | | | | |
|---|---|---|---|---|
| (last) | پچھلا | ← | (behind) | پیچھے |
| (hazy) | دھندھلا | ← | (haze) | دھندھ |
| (golden) | سنہرا | ← | (gold) | سونا |
| (silver) | رپہلا | ← | (rupee) | روپیا |

*F. Given the meaning of the word on the right, guess the meaning of the word on the left.*

| | | | |
|---|---|---|---|
| بلونت | ← | (power) | ۱۔ بل |
| رسونت | ← | (juice, essence; pleasure) | ۲۔ رس |
| دھرم ونت | ← | (dharma; righteousness) | ۳۔ دھرم |
| اگلا | ← | (ahead, next) | ۴۔ آگے |
| اکہرا | ← | (one) | ۵۔ ایک |

## 3.39 Diminutive Suffixes

The most common diminutive suffix in Urdu is simply the feminine marker ی. When applied to animals, it may suggest either natural gender or diminution. When applied to inanimate objects, it suggests diminution.

| | |
|---|---|
| (small bowl) کٹوری | (bowl) کٹورا |
| (small cup) پیالی | (cup; bowl) پیالہ |

*A. Use the diminutive suffix to form diminutive counterparts of the following.*

| | | | |
|---|---|---|---|
| (spoon, tablespoon) | ۲۔ چمچہ | (account; day-book; note) | ۱۔ چٹھا |
| (cable, thick rope) | ۴۔ رسّا | (leaf) | ۳۔ پتّا |
| (mountain) | ۶۔ پہاڑ | (shoe) | ۵۔ جوتا |

### The Diminutive Noun with چی [-chī]

Occasionally, Urdu produces further diminution of the Persian diminutive suffix چہ [cha] by changing it to the feminine چی. This is in keeping with Urdu's pattern of diminution by the feminine gender; for example, جوتا (shoe) and جوتی (small shoe).

| | | | | |
|---|---|---|---|---|
| (small pot) | دیگچی | ← | (pot) | دیگ |

*B. Form the diminutive noun using چی. Then guess the meaning of the resulting noun.*

۱۔ صندوق (chest, case)

## The Colloquial Diminutive یا [-iyā]

Diminutive nouns ending in this suffix are almost always grammatically feminine in Urdu. Note that suffixation results in the shortening of the long vowel in the initial syllable. This suffix is particularly common in registers of Urdu that echo local dialects and is often found in idioms, poetry, and classic film songs that evoke this context.

آنکھ (eye) انکھیا (eye)

Nouns of this form are pluralized by suffixing ں (or, considered differently but to the same effect, by dropping ا and suffixing the feminine plural suffix اں-).

انکھیا (eye) انکھیاں (eyes)

*C. Form colloquial diminutives from the following nouns. Be sure to shorten long vowels where appropriate.*

۱۔ ڈبا (box) ۲۔ پھوڑا (sore, boil) ۳۔ آم (mango)

۴۔ پنکھ (wing, feather) ۵۔رات (night) ۶۔ بات (matter, word)

## The Affective Diminutive ر [-ar] ڑ [-aṛ] را [-rā] ڑا [-ṛā] and occasionally لا [-lā] or ل [-al]

These suffixes are are all Prakritic and, although diminutive in principle, this family of suffixes may also convey an emotional attitude of adoration or cuteness about the object rather than an actual diminution.

مکھ (face) مکھڑا (mouth, face)

بچھ (calf) بچھڑا (calf)

These suffixes are among the most emotive and colorful in Urdu. The following word is often used to tease friends or family:

چھوچھا (empty, vacuous; mean) چھچھورا (foolish)

Consider the following chart, which reviews vocabulary related to the verb تھاپنا [thāpnā] (to tap, beat, pat). Note the differences among the various derived nouns. Pay close attention to the meaning conveyed by the affective diminutive.

تھپکنا (to pat a child to sleep; to soothe)

تھپک (a tap, pat)

| | |
|---|---|
| تھاپنا | (to pat, tap, beat) |
| تھاپا | (paw-print; hand-print; a mark) |
| تھاپ | (tap, pat, slap; strike of a drum) |
| تھپڑ / تھپیڑ / تھپیڑا | (slap, smack) |
| تھپڑی | (clapping of the hands; slap of the hands) |

The diminutive suffixes ری, ڑی, or لی are also commonly used.

| | | | |
|---|---|---|---|
| پنکھ | (feather, wing) | پنکھڑی | (petal, leaf of a flower) |

*D. Use the suffix ڑا to derive the corresponding diminutive nouns from the following words and give their meanings.*

| | | | |
|---|---|---|---|
| ۱۔ ٹک | (a little, a bit) | ۲۔ جیو | (life, soul) |

*E. Read the following list of words and their meanings. What inferences can you draw about the registers in which this suffix is used and the connotations that it carries?*

| | | | |
|---|---|---|---|
| تگڑا | (stout; strong, robust) | تھمڑا | (thick, corpulent) |
| تھوڑا | (little, small) | | |
| چھیچھڑا | (refuse [from meat]) | | |
| جھکڑا | (nonsense prattle; a rigmarole) | | |
| چھوچھا | (empty) | چھچھورا | (puerile; stupid) |
| جیو | (life) | جیوڑا | (life; beloved; pleasure) |
| دکھ | (pain) | دکھڑا | (great, constant suffering) |
| پوت | (child) | پوتڑا | (a diaper-cloth) |
| جبھا | ([rare in Urdu] jaw) | جبڑا | (jaw, lower part of the face) |

*F. Use the suffix ڑی to derive diminutive nouns. Shorten long vowels in initial syllables except in 2.*

| | | | | | | | |
|---|---|---|---|---|---|---|---|
| ۱۔ آنت | (intestine) | ۲۔ اوجھ | (intestine) | ۳۔ تاگا | (thread) | ۴۔ پلہ | (scale) |
| ۵۔ آنکھ | (eye) | ۶۔ راب | (molasses) | ۷۔ پٹ | (slab) | ۸۔ پاگ | (large turban) |

### The Diminutives لا [-ulā], ولا [-aulā, olā], وڑا [-auṛā, oṛā], ورا [-aurā, -aurī]

(a small bedstead, small cot) کھٹولا ← (cot, bedstead) کھاٹ

(betel leaf prepared to be chewed and swallowed) گلوڑی

*G. Given the meaning of the word on the right, guess the meaning of the word on the left.*

ہچکولا ← (jerk) ۲۔ ہچکا    سپولا ← (snake) ۱۔ سامپ

### Relative Diminutives with یل [-el] and یلی [-elī]

(female's female friend) سہیلی    (female's female friend) سکھی

(palm) ہتھیلی    (hand) ہاتھ

### Relative Diminutive Suffix ت [-at]

This suffix forms abstract nouns.

(hue, tone [esp. of skin]) رنگت    (color) رنگ

### Relative Diminutives with the Suffix کی [-kī]

This suffix is sometimes used to form diminutive verbal nouns. Compare with similar nouns formed with کا [kā].

(a dive; a dunk) ڈبکی    (to be immersed, drown) ڈوبنا

*H. Given the meaning of the word on the right, guess the meaning of the word on the left.*

پھرکی ← (to turn) ۱۔ پھرنا

## 3.40 Feminine Suffixes

The most common feminine suffix in Urdu is ی [-ī].

(girl) لڑکی    (boy) لڑکا

This suffix is etymologically related to the colloquial suffix یا [iyā].

(bitch) کُتیا    (male dog) کُتّا

*A. Given the meaning of the word on the right, guess the meaning of the word on the left.*

بڑھیا    (an old man) ۱۔ بوڑھا

### The Femininizing ن- Suffixes

Urdu uses several related suffixes to produce feminine nouns. Among the most common of these suffixes is ن [-an, -in]. This suffix is comparable to the English suffixes -ess, -woman, etc. Note that word-final long vowels such as ا and ی in the masculine word are typically elided. Suffixation may involve vowel shortening, but does not require it.

| | | | |
|---|---|---|---|
| سنار | (goldsmith) | سنارن | (lady goldsmith; wife of a goldsmith) |
| ناگ | (snake) | ناگن | (female snake) |
| دلہا | (husband) | دلہن | (wife) |

This suffix is also found in feminine personal names.

| | | | |
|---|---|---|---|
| رحیم | (Rahim) | رحیمن | (Rahiman) |

*B. Use the suffix ن to form the female counterparts of the following nouns.*

| | | | | | | | |
|---|---|---|---|---|---|---|---|
| ۱۔ بڑھئی | (carpenter) | ۲۔ اہیر | (cowherd) | ۳۔ جمعدار | (sweeper) | ۴۔ لوہار | (ironsmith) |
| ۵۔ کمہار | (potter) | ۶۔ دھوبی | (washerman) | ۷۔ کہار | (bearer) | ۸۔ بیوپار | (trader) |
| ۹۔ ڈاکو | (robber) | ۱۰۔ سیار | (jackal) | | | | |

## The Suffix ائن / اين [-āin, -āyan]

This suffix typically marks the feminine gender, especially that of social groups and professions. Suffixation does not require vowel shortening. Note that word-final long ی [ī] is elided.

| | | | |
|---|---|---|---|
| چودھری | (headman) | چودھرائن | (headman's wife; headwoman) |

*C. Use the suffix ائن to form the corresponding female of the given noun and give its meaning.*

| | | | | | | | |
|---|---|---|---|---|---|---|---|
| ۱۔ پنڈت | (pandit) | ۲۔ اوجھا | (diviner) | ۳۔ قصائی | (butcher) | ۴۔ حلوائی | (confectioner) |
| ۵۔ ٹھاکر | (boss) | | | | | | |

## The Suffix نی [-nī]

Like the other suffixes discussed here, this one, too, marks the feminine counterpart to masculine nouns. One of its many uses is as the preferred marker for the female form of animals. Suffixation does not require vowel shortening.

| | | | | |
|---|---|---|---|---|
| اونٹ | (camel) | ← | اونٹنی | (female camel) |
| استاد | (master) | ← | استانی | (mistress) |

*D. Use the suffix form نی to form the female counterpart of the following nouns.*

| | | | | | |
|---|---|---|---|---|---|
| (commander; Sikh) | ٣۔ سردار | (elephant) | ٢۔ ہاتھی | (peacock) | ١۔ مور |
| | | | | (menial servant) | ٤۔ نفرا |

**The Suffix انی [-ānī]**

The final suffix in this group likewise forms female counterparts. In this case, most of the nouns refer to humans. Suffixation does not require vowel shortening.

| | | | |
|---|---|---|---|
| (husband's [younger] brother's wife) | دیورانی | (husband's [younger] brother) | دیور |

*E. Derive the feminine counterparts of the following words using the suffix انی [-ānī] and give the meaning of the resulting word.*

| | | | | | |
|---|---|---|---|---|---|
| (husband's elder brother) | ٣۔ جیٹھ | (servant) | ٢۔ نوکر | (merchant) | ١۔ سیٹھ |
| | | (headman) | ٥۔ چودھری | (boss) | ٤۔ ٹھاکر |

## 3.41 Noun Pairs and Hindi Idioms

Now that we have covered the forms of most Urdu nouns, we shall turn our attention briefly to some of the ways in which Urdu builds idioms from its vast vocabulary in the Hindi register. One of the most interesting ways is by pairing. Consider the following nouns, which are built of verb pairs conjugated in the simple past tense.

| | | | |
|---|---|---|---|
| ([that which has been] eaten and drunk) | کھایا پیا | پینا | کھانا |
| ([that which has been] spoken and heard) | کہا سنا | سُننا | کہنا |

In many cases, the main meaning of the compound is found in the first element of the pair and the second element lends color.

| | | | | | |
|---|---|---|---|---|---|
| (remaining, surviving, residual) | رہا سہا | (to endure) | سہنا | (to remain) | رہنا |

Some pairs of verbs have become so closely associated that they are often the basis of multiple compounds. Note that the part of speech of the verbal nouns or adjectives determines the part of speech of the compound.

| | | | | | |
|---|---|---|---|---|---|
| (food and drink; cuisine) | کھان پان | (to drink) | پینا | (to eat) | کھانا |
| (lifestyle) | رہن سہن | (to endure) | سہنا | (to live) | رہنا |

As is obvious from the above compounds, the pairing of nouns in Urdu often yields a term the sense of which is greater than the sum of its parts.

| | | | | | |
|---|---|---|---|---|---|
| ملنا | (to meet) | جلنا | (to be united) | میل جول | (association) |
| بولنا | (to speak) | چلنا | (to move) | بول چال | (conversation; idiom, parlance) |

Some pairs retain verbs that have become rare or archaic.

| | | | | | |
|---|---|---|---|---|---|
| بھولنا | (to forget, mistake) | بِسرنا | (archaic)(to forget) | بھولا بسرا | (long forgotten) |

*A. Given the meaning of the word or words on the right, estimate the meaning of the pairs on the left.*

| | | | | |
|---|---|---|---|---|
| ۱۔ پڑھنا | (to read) | لکھنا | (to write) | پڑھا لکھا |
| ۲۔ لوٹنا | (to steal) | مارنا | (to strike) | لوٹ مار |
| ۳۔ کھیلنا | (to play) | کودنا | (to jump) | کھیل کود |
| ۴۔ بھولنا | (to forget) | چوکنا | (to blunder) | بھول چوک |
| ۵۔ بھاگنا | (to run) | دوڑنا | (to race) | بھاگ دوڑ |
| ۶۔ سوجھنا | (to be seen) | بوجھنا | (to understand) | سوجھ بوجھ |
| ۷۔ کاٹنا | (to cut) | چھانٹنا | (to clip) | کاٹ چھانٹ |
| ۸۔ بتانا | (to tell) | چیتنا | (to think) | بات چیت |
| ۹۔ چھاننا | (to sift) | بیننا | (to pick up, gather) | چھان بین |
| ۱۰۔ سمجھنا | (to understand) | بوجھنا | (to comprehend) | سمجھ بوجھ |

## Pairs Built from a Common Verb

A second kind of coumpound is built from words derived from the same verb. Once again, the meaning of the resulting pair is often greater than the sum of its parts; that is, it is semantically more extensive.

One way to form such words is to conjoin two verbal nouns with similar meanings. In these cases, the meaning of the resulting phrase is closely tied to the first word in the pair, the second element adding color or breadth.

| | | | |
|---|---|---|---|
| چلنا | (to move, go) | چال چلن | (conduct, behavior) |

Another is to combine verbal nouns derived from two different levels of transitivity (e.g. intransitive-transitive; passive-active) of the verb or causality (e.g. transitive-causitive). The meaning of these words is typically close to that of the first word in the pair, but often suggest that more people than just the agent of the first word are involved in the action or emphasize thoroughness.

| (departure; transit) | چل چلاؤ | (to move, go) | چلنا |
|---|---|---|---|

Such compounds may also be the basis of adjectives formed with participles.

| (to make hear, recite) | سنانا | (to hear) | سننا |
|---|---|---|---|
| | | (hearsay, rumor) | سنی سنائی بات |

A third common combination involves the masculine and feminine past participles of the verb. These often imply an intensity of action.

| (staring, gazing; observation) | دیکھا دیکھی | دیکھنا |
|---|---|---|

The final forms that we will note here are those that do not follow a set pattern, but involve two words derived from the same verb.

| (a maze) | بھُول بھُلَیاں | (to forget) | بھولنا |
|---|---|---|---|
| (openly) | کھُلَم کھُلّا | (to open) | کھلنا |

*B. Given the meaning of the verb on the right, estimate the meaning of the word on the left.*

| رکھ رکھاؤ | (to keep) | ۲۔ رکھنا | میل ملاپ | (to meet) | ۱۔ ملنا |
|---|---|---|---|---|---|
| گرما گرمی | (to heat) | ۴۔ گرمانا | چلا چلی | (to move, leave) | ۳۔ چلنا |
| | | | بنا بنایا | (to be made) | ۵۔ بننا |

## 3.42 Rhymed Pairs

Some nouns are formed by pairing a noun with a rhyming word. Sometimes, the rhyming word has an independent existence which colors the meaning of the new word. Compare with the English "wear and tear." The meanings of these compounds tend to be greater than the sum of their parts.

| (intellect, intelligence) | سوجھ بوجھ | (to comprehend) | بوجھنا | (to appear) | سوجھنا |
|---|---|---|---|---|---|

In many cases, the meaning of the rhyming word is irrelevant to the meaning of the phrase, even if it has an independent existence. In these cases, it simply augments, colors, or gives mood to the main word. Among the most common patterns for pairing is the substitution of the long vowel in the first pattern with ا [ā] in the second. The effect of the rhyming word is similar to the English "and so on" or "and what have you."

| | | | | | |
|---|---|---|---|---|---|
| پوچھنا | (to ask) | پاچھنا | (to cut) | پوچھ پاچھ | (investigation, inquiry; scrutiny) |
| چھیڑنا | (to tease) | چھاڑنا | (to leave) | چھیڑ چھاڑ | (teasing) |
| بیچنا | (to sell) | باچنا | (to read) | بیچ باچ کر | (investigation, inquiry; scrutiny) |

A second trend is to build compounds from one meaningful term and one meaningless one. The effect of the nonsensical term is likewise similar to the English "and so on" or "and what have you." Sometimes, its idiomatic force is similar the dismissive "or whatever." Often, these compounds are used for humorous effect. In terms of form, the first consonant of the rhyming word is most commonly replaced by و [v] or ش [sh] Compare with the English "palsy-walsy."

چائے وائے (tea and such)

پارٹی وارٹی (party and what have you)

پڑھنا وڑھنا (studying or whatever)

گانے شانے (songs and what have you)

Some rhymed pairs often have idiomatic meanings. The following is built of two meaningful elements.

ایسا ویسا (disreputable; improper; of little worth)

*A. Read the following couplets by Inshā and Dāġh and translate them into English. Try to capture the rhetorical nuances of the rhyming pairs.*

اب چھیڑ چھاڑ کی غزل انشا اک اور لکھ
ہیں لاکھ شوخیاں تری نوک قلم کے ساتھ

ایسے ویسوں سے کیا ملے کوئی
ایرے غیرے ہیں تیری محفل میں

*B. Use a dictionary to learn about the following pairs.*

۱۔ جوڑ توڑ ۲۔ چھوڑ چھاڑ ۳۔ کھاؤ اڑاؤ ۴۔ اناپ شناپ ۵۔ اٹک ڈھٹک

## 3.43 Word Pairs and Urdu Idioms

The word forms covered in this unit appear in a large number of Urdu idioms and proverbs. In this section, we shall study some idioms that include repetition, rhyme, or word pairs.

Translate each of the following Urdu idioms literally into English. Then choose the English idiom that most closely approximates it.

۱۔ جیسا دیس ویسا بھیس

(All countries are a wise man's home.)

(When in Rome, do as the Romans.)

(In every country, the sun rises in the morning.)

۲۔ جیسی کرنی ویسی بھرنی

(Covetousness is always filling a bottomless vessel.)

(You reap what you sow.)

(Begun is half done.)

۳۔ جنگل میں منگل

(Tuesday in the desert.)

(Cheaters never prosper.)

(Happy despite unfavorable circumstances.)

۴۔ اپنا کیا دھرا سب بیکار ہونا

(For all one's efforts to come to naught.)

(For one's idea not to be implemented.)

(To meet with opposition.)

۵۔ خدا بھرے کو بھرتا ہے

(Fair words don't fill the pockets.)

(God fills the full.)

(Better God than gold.)

۶۔ مان نہ مان میں تیرا مہمان

(He who has gold is a welcome guest.)

(Ready or not, here I come.)

(Unbidden guests are often welcome when gone)

۷۔ جہاں چاہ وہاں راہ

(Better to have than to wish.)

(A beaten path is a safe one.)

(Where there's a will, there's a way)

۸۔ سانچ کو آنچ نہیں

(Truth knows no fear.)

(Where there's smoke, there's fire.)

(Truth never grows old.)

۹۔ اونچی دکان پھیکا پکوان

(All that glitters isn't gold.)

(Corruption wins not more than honesty.)

(The truth is a bitter pill to swallow.)

۱۰۔ جان ہے تو جہان ہے

(Health is wealth.)

(The world has people of all sorts.)

(Better to live well than long.)

## 3.44 Suggestions for Further Study

Since the Hindi element is in many ways the structural backbone of Urdu, virtually any text in Urdu will contain copious amounts of vocabulary in this register. The following texts are recommended for their balance of Hindi elements with others and because the use of Hindi registers in them is especially rich. ʿIṣmat Chughtāʾī, *Ṭeṛhī Lakīr*; ʿIṣmat Chughtāʾī, *Kāġhażī Hai Pairahan*; Mīrājī, *Mīrājī ke Gīt*; Premchand, *Godān*; Qurrat ul-ʿAin Ḥaidar. *Āg kā Daryā;* Ibn-e Ṣafī. *Jāsūsī Dunyā*.

# UNIT 4

# THE PERSIAN ELEMENT

Although a large number of words borrowed into Urdu are Arabic in origin, many of them have entered Urdu not directly from Arabic, but through Persian. The importance of Persian as the conduit of a large number of words is evinced by the form of certain Arabic words, such as تماشا and تحاشا, whose form is unique to Urdu and Persian. (In Arabic, they are written and pronounced as تماشی and تحاشی.)

As the language of administration and literary arts at the courts of the Delhi Sultanate and Mughals, a classical language during the British-colonial period, and a language of classical study, cultural capital, religious significance, and academic interest since the formation of India and Pakistan, Persian has occupied a central position in the linguistic history and intellectual life of South Asia for more than half a millenium. Its impression on Urdu has been especially profound, since many early Urdu writers drew inspiration from the forms, themes, and vocabulary of Persian literature. This unit introduces students to the ways in which Persian is used in Urdu, beginning with basic morphological elements and advancing to an introduction to Persian proverbs and poetry.

Before beginning, readers should familiarize themselves with the following key terms, which are among the most commonly used Persian words and phrases in Urdu. They, their relatives, and the word-building patterns that they exhibit will be among the main points of focus in this unit.

| | | | | | | | |
|---|---|---|---|---|---|---|---|
| (effort) | کوشش | (life) | زندگی | (age, time) | زمانہ | (heart) | دل |
| (proceeding, activity) | کارروائی | (perhaps) | شاید | (happiness) | خوشی | (happy) | خوش |
| (young, youth) | نوجوان | (never) | ہرگز | (salary) | تنخواہ | (successful) | کامیاب |
| (magician) | جادوگر | (mad, insane) | دیوانہ | (animal) | جانور | (discovery) | دریافت |
| (my dear; beloved) | جانِ من | (past, bygone) | گذشتہ | (journalist) | نامہ نگار | (supervision) | نگرانی |

## 4.1 Recognizing Persian Words

There are several signs that an Urdu word is of Persian origin. The most obvious is the presence of the letter ژ, which is unique to Persian words (and a handful of English borrowings) in Urdu.

The easiest way to identify a Persian word in Urdu apart from knowledge of Persian forms is by process of elimination. If a word lacks tell tale Indic letters, contains a letter representing a sound that is not Indic, and contains a letter that is not found in Arabic, it is probably Persian. The tell tale Indic letters are the retroflexes ٹ ڈ ڑ and the ھ of aspiration. Words with these letters are Indic and never borrowed from Persian. An example of a non-Indic sound is z. Recall that Urdu has four letters representing this sound, three of which are borrowed exclusively from words of Arabic origin (except for rare cases in which ذ is used in Persian words). This leaves ز as the letter for a Persian z. The Urdu letters representing sounds not classically found in Indic languages and not borrowed exclusively from Arabic are

خ ز ژ غ ق

Because these letters, with the exception of ژ, are also found in Arabic words, their presence alone in is not necessarily an indication of Persian origin. However, when any of these letters is found in a word that also contains letters *not* found in Arabic, we may assume that the word is Persian. (Of course, the word may also be borrowed from another language, such as Turkish, but the proportion of such words in Urdu is small.) The Urdu letters found in Persian, but not found in Arabic, are

پ چ گ و ["o" only] ے ["e" only]

By the letters ے [e] and و [o] are meant **only these two specific vowel sounds**. Arabic lacks them, but it *does* have the equivalents of ے [ai] ی [ī] و [au] and و [ū]; for example, the Arabic words خیر (k̤hair), کبیر (kabīr), یوم (yaum), and مشہور (mashhūr).

When a word contains both a letter from the first row (خ ز ژ غ ق) *and* a letter from the second (پ چ گ و ے), where و is [o] and ے is [e], it is safe to assume that it is a Persian word. For example, the word چیز (thing) contains the non-Indic letter ز and the non-Arabic letter چ and we can therefore correctly infer that it is a Persian word. Likewise, خیز [k̤hez] (-rising; -raising) contains two non-Indic letters ز and خ as well as the non-Arabic vowel "e" and we can therefore correctly infer that it, too, is Persian. By contrast, the word باگ (rein) contains the non-Arabic letter گ, but lacks a non-Indic letter and could therefore be either Indic or Persian. (It is Indic.) By contrast, the word خزف (pottery) contains all non-Indic letters, but since it lacks a non-Arabic one, it could be either Arabic or Persian. (It is Arabic.)

Some words that contain what are here called "non-Indic" letters are in fact Indic words. This may seem unintuitive, indeed self-contradictory, but the long history of contact among Persian and Indic languages has led to the adoption of non-Indic letters and sounds into Indic languages. For example, the words غنڈا (gangster; lout, bully) and چٹخارا (the smacking of the mouth when eating; the taste in one's mouth) contain the non-Indic letters غ and خ along with the Indic ٹ and ڈ. Some writers may prefer غ and خ instead of the Indic گ and کھ, but Urdu writers and speakers have written and pronounced غنڈا this way since at least the eighteenth century and چٹخارا since at least the nineteenth. It may make sense from a classicist's perspective to consider خ and غ as non-Indic, since Sanskrit, for example, lacks them, but, seen from Urdu's perspective, this label is somewhat misleading.

Note also that the guidelines suggested here apply to Urdu because most of Urdu's non-Arabic, non-Indic vocabulary comes from Persian. Likewise, there is a small number of Turkish words that might seem to be Persian; for example, چوغا (a kind of cloak). Thus, these guidelines for identifying Persian loanwords are simply a helpful starting point. By closely studying the Persian patterns of word-building surveyed in this unit, you will be able to identify Persian loanwords with confidence and ease.

*A. Use the guidelines in this section to help you determine which of the following must be Persian (or are at least very likely to be). (Note that not all words are Persian.)*

[sīrat] سیرت    [fauz] فوز    سچ    گداز    مجاز    اتفاق    چرخ    باغ    چمڑا

[soz] سوز    [doz] دوز    گستاخ    زد    گز    گڑ    چاقو    مژگاں    پختہ

[ḳhorāk] خوراک    [furoġh] فروغ    احتراز    ساز    پیاز    غڑپ    پرداز    غیر    چراغ

## 4.2 Overview of Simple and Compound Persian Words

Most Persian words can be divided into two kinds, simple and compound.

Simple words comprise only one independently meaningful element. Here are three examples:

(smell) بو    (happiness) خوشی    (fine, nice, good) خوش

Compound words comprise more than one independently meaningful element. For example, the simple adjective and nouns above can be combined to form a compound adjective or noun.

(sweet aroma, fragrance) خوشبو ← (smell) بو (fine, good, nice) خوش

Persian compounds may built of adjectives, nouns, and participles.

(washroom) غسل خانہ ← (house) خانہ (bathing) غسل

(knowledge-loving) علم دوست ← (friend) دوست (knowledge) علم

(pleasant) خوش مزاج ← (temperament) مزاج (fine) خوش

(calligrapher; penman) خوش نویس ← (-writing/-writer) نویس (fine) خوش

*A. Read the following compound words aloud and identify the simple words from which they are built.*

بدبو　　خوبصورت　　بدصورت　　روشن خیال　　خود غرض　　کمبخت　　نیکدل

*B. Combine the simple nouns and adjectives to form compound nouns and/or adjectives. Guess their meanings and check your guesses in an Urdu dictionary.*

| | | | |
|---|---|---|---|
| ۱۔ خوب (fine) | صورت (form) | ۲۔ خوش (fine) | حال (state) |
| ۳۔ بد (bad) | صورت (form) | ۴۔ بد (bad) | حال (state) |

## 4.3 Persian Nominal Suffixes—Simple Persian Nouns and Adjectives

Like English and other Indo-European languages, Persian forms words through prefixation, suffixation, and the combination of words or word-elements. The most common Persian suffixes are surveyed here.

### The Relative Noun with ہ [ā]

Relative nouns are formed by suffixing ہ to a noun or adjective. The resulting word is typically close in meaning to the root word, sometimes instrumental, and occasionally diminutive. The resulting word will always be a noun.

| | | | |
|---|---|---|---|
| دہان (mouth) | ← | دہانہ | (mouth [of a river, water-bag, drain]; bit [of a bridle]) |
| ہفت (seven) | ← | ہفتہ | (week; Saturday) |

*A. Form the relative nouns of the following words with ہ. Then choose the best meaning from those given.*

| | | | | | |
|---|---|---|---|---|---|
| ۱۔ پنج (five) | ← | ______ | (decimal) | (finger) | (paw) |
| ۲۔ پیش (before, in front of) | ← | ______ | (rear) | (profession) | (forthright) |
| ۳۔ خُرد (small) | ← | ______ | (tiny) | (tower) | (a small piece) |
| ۴۔ روز (day) | ← | ______ | (night) | (daily) | (day of fasting) |
| ۵۔ لال (red | ← | ______ | (tulip) | (courage) | (reddish) |
| ۶۔ دست (hand) | ← | ______ | (deftness) | (handy) | (handle) |

### The Relative Noun with انہ [-ānā]

Occasionally, the relative noun is formed by suffixing انہ to a noun or adjective.

| | | | |
|---|---|---|---|
| دست (hand) | ← | دستانہ | (glove) |
| شکر (sugar) | ← | شکرانہ | (a dish made of rice, ghee, and sugar) |

*B. Form the relative nouns of the following words with انہ. Then choose the meaning from those given.*

| | | | | | | |
|---|---|---|---|---|---|---|
| (lawyer) | (fine) | (lawful) | ______ | ← | (crime) | ۱۔ جرم |
| (arrival) | (dismissed) | (parting present) | ______ | ← | (departure) | ۲۔ رخصت |
| (engagement) | (instrument played at a wedding) | ______ | ______ | ← | (wedding) | ۳۔ شادی |
| (grateful) | (love) | (a gift for thanks) | ______ | ← | (thanks) | ۴۔ شکر |

## The Diminutive Noun with ک [-ak]

Diminutive nouns are occasionally formed by suffixing ک [ak].

| | | | | |
|---|---|---|---|---|
| (small worm; firefly) | کِرمک | ← | (worm) | کِرم |

This suffix is sometimes used to form relative nouns. In these cases, the noun often carries either a concrete or specialist meaning. Abstraction is rare.

| | | | | |
|---|---|---|---|---|
| (syphilis) | آتشک | ← | (fire) | آتش |

Occasionally, relative nouns formed with this suffix refer to an action associated with the noun.

| | | | | |
|---|---|---|---|---|
| (knocking, rapping) | دستک | ← | (hand) | دست |
| (ignition) | اشتعالک | ← | (ignition) | اشتعال |

*C. Form the diminutive relative nouns of the following words using ک. Then choose the most likely meaning from the options given.*

| | | | | | | |
|---|---|---|---|---|---|---|
| (jewelry) | (chest) | (small box) | ______ | ← | (box) | ۱۔ دُرج |
| (fatigue) | (wink) | (fountain) | ______ | ← | (eye) | ۲۔ چشم |
| (visible) | (a visionary) | (spectacles) | ______ | ← | (eye) | ۳۔ عین |
| (lowly man) | (manly) | (emasculation) | ______ | ← | (man) | ۴۔ مرد |
| (pipeline) | (tubular) | (arrow) | ______ | ← | (pipe, tube) | ۵۔ ناو |

## The Diminutive Noun with چہ / یچہ [-chā / īchā]

Diminutive nouns are sometimes formed using these suffixes. Note that ہ [a] is dropped from the end of the root word. Nouns built with this suffix are rarely, if ever, abstract.

| | | | | | | | |
|---|---|---|---|---|---|---|---|
| | | (small opening; vent) | دریچہ | ← | | (door) | در |
| | | (diary) | روزنامچہ | ← | | (daily paper) | روزنامہ |
| (plum) | آلوچہ | ← | (plum) | آلو بخارا | | (P: plum; U: potato) | آلو |

*D. Form the diminutive noun using چہ (or ـچہ in the case of #5). Then choose the most likely meaning of the resulting noun.*

| | | | | | | |
|---|---|---|---|---|---|---|
| (notebook) | (letter) | (a folder) | _____ | ← | (book) | ۱۔ کتاب |
| (roundabout) | (vagabond) | (alley) | _____ | ← | (road, lane) | ۲۔ کو |
| (proximity) | (incomplete) | (short-sword) | _____ | ← | (half) | ۳۔ نیم |
| (a utensil) | (a stove) | (small pot) | _____ | ← | (pot) | ۴۔ دیگ |
| (a small garden) | (a field) | (a lawn) | _____ | ← | (garden) | ۵۔ باغ |

## Agentive Suffixes

Persian forms a large number of agentive nouns and adjectives by suffixation. This section surveys the most common ones in Urdu.

The following suffixes are all related to the verbs آوردن [āvardan/āvurdan] (to bring) and بردن [burdan] (to take, carry). They are especially productive in Urdu and carry a sense of possession or performance.

[-yār] یار- [-var] ور- [-vār] وار- [-er] یر- [-ār] ار- [-āvar] اور-

Here follow examples:

| | | | | |
|---|---|---|---|---|
| (strong) | زور آور | ← | (strength) | زور |
| (leader, commander, general; lit. year-possessor) | سالار | ← | (year) | سال |
| (animal) | جانور | ← | (life) | جان |
| (courageous) | دلیر | ← | (heart) | دل |
| (a candidate) | امیدوار | ← | (hope) | امید |
| (king) | شہریار | ← | (city) | شہر |

*E. Combine the word on the right with the possessive-agentive suffix. Then choose the best meaning.*

| | | | | | | | |
|---|---|---|---|---|---|---|---|
| (wealthy) | (God) | (fortunate) | ________ | ← | یار | (luck) | ۱۔ بخت |
| (sleepy) | (friendly) | (intelligent) | ________ | ← | یار | (awareness) | ۲۔ ہوش |
| (broken) | (guilty) | (judge) | ________ | ← | وار | (fault) | ۳۔ قصور |
| (worth) | (judgment) | (worthy) | ________ | ← | وار | (requital) | ۴۔ سزا |
| (hat) | (soldier) | (leader) | ________ | ← | ور | (head) | ۵۔ سر |
| (king) | (book) | (poet) | ________ | ← | ور | (speech) | ۶۔ سخن |
| (senior) | (wealthy) | (powerful) | ________ | ← | ور | (power) | ۷۔ طاقت |
| (poor) | (fortunate) | (profit) | ________ | ← | ور | (fortune) | ۸۔ بہرہ |

## The Agentive Suffix بان [-bān]

This suffix and its cousin وان form agentive nouns and adjectives. They are comparable to the English -keeper. Note that the Persian بان (-keeper) is etymologically connected to وان (compare with Sanskrit वान् [vān]) and that both are found in Indic languages. This makes it difficult to say with certainty in many cases, especially in cases when the suffix is applied to an English borrowing, whether it has been borrowed from Persian, Sanskrit, or Prakrit. In fact, one might argue that the suffixes in these languages are so close, and the linguistic traditions so intertwined, that, in this case, the distinction is not meaningful.

| | | | | |
|---|---|---|---|---|
| (gardener) | باغبان | ← | (garden) | باغ |
| (kind; a kind person, friend) | مہربان | ← | (kindness) | مہر |
| (coachman) | کوچوان | ← | (coach) | کوچ |
| (coachman, driver) | گاڑی بان | ← | (coach) | گاڑی |

*F. Form agentive nouns or adjectives by suffixing بان [bān] to the following words. Then give their meanings. Some of the meanings of these words are highly idiomatic, so be sure to check your guesses in an Urdu dictionary.*

| | | | | | | | | | |
|---|---|---|---|---|---|---|---|---|---|
| (support) | ۵۔ پشتی | (protection) | ۴۔ پاس | (wind) | ۳۔ باد | (table) | ۲۔ میز | (door) | ا۔ در |
| (sight) | ۱۰۔ نگاہ | (passage) | ۹۔ گذر | (dog) | ۸۔ سگ | (shade) | ۷۔ سایہ | (boat) | ٦۔ کشتی |

## The Agentive Suffix of Occupation چی [-chī]

This suffix, which Persian borrows from Turkish, forms agentive nouns of profession, occupation, or habit and is comparable to the English suffix -er. Note that suffixation requires ہ to be dropped from the end of the word and may affect internal vowel patterns.

| | | | | |
|---|---|---|---|---|
| (tabla player) | طَبلچی | ← | (tabla) | طبلہ |

Some examples are quite idiomatic.

| | | | | |
|---|---|---|---|---|
| (a cook, a chef; lit. one who is trusted) | باورچی | ← | (trust) | باور |

*G. Form agentive nouns or adjectives by suffixing چی to the following words. Then estimate their meanings.*

| | | | | | |
|---|---|---|---|---|---|
| (clarion) | ۳۔ سُرنا | (target) | ۲۔ نشانہ | (rifle) | ا۔ بندوق |
| | | (kettle-drum) | ۵۔ نقارہ | (opium) | ۴۔ افیم |

### The Agentive Suffixes گر [-gar] گار [-gār] کار [-kār]

These agentive suffixes are perhaps the most common in Persian. They are cognate with a large number of words in Persian, Sanskrit, and Urdu meaning "to do" and hence are comparable with the English -er, -doer, and -maker, and -smith. Words formed with these suffixes may be nouns or adjectives (or both).

| | | | | |
|---|---|---|---|---|
| (self-working; automatic, automated) | خودکار | ← | (self) | خود |
| (God) | پروردگار | ← | (raised, protected) | پرورده |
| (magician) | جادوگر | ← | (magic) | جادو |
| (successful, useful; a workman) | کارگر | ← | (work) | کار |

*H. Form agentive nouns or adjectives with the given suffix, then guess the meaning of the resulting word.*

| | | | | | | | | |
|---|---|---|---|---|---|---|---|---|
| گر | (gold) | ۳۔ زر | گر | (power) | ۲۔ توان | گر | (game) | ا۔ بازی |
| گار | (torment) | ۶۔ ستم | گار | (help) | ۵۔ مدد | گر | (trade) | ۴۔ سودا |
| | | | کار | (act, performance) | ۸۔ ادا | کار | (art) | ۷۔ فن |

## Adjectival Suffixes

The following suffixes form adjectives that connote appearance, feeling, quality, or state.

### The Suffixes of Character ین [-īn] گین [-gīn] ینہ [-īnā] گینہ [-gīnā]

These suffixes give the sense of being possessed or full of, or characterized by, a particular quality. Compare with the English -ful, -like, and -y, and the Latin -ous.

| | | | | |
|---|---|---|---|---|
| (grievous, sorrowful) | غمگین | ← | (grief, sorrow) | غم |
| (colorful) | رنگین | ← | (color) | رنگ |
| (old) | دیرین | ← | (long while) | دیر |

Often, these adjectival suffixes are combined with the nominalizing suffix ہ.

| | | | | | | | |
|---|---|---|---|---|---|---|---|
| (woolen cloth) | پشمینہ | ← | (woolen) | پشمین | ← | (wool) | پشم |
| (a mirror; lit. possessed of water-like qualities [luster]) | | | | آبگینہ | ← | (water) | آب |

Sometimes, the suffixes ینہ and گینہ generate adjectives.

| | | | | |
|---|---|---|---|---|
| (old) | دیرینہ | ← | (long while) | دیر |

Abstract nouns can be formed from these adjectives by suffixing ی.

غم (sorrow) ← غمگین (sorrowful) ← غمگینی (sorrowfulness)

*I. Form adjectives or nouns from the following nouns using the suffix on the left and give their meaning.*

۱۔ خَشم (wrath) گین ۲۔ شرم (shame) گین ۳۔ سنگ (stone) ین

۴۔ آتش (fire) ین ۵۔ شوق (interest) ین ۶۔ کم (less, low) ینہ

## The Suffixes of Possession مند [-mand] and وند [-vand]

These suffixes form adjectives, and occasionally nouns, describing the possession of a particular quality.

عقل (intellect) ← عقل مند (intelligent)

سود (profit) ← سود مند (profitable)

خدا (lord) ← خداوند (possessor; Lordship)

Abstract nouns are formed by suffixing ی.

عقل مند (intelligent) ← عقل مندی (intelligence)

*J. Form adjectives from the following nouns using مند , then form the abstract noun. Give the meaning of both.*

۱۔احسان (favor, obligation) ۲۔ رضا (will) ۳۔ حاجت (need) ۴۔ خرد (wisdom)

۵۔ دانش (knowledge) ۶۔ دولت (wealth) ۷۔ فکر (worry, thought) ۸۔ ہنر (skill)

## The Adjectival and Adverbial Suffix انہ [-āna]

This suffix is ubiquitous in Urdu and conveys a sense of manner. Compare with the English -ly.

دوست (friend) ← دوستانہ (friendly)

طالب علم (student) ← طالب علمانہ (student-related; student-like; in the manner of a student)

When انہ is suffixed to a word ending in ہ [ā], the ہ is dropped and گ is infixed.

بچہ (child) ← بچگانہ (child-like; childish)

*K. Form adjectives from the following nouns using انہ and give the meaning of the resulting word.*

۱۔ مست (intoxicated) ۲۔ سال (year) ۳۔ شاہ (king) ۴۔ عاشق (lover) ۵۔ مرد (man)

## Adjectives of Quality with ناک [-nāk]

This suffix typically forms adjectives of quality. These are most often, but not always, negative in connotation. Compare with English -laden, -ful.

افسوس (regret) ← افسوسناک (regretful)

شرم (shame) ← شرم ناک (shameful)

*L. Form adjectives from the following nouns using the suffix ناک and give the meaning of the resulting word.*

۱۔ خوف (dread) ۲۔ الم (trajedy) ۳۔ غم (grief) ۴۔ ہوس (lust) ۵۔ تاب (shine)

## Suffixes of Resemblance and Character سار [-sār] وش [-vash] مان [-mān] منش [-manish]

These suffixes, which are relatively rare, form adjectives and nouns of resemblance. Compare with English -like.

خاک (dust) ← خاکسار (humble; lit. like dust)

ماہ (moon) ← ماہ وش (moon-like; beautiful)

آس (millstone) ← آسمان (lit. millstone-like; the sky)

بزرگ (great) ← بزرگ منش (magnanimous)

*M. Form adjectives from the following nouns using the suffix given and give the meaning of the resulting word.*

۱۔ شرم (shame) سار ۲۔ پری (fairy) وش ۳۔ مہر (sun) وش

۴۔ شاد (happy) مان ۵۔ صوفی (Sufi) منش

## Adjectives of Color with فام [-fām]

Compare with English -hued.

سفید (white) ← سفید فام (white/fair-colored)

*N. Form adjectives from the following nouns using the suffix فام and give the meaning of the resulting word.*

۱۔ سیاہ (black) ۲۔ گل (rose) ۳۔ لعل (ruby) ۴۔ لالہ (tulip) ۵۔ مشک (musk)

## 4.4 Persian Suffixes of Place

### The Suffix of Place or Time گاہ [-gāh]

This suffix can refer to both space and time. It is often used to form abstract nouns. Note that it can be written either adjoined to the word or separate from it.

| | | | | |
|---|---|---|---|---|
| خواب | (dream, sleep) | ← | خوابگاہ | (bedroom) |
| شام | (evening) | ← | شامگاہ | (eventide) |
| ہر | (every) | ← | ہر گاہ | (wherever; whenever; always; everywhere) |

Many of words formed with گاہ have idiomatic meanings:

| | | | | |
|---|---|---|---|---|
| در | (in; door) | ← | درگاہ | (a shrine) |
| سجدہ | (prostration) | ← | سجدہ گاہ | (place of prostration; soil from Karbala onto which Shias especially prostrate) |

*A. Use گاہ to form the nouns of place from the following words and give their meanings.*

۱۔ عید (Eid) ۲۔ تعلیم (education) ۳۔ درس (lesson, class) ۴۔ آرام (rest)

### The Suffix of Place خانہ [-khānā]

This ubiquitous suffix indicates a place, especially a physical one. This often distinguishes it from گاہ, which tends toward abstraction.

| | | | | |
|---|---|---|---|---|
| شراب | (wine) | ← | شراب خانہ | (wine-tavern) |
| آئینہ | (mirror) | ← | آئینہ خانہ | (a house or hall of mirrors) |

*B. Form the noun of place with the following words using خانہ. Then give their meaning.*

۱۔ مے (wine) ۲۔ بت (idol) ۳۔ قید (imprisonment) ۴۔ مہمان (guest) ۵۔ کتب (books)

### The Suffix of Place کدہ [-kadā]

This suffix typically connotes abstract, literary, or poetic registers or contexts and is thus distinguished from خانہ. It is used in a much smaller number of compounds than خانہ, but is nonetheless frequent.

| | | | | |
|---|---|---|---|---|
| بت | (idol) | ← | بت کدہ | (idol-house) |
| مے | (wine) | ← | مے کدہ | (wine-tavern) |

*C. Form the noun of place from the following words with کدہ. Then give their meaning.*

۱۔ ماتم (mourning) ۲۔ آتش (fire) ۳۔ خم (wine) ۴۔ صنم (idol) ۵۔ عشرت (pleasure)

## The Suffix of Land or Region ستان [-stān / istān]

This suffix is regularly encountered in the names of countries. When suffixed to a word ending in a consonant, it is pronounced istān. When suffixed to a word ending in a vowel, the initial i is dropped and the suffix is pronounced stān. Compare with the English -land.

پاک (pure) ← پاکستان (Pakistan)

پری (fairy) ← پرستان [parīstān] (fairyland)

*D. Form the noun of place or time from the following words with ستان. Then give their meaning.*

۱۔ گل (rose) ۲۔ تاجک (Tajik) ۳۔ شکر (sugar)

۴۔ کوہ (mountain) ۵۔ قبر (grave) ۵۔ بو (fragrance)

*E. Use English and Urdu maps to find all the names of countries ending in -istān and note their locations.*

## The Suffix of Abundance زار [-zār]

This suffix conveys the sense of a abundance or overgrowth.

چمن (grass) ← چمن زار (meadow)

خار (thorn) ← خار زار (briar patch, thicket; a place full of thorns)

Sometimes, this suffix changes to سار.

شاخ (branch) ← شاخسار (bower)

کوہ (mountain) ← کوہسار (mountain range; mountainous region)

*F. Form the noun of place or time from the following words with زار. Then give their meaning.*

۱۔ لالہ (red poppy; tulip) ۲۔ گل (rose) ۳۔ سبزہ (green)

## The Suffix of Settlement or Population آباد [ābād]

This suffix is regularly encountered in the names of populated areas, such as cities and towns. Compare with the English -town, -ville. It is often written in its independent form (آباد), but is sometimes suffixed as اباد [-ābād].

اسلام (Islam) ← اسلام آباد (Islamabad)

مراد (Murad) ← مراد آباد (Muradabad)

*G. Use a map of South Asia to locate the names of five major cities whose names end in this suffix.*

## The Suffix of Receptacle دان [-dān]

This is often used to indicate a container or receptacle.

گل (rose) ← گلدان (vase)

نمک (salt) ← نمکدان (salt-dish)

*H. Form nouns of place from the following words with دان. Then give their meaning.*

۱۔ پان (paan) ۲۔ پھول (flower) ۳۔ پیک (spittle) ۴۔ قلم (pen, quill) ۵۔ کوڑا (rubbish)

## The Rare Suffix of Place شن [-shan]

This suffix is used in only one Urdu word. Its etymology is mysterious.

گل (rose) ← گلشن (rose-garden)

## Multiplicity

Some nouns take more than one suffix. In such cases, the difference among the resulting compounds is typically one of connotation rather than denotation.

مے (wine) ← مے خانہ or مے کدہ (wine-tavern)

بت (idol) ← بت خانہ or بت کدہ (idol-house)

In these cases, خانہ tends to carry a broad connotation and used in both concrete and abstract nouns, while کدہ typically carries literary or poetical senses. This is not a hard rule, of course. There are many poems in which مے خانہ has poetic and literary connotations. Context will typically determine the sense.

*I. Explain the differences in sense among the following words, all of which are often translated into English as "garden."*

گل (rose) ← گلزار گلشن گلستان

*J. Here follow the names of literary works in Persian and Urdu whose names exhibit the suffixes surveyed here. Give literal and idiomatic translations of their meanings. Then learn a bit about them by searching online or in a library. Note that the Persian texts have left an indelible impression on Urdu literature.*

گلستان بوستان بہارستان خیالستان شبستان چمنستان شعرا

گلشن بے خار گلزار نسیم نالہ زار انجم کدہ صنم خانۂ عشق پری خانہ

میرے بھی صنم خانے

## 4.5 The Suffix ی

This is among the most versatile and frequently used Persian suffixes in Urdu. It can be used to form both adjectives and nouns.

When suffixed to nouns, it typically forms relative adjectives.

| | | | | |
|---|---|---|---|---|
| (of or from Shiraz; Shirazi) | شیرازی | ← | (Shiraz) | شیراز |
| (familial, hereditary, ancestral) | خاندانی | ← | (family) | خاندان |

When suffixed to some nouns, especially agentive ones, it can form abstract relative nouns.

| | | | | |
|---|---|---|---|---|
| (poetry) | شاعری | ← | (poet) | شاعر |
| (slavery) | غلامی | ← | (slave) | غلام |

When suffixed to adjectives, it typically forms relative (usually abstract) nouns.

| | | | | |
|---|---|---|---|---|
| (happiness) | خوشی | ← | (happy, good) | خوش |
| (beauty) | خوبصورتی | ← | (beautiful) | خوبصورت |

Nouns and adjectives ending in ہ [a] drop the ہ and take گی. For example:

| | | |
|---|---|---|
| (servitude; devotion) بَندگی | ← | (servant; devotee) بَندہ |
| (life) زِندگی | ← | (alive) زِندہ |

This pattern is also used to form abstract nouns from Arabic nouns ending in ہ:

| | | | | |
|---|---|---|---|---|
| (courageousness) | اعلیٰ حوصلگی | ← | (courage; fortitude) | حوصلہ |

*A. Form nouns from the following adjectives and nouns using the patterns discussed in this section. Then guess the meanings of the new words and check your guesses in an Urdu dictionary.*

| | | | |
|---|---|---|---|
| (fine, good) | ۲۔ خوب | (bad) | ۱۔ بد |
| (stuck, affixed) | ۴۔ چسپیدہ | (slow[ly]) | ۳۔ آہستہ |
| (prisoner) | ۶۔ اسیر | (mendicant; fakir) | ۵۔ فقیر |
| (present, existent) | ۸۔ موجودہ | (excellent) | ۷۔ عمدہ |
| (mad, insane) | ۱۰۔ دیوانہ | (manly) | ۹۔ مردانہ |

## 4.6 Comparatives and Superlatives

The Persian comparative تر and superlative ترین suffixes are regular and easy to recognize. Study the following:

(worst) بدترین ← (worse) بدتر ← (bad) بد

(best) بہترین ← (better) بہتر ← (good) بہ

ی is sometimes suffixed to the comparative to form an abstract noun.

(betterment) بہتری ← (better) بہتر

*A. Write the comparative and superlative forms of the Persian adjectives. Then nominalize the comparative. Give their meanings.*

(on, over, above) ۲۔ بر (less, few) ۱۔ کم

## 4.7 Persian Plurals

Persian words, especially those referring to human beings, are often pluralized with the suffix اں [-ān], sometimes spelled and pronounced ان [-ān].

(men) مرداں ← (man) مرد

(elders) بزرگاں ← (elder) بزرگ

(well-wishers) خیرخواہاں ← (well-wisher) خیرخواہ

When اں appears in a word to which iẓāfat attaches, it must be spelled and pronounced انِ [ān-e], since a consonant is required to carry the vowel ِ [e].

(the elders/great figures of the religion) بزرگانِ دین

This suffix is also applied to words of Arabic origin, especially in terms or phrases that include Persian grammatical constructions (such as iẓāfat).

(possessors of taste; connoisseurs) صاحبانِ ذوق ← (lord; possessor) صاحب

If a word ends in the vowel ہ [ā], the ہ is dropped and گاں or گان is suffixed. Note that اں is gender-neutral and therefore not used to form plurals of words in which ہ marks feminine personal gender in Arabic (for example, والدہ is *not* pluralized as والدگاں).

(children) بچگاں ← (child) بچہ

(servants; devotees) بندگاں ← (servant; devotee) بندہ

*A. Pluralize the following nouns using the appropriate form of ان and give their meanings.*

۱۔ عاشق (lover) ۲۔ خوب (fine) ۳۔ رفتہ (adj. gone) ۴۔ دلدادہ (n. enthusiast, fan)

۵۔ خواجہ ([lord, master; a title [especially of Sufis]) ۶۔ بادشاہ (emperor)

## The Non-Human Pural Suffix ہا [-hā]

Like Persian, Urdu uses this suffix to pluralize words that refer to inanimate objects, especially in names or phrases in which other Persian grammatical elements are found (such as iẓāfat). For example:

ریاست (state) ← رِیاسَت ہائے مُتحدۂ اَمریکہ (The United States of America)

When suffixed to words related to time, this plural suffix implies countlessness. It may also connote exaggeration.

بار (occasion, time) ← بارہا (lit. many times; repeatedly)

*B. Pluralize the following words using ہا and guess their meanings.*

۱۔ ہزار (thousand) ۲۔ صد (hundred)

## The Plural Suffix جات [-jāt]

The third Persian plural suffix which Urdu borrows is جات [-jāt]. Some philologists believe that this is in fact a Persianized form of the Arabic plural suffix ات [-āt]. The suffix جات [jāt] is used exclusively with words ending in ہ that refer to inanimate objects, though not all such words are pluralized in this manner.

There are two ways to write the suffix. The ہ may be dropped to form the plural:

نقشہ (map) ← نقشجات (maps)

Alternatively, جات may be written separately:

نسخہ (copy, edition; recipe; prescription) ← نسخہ جات (copies, etc.)

Note that in both cases the preceding syllable retains the vowel a (naqsha-jāt; nusḳha-jāt).

*C. Pluralize the following nouns with جات and give their meanings.*

۱۔ حوالہ (reference) ۲۔ گوشہ (corner) ۳۔ میوہ (fruit)

۴۔ نوشتہ ([a] written [text]) ۵۔ صوبہ (province, district)

## 4.8 Persian Verbs in Urdu

Although the infinitive forms of Persian verbs are rarely used in Urdu, it is useful to recognize them for the purpose of vocabulary acquisition, since a substantial number of Urdu words are derived from them. Fortunately, Persian infinitives, like Persian verbs in general, follow predictable patterns. For example, all Persian infinitives end in ن [-an]. Comparative study of Persian verbs reveals a number of vowel patterns that can be used to group Persian verbs. The following chart reviews the most common ones.

| (to adhere) | چسپیدن | (to have) | داشتن | (to lose, to play) | باختن |
|---|---|---|---|---|---|
| (to buy) | خرِیدن | (to pass [something]) | گُذاشتن | (to cast, to throw) | انداختن |
| (to arrive) | رسیدن | (to portray; to write) | نِگاشتن | (to make) | ساختن |
| (to fall) | اُفتادن | (to pass) | گُزشتن | (to recognize) | شناختن |
| (to set, place) | نہادن | (to turn; to become) | گشتن | | |
| | | | | (to ignite) | افروختن |
| (to order | فرمُودن | (to write) | نوِشتن | (to burn) | سوختن |
| (to rob) | رُبُودن | | | (to learn, to teach) | آموختن |
| (to show) | نمُودن | | | | |
| | | | | (to pour) | ریختن |
| (to be) | بُودَن | | | | |
| | | | | (to rouse) | انگیختن |
| | | | | (to mix) | آمیختن |
| (to turn [something]) | گرداندن | | | | |
| | | (to shine, burn) | تافتن | (to rise) | خاستن |
| (to cause to pass) | گُذراندن | | | | |
| | | (to acquire) | یافتن | (to decorate) | آراستن |
| (to cause to burn) | سوزاندن | | | | |
| | | (to make haste) | شتافتن | (to want, desire) | خواستن |
| (to read) | خواندن | | | | |
| | | (to sew) | بافتن | (to seek) | جُستن |
| | | (to split) | شگافتن | (to wash) | شُستن |
| (to take, bear) | بُردن | | | | |
| (to eat) | خوردن | | | | |
| | | (to disturb) | آشُفتن | (to sit) | نشستن |
| (to give) | دادن | | | | |
| | | (to beat, pound) | کوفتن | (to know) | دانستن |
| (to do) | کردن | | | | |
| | | (to speak) | گُفتن | | |
| (to die) | مُردن | | | | |
| | | | | (to break) | شکستن |
| (to strike) | زَدَن | | | | |
| | | (to deceive, charm) | فریفتن | | |
| (to happen) | شُدَن | | | | |
| | | | | (to close, seal) | بستن |
| (to come) | آمدن | | | | |
| | | (to go) | رَفتن | | |
| (to see) | دیدن | | | | |
| | | (to take) | گِرفتن | | |

### Infinitive Patterns

The Persian infinitive follows a set of regular rules. The first is that all infinitives end either in دن or تن. The second is that تن verbs are preceded by an unvoweled consonant (-ḳhtan, -stan, -shtan, -ftan) while some دن verbs are preceded by a long vowel (ādan, ūdan, īdan) and others are not (-ndan, -rdan, -adan, -udan).

### The Causative Verb Ending اندن [-āndan] or انیدن [-ānīdan]

To form causative verbs, Persian suffixes ان [-ān] to the present stem and suffixes the verbal ending دن [-dan] or یدن [-īdan].

| | | | | |
|---|---|---|---|---|
| (to [cause to] boil) | جوشاندن | ← | (to boil) | جوشیدن |
| (to explain) | فہمانیدن | ← | (to understand) | فہمیدن |

### The Ending یدن [-īdan]

This is the standard verbalizing suffix in Persian (and the Urdu words derived from the large group of Perisan verbs that it forms). Consider the following Persian verbs, which have been formed by suffixing یدن [-īdan] to an Arabic noun.

| | | | | | | | |
|---|---|---|---|---|---|---|---|
| (sought) | طلبیدہ | ← | (to seek) | طلبیدن | ← | (seeking) | طلب |
| (deadness) | فوتیدگی | ← | (to die) | فوتیدن | ← | (death) | فوت |

### Persian Infinitives as Nouns

In Urdu, as in Persian, infinitives can be used as gerunds, especially in literary contexts or as parts of compounds and phrases.

(the blink of an eye) چشم زدن

### Inifinitives and Nouns of Worth or Fitness

Suffixing ی to the infinitive form of a Persian verb can produce Urdu words that give the sense of worth, fitness, or ability:

| | | | | |
|---|---|---|---|---|
| (readable, legible; a part of the Quran read daily) | خواندنی | ← | (to read) | خواندن |
| (worth seeing) | دیدنی | ← | (to see) | دیدن |

It can also produce idioms:

| | | | | |
|---|---|---|---|---|
| (income) | آمدنی | ← | (to come) | آمدن |

*A. Given the meaning of the verb on the right, select the meaning of the word on the left.*

| | | | | | |
|---|---|---|---|---|---|
| (fit to go; departing; fleeting) | (gone; fled) | رفتنی | ← | (to go) | ۱۔ رفتن |
| (hazardous; dangerous) | (fit, deserving to be burnt) | سوختنی | ← | (to burn) | ۲۔ سوختن |
| (free; inexpensive) | (obtainable; a loan) | یافتنی | ← | (to obtain) | ۳۔ یافتن |
| (fit to be cut; in need of being cut) | (fragile; unstable) | بریدنی | ← | (to cut) | ۴۔ بُریدن |

*B. Form the noun of fitness of the following verbs and guess their meanings.*

(to eat) ۴۔ خوردن (to pass) ۳۔ گذشتن (to reach) ۲۔ رسیدن (to strike) ۱۔ زدن

## 4.9 The Persian Past Stem

The past stem of a Persian verb is easy to recognize. It is formed simply by dropping the ن [-an] ending of the infinitive.

| | | | | | |
|---|---|---|---|---|---|
| دانستن | ← | دانست | رسیدن | ← | رسید |
| نشستن | ← | نشست | بودن | ← | بود |

Persian past stems are ubiquitous in Urdu. Many of them are used as simple nouns:

| | | | | |
|---|---|---|---|---|
| دانستن | (to know) | ← | دانست | (knowledge, awareness; lit. that which is known) |
| نشستن | (to sit) | ← | نِشست | (sitting; a session; a seat) |

*A. Write the past stem of the all the verbs in the chart above that share a past-stem ending with at least two other verbs (e.g. شاخت انداخت ساخت).*

## 4.10 Simple Nouns Adjectives, and Adverbs from the Past Stem

Simple nouns, adjectives, and adverbs can be derived from the past stem in a number of ways.

### The Past Stem as a Noun

The past stem is often used as a noun in Urdu. Its meaning is typically gerundive, denoting the action of the infinitive. Compare with English gerunds endings in -ing (such as "asking" from "to ask").

| | | | | |
|---|---|---|---|---|
| خریدن | (to purchase) | ← | خرید | (buying; cost; that which is sold) |
| دیدن | (to see) | ← | دید | (seeing, vision; inspection) |

*A. Using the definitions for the Persian verbs listed above, guess the meaning of the following nouns. Check your guesses in an Urdu dictionary.*

| | | | |
|---|---|---|---|
| ۱۔ رسید | ۲۔ زد | ۳۔ ساخت | ۴۔ نمود |
| ۵۔ ریخت | ۶۔ شناخت | ۶۔ کوفت | ۷۔ بود |

*B. Memorize the following common Urdu phrases, both of which include the past stem(s) of a Persian verb.*

۱۔ نمود و بود (existence, persistence) ۲۔ آمد و رَفت (coming and going; traffic)

## Persian Past Participles (Past Stem + ہ)

The past participle is formed by suffixing ہ [-ā] to the past stem. This is akin to the English -ed and its various forms (e.g. mark ⟶ marked; do ⟶ done). Although the basic sense of past participles is adjectival, they may also be treated as nouns (compare with English "the marked"; "the done") or adverbs. Here are some examples.

| | Past Participle | | Past Stem | | | Infinitive |
|---|---|---|---|---|---|---|
| (passed, bygone; the past) | گذشتہ | ← | گذشت | ← | (to pass) | گذشتن |
| (knowingly) | دانستہ | ← | دانست | ← | (to know) | دانستن |
| (selected, select; favored, favorite) | پسندیدہ | ← | پسندید | ← | (to select) | پسندیدن |

*C. Write the past participle of the following verbs. Use the chart of infinitives to infer their literal meanings.*

۱۔ آراستن ۲۔ بستن ۳۔ گذشتن ۴۔ نوشتن ۵۔ مردن ۶۔ زدن ۷۔ شدن ۸۔ دیدن ۹۔ رسیدن ۱۰۔ ساختن ۱۱۔ ریختن ۱۲۔ جوشاندن

## Past-Stem Nouns with the Suffix ار [-ār]

Another common way that Persian (and Urdu) derive simple nouns from past stems is by suffixing ار [ār]. The resulting nouns typically refer to state or quality associated with the action of the verb.

| | | | | | | |
|---|---|---|---|---|---|---|
| (speed; gait) | رفتار | ← | رفت | ← | (to go) | رفتن |

They may also be agentive nouns (-er) or adjectives (-ing).

| | | | | | | |
|---|---|---|---|---|---|---|
| (worshipper) | پرستار | ← | پرست | ← | (to worship) | پرستن |

Occasionally, they are adjectival and similar in sense to the past participle (-ed). These may also be nominalized ("the -ed").

| | | | | | | |
|---|---|---|---|---|---|---|
| (seized) | گرفتار | ← | گرفت | ← | (to seize) | گرفتن |

*D. Form verbal nouns from the following verbs by suffixing ار [ār] to the past stem. Use the clues in parentheses to help you guess the meaning of the resulting noun.*

| | | | |
|---|---|---|---|
| (agentive noun) | ۲۔ خریدن | (noun) | ۱۔ دیدن |
| (agentive adjective) | ۴۔ نمودن | (noun) | ۳۔ گفتن |
| | | (nominalized adjective) | ۵۔ مُردن |

## 4.11 The Persian Present Stem in Urdu

The present stem of Persian verbs almost always begins with the initial letters of the infinitive form and past stem. It differs from the past stem in that it drops the end of the past stem and typically adds a consonant or changes a vowel. This may seem confusing at first, but comparative study reveals regular or nearly regular patterns in the formation of most present stems from Persian verbs. The following chart shows the relationship between past and present stems. The present stem appears to the left of the arrows.

| Present Stem | ← | Past Stem |
|---|---|---|
| باز | ← | باخت |
| انداز | ← | انداخت |
| ساز | ← | ساخت |
| | | |
| شناس | ← | شناخت |
| | | |
| افروز | ← | افروخت |
| سوز | ← | سوخت |
| آموز | ← | آموخت |
| | | |
| ریز | ← | ریخت |
| انگیز | ← | انگیخت |
| آمیز | ← | آمیخت |
| خیز | ← | خاست |
| آرا | ← | آراست |
| خواه | ← | خواست |
| | | |
| جُو | ← | جُست |
| شُو | ← | شُست |
| | | |
| نشیں | ← | نشِست |
| داں | ← | دانست |
| | | |
| شکن | ← | شکست |
| | | |
| بند | ← | بست |

| Present Stem | ← | Past Stem |
|---|---|---|
| دار | ← | داشت |
| گذار | ← | گذاشت |
| نِگار | ← | نِگاشت |
| | | |
| گذر | ← | گذشت |
| گرد | ← | گشت |
| | | |
| نویس | ← | نوِشت |
| تاب | ← | تافت |
| یاب | ← | یافت |
| شتاب | ← | شتافت |
| | | |
| آشوب | ← | آشُفت |
| کوب | ← | کوفت |
| گو | ← | گفت |
| | | |
| فریب | ← | فریفت |
| | | |
| رَو | ← | رفت |
| گیر | ← | گِرِفت |
| | | |
| باف | ← | بافت |
| شگاف | ← | شگافت |

| Present Stem | ← | Past Stem |
|---|---|---|
| چسپ | ← | چسپید |
| خر | ← | خرید |
| رس | ← | رسید |
| | | |
| افت | ← | افتاد |
| نہہ | ← | نہاد |
| | | |
| فرما | ← | فرمود |
| ربا | ← | ربود |
| نما | ← | نمود |
| | | |
| باش | ← | بُود |
| | | |
| گرداں | ← | گرداند |
| گذراں | ← | گُذراند |
| سوزاں | ← | سوزاند |
| | | |
| خواں | ← | خواند |
| | | |
| بَر | ← | بُرد |
| خور | ← | خورد |
| ده | ← | داد |
| کُن | ← | کرد |
| میر | ← | مُرد |
| زَن | ← | زَد |
| شَو | ← | شُد |
| آ | ← | آمد |
| بیں | ← | دید |

*A. Patterns. Scan the chart to find regular, predictable patterns which obtain between past and present stems. Use the groupings to guide you. Then write the patterns in the space provided. The first two have been done for you.*

...اخت ← ... از

... وخت ← ... وز

There are occasional exceptions to the regular vowel and consonant patterns that obtain between past and present participles.

فروختن ← فروخت ← فروش

شناختن ← شناخت ← شناس

Even in these examples, however, we note some resemblance to the standard pattern, since س is the unvoiced counterpart of the standard ز (compare with اختن ← از) and ش is the sibilant sibling of س. As exceptions go, they aren't very exceptional.

Sometimes, more than one present stem is associated with a single past stem. Many of these are actually derived from related verbs, often archaic or obsolete, with similar or identical meanings.

خوردن ← خور خوار (from خواردن)

گذاشتن ← گذار گسار (from گساردن)

The regularity of Persian verb forms also allows for one present stem to be used in multiple verbs (and hence for it to have multiple corresponding past stems).

فریب ← فریفتن فریبیدن ← فریفت فریبید

کوب ← کوفتن کوبیدن ← کوفت کوبید

*B. Use the chart of stems and the rules surveyed here to infer the present stem corresponding to the following past stems.*

۱۔ کُشُود ۲۔ رُبُود ۳۔ پِنداشت ۴۔ کاشت ۵۔ دوخت ۶۔ سوخت

۷۔ ریخت ۸۔ آویخت ۹۔ فہمید ۱۰۔ کشید ۱۱۔ پرداخت ۱۲۔ گداخت

*C. Write the past stem corresponding to the present stem.*

۱۔ اندوز ۲۔ افروز ۳۔ گُمار ۴۔ گوار ۵۔ آزما ۶۔ افزا

۷۔ آویز ۸۔ گُریز ۹۔ پوش ۱۰۔ بُر ۱۱۔ نواز ۱۲۔ پرداز

## 4.12 Present Stem Simple Nouns

Persian derives nouns and adjectives from the present stem in a number of ways. The following sections survey the patterns most commonly used in Urdu.

## The Present Stem as a Noun

Sometimes the present stem is used as a noun by itself. Typically, these convey the action of the verb and are therefore similar to English gerunds ending in -ing (e.g. to go, going; to eat, eating).

| | | | | |
|---|---|---|---|---|
| (burning; love, ardor) | سوز | ← | (to burn) | سوختن |
| (melting, melted; anguish) | گداز | ← | (to melt) | گداختن |

### Active participles ندہ [-indā]

Following Persian, Urdu forms active participles by suffixing ندہ [-indā] to the present stem. This is analogous to the English -er ending, as in do ⟶ doer. Note that if a present stem ends in a long vowel, the suffix changes to either ئندہ [-indā] or یندہ [-yindā]. The former is typically used with stems ending in ا [ā], the latter with those ending in و [o, ū].

| Noun | | | Present Stem | | Verb | |
|---|---|---|---|---|---|---|
| (bird) | پرندہ | ← | پر | ← | (to fly; to flutter) | پریدن |
| (resident, citizen) | باشندہ | ← | باش | ← | (to be) | بودن |
| (n. the future; adv. in the future) | آئندہ | ← | آ | ← | (to come) | آمدن |

The active participle, like all other nouns ending in ہ which refer to sentient beings, is pluralized by dropping ہ and suffixing گاں or گان.

| | | | | |
|---|---|---|---|---|
| (residents) | باشندگاں | ← | (resident) | باشندہ |

*A. Write the singular and plural forms of the active participle of the following verbs and give their meanings. Use the regular patterns or the chart of present and past stems to resolve ambiguities.*

۱۔ نمودن (to exibit, represent) ۲۔ نوشتن (to write) ۳۔ خواندن (to read) ۴۔ کردن (to do)

۵۔ دادن (to give) ۶۔ گفتن (to say) ۷۔ رفتن (to go) ۸۔ دیدن (to see)

۹۔ دانستن (to know) ۱۰۔ نگاشتن (to write)

*B. Read and translate the following Persian idiom, which is commonly used in Urdu.*

۱۔ جویندہ یابندہ

## Adjectives and Nouns of Agency with ا [ā]

Suffixing ا [ā] to the present stem forms agentive adjectives in Persian (compare with English -ing). Sometimes, these adjectives are nominalized. When the verb stem ends in a vowel, ی is infixed and the suffix changes to یا [yā]. Thus, with regard to the verb توانستن (to be able), by suffixing ا to the present stem توان, we are left with توانا (powerful, strong). Likewise, suffixing ا to گو (the present stem of گفتن [to speak]) yields گویا (speaking [not mute]; a speaker; idiom. "as if to say," "you might say").

| | | | | | | |
|---|---|---|---|---|---|---|
| توانستن | (to be able) | ← | توان | ← | توانا | (powerful, strong) |
| گفتن | (to say) | ← | گو | ← | گویا | (speaking; speaker; idiom. "as if") |

Abstract nouns can be formed from nouns of agency by suffixing ی [ī]:

| | | | | |
|---|---|---|---|---|
| توانا | (strong, powerful) | ← | توانائی | (capability, power) |
| گویا | (speaking [adj.]; speaker) | ← | گویائی | (speaking [n.]; speech; the ability to speak) |

*C. From the following infinitives, derive the present stem, the adjective or noun of agency, and the abstract noun give their meanings. Whether the noun of agency is an adjective, noun, or both is indicated in parentheses.*

| | | | | | |
|---|---|---|---|---|---|
| ۱۔ دانستن | (to know, to be wise) | (adj./n.) | ۲۔ شناختن | (to recognize) | (adj./n.) |
| ۳۔ رسیدن | (to reach) | (adj.) | ۴۔ دیدن | (to see) | (adj.) |
| ۵۔ گرفتن | (to grasp, seize) | (adj./n.) | ۶۔ رفتن | (to go, pass) | (adj.) |
| ۷۔ جستن | (to seek) | (adj./n.) | | | |

## Agentive Adjectives and Adverbs with اں [-āñ]

Persian forms imperfective participles by suffixing اں [-āñ] to a present stem. This is comparable to suffixing -ing in English (e.g. work ⟶ working). The resulting word is typically treated as an adjective or adverb in Urdu. Note that if the verb stem ends in ا [ā], ی (y) is infixed and the suffix becomes یاں [-yāñ].

| | | | | | | |
|---|---|---|---|---|---|---|
| سوختن | (to burn) | ← | سوز | ← | سوزاں | (burning; affecting) |
| نمودن | (to show) | ← | نما | ← | نمایاں | (conspicuous, outstanding) |
| رفتن | (to go) | ← | رو | ← | رواں | (going, flowing) |

Adjectives of this group are sometimes nominalized by suffixing ی [ī]. In such cases, ں becomes ن.

| | | | | |
|---|---|---|---|---|
| رواں | (going, flowing) | ← | روانی | (fluency) |

*D. Write the agentive adjectives of the following verbs using اں and give their meanings.*

| | | | | | | | |
|---|---|---|---|---|---|---|---|
| ۱۔ گذشتن | (to pass) | ۲۔ افتادن | (to fall) | ۳۔ خاستن | (to rise) | ۴۔ تافتن | (to shine) |
| ۵۔ کوفتن | (to beat) | ۶۔ بُریدن | (to cut, slice) | ۷۔ گفتن | (to speak) | ۸۔ خواستن | (to desire) |

## Verbal Nouns with ش [-ish]

Suffixing this to the present stem forms verbal nouns. Most of these nouns are best defined as the action or state associated with the performance of the verb. All nouns in this pattern are grammatically feminine in Urdu. Note that when the verb stem ends in a vowel, hamza is infixed.

(request) گذارِش ← گذار ← (to pass) گذاشتن

(order) فرمائش ← فرما ← (to order) فرمودن

*E. Form the abstract verbal noun of the verb on the right. Then guess its meaning.*

۱۔ سوختن (to burn) ۲۔ دانستن (to know) ۳۔ رفتن (to go) ۴۔ نمودن (to exibit)

۵۔ کوشیدن (to attempt) ۶۔ خواستن (to desire) ۷۔ نگاشتن (to write) ۸۔ بستن (to compose)

## Verbal Nouns with اک [-āk]

The verbal nouns formed by suffixing this to the present stem tend to refer to the instrument because of, or by means of which, the action of the verb takes place. Hence, پوشاک (clothing) is the means by which one covers (پوشیدن) oneself and سوزاک (gonorrhea) is the cause or means of the sensation of burning (سوختن).

(clothing) پوشاک ← پوش ← (to cover) پوشیدن

(gonorrhea) سوزاک ← سوز ← (to burn) سوختن

Only a few such words are used in Urdu, but some of them are very common.

*F. Form verbal nouns from the present stem of the verb on the right using اک [-āk]. Then give its meaning.*

۱۔ خوردن (to eat) ۲۔ تپیدن (to be warm)

## Relative Nouns with ہ [-ā]

Relative nouns are formed by suffixing ہ to the present stem. These are often instrumental, primarily denoting the action or object by which the verb is completed. It may also refer to an object or action which requires the completion of the action of the verb. Hence, an اندازہ (estimate) is an action that requires one to cast (انداختن) an instrument of measurement and a شمارہ (number) is the instrument by which a person counts (شمردن). Many of these are also conceivable as objects of the verbs. Thus, one hazards or casts a guess or estimate and likewise counts the numbers of things.

(estimate) اندازہ ← انداز ← (to cast) انداختن

(number) (e.g. of a magazine) شُمارہ ← شُمار ← (to count) شُمُرَدن

*G. Using ہ, write the present-stem relative verbal noun of the verb on the right. Then choose the most likely meaning from those given on the left.*

| | | | | | | |
|---|---|---|---|---|---|---|
| (story) | (a smile) | (humor) | ________ | ← | (to laugh) | ۱۔ خندیدن |
| (passage) | (a boat) | (money) | ________ | ← | (to pass) | ۲۔ گذاشتن |
| (paper) | (the fist) | (a fragment) | ________ | ← | (to scatter) | ۳۔ ریختن |
| (party) | (mixture) | (spoon) | ________ | ← | (to mix) | ۴۔ آمیختن |
| (wardrobe) | (closet) | (earring) | ________ | ← | (to hang) | ۵۔ آویختن |
| (to laugh) | (recording) | (clod-breaker) | ________ | ← | (to beat) | ۶۔ کوبیدن |

*Review Exercise. Recognizing the relationship between a word and the present stem. All of the words below are nouns or adjectives formed from the present stem of a verb. Write the present stem (removing any suffixes if necessary). Then write the past stem.*

| | | | |
|---|---|---|---|
| ۴۔ انداز | ۳۔ ساز | ۲۔ اندازہ | ۱۔ تابہ |
| ۸۔ جویا | ۷۔ دانا | ۶۔ شرمندہ | ۵۔ درِندہ |
| ۱۲۔ سازش | ۱۱۔ خواہش | ۱۰۔ رساں | ۹۔ چسپاں |
| ۱۶۔ گیرا | ۱۵۔ جویا | ۱۴۔ تپاک | ۱۳۔ خوراک |

*H. Choose three present stems in the present-stem chart above and use a dictionary to find all the present-stem nouns that are derived from them in Urdu. Record the connections and compare them with the meanings of the suffixes discussed in this section.*

## 4.13 Compound Words from the Past Stem

Persian forms compound words by combining simple elements. For example:

(fragrance, sweet smell) خوشبو ← (odor) بو (pleasant) خوش

In the following sections, we shall examine the ways that compound words are derived from Persian verbal elements.

### Past Stem Compounds

Many compound words are formed by suffixing the simple past stem to a word to yield nouns, adjectives, and occasionally adverbs. The use of the past stem often imparts a sense of a completed action to the resulting compound.

| | | | | | | |
|---|---|---|---|---|---|---|
| (self-written; autobiography) | خود نوشت | ← | (to write) | نوشتن | (self) | خود |
| (contract; settlement) | قرارداد | ← | (to give) | دادن | (rest, fixity) | قرار |

The following chart surveys some of the ways in which the past stem of the verb داشتن (to have, keep, hold; consider) is used to form compound nouns.

| | | | | |
|---|---|---|---|---|
| (hope, desire; trust) | چشم داشت | ← | (eye) | ۱۔ چشم |
| (care, service; favor) | خاطر داشت | ← | (mind, will) | ۲۔ خاطر |
| (a summons) | طلب داشت | ← | (demand) | ۳۔ طلب |
| (a petition) | عرض داشت | ← | (request; address) | ۴۔ عرض |
| (protection, supervision) | نگاه داشت | ← | (sight) | ۵۔ نگاہ |
| (memory; memorandum; note) | یادداشت | ← | (memory) | ۶۔ یاد |

The following list surveys the ways in which the stem of the verb زدن (to strike) is used to form compound adjectives.

| | | | | |
|---|---|---|---|---|
| (committed, occurred [as an error]) | سرزد | ← | (head) | ۱۔ سر |
| (heard; that which is heard) | گوش زد | ← | (ear) | ۲۔ گوش |
| (named, designated; appointed) | نام زد | ← | (name) | ۳۔ نام |

*A. Combine the term on the right with the past stem to form compound nouns. Then guess their meanings and check your guesses in a dictionary. The resulting compound's part of speech (noun, adjective, or both) is indicated in parentheses.*

| | | | | | | | |
|---|---|---|---|---|---|---|---|
| (n.) | خرید | (fine, happy) | ۲۔ خوش | (n.) | آمد | (in front of) | ۱۔ پیش |
| (adj./n.) | بود | (not) | ۴۔ نا | (adj.) | نمود | (bad) | ۳۔ بد |
| (adj.) | نہاد | (name) | ۶۔ نام | (n.) | نہاد | (heart) | ۵۔ دل |
| (adj.) | داد | (god) | ۸۔ خدا | (n.) | بُرد | (hand) | ۷۔ دست |
| (n.) | گذاشت | (back, behind) | ۱۰۔ وا | (n.) | گذاشت | (down) | ۹۔ فرو |
| (adj.) | یافت | (not) | ۱۲۔ نا | (n.) | یافت | (again, back) | ۱۱۔ باز |
| (n.) | دید | (just action) | ۱۴۔ صواب | (adj.) | زد | (tongue) | ۱۳۔ زبان |
| (adj./n.) | آمد | (head) | ۱۶۔ سر | (n.) | آمد | (pleasant) | ۱۵۔ خوش |
| (adj./n.) | آمد | (new) | ۱۸۔ نو | (adj.) | آمد | (work, use) | ۱۷۔ کار |

## Past Participle Compounds

A large number of compound nouns and adjectives are formed by suffixing the past participle to a noun. These nouns typically convey the sense that the referent is the recipient or object of the action of the verb. Thus, someone who has been struck (زده) by grief (غم) is grief-stricken.

| | | | | | | |
|---|---|---|---|---|---|---|
| (grief-stricken) | غم زده | ← | (struck) | زده | (grief) | غم |
| (heart-burnt; [someone] in love) | دل سوختہ | ← | (burnt) | سوختہ | (heart) | دل |
| (heart-stolen; [someone] in love) | دل ربوده | ← | (stolen) | ربوده | (heart) | دل |

The following list surveys a number of compounds built on the past participle of the verb رسیدن (to reach).

| | | | | |
|---|---|---|---|---|
| (doomed) | اجل رسیده | ← | (the fated time of death) | اجل |
| (disaster-stricken) | آفت رسیده | ← | (trouble, calamity) | آفت |
| (godly; a gnostic) | خدا رسیده | ← | (god) | خدا |
| (oppressed, tormented) | ستم رسیده | ← | (oppression, torment) | ستم |
| (tyrannized) | ظلم رسیده | ← | (tyranny) | ظلم |
| (aged) | عمر رسیده | ← | (age, lifetime) | عمر |
| (immature, imperfect) | نا رسیده | ← | (not; un-) | نا |

To form abstract nouns from past-participle compounds, follow the rule for words ending in ه by dropping ه and suffixing گی.

| | | | | |
|---|---|---|---|---|
| (grief) (lit. grief-stricken-ness) | غمزدگی | ← | (grief-stricken) | غم زده |
| (immaturity, imperfection) | نارسیدگی | ← | (not realized, incomplete) | نا رسیده |

When these compounds refer to people, they are pluralized with گاں [-gāñ] after dropping ه.

| | | | | |
|---|---|---|---|---|
| (the grief-stricken) | غمزدگاں | ← | (grief-stricken) | غم زده |
| (the oppressed) | ستم رسیدگاں | ← | (oppressed) | ستم رسیده |

*B. Combine the following nouns or adjectives with the past participle of the given verb to form compound nouns and/or adjectives. Give the meaning of the resulting compounds. Then form abstract nouns using the suffix* گی *and give the meaning of the resulting abstract noun. Check your guesses in a dictionary.*

| | | | | | |
|---|---|---|---|---|---|
| یافتن | (certificate, certification) | ۲۔ سند | یافتن | (education) | ۱۔ تعلیم |
| زدن | (terror) | ۴۔ دہشت | زدن | (astonishment) | ۳۔ حیرت |
| دیدن | (the world) | ۶۔ جہاں | زدن | (flood) | ۵۔ سیلاب |

| | | | | | |
|---|---|---|---|---|---|
| ۷۔ نا | (not) | دیدن | ۸۔ فریب | (deceit) | خوردن |
| ۹۔ کِرم | (worm) | خوردن | ۱۰۔ سفر | (travel) | کردن |
| ۱۱۔ نا | (not) | کردن | ۱۲۔ دل | (heart) | شکستن |
| ۱۳۔ پا | (foot) | شکستن | ۱۴۔ دست | (hand) | بستن |
| ۱۵۔ یخ | (ice) | بستن | ۱۶۔ بھرتی | (enlistment) | شدن |
| ۱۷۔ شادی | (marriage) | شدن | ۱۸۔ دل | (lost) | دادن |
| ۱۹۔ نیم | (half) | مردن | ۲۰۔ جان | (spirit, life) | سوختن |

## 4.14 Present-Stem Compound Nouns

Urdu frequently uses Persian present stems as the second element in compounds to form nouns and adjectives. When used in this way, the present stem functions as an agentive suffix (compare with the English -er or -ing) that specifies the nature of the actor. Thus, a سبزی خور is a vegetable (سبزی) eater (خور) and someone who is خوددار is a self (خود) possessor (دار) or self-possessing. Note that compounds of this kind may be treated as nouns or adjectives (or both).

خوردن (to eat) ⟵ خور (-eater, -eating) ⟵ سبزی خور (vegetarian)

داشتن (to hold) ⟵ دار (-holder, -holding) ⟵ خود دار (self-possessing)

### A Note on Present Stem Nouns and Urdu Idiom

Knowing the literal meaning of the elements in Persianate compounds can facilitate predicting and understanding their idiomic meaning and use in Urdu. For example, although سبزی خور means vegetarian, it is considered ineloquent by some to say سبزی خور کھانا (lit. "vegetarian food") because this literally means "vegetable-eating food." (Vegetarian food is simply سبزی or perhaps دال سبزی.) Another example of the way that the present stem shades the meaning of vocabulary can be seen in the different senses of the following compounds.

تاریخ (history) ⟵ دانستن (to know) ⟵ تاریخ داں (historian)

تاریخ (history) ⟵ نوشتن (to write) ⟵ تاریخ نویس (historiographer)

Although both words roughly mean "historian" in Urdu, like the English "historian" and "historiographer," they have different senses. In Urdu, تاریخ داں connotes a master of historical information and the academic subject of history, while تاریخ نویس refers to an author of historical works. The latter may also suggest someone who records dates, or an author of the genre of poetry called *tarīḳh*, in which chronograms are written using the science of Arabic numerology.

Read the following chart, which surveys present-stem compounds built from the word دل (heart) and the present stems of various verbs. Consider the ways in which each verb shades the meaning of the compound. Note that abstract nouns can be formed from all compounds by suffixing ی. Also note that the present stem is sometimes attached to the first element and at other times written separately.

| | | | | | |
|---|---|---|---|---|---|
| (comfort, satisfaction) | دلاسا | ← | (to soothe) | آسودن | دل |
| (brave) | دلاور | ← | (to bring) | آوردن | دل |
| (delightful) | دل آویز | ← | (to suspend) | آویختن | دل |
| (attractive; the beloved) | دلبر | ← | (to carry, take) | بردن | دل |
| (darling [used with one's children]) | دل بند | ← | (to seal) | بستن | دل |
| (agreeable, pleasant) | دل پذیر | ← | (to accept) | پذیرفتن | دل |
| (pleasing) | دل پسند | ← | (to select) | پسندیدن | دل |
| (pleasing; cajoling; cajoler) | دل جو | ← | (to seek) | جُستن | دل |
| (interesting, pleasant) | دلچسپ | ← | (to stick) | چسپیدن | دل |
| (irritating; excruciating) | دل خراش | ← | (to scratch) | خراشیدن | دل |
| (desired, desirable) | دل خواہ | ← | (to desire) | خواستن | دل |
| (charming; a beloved) | دل دار | ← | (to possess) | داشتن | دل |
| (zealous, passionate) | دل دہ | ← | (to give) | دادن | دل |
| (painful) | دل دوز | ← | (to pierce, sew) | دوختن | دل |
| (alluring; the beloved) | دل ربا | ← | (to steal) | ربودن | دل |
| (pleasant) | دل ساز | ← | (to make) | ساختن | دل |
| (sympathetic; sympathizer; painful; ardent) | دل سوز | ← | (to burn) | سوختن | دل |
| (alluring, enchanting) | دل فریب | ← | (to deceive) | فریفتن | دل |
| (attractive) | دل کش | ← | (to draw) | کشیدن | دل |
| (entertaining, exciting, thrilling) | دل کشا | ← | (to open) | کشودن | دل |
| (moving, touching, pathetic) | دل گداز | ← | (to melt) | گداختن | دل |
| (impressive, agreeable) | دل نشین | ← | (to sit) | نشستن | دل |
| (soothing; beloved) | دل نواز | ← | (to care for) | نواختن | دل |

### Abstract Nouns from the Agentive Compound

Suffixing ی to compound nouns produces abstract nouns.

| | | | | |
|---|---|---|---|---|
| (self-possession, autonomy) | خود داری | ← | (self-possessing) | خود دار |
| (vegetarianism) | سبزی خوری | ← | (vegetarian) | سبزی خور |
| (rulership) | فرمان روائی | ← | (ruler) | فرمان روا |

*A. Combine the following nouns with the present stems of the following verbs to form compound nouns or adjectives. Guess the meaning of the new word based on the meaning of the noun and the verb from which the active stem is derived. Then form the abstract noun of each and guess its meaning, too. Check your guesses in a dictionary.*

| | | | |
|---|---|---|---|
| (to disturb) | آشفتن | (the world) | ۱۔ عالَم |
| (to illuminate) | افروختن | (the world) | ۲۔ عالم |
| (to seize) | گرفتن | (the world) | ۳۔ عالم |
| (to have, keep) | داشتن | (kindness, obligation) | ۴۔ منت |
| (to recognize) | شناختن | (kindness, obligation) | ۵۔ منت |
| (to draw, take) | کشیدن | (kindness, obligation) | ۶۔ منت |
| (to break) | شکستن | (mind, heart) | ۷۔ خاطر |
| (to draw, take) | کشیدن | (mind, heart) | ۸۔ خاطر |
| (to sit) | نشستن | (mind, heart) | ۹۔ خاطر |
| (to have) | داشتن | (life, spirit) | ۱۰۔جان |
| (to play, gamble, lose) | باختن | (life, spirit) | ۱۱۔ جان |
| (to give, grant) | بخشیدن | (life, spirit) | ۱۲۔ جان |

## 4.15 Persian Compounds Continued

Persian may also combine elements other than nouns (such as prepositions) with verbal elements (e.g. past and present stems, participles) to form compound words.

| | | | | | | |
|---|---|---|---|---|---|---|
| (import; income) | درآمد | ← | (to come) | آمدن | (in) | در |
| (export; expenditure) | برآمد | ← | (to come) | آمدن | (above, on) | بر |

Here is a list of Urdu nouns derived from Persian verbs compounded with باز (again, back). Note how each type of verbal element affects the meaning.

| | | | | | |
|---|---|---|---|---|---|
| (return; echo) | بازگشت | ← | (to turn) | گشتن | (again, back) باز |
| (inquiry, investigation) | بازپرس | ← | (to ask) | پرسیدن | (again, back) باز |
| (inquiry, request for return) | بازخواست | ← | (to want; to ask for) | خواستن | (again, back) باز |
| (inquirer) | بازخواہ | ← | (to ask) | خواستن | (again, back) باز |
| (return) | باز آمد | ← | (to come) | آمدن | (again, back) باز |
| (repossession, retrieval) | بازیافت | ← | (to obtain) | یافتن | (again, back) باز |

*A. Form compounds using the word on the right and the indicated stem or participle of the verb on the left, then guess their meanings. Check your guesses in an Urdu dictionary.*

| | | | |
|---|---|---|---|
| (past stem) | (to come) | آمدن | ۱۔ پیش (fore/front) |
| (present stem) | (to bind) | بستن | ۲۔ پیش (fore/front) |
| (present stem) | (to see) | دیدن | ۳۔ پیش (fore/front) |
| (present stem) | (to go) | رفتن | ۴۔ پیش (fore/front) |
| (past participle) | (to go) | رفتن | ۵۔ پیش (fore/front) |
| (present stem) | (to draw) | کشیدن | ۶۔ پیش (fore/front) |
| (present stem) | (to say) | گفتن | ۷۔ پیش (fore/front) |

## 4.16 Negation and Nouns

Persian verbs are negated by the prefixation of either م [ma] in the imperative or ن [na]. These appear in a number of common Urdu idioms.

| | | | | | |
|---|---|---|---|---|---|
| (unavoidably; unnecessarily; like it or not) | خواہ مخواہ | ← | خواہ | ← (to desire) | خواستن |
| (struggle, back-and-forth) | کشمکش | ← | کش | ← (to pull) | کشیدن |
| | | (God forbid) | خدانخواستہ | ← (to desire) | خواستن |

Nouns can be negated by prefixing نا [nā].

| | | | | |
|---|---|---|---|---|
| (annihilated; non-existent) | نابود | ← | (being, existence) | بود |
| (unsighted, blind) | نابینا | ← | (sighted) | بینا |

*A. Indicate the absence or reversal of the following using the negative prefix نا [nā]. Guess the meaning of the resulting word.*

| | | | | | |
|---|---|---|---|---|---|
| (studied; summoned) | ۳۔ خواندہ | (desired) | ۲۔ خواستہ | (choice, favor) | ۱۔ پسند |
| (knowingly) | ۶۔ دانستہ | (-knower) | ۵۔ داں | (possession) | ۴۔ دار |
| | | | | (worthy, proper) | ۷۔ شائستہ |

*B. Analyze the following Urdu idiom by giving the meaning of each of its parts. Then guess its meaning. Use the word bank to help you.*

ناگفتہ بہ

گفتن (to say, speak) بہ (good, better)

## 4.17 Non-Verbal Compounds

A number of Persian particles and prepositions are used as elements of compound words and should therefore be memorized. Here follows a chart listing some of the most common along with examples of their use.

| | | | | | | | |
|---|---|---|---|---|---|---|---|
| ب / بہ | (with, by, to) | با | (with) | بے | (without) | نا | (not) |
| بجا | (apropos) | باخبر | (informed) | بے خبر | (clueless) | ناامید | (hopeless) |
| بہر حال | (in any case) | با ادب | (polite) | بے ادب | (unmannerly) | نا مرد | (unmanly) |
| بہ آسانی | (easily) | با وفا | (faithful) | بے وفا | (unfaithful) | ناراض | (upset; unwilling) |

| | | | | | | | |
|---|---|---|---|---|---|---|---|
| بر | (on) | از | (from, by) | در | (in) | تا | (until, so) |
| بر ہم | (jumbled) | از حد | (extremely) | در اصل | (actually) | تاکہ | (so that) |
| بروقت | (on time) | از راہِ | (by way of) | در پیش | (in front) | تاحال | (till now) |
| بر محل | (opportune) | از بر | (by heart) | درمیان | (in the middle) | تاہم | (even so; still) |

| | | | |
|---|---|---|---|
| پیش | (before, in front of) | پس | (behind) |
| پیش لفظ | (foreword) | پس نوشت | (postscript; P.S.) |
| پیش نماز | (leader in prayer) | پس انداز | (savings) |
| پیش منظر | (foreground) | پس منظر | (background) |

| | | | |
|---|---|---|---|
| پست | (low, below) | بلند | (high, above) |
| پست قامت | (short) | بلند قامت | (tall) |
| پست ہمت | (cowardly) | بلند ہمت | (courageous) |

| | |
|---|---|
| ہم | (also, same) |
| ہم راہ | (fellow traveler; along with) |
| ہمسفر | (fellow traveler) |
| ہم معنی | (synonymous) |

*A. Form non-verbal compounds using the term on the right and the word on the left. Then choose the most likely meaning from the options below.*

| | | | |
|---|---|---|---|
| ۱۔ پیش (fore/front) | آب (water) | ۲۔ پیش (fore/front) | قدم (step) |
| ۳۔ پیش (fore/front) | گاہ (place) | ۴۔ پیش (fore/front) | منظر (scene) |
| ۵۔ پیش (fore/front) | خدمت (service) | | |

ا۔ urine　　ب۔ court　　پ۔ leader　　ت۔ servant　　ٹ۔ foreground

## Compounds of Entirety with تا [tā]

Many Urdu compounds are formed by infixing تا [tā] (to, until) between two nouns. In such cases, the ت is often dropped. When the same word is repeated, the sense is often of continuation, entirety, fullness, or variety. The resulting words are often adjectives. Thus, something that is لب (edge, lip) تا (to) لب (edge, lip) is brimful or replete.

| | | | | | |
|---|---|---|---|---|---|
| لب (lip, edge) | تا | لب | ← | لبالب | (brimful, replete) |
| رنگ (color) | تا | رنگ | ← | رنگارنگ | (of many colors; diverse) |

In some cases, the ت may be retained to distinguish an idiomatic sense.

| | | | | | |
|---|---|---|---|---|---|
| سر (head) | تا | پا (foot) | ← | سراپا | (stature, body; from head to foot, entirely) |
| سر (head) | تا | پا (foot) | ← | سرتاپا | (from head to foot, entirely) |

*B. Form compounds of entirety from the following words by infixing* ا *between the word repeated, as in* رنگارنگ*.*

| | | |
|---|---|---|
| ۱۔ سر (head, edge, end) | ۲۔ گون (hue; kind, mode) | ۳۔ دم (breath, moment) |
| ۴۔ کش (draw, pull, tug) | ۵۔ بر (side, breast) | ۶۔ نصف (half) |

# 4.18 Persian Nouns and Urdu Gender

Persian does not have grammatical gender except in the case of gender markings borrowed from Arabic (e.g. والد / والدہ). But because Urdu does observe grammatical gender, it assigns gender to all borrowed Persian nouns, and in some cases the pattern of assignment is regular.

## Verbal Nouns Ending in ش [-ish]

All Persian verbal nouns ending in ش [-ish] are feminine in Urdu. Use the following words in a sentence or phrase that reflects their gender.

۱۔ دانش　　۲۔ خواہش　　۳۔ آزمائش　　۴۔ سوزش　　۵۔ کوشش

### Past-Stem Verbal Nouns

All past-stem verbal nouns ending in ید [īd] and یخت [ekht], nearly all past stems ending in ت (with very few exceptions), and, indeed, most past stems in general, are feminine. Read the following past stems, all of which are feminine, and then use them in a sentence or phrase that reflects their gender.

۱۔ دید ۲۔ خرید ۳۔ کشید ۴۔ شکست ۵۔ دانست

### Present Stem + ہ [-ā]

Following regular patterns of Urdu gender, verbal nouns formed by suffixing ہ [ā] to the present stem are masculine. Read the following and use them in a way that reflects their gender.

۱۔ شمارہ ۲۔ ریزہ ۳۔ اندازہ ۴۔ نشانہ ۵۔ آمیزہ

### Past Participle

Following regular patterns of Urdu gender, the past participle, when nominalized, is, with very rare exception, masculine. Use the word گوفتہ in a sentence that reflects its gender.

### Nouns ending in ی

Following Urdu patterns of marked gender, Persian nouns ending in ی are typically treated as feminine. Such nouns include abstract nouns of compound nouns (e.g. خود داری) and simple nouns (e.g. خوبی, بندگی). Revisit one of the sections on abstract nouns above and use five words in a sentence that reflects their gender.

### Nouns of Place with گاہ [gāh]

All nouns of place ending in گاہ are feminine in Urdu. Use the following words in sentences or phrases to reflect their gender.

۱۔ تعلیم گاہ ۲۔ درس گاہ ۳۔ خواب گاہ ۴۔ در گاہ ۵۔ عبادت گاہ ۶۔ گذر گاہ

## 4.19 Urdu Idioms and Persian Grammar

Many Urdu phrases and idioms borrowed from Persian are used across a range of contexts, from literary writing to everyday speech. It is therefore useful for Urdu students wishing to build a large and rich vocabulary in Urdu to familiarize themselves with the basic elements of Persian grammar.

## 4.20 اضافت [iẓāfat]

The iẓāfat (sometimes iẓāfah) (lit. augmentation) is a Persian grammatical element that is found in all registers of Urdu. In form, it is an enclitic pronounced [e] that is suffixed to the first of two connected words. It can be spelled three different ways.

1. The most common is as the diacritical marker *zer* ِ [e]. For example, طالبِ علم [ṭālib-e ʻilm] (lit. seeker of knowledge; student).
2. If a word ends in the long vowels ا [ā] or an و [o, ū] iẓāfat is spelled ئے (or ے). For example, دعائے خیر [duā-e ḳhair] (lit. good prayer; well-wishing), کوئے یار [kū-e yār] (the lane of the beloved). If a word ends in the long vowel و [au], the iẓāfat is written under the و and the au is pronounced "av." For example, پرتو [partau] (ray) becomes پرتوِ نور [partav-e nūr] (ray of light) and خسرو [ḳhusrau] (king) becomes خسروِ عالم [ḳhusrav-e ʻālam] (king of the world).
3. If a word ends in ہ pronounced as a vowel [ā], iẓāfat is spelled as a hamzah ء written above ہ. For example, درجۂ اول [darjā-e avval] (first degree/level/class). Note that if a word ends in the breathy consonant ہ [h], iẓāfat is written as ِ (zer). Thus, ماہِ تمام [māh-e tamām] (full moon).

### Three Kinds of Iẓāfat

Most iẓāfat constructions can be divided into three kinds: noun-noun; noun-adjective; and adjective-noun.

## 4.20.1 Noun-Noun Iẓāfat

When iẓāfat connects two nouns, it performs a genitive function. That is, it indicates a relationship of either possession or composition of the former by the latter.

| | | | | |
|---|---|---|---|---|
| (student; lit. seeker **of** knowledge) | طالبِ علم | ← | (knowledge) علم | (seeker) طالب |
| (a goblet **of** wine) | جامِ شراب | ← | (wine) شراب | (goblet) جام |

Although by its very nature an iẓāfat construction comprises at least two words, the term itself often carries the meaning of a single word. In the example above, طالبِ علم can be considered as a single word meaning "student" and is often treated as such in terms of idiom and grammar. Note that iẓāfat and the Urdu genitive (کا) are not idiomatically interchangeable. That is, many common Urdu words built around iẓāfat change their meaning or become unidiomatic if کا is substituted:

| | | |
|---|---|---|
| (a seeker/demander of knowledge) | علم کا طالب | (a student) طالبِ علم |

Also note that Urdu iẓāfat constructions have the same word order as English genitive ("of") constructions, but the opposite order of a standard of Urdu genitive کا (kā) construction.

Note that Iẓāfat phrases are often fixed idioms in Urdu whose sense may not strictly adhere to their literal meaning. Consider the following example of a noun-noun iẓāfat which is treated as an adjective in Urdu:

قدّ (height) آدم (Adam; mankind) ← قدِ آدم (lifesize)

Although according to the rules of iẓāfat discussed here, قد آدم should be a noun, it is used as an adjective in Urdu:

قد آدم تصویر (a life-size painting [lit. a painting the height of a man])

*A. Combine the following nouns using iẓāfat and give the meaning of the resulting compound.*

۱۔ نقش (impression) پا (foot)

۲۔ وِصال (union) یار (beloved)

۳۔ آب (water) حیات (life)

۴۔ دیوان (collected poems) غالب (Ghalib)

۵۔ یوم (day) آزادی (freedom)

A special kind of noun-noun iẓāfat begins with a nominal Arabic phrase that functions similarly to an English prefix. In the following example, the initial phrase مابعد literally means "what (ما) [is] after (بعد)," but functions more like the English prefix "meta-."

مابعدِ (post-, meta-) طبیعیات (physics) مابعدِ طبیعیات (metaphysics)

*B. Combine the following nouns using iẓāfat and give the meaning of the resulting compound.*

۱۔ مابعدِ (post-, meta-) جدیدیت (modernity)

۳۔ مافوقِ (super-) فطرت (nature)

*C. Read the following idioms and use the word banks to translate them literally. Idiomatic translations have been given.*

۱۔ خوابِ خرگوش (a very deep or negligent slumber)

خواب (sleep, dream) خرگوش (rabbit)

۲۔پسر نوح (an arrogant or disobedient son)

پِسَر (son) نُوح (Noah)

۳۔ ہِمّتِ مرداں مددِ خدا (God helps the brave.)

ہِمَّت (courage; fortitude) مرداں (men) مدد (help) خدا (God)

*D. A final point to keep in mind is the iẓāfat, while borrowed from Persian, is not used exclusively with Perso-Arabic registers in Urdu. Read the following title of a popular Bollywood film song and translate it into English.*

دردِ ڈسکو

## 4.20.2 Noun-Adjective Iẓāfat

When iẓāfat connects an adjective and a noun, it does not have a translatable meaning, but rather serves simply as a means to join the words:

| | | | | | | | |
|---|---|---|---|---|---|---|---|
| (the great[est] mughal) | مغلِ اعظم | ← | (great[est]) | اعظم | (mughal) | مغل |
| (exalted sir) | جنابِ عالی | ← | (high, exalted) | عالی | (sir) | جناب |

*A. Combine the following nouns and adjectives using iẓāfat, then translate the resulting idioms literally into English.*

| | | | | | | | |
|---|---|---|---|---|---|---|---|
| (long) | دراز | (lifespan) | ۲۔ عمر | (noble) | شریف | (name) | ۱۔ اسم |
| (first) | اوّل | (day) | ۴۔ روز | (evil) | بد | (eye) | ۳۔ چشم |
| (naive) | نادان | (heart) | ۶۔ دل | (young) | جوان | (man) | ۵۔ مرد |

*B. Translate the following common Urdu idiom into English literally, then memorize it. The idiomatic meaning has been given for you.*

چشم بد دور (Away with the evil eye!)

| | | | | | |
|---|---|---|---|---|---|
| (far) | دور | (bad) | بد | (eye) | چشم |

## 4.20.3 Adjective-Noun Iẓāfat

In some cases, the first element in an iẓāfat construction is an adjective. In such cases, the resulting phrase is adjectival. The two most common are the words قابل (capable, worthy) and لائق (capable, worthy).

| | | | | | | |
|---|---|---|---|---|---|---|
| (praiseworthy) | قابلِ تعریف | ← | (praise) | تعریف | (worthy) | قابل |
| (commendable) | لائقِ تحسین | ← | (commendation) | تحسین | (worthy) | لائق |

Note that, in most if not all cases, the governed adjective carries an agentive sense. Some linguists and grammarians might prefer to categorize adjective-noun iẓāfat constructions under the noun-noun heading, since, strictly speaking, words like قابل may be treated as either adjectives or nouns. They may therefore be considered to be implicitly nominalized for the sake of the iẓāfat. What is important for our purposes is to recognize that iẓāfat constructions which begin with words like قابل and لائق that are generally considered to be adjectives regularly yield adjectival phrases.

A second point to note is that these constructions closely follow a similar pattern of iẓāfat constructions found in Arabic, which use the definite article ال. For example

| | | | | | |
|---|---|---|---|---|---|
| (blind) | فاقد البصر | (vision) | بصر | (lacking) | فاقد |

*A. Combine the following adjectives and nouns using iẓāfat, then translate the meaning of the resulting compound.*

| | | | | | | | |
|---|---|---|---|---|---|---|---|
| (credence, belief) | اعتبار | (worthy) | ۲۔ قابل | (objection) | اعتراض | (worthy) | ۱۔ قابل |
| (acceptance) | قبول | (unable) | ۴۔ ناقابل | (reliance) | اعتماد | (unworthy) | ۳۔ ناقابل |
| (attention) | توجہ | (worthy) | ۶۔ لائق | (affliction) | بلا | (captive) | ۵۔ گرفتار |

## 4.21 Persian Conjunctions

Another Persian grammatical element ubiquitous in Urdu is the conjunction و [o]. Although written separately from the words that it connects, و is always pronounced as if suffixed to the word that precedes it. Thus, آب و ہوا (climate; lit. water and air), is pronounced ābohavā (often transliterated as āb-o-havā).

In its basic sense, و is synonymous with the English "and." However, idiomatically, it is used to produce fixed idioms and phrases the whole sense of which is typically greater than the sum of their parts. In other words, whereas the Hind-Urdu اور [aur] simply adds one and one to make two, و adds one and one to make three.

| | | | | | | |
|---|---|---|---|---|---|---|
| (climate, atmosphere) | آب و ہوا | ← | (air) | ہوا | (water) | آب |
| (time) | ماہ و سال | ← | (year) | سال | (month) | ماہ |

*A. Practice reading and pronouncing the following phrases.*

| | | | |
|---|---|---|---|
| آمد و رفت | تر و تازہ | بند و بست | خواب و خیال |
| چون و چرا | جاہ وجلال | سر و سامان | دست و بازو |
| | سردی و گرمی | کم و بیش | سیر و تفریح |
| | دیدہ و دانستہ | خرید و فروخت | باغ و بہار |

*B. Conjoin the following words. Then estimate the meaning of the resulting compound.*

| | | | | | | | |
|---|---|---|---|---|---|---|---|
| (grandeur) | شوکت | (glory) | ۲۔ شان | (night) | شب | (day) | ۱۔ روز |
| (mind) | دماغ | (heart) | ۴۔ دل | (wailing) | زاری | (weeping) | ۳۔ گریہ |
| | | | | (sky) | سما | (earth) | ۵۔ ارض |

## Conjunctions and Verb Stems

The present and past stems of Persian verbs, quite often those of the same verb, are regularly conjoined to form compounds using و, the sense of which is often abstract. Read and consider the following stems and compounds.

(arrangement[s]) بند و بست ← (past stem) بست (pres. stem) بند ← (to close) بستن

(residence; lifestyle) بود و باش ← (present stem) باش (past stem) بود ← (to be) بودن

In some cases, the resulting word has a special spelling:

(conversation) گُفتگو ← گفت و گو ← (present) گو (past) گفت ← (to speak) گفتن

The stems of complementary verbs are also often paired to achieve a similar effect:

| | | | | | | |
|---|---|---|---|---|---|---|
| (conversation, discourse) | گفت و شنید | ← | (to listen/hear) | شنیدن | (to speak) | گفتن |
| (pathos; affect; anguish) | سوز و گداز | ← | (melting) | گُداختن | (burning) | سوختن |

*C. Conjoin the following words from identical or complementary verbs, then give their meanings. Hints are given in parentheses.*

| | | | | |
|---|---|---|---|---|
| | (going) | رفت | (coming) | ۱۔ آمد |
| (same pattern as گُفتگو) | (searcher) | جو | (searching) | ۲۔ جست |
| (adv.) | (known) | دانستہ | (seen) | ۳۔ دیدہ |
| | (safeguarding) | پرداخت | (holding) | ۴۔ داشت |
| | (selling) | فروخت | (buying) | ۵۔ خرید |

## 4.22 Persian Pronouns

### Personal Pronouns and Possession

Read the following list of Persian personal pronouns. Then read the list of Urdu phrases in which they are used.

| | | | |
|---|---|---|---|
| (we) | ما | (I) | من |
| (you) (formal) | شُما | (you) (informal) | تو |
| (they) | ایشان | (he, she, it) | او / وی or وے |
| (this / those) | این or ایں / اینہا | (that / those) | آن or آں / آنہا |

من و توئی (lit. "I and thou-ness"; idiom. a sense of difference or distinction; duality)

ما و من (lit. we and I; egotism, selfishness)

ما و شما (lit. we and you; everyone and anyone)

ہمہ شما (lit. all of you; everyone and anyone)

آں حضرت (lit. that gentleman; idiom. the Prophet of Islam)

علاوہ بریں (apart from this)

این و آن (this and that; everyone and everything, great and small)

ہمہ اوست (All is he.) (said of God)

جانِ من (lit. life of me; my dear, my beloved)

The last example illustrates the way in which Persian forms possessive constructions using pronouns. On this pattern, one can form possessives such as جانِ او (his life) and جانِ ما (our life).

*A. The following are sometimes used as headings in correspondence. Translate them literally into English on the pattern of جانِ من (my dear).*

۱۔ عزیز من ۲۔ جناب من ۳۔ برادر من

*B. The following idiom is used to express consent. Read it and translate it literally into English.*

۱۔ چشم ما روشن دل ما شاد

## Interrogative Pronouns

The interrogative pronouns are also frequently encountered in Urdu phrases.

(who) کہ (what) چہ (where) کجا (when) کَی / کے (why) چرا (how) چوں

Consider the following idioms:

چون و چرا / چوں چرا (how and why; disputing, questioning)

چوں کہ (because)

اگرچہ (although, even if)

تا کجا (to what extent?)

The locative interrogative کجا (where) is used in parallel clauses to indicate the incomparability of two things. (Compare with the Urdu --- کہاں --- کہاں.) For example:

کجا ذرہ کجا خورشید (lit. where the mote, where the sun?) (the high and the low can't be compared)

*C. Translate the idiom on the right literally into English. Then estimate its idiomatic meaning.*

۱۔ کجا شیرِ نر کجا بچۂ خر

## 4.23 Persian Verbs

The following chart reviews the conjugation of the Persian verb بودن in the present and past tenses. Recall its present باش and past بود stems.

**Present**

| | | | |
|---|---|---|---|
| (we are) | باشیم | (I am) | باشم |
| (you are) (pl.) (s. formal, polite) | باشید | (you are) (s.) (informal) | باشی |
| (they are) | باشند | (he/she/it is) | باشد / بُوَد |

**Past**

| | | | |
|---|---|---|---|
| (we were) | بودیم | (I was) | بودم |
| (you were) (pl.) (s. polite, formal) | بودید | (you were) (s.) (informal) | بودی |
| (they were) | بودند | (he/she/it was) | بُود |

This chart demonstrates two important facts about Persian verbs. First, they are conjugated by suffixing particles to the present and past verb stems. Second, the patterns of suffixation are nearly identical in the past and present tenses. The only difference is found in the third person singular (he/she/it). In the present tense, د [ad] or ید [yad] in case the stem ends in a vowel, is suffixed to the present stem, while, in the past, the past stem alone is used without a suffix. (The suffixes ی (ī) and ا (ā) are sometimes used, and may be encountered in classical contexts.)

The present tense in Persian may also be formed by prefixing می or مے to the verb.

| | | | |
|---|---|---|---|
| (we are) | می باشیم | (I am) | می باشم |
| (you are) (pl.) (s. polite, formal) | می باشید | (you are) (s.) (informal) | می باشی |
| (they are) | می باشند | (he/she/it is) | می باشد |

Study the following chart, which lists the suffixes used in the present and past tenses of Persian verbs. Pronunciations are in brackets and meanings are in parentheses.

| Plural | | | Singular | | | Present |
|---|---|---|---|---|---|---|
| (we are) | [-īm] | یم | (I am) | [-am] | م | 1st person |
| (you are) | [-īd] | ید | (you are) | [-ī] | ی | 2nd person |
| (they are) | [-and] | ند | (he/she/it is) | [-ad] | د | 3rd person |

| Plural | | | Singular | | | Past |
|---|---|---|---|---|---|---|
| (we were) | [-īm] | یم | (I was) | [-am] | م | 1st person |
| (you were) | [-īd] | ید | (you were) | [-ī] | ی | 2nd person |
| (they were) | [-and] | ند | (he/she/it was) | [past stem] | | 3rd person |

*A. Conjugate the following verbs in the simple present and simple past tenses. Use pronouns. The first verb has been conjugated into the first-person past and present tenses to guide you.*

| | | | | | | | |
|---|---|---|---|---|---|---|---|
| (to become) | ۴۔ شدن | (to say) | ۳۔ گفتن | (to do) | ۲۔ کردن | (to know) | ۱۔ دانستن |
| | | | | (I knew) | من دانستم | (I know) | ۱۔ من (می) دانم |

## The Stative Present (To Be)

The verb "to be" (بودن) is exceptional in Persian because it has two present-tense forms: the present stem (باش) (used for habitual, subjunctive, and sometimes stative senses) and the stative (I am, we are, etc.). One way to form the latter is with the following suffixes. With the exception of the third person, the suffixes used are the same as those used to conjugate the present tense. When the word to which they are suffixed ends in a vowel sound (e.g. ہ [ā]), they are sometimes spelled with a prefixed ا [a]. Study the following chart:

| Plural | | | Singular | | | Person |
|---|---|---|---|---|---|---|
| (we are) | [-īm] | یم | (I am) | [-am] | م | 1st person |
| (you are) | [-īd] | ید | (you are) | [-ī] | ی | 2nd person |
| (they are) | [-and] | ند | (he/she/it is) | [ast] | است | 3rd person |

Here is how the concept is applied using the adjectives خوب (well, fine) and خستہ (tired) in the present tense.

| Plural | | | Singular | | | Person |
|---|---|---|---|---|---|---|
| (We are well.) | [ḳhūbīm] | خوبیم | (I am well.) | [ḳhūbam] | خوبم | 1st |
| (You are well.) | [ḳhūbīd] | خوبید | (You are well.) | [ḳhūbī] | خوبی | 2nd |
| (They are well.) | [ḳhūband] | خوبند | (He/she/it is well.) | [ḳhūb ast] | خوب است | 3rd |
| (We are tired.) | [ḳhasta-īm] | خستہ ایم | (I am tired.) | [ḳhasta-am] | خستہ ام | 1st |
| (You are tired.) | [ḳhasta-īd] | خستہ اید | (You are tired.) | [ḳhasta-ī] | خستہ ای | 2nd |
| (They are tired.) | [ḳhasta-and] | خستہ اند | (He/she/it is tired.) | [ḳhasta ast] | خستہ است | 3rd |

Incidentally, the past participle in combination with the stative suffix is how the present perfect tense is formed in Persian. Verbs in this conjugation can therefore be translated using "to have" or "to be" depending on the meaning of the main verb. For example, خستہ might be translated as "I have become tired," and so on. Likewise, من آمدہ ام (I have come) and so on. The past perfective (English "I had," etc.) is formed by replacing the stative suffix with the past form of بودن. For example, من خستہ بودم (I had become tired), من آمدہ بودم (I had come), تو آمدہ بودی (you had come), and so on.

*B. Form present-tense stative (I am …, etc.) or perfective (I have …, etc.) of the following for all pronouns and give their meanings.*

| | | | | | | | |
|---|---|---|---|---|---|---|---|
| (seen) | ۴۔ دیدہ | (gone) | ۳۔ رفتہ | (intoxicated) | ۲۔ مست | (happy) | ۱۔ شاد |

A final way to form the stative present is with the verb ہستن (to exist).

| | | Plural | | | Singular |
|---|---|---|---|---|---|
| (We are/exist.) | [mā hastīm] | ما ہستیم | (I am/exist.) | [man hastam] | من ہستم |
| (You are/exist.) | [shumā hastīd] | شما ہستید | (You are/exist.) | [to hastī] | تو ہستی |
| (They are/exist.) | [īshān hastand] | ایشان ہستند | (He/she is/exists.) | [ū hast] | او ہست |

Note that Persian has four ways to express the sense "he/she/it is," all of which are regularly encountered in Urdu phrases borrowed from Persian:

است　　ہست　　بُوَد　　(می) باشد

In general, باشد and بُوَد are habitual, ہست is existential, and است is stative. Consider the following:

| | | |
|---|---|---|
| | (He/she is [generally] [or may be] fine.) | او خوب باشد |
| | (He/she is [generally] fine.) | او خوب می باشد |
| (literary or archaic) | (He/she is [generally] fine.) | او خوب بُوَد |
| (He/she is indeed fine.) | (Used for emphasis or to refute doubt.) | او خوب ہست |
| | (He/she is fine.) | او خوب است |

If the elements of Persian verbs, pronouns, and personal suffixes sound and look familiar, it is because they are cognate with those in other Indo-European languages, including English. Compare the following cognates:

| Persian | English |
|---|---|
| است | is |
| ام | am |
| ات | art |

*C. Form sentences using ہستن (to exist) with the following words and give their meanings.*

| | | | |
|---|---|---|---|
| (student) | ۲۔ طالب علم | (human being) | ۱۔ انسان |

## Negation

All tenses can be negated with ن.

| | |
|---|---|
| نمی روم | (I do not go. / I am not going.) |
| نروم | (I do not go. / I am not going/ may not go.) |
| نرفتم | (I did not go.) |
| نمی رفتم | (I did not used to go. / I was not going. / I would not have gone.) |
| نرفتہ ام | (I have not gone.) |
| نرفتہ بودم | (I had not gone.) |
| نرفتہ باشم | (I may not have gone.) |
| نخواہم رفت | (I will not go.) |

The stative present is typically negated with the same suffixes affixed to نیست [nīst]:

| | | | | |
|---|---|---|---|---|
| 1st person | نیستم | (I am not.) | نیستیم | (We are not.) |
| 2nd person | نیستی | (You are not.) | نیستید | (You are not.) |
| 3rd person | نیست | (He/she/it is not.) | نیستند | (They are not.) |

The stative past is negated using بودن (to be). For example, من استاد نبودم (I was not a/the master/ professor.) and so on.

*D. Form present-tense and past-tense negative stative sentences (I am not, you are not; I was not, you were not, and so on) for all pronouns using the following words.*

| | | | |
|---|---|---|---|
| ا۔ طالب علم | (student) | ا۔ خوش | (happy) |

## The Imperative and the Subjunctive

The imperative for تو is simply the present stem. The imperative for شما is the stem plus the suffix ید [īd].

| | | | |
|---|---|---|---|
| باش | (Be!) (s.) (informal) | باشید | (Be!) (pl.) (s. formal, polite) |

The imperative is often formed by prefixing ب to the present stem.

| | | | |
|---|---|---|---|
| برو | (Go!) (s.) (informal) | بروید | (Go!) (pl.) (formal, polite) |
| بیا | (Come!) (s.) (informal) | بیائید | (Come!) (pl.) (formal, polite) |

The following Urdu idioms are built on the imperative of the verb بودن (to be). The last of this group is an interesting word. It is built of two words, شاد (happy) (truncated to شا) and باش (be!).

| | | | |
|---|---|---|---|
| (lit. "be ready"; idiom. an attendant) | حاضر باش | (Go away!) | دور باش |
| (Bravo!) | شاباش | (Attention!) | ہوشیار باش |

The subjunctive can be indicated by prefixing ب.

| | | | | |
|---|---|---|---|---|
| (We may go.) | برویم | (I may go.) | بروم | 1st person |
| (You may go.) | بروید | (You may go.) | بروی | 2nd person |
| (They may go.) | بروند | (He/she/it may go.) | برود | 3rd person |

For example, read the following sentence, which ends in the subjunctive.

(It is better that he go.) بہتر است کہ برود

Perfective subjunctives are formed by combining past participles with the present tense of بودن (stem باش). Note that ب is never prefixed to باش in the subjunctive.

| | | | | |
|---|---|---|---|---|
| (We may have.) | داشتہ باشیم | (I may have.) | داشتہ باشم | 1st person |
| (You may have.) | داشتہ باشید | (You may have.) | داشتہ باشی | 2nd person |
| (They may have.) | داشتہ باشند | (He/she/it may have.) | داشتہ باشد | 3rd person |

*E. Form imperatives for* تو *and* شما *using the following verbs.*

| | | | |
|---|---|---|---|
| (to go) | ۲۔ رفتن | (to know) | ۱۔ دانستن |

*F. Complete the following sentence with the subjunctive for all six pronouns using the following verbs. The first has been done for you.*

(to go) ۱۔ رفتن ممکن است کہ

(It is possible that I may go.) ۱۔ ممکن است کہ بروم

## Persian Idioms

Read the following Persian saying, which is commonly used in literary registers of Urdu in response to praise. It is taken from the *Gulistān*.

(I am that which I know [myself to be].) من آنم کہ من دانم

The saying conveys the idea that the speaker is intimately aware of his own faults or limitations. That is, "I know what I am. (Your praise is too kind.)" Having studied the sections above, you can easily parse the Persian:

| I know | I | which | am that | I |
|---|---|---|---|---|
| دانم | من | کہ | آنم | من |

Everyday Urdu idioms can also be built from conjugated Persian verbs. The following idiom is particularly delightful:

(chit-chat) چہ میگوئیاں

You can now analyze this idiom:

| اں | ئی | گو | می | چہ |
|---|---|---|---|---|
| (Urdu pl.) | (2nd person present) | (present stem) | (present enclitic) | (what) |

Thus, the literal meaning of this word is "what-do-you-say-s." Urdu has treated the entire Persian phrase چہ می گوئی (what do you say?) as a marked feminine noun and pluralized it with اں [āñ].

*G. Translate the following idioms literally into English. Then choose the most appropriate idiomatic meaning. Use the word bank to assist you.*

| | | | |
|---|---|---|---|
| (you barely made it) | (welcome) | ____________ | ا۔ خوش آمدید |
| (no reply) | (I'm speechless) | ____________ | ۲۔ جواب ندارد |
| (perfect) | (perhaps) | ____________ | ۳۔ شاید |
| (forsakenness) | (sush!) | ____________ | ۴۔ کس مپرسی |

| | | | | | | | |
|---|---|---|---|---|---|---|---|
| (to have) | داشتن | (reponse) | جواب | (to come) | آمدن | (happy) | خوش |
| | | (to ask) | پرسیدن | (someone) | کس | (to suit; to be right) | شایستن |

*H. The following idioms are often used in Urdu. Translate them literally into English. Then choose the most appropriate idiomatic translation.*

ا۔ دیر آید درست آید

All's well that ends well.

At last!

That which is long come is well come.

۲۔ یک نشُد دو شُد

One good turn deserves another.

One and one make two.

Things just went from bad to worse.

۳۔ نقل کُفر کُفر نباشد

Heresy is unforgivable.

Heresy lies in copying the words of others.

There's no heresy in repeating heresy.

۴۔ نمی دانم چہ منزل بود شب جائے کہ من بودم

I don't know where I was last night.

I don't know where to go at night.

I don't know where you were last night.

۵۔ سگ باش برادر خرد مباش

Be a dog, but don't be a younger brother.

You are the younger brother of a dog.

You are a dog without a younger brother.

## 4.24 Persian Prepositions

Urdu regularly uses Persian prepositions in fixed idioms and as independent words.

| | | | |
|---|---|---|---|
| از | (from, by) | بہ / ب | (with, to, by, in) |
| با | (with) | بے | (without) |
| در | (in) | بر | (on) |
| تا | (up to) | | |

Read the following common idioms in which Persian prepositions are used:

| | | | |
|---|---|---|---|
| کم از کم | (at very least) | بہر حال | (in any case [lit. in every circumstance]) |
| با محاورہ | (idiomatic [lit. with idiom]) | بے فائدہ | (pointless; profitless) |
| در حقیقت | (in reality; in fact) | برباد | (destroyed; lit. "on the wind") |
| سرتاپا | (completely; from head to foot) | | |

Some Persian prepositions are compounds:

| | | | |
|---|---|---|---|
| (middle; between, among) | درمیان | (instead of; lit. in place of) | بجائے |
| (by means of) | بذریعہ | (contrary to) | برخلاف |

Compound prepositions are often written in Persian iẓāfat constructions:

| | | | |
|---|---|---|---|
| (itself; lit. in its own place) | بجائے خود | (by [means of] train) | بذریعہ ٹرین |

## Persian Postpositions and Circumposition

Persian also uses postpositions, though their number is small. Here follow the two commonest used with خُدا (God).

| | | | | | | |
|---|---|---|---|---|---|---|
| (For God's sake!) | خدا را | ← | (to, for) | را | (God) | خدا |
| (O God!) | خدایا | ← | (vocative) | یا | (God) | خدا |

Classical Persian also uses circumposition, which is when both a postposition and a preposition are used at the same time to modify a noun. For example, the object of را is sometimes preceded by a preposition, مر.

(For God's sake!) مر خدا را

Persian prepositions can also be converted into postpositions by circumposition. A typical case sees the preposition ب or بہ used before the noun and the preposition shifted after it. Compare the following.

| Classical circumposition | | Standard Persian | |
|---|---|---|---|
| (in the sea) | بہ دریا در | (in the sea) | در دریا |

*A. Read the following Persian idioms and their English translations. Underline the Persian preposition and give the meaning of the prepositional phrase.*

| | |
|---|---|
| (a corpse in the hand of the living) | ۱۔ مُردہ بدستِ زندہ |
| (alive in the grave) | ۲۔ زندہ در گور |
| (a punch after the battle) | ۳۔ مشت بعد از جنگ |
| (an impression on water; said of something that is fleeting) | ۴۔ نقش بر آب |
| (hand at work, heart with the beloved; neglecting the task at hand) | ۵۔ دست بہ کار و دل بہ یار |

## 4.25 The Possessive Enclitic

Read the following enclitic suffixes, which are used to express possession. They are suffixed to the word کتاب (book) for the sake of example.

| | | | | | |
|---|---|---|---|---|---|
| [-imān] | مان | ما | [-am] | م | من |
| [-itān] | تان | شما | [-at] | ت | تو |
| [-ishān] | شان | ایشان | [-ash] | ش | او |

| | | | |
|---|---|---|---|
| (our book) | کتابمان | (my book) | کتابم |
| (your book) (pl.) (s. formal, polite) | کتابتان | (your book) (s. informal) | کتابت |
| (their book) | کتابشان | (his/her/its book) | کتابش |

*A. Use the chart above to form possessives of the following nouns for all pronouns (I, we, you [s.], you [pl.], he/she/it, and they). Be sure to give their meanings.*

۱۔ استاد　　۲۔ دوست　　۳۔ نام

## 4.26 More Persian Syntax in Urdu

In many ways, Persian syntax closely resembles Urdu. Standard word order is subject-object-verb. Verb declension specifies number, person, and tense. Unlike Urdu (but like English), Persian typically uses prepositions and lacks grammatical gender.

### The Postposition را [rā]

The postpositional enclitic را [rā] always follows the noun it modifies and can be translated as for, to, or of, depending on context.

| | |
|---|---|
| (For God's sake!) | خدارا |
| (for what; why) | چرا |

The pronouns take a special form when modified by را:

| | | | |
|---|---|---|---|
| (for/to/of us) | مارا | (for/to/of me) | مرا |
| (for/to/of you) (pl.) | شما را | (for/to/of you) (s.) | ترا |
| (for/to/of them) | ایشان را | (for/to/of him/her/it) | اورا / ورا / وے را |

Consider the following line by Sa'dī:

Neither the dignity **of** the small remains nor that **of** the great.　　نہ کہ را منزلت ماند نہ مہ را

### The Indefinite Suffix ی [ī] or ے [e]

Another feature of Persian syntax ubiquitous in Urdu idioms borrowed from Persian is the indefinite suffix spelled and pronounced either ی [ī] or ے [e]. When suffixed to ہ , it is sometimes spelled as a hamza ء above the ہ (just like iẓāfa). It indicates indefiniteness (compare with the English indefinite article "a").

ده درویش در گلیمے نخسبند ودو بادشاہ در اقلیمے نگنجند

Ten dervishes may fit in a blanket, but two emperors won't fit in a (single) clime.

چو کاری بے فضول من بر آید　　　مرا در وی سخن گفتن نشاید

When a task has been done without my involvement,
It isn't proper for me to speak a word about it.

*A. Translate the following aphorisms literally into English. Use the word banks for each to help you.*

۱۔ چراغ مفلساں نورے ندارد

| | | | |
|---|---|---|---|
| چراغ | (lamp) | مفلس | (poor person) |
| نور | (light) | داشتن | (to have) |

۲۔ چو از قومے یکے بے دانشی کرد
نہ کہ را منزلت ماند نہ مہ را

| | | | |
|---|---|---|---|
| چو | (when) | از | (from) |
| قوم | (community) | یک | (one) |
| بے دانشی | (lack of wisdom) | کردن | (to do) |

## 4.27 Persian in Urdu vs Modern Standard Persian

Persian idioms in Urdu are often written and pronounced in ways that may surprise readers who are familiar with modern Persian. We have already encountered the prefix بے [be], which is typically written and pronounced in modern Persian as بی [bī]. Similar differences are found in other aspects of Persian grammar as used in Urdu. For example, the Persian indefinite or relative suffix ی—e.g. کتابی (a book; the book that …)—is often written and pronounced as ے [e]. Likewise, the interrogative کی [kai] (when) is often written as کے.

Similarly, the second-person verbal suffixe ی which in modern standard Persian is pronounced as ī (e.g. باشی بودی) is sometimes written and pronounced as ے [e] in Urdu:

| | |
|---|---|
| باشے | [bāshe] |
| بودے | [būde] |

Another difference between modern Persian and Urdu orthography concerns the spelling and pronunciation of iẓāfat. Compare the following:

| | Modern Persian |
|---|---|
| [ba-rūye kār] | بروِی کار |
| | Classical Persian/Urdu |
| [ba-rū-e kār] | بروئے کار |

**Persian Archaims and Poetic Language**

A large number of Urdu idioms, maxims and aphorisms are borrowed from Persian poetry. In order to overcome the strictures of meter, poets employ contractions of common phrases. These are unique to verse, but, thankfully, they are quite intuitive.

| | | | | |
|---|---|---|---|---|
| | کاں | ← | (… that that/those) | کہ آں |
| | کیں | ← | (… that this/these) | کہ ایں |
| [zi] | ز | ← | (from) | از |

The ا in است is often dropped:

| | |
|---|---|
| (Everything that comes from friends is good.) | ہرچہ از دوست رسد نیکوست |

Another feature of classical Persian verse is the portability of possessive suffixes and their use as object markers. This can sometimes be confusing to new students. Consider the following common Urdu idiom.

خاکم بدہن

Said when uttering something negative or impudent, the literal meaning appears to be "my dust in mouth." However, the possessive م has been shifted from its logical position in دہنم (my mouth), thus yielding "dust in my mouth."

*A. Read the following couplet by Sadi, underline any shortened elements, and write them out completely.*

اے مرغ سحر عشق ز پروانہ بیاموز

کاں سوختہ را جاں شد و آواز نیامد

O bird of the morning, learn love from the moth,

For that burnt one lost his life and not a sound emerged.

## 4.28 Persian Proverbs and Aphorisms in Urdu

You now have all the tools you need to appreciate the range of Persian language and idioms used in Urdu, from everyday phrases to quotations from classical Persian literature. The following exercises review the Persian grammar and word-building surveyed in this unit.

*A. Translate the following idioms literally into English. Use the word banks to help you. An idiomatic explanation is given in parentheses to facilitate comprehension of their sense. These idioms are quite common in Urdu. One reads them in books, uses them in conversation across a range of contexts, and hears them in Bollywood films.*

۱۔ ہنوز دہلی دور است (The goal remains far ahead.)

| | | | |
|---|---|---|---|
| ہنوز | (still) | دہلی | (Delhi) |
| دور | (far) | | |

۲۔ گربہ کشتن روز اول (Assert authority from the outset.)

| | | | |
|---|---|---|---|
| گربہ | (cat) | کشتن | (kill) |
| روز | (day) | اول | (one) |

۳۔ از ماست کہ بر ماست (We are responsible for our own state.)

| | | | |
|---|---|---|---|
| ما | (we) | کہ | (that, which) (conjunction) |

۴۔ کوہ کندن و کاہ بر آوردن (Said to describe a massive undertaking with little pay-off.)

| | | | |
|---|---|---|---|
| کوہ | (mountain) | کندن | (to dig) |
| کاہ | (straw) | بر آوردن | (produce) |

۵۔ محتسب را درون خانہ چہ کار (Said to indicate that a person has no right to interfere.)

| | | | |
|---|---|---|---|
| محتسب | (policeman) | درون | (inside) |
| خانہ | (house) | کار | (task, business) |

۶۔ ہر فرعونے را موسیٰ (Someone eventually comes to destroy even the most powerful.)

| | | | |
|---|---|---|---|
| فرعون | (Pharoah) | موسیٰ | (Moses) |

۷۔ اے وقت تو خوش کہ وقت ما خوش کردی (Used to express gratitude for good news. Often written in letters.)

۸۔ پدرم سلطان بود (Said, typically sarcastically, in response to boasting about ancestors.)

| | | | |
|---|---|---|---|
| پدر | (father) | سلطان | (sultan) |

۹۔ جمال ہمنشیں در من اثر کرد (Said in response to praise or criticism.)

| | | | |
|---|---|---|---|
| جمال | (beauty) | ہمنشیں | (companion; lit. fellow sitter) |

۱۰۔ آمدم بر سر مطلب (Said when turning to the main point of a discussion.)

سر (top, edge) مطلب (point, purpose)

۱۱۔ شنیدہ کے بود مانند دیدہ (Said to emphasize the importance of witnessing things first-hand.)

شنیدن (to hear) کے (when)
مانند (like) دیدن (to see)

۱۲۔ مترس از بلائے کہ شب درمیان است (Used to tell others not to worry, since things may change.)

ترسیدن (to fear) بلا (affliction)
شب (night) درمیان (between)

۱۲۔ ہر کمالے را زوالے ہر بہارے را خزاں (All good things come to an end.)

کمال (perfection) زوال (decline)
بہار (springtime) خزاں (autumn)

## 4.29 Suggestions for Further Study

Students of literary Urdu are unlikely to have trouble finding texts rich in Persian and Persianate vocabulary. The following texts are specifically suggested because they not only include Persian words, but Persian phrases and passages as well. Aḥmad Ḥusain Amjad, *Rubāʿiyāt-e Amjad* (Hyderabad, 1968); Mīr Anīs, *Marāsī-e Anīs* (Badayun: Nizami Press, 1921) (various editions); Muḥammad Ḥusain Āzād, *Āb-e Ḥayāt* (Lahore: Victoria Press, 1880) (various editions); Alṭāf Ḥusain Ḥālī, *Dīvān-e Ḥālī maʿ-e Muqaddamah-e Shiʿr o Shāʿirī* (Kanpur: Nāmī Press, 1892); Mīr Ḥasan, *Siḥr ul-Bayān* (Lahore, 1966) (various editions); Shiblī Nuʿmānī, *Shiʿr ul-ʿAjam*, 5 vols (1909–21).

# UNIT 5

# THE SANSKRIT-PRAKRIT ELEMENT

Urdu and Sanskrit are members of the Indo-European language family and have long, interconnected histories of geographical, cultural, and linguistic interaction. Urdu borrows a great deal of Sanskritic vocabulary through Prakrit. It also borrows some words from Sanskrit directly. And many Urdu and Sanskrit words share Proto-Indo-European etymons. This unit surveys some of the most common linguistic elements that link Urdu and Sanskrit (and Prakrit). The division of Urdu and Hindi in terms of Perso-Arabic and Sanskritic vocabulary has often obscured the importance of Sanskrit and Prakrit as a source of vocabulary in Urdu. But the fact remains that Urdu includes a massive amount of Sanskrit vocabulary, both through its own traditions and through borrowings from Sanskritized Hindi. From news and television programs in India and Pakistan to classical poetry and Bollywood lyrics, Sanskrit and Sanskritic words make up a substantial proportion of Urdu vocabulary.

Grammarians typically divide Sanskritic vocabulary in Urdu into two categories: تتسم [tatsam(a)] and تدبھو [tadbhav(a)]. Tatsam indicates Sanskrit vocabulary whose form in Urdu is the same as in Sanskrit. This may be because Urdu borrowed the words directly from Sanskrit. It may also be because the form of the words did not change despite the process of borrowing and loaning that led them to Urdu. Many words that travel indirectly from Sanskrit to Urdu, usually through Prakrit, show only slight changes. The only difference between the tatsam and tadbhav may be the pronunciation of a single letter. Such words are sometimes called semi-tatsam; for example, the tatsam ولاس [*vilās*] and semi-tatsam بلاس [*bilās*]. By contrast, tadbhav refers to vocabulary related to Sanskrit, but whose form has changed significantly, usually through long histories of borrowing, loaning, interaction, and linguistic change. The relationship between tatsam and tadbhav vocabulary is not always immediately obvious; for example, that between the tatsam کرم [karm] (action, deed) and its tadbhav relative کام [kām] (work). However, the differences between tatsam and tadbhav words are largely determined by predictable patterns. Familiarity with these patterns allows us to recognize the relationship between tadbhav and tatsam words and enrich our understanding of the meaning and history of Urdu words.

From Sanskrit's perspective, the relationship between tatsam and tadbhav vocabulary is characterized as the relationship of change from the former to the latter. This attitude is enshrined in the terms themselves. "Tatsam" means "that" (tat) "same" (sam), that is, "the same as it is (in Sanskrit)." "Tadbhav" means "that" (tad) "arising from" (bhav), that is, words that are derived or evolved from Sanskrit. This is a productive and useful model for thinking about the relationship between tatsam and tadbhav vocabulary. But it has also mislead scholars to think that all tadbhav vocabulary is derived from Sanskrit or reflects corrupt forms of it. The truth is much more complicated. Sanskrit, the literal meaning of which is "make (kṛ) together (saṃ)" or "composed," is a formalized language based on spoken forms of Proto-Indo-European languages. Tadbhav words typically come through the Prakrits, which were vernacular, spoken languages that were likewise derived from Proto-Indo-European, existed alongside Sanskrit, and formed the basis of what we recognize as Indic vernacular languages such as Hindi and Urdu today. The differences that we find between tatsam and tadbhav vocabulary are thus not necessarily linear changes to an original Sanskrit loanword as it passed through Prakrit into Urdu. This unit will use the words "variation," "difference," and "change" to refer to the relationships between Sanskritic tatsam and Prakritic tadbhav vocabulary, but it is important to remember that the differences themselves reflect a complicated history of linguistic evolution and interaction that none of these words accurately captures.

Although Urdu uses a much greater number of tadbhav words than tatsam ones, familiarity with both is essential for Urdu learners. Tatsam vocabulary is found in a wide range of literary and cultural contexts and registers. Urdu users encounter it in personal names, the technical terminology of Indic philosophy and Hindu religious traditions, political language in postcolonial India, Indian television, Bollywood films, and some forms of Urdu poetry. By studying tatsam word-building and tadbhav sound change, Urdu students will learn to recognize the underlying structures of words and to appreciate nuances in their meanings. They will also find it easier to remember them. Another advantage of studying tatsam and tadbhav patterns in Urdu is that it leads to easier recognition of Sanskritic-Prakritic vocabulary in other Indic languages that are closedly tied to Urdu culture, such as Avadhi, Braj Bhasha, Gujarati, Panjabi, and Sindhi, to name just a few. Since the unit on "The Hindi Element" has already surveyed a great deal of tadbhav vocabulary, readers are encouraged to review that unit before and after studying the lessons in this one.

The following couplet exemplifies the centuries-long use of Sanskritic tatsam and tadbhav words alongside Hindi-Urdu and Perso-Arabic vocabulary in Urdu. It is the first couplet in the *Dīvān* (compiled poems) of Qulī Quṭb Shāh (1566–1613). The *Dīvān* is generally recognized today as the first to be compiled in Urdu.

چندر سور تیرے نور تھے نس دن کوں نورانی کیا (By your light, the sun and moon have illuminated night and day.)

تیری صفت کن کر سکے توں آپی میرا ہے جیا (Who can describe you? You alone are my life.)

This poem, typically read as a حمد (a poem written in praise of God), combines the tatsam words سوُر (sun) and دن (day), the semi-tatsam or tadbhav words چندَر (moon) and نس (night) and جیا (life, soul), Hindi-Urdu tadbhav vocabulary such as تھے (cf. سے) (from) and تیرا (your), and Perso-Arabic vocabulary such as صفت (attribute; description; praise) and نورانی (illuminated).

## Sanskrit Words in Everyday Urdu

For mostly political reasons, Hindi and Urdu identies have largely been tied to vocabulary and their relationships to classical literary traditions: Sanskrit for Hindi; Perso-Arabic for Urdu. Efforts to avoid one register of vocabulary or the other have never succeeded, but attitudes about linguistic purity and derivation that were formed in the colonial period have largely become conventional wisdom in the postcolonial one. It is common to read and hear ideas such as that the Arabic word حرف (letter) is an Urdu word whereas the Sanskrit اکشر (letter) is not. The rationale that underlies this claim is that حرف is a Perso-Arabic word (and therefore Urdu) and اکشر is a Sanskrit word (and therefore Hindi). This rationale has led to the exclusion of certain forms of literary and linguistic education in Urdu, much to the detriment of students. Here follow two everyday Urdu idioms that include Sanskrit borrowings, including اکشر. The Sanskrit borrowings and their English parallels are in bold.

| | |
|---|---|
| (A black **letter** is equal to a water buffalo.)<br>(A reference to illiteracy and foolishness. Often used sarcastically.) | کالا **اکشر** بھینس برابر |
| (lit. "**body** turnaround")<br>(An about-face or complete change.) | **کایا** پلٹ |

Neither idiom survives if the Perso-Arabic equivalent of the Sanskrit is substituted.

## Note on the Urdu Pronunciation and English Spelling of Sanskrit words

This unit will present Sanskrit spellings and transliterations in accordance with standard Urdu pronunciation. Transliterations do not add the typical "a" at the end of Sanskrit words, since Urdu speakers do not pronounce this letter except in special contexts (such as the recitation of Sanskrit texts). Thus, in this section, رام will be transliterated as Rām (not Rāma), راگ as rāg not rāga, and so on.

The reason why the standard English transliteration of Sanskrit includes the short "a" vowel ending is that the vowel plays an important role in the rules that govern the combination of words and particles in Sanskrit. We shall study these rules, called *sandhi*, in some detail. For our purposes, what is important to keep in mind is that most words pronounced without a vowel ending in Urdu (such as راگ and رام), for the purpose of *sandhi*, end in the short vowel (a) in Sanskrit (hence rāga, Rāma), which represents the stem form of the noun.

The Urdu script does not distinguish among many of the phonemes that are distinguishable in the Nagari script (the most widely used script for Sanskrit). Similarly, in everday speech, most Hindi-Urdu speakers (except in special circumstances) do not pronounce several sounds that are represented in Nagari letters (e.g. the retroflex or palatal sh ष and n ण).

For this reason, the name कृष्ण, although spelled with two retroflex consonants, is typically pronounced without the retroflexes as کرشن [krishn], though Urdu speakers have also long pronounced this word as کِشَن [kishan] or کسن [kisan], and so on. This is because the vocalic *ṛ* in Sanskrit is lost in the Prakrits, from which many classical Urdu forms of Sanskritic vocabulary are derived.

## 5.1 Connections and Cognates

In order to recognize the connections among tadbhav and tatsam vocabulary, one must develop familiarity with some of the most common predictable patterns of sound change or variation between them. For example, the most commonly used verb in Urdu, ہونا (to be), and its many relatives share a Proto-Indo-European etymon with the Sanskrit word بھو (being) and demonstrates the regular change whereby an aspirated consonant Sanskrit is dropped and only the aspiration itself, *h*, remains in Urdu. This and other patterns of change provide us with a point of comparison from which to recognize other words similarly related to the Sanskrit (and therefore to the Urdu word). Most Sanskritic words in Urdu are not borrowings, but cognates whose relationship to Sanskrit is typically indirect and often difficult to recognize without studying these patterns.

The following chart introduces students to the Sanskrit relatives of four of the most commonly used words in Urdu:

| Other Urdu Cognates | | Sanskrit | | Urdu |
|---|---|---|---|---|
| کرنا | [kṛi] (to do) | کرِ | | کا |
| منجھلا | [madhya] (middle) | مدھیہ | (in) | میں |
| | [apar] (later, further) | اپر | | اور |
| یاترا | [yā] (to go) | یا | | جانا |

The following chart surveys some of the most commonly used Urdu verbs and their Sanskrit relatives. It demonstrates some of the phonemic differences between Sanskrit and Urdu words borrowed from Prakrit. For example, ی [y] and ج; ش and کھ; and ش and س. It also demonstrates how productive a knowledge of Sanskrit can be for students interested in studying the relationships among Urdu words.

| Other Urdu Cognates | Sanskrit Root | Urdu |
|---|---|---|
| بھاو / بھون / بود | بھو | ہونا |
| کار / کام / کرم (karma) | کرِ | کرنا |
| برات / یاترا or انجام / جگت / گنگا / گنوانا / ہنگام / ہنگامہ / گُم / گاڑی | یا or گم | جانا، گیا |

| | | |
|---|---|---|
| دینا | دا | بادل / داد / دائی / دَیا / دان |
| رہنا | رہ or رکش | رہا / راز |
| کہنا | کتھ | کتھا / کتھک |
| لینا | لبھ | لادنا / لابھ |
| دیکھنا | درِش | درشٹی / درشن |
| چلنا | چل | چالاک |
| رکھنا | رکش | انگرکھا / راکھی / رکشا بندھن |
| لگنا | لگ | لاگ / بلکنا / سلگنا |
| جاننا | جنا | اجنبی / اچانک / پہچان / سیانا / شناخت / گیان / ناپنا |
| سننا | شرُ | سرود / سروش / شرتی / شنید |

A large number of Urdu verbs are related to Sanskrit compounds in which the root کری / کر (to do) is suffixed to another root. In Urdu, the result is a verb whose stem ends in ک or گ and sometimes ر or ڑ. The number of such verbs is enormous and has parallels in Sanskrit, in which nouns are compounded with kṛi to form compound verbs. The following list lists some of them, but is far from exhaustive. Look up five words in Platts' dictionary and learn something about their roots.

اُبکنا اٹکنا اُکتنا اُکتارنا بوکنا پھٹکنا پھاکارنا تھپکنا ٹیکنا جھپکنا جھلکنا

جھوکنا چُٹکنا چگنا چمکنا چھِڑکنا چھلکنا چھینکنا روکنا سرکنا سکڑنا سینکنا کرنا

کڑکنا کھٹکنا کھِسکنا کھنکنا لپکنا مسکرانا ہانکنا ہگنا

The following examples demonstrate how these verbs are formed. Remember that the Sanskrit compounds are not borrowed into Urdu. Instead, they are distant relatives, so to speak, of the Urdu words. Note the different consonants between Urdu and Sanskrit.

| Sanskrit | | | | Urdu | | |
|---|---|---|---|---|---|---|
| اُد | (up, out) | وم | (to vomit) | کر ← | ابکنا | (to vomit) |
| جھمپ | (leaping) | کر | | ← | جھپکنا | (to wave; to close the eyes; to pounce upon) |
| سپرِش | (touching) | کر | | ← | چھڑکنا | (to sprinkle, scatter) |
| سوِد | (being hot) | کر | | ← | سینکنا | (to toast, to warm) |
| ہد | (to defecate) | کر | | ← | ہگنا | (to defecate) |

Consider the following set of words. The relationships among them may not be immediately obvious, but awareness of their etymological connection to the Sanskrit سْتوک स्तोक [stok(a)], meaning very small, little, and the various regular patterns of difference that obtain between Sanskrit words and their Urdu relatives makes the connection clear.

(a bit) تھوڑا (a small piece) ٹکڑی (a piece) ٹکڑا (a little) ٹک

The following section, adapted mostly from Beams, will review some of the most important differences in spelling and pronunciation between Sanskrit tatsam words and Sanskritic tadbhav (or semi-tatsam) vocabulary. By developing familiarity with the predictable patterns of change between Sanskrit and Urdu, we will quickly learn to recognize relationships that might otherwise not be obvious; for example, the connection between the Sanskrit-tatsam مارگ (path, road) and the Sanskritic-tadbhav مانگ (a part in the hair), both of which are used in Urdu. In the following sections, words will be categorized as Sanskrit or Urdu, rather than Sanskrit-tatsam and Prakrit-tadbhav for the sake of ease. But remember that many of the words listed as Sanskrit, such as مارگ (path, road), have been borrowed into Urdu and are therefore Urdu words, too.

## 5.2 Patterns of Difference and Change

### 5.2.1 Vowel Quality

Among the most basic and outstanding differences between Prakritic-tadbhav and Sanskritic-tatsam cognates is the quality vowels. Vowel differences can broadly be grouped into three categories: change of one into another; addition or elision; and lengthening or shorting. This section will survey some of the most common changes. You will note that many of these changes are accompanied by changes to consonants, too. We will survey those changes in the next section. Remember, "Sanskrit" and "Urdu" are used here for the sake of ease and clarity. Many of the words listed under "Sanskrit" have been borrowed into Urdu and are therefore Urdu words, too.

One common difference is for the vowel of the second syllable in the Sanskrit-tatsam word to affect the quality of the vowel in the first syllable of the Prakritic-Urdu-tadbhav word. The nature of the vowel change is determined by a set of rules which Sanskritists call guṇa. We will pass over those rules for now.

| Urdu | | Sanskrit |
|---|---|---|
| اُنگُلی | (finger) | اَنگُلی |
| رُت | (season, time) | رِتُ |
| پیڑ | (tree) | پَیڑی |

Note that in the first two cases, the vowel in the second syllable has been displaced to the first. Here are the same words in Roman script.

| Urdu | Sanskrit |
|---|---|
| **u**nglī | ang**u**lī |
| r**u**t | rit**u** |
| p**e**ṛ | patr**ī** |

In the third example, the displaced vowel has in fact followed a rule for vowel combination (which we will study later), whereby the combination of a and ī yields e:

| | | |
|---|---|---|
| p**e**ṛ | a+ī = e | patr**ī** |

Sometimes the difference involves the quality of a vowel. For example, the change from ī to a in the following pair. Note that the Sanskrit word has been borrowed into Urdu.

| | Urdu | | Sanskrit |
|---|---|---|---|
| (to examine) | پَرَکھنا | (examination) | پَرِیکْشا |

Another common difference is the shortening or lengthening of vowels. For example, a long ā may be shortened (along with other changes) to a:

| Urdu | | Sanskrit |
|---|---|---|
| مہنگا | (costly, expensive) | مہارگھ |

Among the most common differences is the lengthening of a short vowel. Such differences are often accompanied by differences in consonants, too, such as the elision of one consonant in a pair or cluster.

| | Urdu | | Sanskrit |
|---|---|---|---|
| (cot) | کھاٹ | (cot) | کھَٹْوا |
| (womb) | کوکھ | (belly) | کُکْشی |
| (bean) | سُیم | (bean) | شِمبا |

There are many ways in which the vowel ـِر [ṛi] in Sanskrit is different in Urdu cognates, but perhaps the most common difference is for it to appear as ـِ [i].

| Urdu | | Sanskrit |
|---|---|---|
| کِسان | (farmer) | کْرِشک |
| تِنکا | (grass, straw) | تْرِن |

Another common difference is for the r to be maintained, but for the short i to change to a, thus to ر [-ar] or sometimes ڑ [-aṛ] in Urdu.

| | Urdu | | Sanskrit |
|---|---|---|---|
| (large) | بڑا | (growth) | وُرِدھ |
| [mar] (to die) (verb stem) | مَر | [mṛi] (to die) (verb stem) | مُرِ |

*A. Match the Sanskrit words on the right to their Urdu cognates. Then explain the differences between them with reference to one of the rules outlined above. Explanations should explain changes to the numbered word. The first has been done for you.*

| | | | | | |
|---|---|---|---|---|---|
| ṛi to ar | گھَر | ا | __ا__ | (home) | ۱۔ گرِہ |
| ____________ | آنسو | ب | ____ | (to do) | ۲۔ کرِ |
| ____________ | مِٹّی | پ | ____ | (tear) | ۳۔ اَشْرُ |
| ____________ | کَر | ت | ____ | (hand) | ۴۔ ہست |
| ____________ | ہاتھ | ٹ | ____ | (mud, soil) | ۵۔ مُرِتِکا |

## Vowel Insertion

Sanskrit favors pairs and clusters of consonants, but these are often broken or reduced in their Urdu cognates. Thus, Urdu cognates of Sanskrit words often differ by the infixation of a short vowel.

| Urdu | | Sanskrit |
|---|---|---|
| بھَگَت | (devotee) | بھَکْت |
| جَنَم | (birth) | جَنْم |

## Elision of Vowels

The elision of initial vowels occurs in Sanskrit as well as in the vernaculars. This means that the relationship between a large number of Urdu words and the Sanskrit prefixes surveyed elsewhere in this unit may not be immediately obvious. Consider the following.

| | Urdu | | Sanskrit |
|---|---|---|---|
| (inside) | بھیتر | (within) | اَبھیَتر |
| (crowd) | بھیڑ | (near) | ابھیرن |

Final vowels may also be elided.

| | Urdu | | Sanskrit |
|---|---|---|---|
| (word, matter) | بات | (speech) | وارتا |
| (sleep) | نیند | (sleep) | نِدرا |

*B. Read the Sanskrit-tatsam words on the right and the Urdu-tadbhav words on the left. Explain differences between the vowels using the information covered in this section.*

| Urdu | | Sanskrit |
|---|---|---|
| دھَرم | (dharma) | ۱۔ دھَرم |
| جَتَن | (endeavor) | ۲۔ یَتْن |
| رَتَن | (jewel) | ۳۔ رَتْن |
| کَلیس | (trouble) | ۴۔ کْلیش |
| بَرَس | (rain, year) | ۵۔ ورْش |
| سینگ | (horn) | ۶۔ شْرِنگ |
| پیٹھ | (back) | ۷۔ پْرِشٹ |

## 5.2.2 Changes to Consonants

Like differences in vowels, differences in consonants, too, can be grouped roughly into three categories: change from one consonant to another; the elision of a consonant; and a change to the quality of a consonant (unvoiced to voiced; unaspirated to aspirated; and so on).

Single initial consonants followed by a vowel rarely vary except in the case of predictable changes in quality (e.g. و to ب). (Initial-position consonant clusters, by contrast, vary considerably.) Changes in the internal consonants of the Sanskrit often involve the aspiration of the initial consonant of the Urdu. In the following pair, the Sanskrit و is predictably made ب in Urdu, and the elision of شْ from the consonant pair شپ [shp] results in the aspiration of the initial consonant, hence بھ.

| | Urdu | | Sanskrit |
|---|---|---|---|
| (vapor) | بھاپ | (vapor) | واشپ |

A similar process is at work in the following pair with the displacement of the aspirate from the final position to the initial consonant.

| | Urdu | | Sanskrit |
|---|---|---|---|
| (house, home) | گھَر | (house) | گْرِہ |

Note the regularity of the change: in gṛi the cluster gr changes to *gar* by the regular patterns of vowel infixation and the change of *ṛi* to ar (see section above). Then the final-position aspirate h is displaced to the initial consonant, *g*, to yield *gh*. Consequently, the Urdu word is *ghar*.

Medial-position consonants show the greatest difference between Sanskrit and Urdu cognates. Urdu words may contain the same consonants as the Sanskrit or differ according to regular and predictable patterns. One common difference is for a medial-position consonant to be elided, sometimes along with a connected vowel or vowels. There is some regularity to the patterns of elision, as some consonants are more likely to be eliminated and others are more frequently maintained. Those which tend to be maintained across Sanskrit-Urdu cognates are ج چ ت پ ٹ ک ج. Note that both Sanskrit words are used in Urdu.

| | Urdu | | Sanskrit |
|---|---|---|---|
| (light, shine) | جوتی / جوت | (light) | جیوتی |
| (mark on the brow) | ٹیکا | (mark on the brow) | تِلَک |

Unvoiced medial- and final-position consonants are often voiced in vernacular Indian languages like Urdu. For example, the letters ک / ٹ in Sanskrit words regularly appear as their voiced counterparts گ / ڈ or ڑ :

| | Urdu | | Sanskrit |
|---|---|---|---|
| (green, leafy vegetable) | ساگ | (vegetable) | شاک |
| (cloth) | کپڑا | (cloth) | کَرپَٹ |

Medial position پ in Sanskrit words often appears as و [v] or و [o] in Urdu.

| | Urdu | | Sanskrit |
|---|---|---|---|
| (to sleep) | سونا | (sleeping) | سوَپن |
| (plus a quarter) | سَوا | (plus a quarter) | سَپادِک |

*A. Match the Sanskrit word on the right to its Urdu cognate. Explain any changes in consonants with reference to the patterns outlined above.*

| | | | | |
|---|---|---|---|---|
| پلنگ | ا | ____ | (crow) | ۱۔ کاک |
| کنگال | ب | ____ | (skeleton) | ۲۔ کنکال |
| کنگن | پ | ____ | (bracelet) | ۳۔ کنکن |
| کاگ | ت | ____ | (bed) | ۴۔ پَریَنک |
| بونا | ٹ | ____ | (pan) | ۵۔ کٹاہ |
| کڑاہی | ث | ____ | (door) | ۶۔ کپاٹ |
| کواڑ | ج | ____ | (sowing) | ۷۔ وَپن |

The elision or omission of consonants is also common. This is especially true of consonants in the final syllable.

| | Urdu | | Sanskrit |
|---|---|---|---|
| (koel) | کوئل | (koel) | کوکِل |
| (crow) | کوّا | (crow) | کاک |

The elision of the initial ک from the agentive suffix کار (-doer, -maker) is characteristic of Urdu vocabulary derived from Sanskrit.

| | | | |
|---|---|---|---|
| (goldsmith) | سونار / سُنار | (goldsmith) | سُوَرن کار |

*B. Read the following pairs of Sanskrit and Urdu words and describe the relationship between them by noting the presence or absence of consonants.*

| | | | |
|---|---|---|---|
| (potter) | کُمہار | (potter) | ۱۔ کُمبھ کار |
| (mother) | مائی | (mother) | ۲۔ ماتا |
| (brother) | بھائی | (brother) | ۳۔ بھراتر |
| (to get) | پانا | (obtaining) | ۴۔ پراپن |
| (to eat) | کھانا | (eating) | ۵۔ کھادن |
| (to cry) | رونا | (crying) | ۶۔ رودن |
| (a well) | کنواں | (a well) | ۷۔ کُوپ |
| (lamp) | دِیا | (lamp) | ۸۔ دیپ |

Initial-position کش [ksh-] in Sanskrit words is generally replaced in Urdu with چھ.

| | Urdu | | Sanskrit |
|---|---|---|---|
| (stamp, seal, impression) | چھاپ | (kshi-; to strike) | کشِ |
| (forgiveness, pardon) | چھما | (forgiveness) | کشما |

Another difference is for the چ in Sanskrit to be replaced by ت in Urdu. This variation is also found among Urdu words. For example:

| | | | | |
|---|---|---|---|---|
| (forty-one, forty-five) | پینتالیس | اکتالیس | (forty) | چالیس |

Changes may also occur between dental and retroflex consonant pairs:

| | Urdu | | Sanskrit |
|---|---|---|---|
| (to determine) | ٹھاننا | (a place) | ستھان |
| (to fall) | پڑنا | (to fall) | پت |
| (to bite) | ڈنسنا | (to bite) | دنش |

The letters and sounds ل and ڈ or ڑ are also found in place of each other:

| | Urdu | | Sanskrit |
|---|---|---|---|
| (game, play, sport) | کھیل | (game, playing, sport) | کریڑا |
| (round) | گول | (ball) | گُڈ |
| (palm-wine) | تاڑی | (palmyra tree) | تال |

Perhaps the most common transformations that occur are those between ل and ر. These letters are also substituted for each other in Urdu dialects and styles, too.

| | Hindi-Urdu Dialect | | Standard Urdu |
|---|---|---|---|
| (plate, dish) | تھاری | (plate dish) | تھالی |

The same is true of ل and ن.

| | Hindi-Urdu Dialect | | Standard Urdu |
|---|---|---|---|
| (Lucknow) | نکھلؤ | (Lucknow) | لکھنؤ |

The case of Lucknow-Nucklow may in fact be a case of inversion, which is also found between Urdu and Sanskrit words.

| | Urdu | | Sanskrit |
|---|---|---|---|
| (to drown) | ڈوبنا | (to drown) | وُرُڈ |

The recognition of the inversion helps us to see how ڈوبنا is connected to the (rare) word بُڑَک (the sound of something falling into water). Note the inversion of ڈ / ڑ and ب.

Among the most common changes is ج in Urdu for ی [y] in Sanskrit.

| | Urdu | | Sanskrit |
|---|---|---|---|
| (yoga; proper; joined) | جوگ | (yoga) | یوگ |
| (to go) | جانا | (to go) | یا |

Also common is the change from و [v] in Sanskrit to ب in Urdu.

| | Urdu | | Sanskrit |
|---|---|---|---|
| (hero) | بیر | (hero) | ویر |

Likewise, the change from ش in Sanskrit to س in Urdu.

| | Urdu | | Sanskrit |
|---|---|---|---|
| (trust, belief) | بسواس / وِسواس | (trust, belief) | وشواس |

The change from م in Sanskrit to نو [ñv] or وں [oñ] (and sometimes simply nasalization) in Urdu is also common.

| | | Urdu | | Sanskrit |
|---|---|---|---|---|
| (dark-complexioned) | سانولا | سیام | (dark, black) | شیامل |
| | (village) | گاؤں | (village) | گرام |

One remarkable tendency is for the sibilants (ش and س) in Sanskrit to vary as ہ or خ or to be elided in other Perso-Indic languages. This is found not only in Urdu, but also in Persian and characterizes the relationship between a large number of Sanskrit words and their Persian cognates used in Urdu.

| | | | Persianate Urdu | | Sanskrit |
|---|---|---|---|---|---|
| (week) | ہفتہ | (seven) | ہفت | (seven) | سپت |
| | | (dry) | خشک | (dry) | شُشک |
| | | (ten) | دہ | (ten) | دَش |

Another common variation is that between the retroflex or palatal ش in Sanskrit and کھ in Urdu.

| | Urdu | | Sanskrit |
|---|---|---|---|
| (language) | بھاکھا | (language) | بھاشا |
| (poison) | بِکھ / بِس | (poison) | وِش |

Another change is the tendency for aspirated consonants (e.g. گھ, تھ, دھ, بھ) to appear as ہ in Urdu, the consonant being elided. We have already seen this in the difference between the Sanskrit کمبھ کار [kumbh-kār] and the Urdu کمہار [kumhār] (note the elision of b and the retention of h).

| | Urdu | | Sanskrit |
|---|---|---|---|
| (rain, mist, drizzle) | مینہ | (cloud) | میگھ |
| (to praise) | سراہنا | (to praise) | شلاگھ |

*C. Read the following pairs of Sanskrit and Urdu words. Explain the differences using the patterns discussed above as guides.*

| | | | |
|---|---|---|---|
| بہرا | (deaf) | بدھر | ۱۔ |
| دہی | (yogurt) | دَدھی | ۲۔ |
| بہُو | (wife; daughter-in-law) | وَدھو | ۳۔ |
| گہرا | (deep; grave; serious) | گمبھیر | ۴۔ |
| اہیر | (cowherd) | آبھیر | ۵۔ |
| ہو | (to be, become) | بھُو | ۶۔ |
| ہانڈی | (pot) | بھانڈ | ۷۔ |
| سُہاگ | (beauty) | سَوبھاگیہ | ۸۔ |
| کنول | (lotus) | کمل | ۹۔ |
| دھواں | (smoke) | دھوم | ۱۰۔ |
| برس | (rain; year) | ورش | ۱۱۔ |

Among the most important and regular patterns of difference between Sanskrit and Urdu is that which concerns Sanskrit consonant clusters. One can distinguish among kinds of clusters and similarly predict the ways in which Urdu forms derived from the same etymon will appear. The rules governing the kinds of consonants that are assimilated or elided, and the types of clusters which are subjected to the changes, are quite complex. Because our focus is mainly on recognizing connections among words for the purpose of vocabulary acquisition and retention, we will only broadly survey the three main patterns that are observed.

The first pattern is that the Sanskrit cluster is predictably paralleled by the elision of one letter and (usually) the lengthening of the preceding vowel in the Urdu cognate.

| | Urdu | | Sanskrit |
|---|---|---|---|
| (milk) | دودھ | (milk) | دُگدھ |

In the preceding example, the first element of the cluster, گ, has been elided and the preceding short vowel, ُ, has been lengthened to و [ū]. The same kind of elision is found in the following example. This time, the d is elided from the pair dg:

| Sanskrit | | Urdu | |
|---|---|---|---|
| اُدْگار | (spitting) | اُگال | (spitting) |

The preceding example belongs to a large group of Urdu words related to Sanskrit words that begin with the prefixes اُد or اُت, both of which convey a sense of upward movement. The elision of the d or t explains why a number of Urdu verbs whose meanings convey a sense of upward motion begin with اُ [u]. Here is another example.

| Sanskrit | | Urdu | |
|---|---|---|---|
| اُتّھان | (rising up) | اُٹھنا | (to arise) |

The next example is especially interesting, since it actually demonstrates two patterns. The first is the elision of the final ر. The second is a change in the nasalized vowel from the dental nasal ن to a nasalization of the elongated vowel, hence ں. This change is quite subtle and not universally pronounced by Urdu speakers, but it is a regular pattern that characterizes the relationship between tadbhav and tatsam registers.

| | | | |
|---|---|---|---|
| چَندر | (moon) | چاند | (moon) |

Here follow more examples:

| Sanskrit | | Urdu | |
|---|---|---|---|
| سکَندھ | (shoulder) | کاندھا / کندھا | (shoulder) |
| کمپن | (shaking, trembling) | کانپنا | (to tremble) |

*D. Read the following pairs and explain the difference between them with reference to the patterns discussed in this section.*

| | | | | |
|---|---|---|---|---|
| ۱۔ | جُمبُ | (jamun fruit) | جامُن | (jamun) |
| ۲۔ | اگنی | (fire) | آگ | (fire) |
| ۳۔ | مُگد | (a type of lentil) | مونگ | (muung daal) |
| ۴۔ | مکتا | (pearl) | موتی | (pearl) |
| ۵۔ | سَپْت | (seven) | سات | (seven) |
| ۶۔ | اُدْگمن | (going up) | اُگنا | (to grow [from soil]) |
| ۷۔ | اُدْجوالن | (heating up) | ابالنا | (to boil) |
| ۸۔ | اُدْبھارن | (raising up) | اُبھارنا | (to raise up) |

One general rule is that the elision of a sibilant (س or ش) from a cluster results in the aspiration of the remaining consonant and the elongation of the preceding short vowel. In the first example below, شُشک [shuṣhk], by removing ش [ṣh] from the pair شک [ṣhk], we are left with شُک [shuk]. By changing ش to س, elongating the vowel to و [ū], aspirating the remaining consonant ک to کھ, and adding an adjectival ending, we arrive at the Urdu word سوکھا, which is itself the root of a handful of other Urdu words.

| | | | |
|---|---|---|---|
| شُشک | (dry) | سوکھا / سوکھنا | (dry / to dry) |
| پَشچِم | (west) | پچھِم | (west) |

The cluster کْش has two frequent parallels in Urdu: چھ and کھ.

| | | | |
|---|---|---|---|
| اَکشی | (eye) | آنکھ | (eye) |
| کْشیر | (milk) | کھیر | (rice pudding) |
| کْشُر | (knife) | چھُری | (knife) |

*E. Read the following set of pairs. Explain the differences between them with reference to the patterns of vowel and consonant change and elision, and aspiration discussed here.*

| | | | | |
|---|---|---|---|---|
| ۱۔ | کُشٹھ | (leprosy) | کوڑھ | (leprosy) |
| ۲۔ | وِرشچِک | (scorpion) | بچھوا | (scorpion) |
| ۳۔ | سپرش | (touching) | پھنسنا | (to be ensnared) |
| ۴۔ | مکشِکا | (fly) | مکّھی | (fly) |
| ۵۔ | کشیتر | (field) | کھیت | (field) |
| ۶۔ | کُکشی | (belly) | کوکھ | (womb) |
| ۷۔ | ہست | (hand) | ہاتھ | (hand) |
| ۸۔ | ہستی | (elephant) | ہاتھی | (elephant) |
| ۹۔ | پْرستر | (stone) | پتّھر | (stone) |
| ۱۰۔ | پُستک | (book) | پوتھی | (book) |
| ۱۱۔ | مستک | (head) | ماتھا | (forehead) |
| ۱۲۔ | ستمبھ | (post) | تھام, تھامنا | (stopping, to stop) |
| ۱۳۔ | مُشٹی | (fist) | موٹھ / موٹھا | (fist) |
| ۱۴۔ | کاشٹ | (wood) | کاٹھ | (wood) |
| ۱۵۔ | پْرِشٹ | (back) | پیٹھ | (back) |

Typically, ر is elided from a cluster and is replaced with nasalization. This variation also involves changes to vowel patterns, especially lengthening and suffixation.

| | | | |
|---|---|---|---|
| کَرکٹ | (crab) | کینکڑا / کیکڑا | (crab) |
| اَرچس | (flame) | آنچ | (flame) |

*F. Read the following pairs and account for the differences between the Sanskrit and the Urdu using the rules discussed so far.*

| | | | | |
|---|---|---|---|---|
| ۱۔ | کرپٹ | (cloth) | کپڑا | (cloth) |
| ۲۔ | کھرجور | (date) | کھجور | (date) |
| ۳۔ | دُربل | (weak) | دُبلا | (thin, emaciated) |
| ۴۔ | ورکر | (goat) | بکرا | (goat) |
| ۵۔ | مارگ | (asking) | مانگ | (request) |
| ۶۔ | مارجن | (rubbing, polishing) | منجن | (polishing, cleaning [teeth]) |
| ۷۔ | سَرُپ | (snake) | سامپ | (snake) |
| ۸۔ | ویاگھُر | (tiger) | باگھ | (tiger) |
| ۹۔ | سَرُو | (all) | سب | (all) |

The changes from Sanskrit clusters ending in ی [y] to their tadbhav-Urdu relatives are regular and predictable: تی [ty(a)] to چ; تھی [thy(a)] to چھ; دی [dy(a)] to ج; and دھی [dhya] to جھ. Hence, in the first example below, the ty in ستیہ [saty(a)] (true) changes to ch and becomes *sach* (true). Note that the ی [y] ending of Sanskrit words is typically spelled یہ in Urdu.

| | | | |
|---|---|---|---|
| ستیہ | (true) | سچ | (true) |
| نرِتیہ | (dance) | ناچ | (dance) |

The variation between the consonants can occur even without ی [y]:

| | | | |
|---|---|---|---|
| بُدھ | (understanding, wisdom) | بُجھنا / بوجھنا | (to understand, to be wise) |
| شُدھ | (pure) | سوجھنا | (to become clear) |

Most Urdu-tadbhav forms of Sanskrit words beginning with پرتی [prati-] reflect the general trend for the initial-position cluster to be broken by the infixation of a vowel, thus parti-. The changes to the vowel and consonant patterns that follow from the infixation are thus often consistent with the patterns تی [ty(a)] is چ and so on.

| | | | |
|---|---|---|---|
| پرتِواسی | (neighbor) | پڑوسی | (neighbor) |

*G. Read the following pairs and explain the variation between the Sanskrit and Urdu words using the patterns discussed in this section.*

| | | | |
|---|---|---|---|
| آج | (today) | ادیہ | ۱۔ |
| بجلی | (lightning) | وِدیُت | ۲۔ |
| منجھلا | (middle, central) | مدھیہ | ۳۔ |
| سانجھ | (night) | سندھیا | ۴۔ |
| (shadow, shade; reflection) | پرچھائیں (reflection) | پرِتچھایا | ۵۔ |

Another common variation is for the cluster رت in Sanskrit to appear as ٹ in Urdu:

| | | | |
|---|---|---|---|
| (cutting) | کاٹ | (cutting) | کرتن |

When the ر follows a dental consonant (ت, د) in a cluster, it is often elided and the dental sometimes becomes retroflex:

| | | | |
|---|---|---|---|
| (spot) | چھینٹ | (spotted) | چِتر |
| (to break) | ٹوٹنا | (breaking) | ترُٹ |

Most often, however, the ر is simply elided:

| | | |
|---|---|---|
| کھیت | (field) | کشیتر |
| پُت / پُوت | (son) | پُتر |

Likewise, the ـیـ [y] at the end of clusters is simply elided.

| | | | |
|---|---|---|---|
| (desert; battlefield) | رن | (desert) | رنیہ |

When a sibilant (ش or س) and n (ن) are paired in Sanskrit, the sibilant is typically elided in Urdu and replaced with ہ following the nasal (ں). For example, from the Sanskrit word سنان [snān] (bathing), we drop س and replace it with نہ [nh], and, with vowel infixation, arrive at the Urdu نہانا [nahānā] (to bathe). The pattern explains why, in some dialects of early moden Hindi-Urdu, the pronunciation of نہانا was nhānā (without the infixed vowel).

| | | | |
|---|---|---|---|
| (to bathe) | نہانا | (bathing) | سْنان |
| (Kanha [Krishna]) | کانھ | (Krishna) | کرشن |

In many cases, when ر is part of a consonant cluster, a vowel is infixed:

| | | | | |
|---|---|---|---|---|
| (archaic) | (to touch) | پَرَسنا | (touching) | سپرش |

*H. Read the following pairs and account for the variations between them using the rules covered in this section.*

| | | | | |
|---|---|---|---|---|
| ۱۔ | وَرتِکا | (quail) | بٹیر | (quail) |
| ۲۔ | مرتِکا | (earth) | مٹّی | (earth, soil, mud) |
| ۳۔ | گَنتری | (mover, goer) | گاڑی | (carriage, cart, car) |
| ۴۔ | راتری | (night) | رات | (night) |

## 5.2.3 Prakritic Pronunciation and Urdu

Urdu takes much of its Sanskrit vocabulary through Prakrit languages and therefore follows the pronunciation of Prakrit, in which the pronunciation of certain Sanskrit letters varies. For example, the retroflex sibilant ष [ṣh] may be pronounced as either the aspirated کھ [kh] or the sibilant ش [sh], whereby sometimes as س [s], in Urdu. Likewise, as in other Prakritic South Asian languages, the letters و [v] and ش [sh] are often pronounced ب and س, respectively, in Urdu. The strength of the Sanskritization movement in India has rendered some of these pronunciations archaic, but for much of the history of Hindi-Urdu, they were considered standard. Thus:

پروت ← پربت (mountain) ← پاربتی [Pārbati]

وشنو ← بسنو [Bisnū] ← بیسنب (Baisnab)

وید ← بید (knowledge) ← بدیا (learning) بدیاوان (scholar)

وشواس ← بسواس (trust)

*A. Read the following excerpt from the maśnavī (rhymed couplets) Siḥr ul-Bayān (1780s) by Mīr Ḥasan. The poem recounts the adventures of a prince and princess in love. In this scene, an heirless king has called a handful of astrologers, including a pandit, for augury. Underline the words that show Prakritic forms of the Sanskrit وچن (word, speech) and وِچار (thought; judgment).*

کیا پنڈتوں نے جو اپنا بِچار — تو کچھ انگلیوں پر کیا پھر شمار

کہا رام جی کی ہے تم پر دَیا — چندرماں سا بالک ترے ہووے گا

مہاراج کے ہوں گے مقصد شتاب — کہ آیا ہے اب پانچواں آفتاب

نکلتے ہیں اب تو خوشی کے بچن — نہ ہو گر خوشی تو نہ ہوں بَرہمَن

## 5.3 Sandhi سندھی

Our discussion of Sanskrit word-building in Urdu begins with what Sanskrit grammarians call sandhī [سندھی] (combination). Like other Indo-European languages, Sanskrit forms vocabulary through combination. Sanskritists distinguish between internal and external sandhi. We will focus on the latter, external sandhī, which describes the changes that occur to vowels and consonants at the point of combination between the last letter of one word and the first letter of another.

### 5.3.1 Sandhi of Vowels

For example, when a word ending in ا [ā] is combined with one beginning in آ [ā], the resulting سندھی or combination is a single ا [ā], as in مہا (great) + آتما (soul) = مہاتما (the great soul). Study the following chart, which surveys the basic and most common سندھی rules for the combination of vowels. Note that in Nagari (the script most often used for Sanskrit), a special character is used for ر [typically transliterated as r̥; in this book, ṛi], which is considered a vowel. Here, this vowel is transliterated into Nastaliq as ری.

| Combined Vowel | | | Initial Vowel | | | End Vowel | |
|---|---|---|---|---|---|---|---|
| [ā] | آ | ← | [a, ā] | ا / آ | + | [a, ā] | اَ / آ |
| [e] | اُے | ← | [i, ī] | اِ / ای | + | [a, ā] | اَ / آ |
| [o] | اُو | ← | [u] | اُ | + | [a, ā] | اَ / آ |
| [ar] | اَر | ← | [ṛi] | ری | + | [a, ā] | اَ / آ |
| [ai] | اَے | ← | [i, e] | اِ / اُے | + | [a, ā] | اَ / آ |
| [ī] | ای | ← | [i, ī] | اِ / ای | + | [i, ī] | اِ / ای |
| [ū] | اُو | ← | [u, ū] | اُ / اُو | + | [u, ū] | اُ / اُو |
| [ṛi] | ری | ← | [ṛi] | ری | + | [ṛi] | ری |
| [ai] | اَے | ← | [e, ai] | اُے / اَے | + | [a] | اَ |
| [au] | اَو | ← | [o, au] | او / اَو | + | [a] | اَ |
| [y] | ی | ← | dissimilar vowel | | + | [i, ī] | اِ / ای |
| [v] | و | ← | | " | + | [u, ū] | اُ / اُو |

Consider the following examples:

| | | | | | | |
|---|---|---|---|---|---|---|
| | **[o]** | **اُو** | **←** | **اُ** | **+** | **اَ** |
| (having a long belly; a name of Ganesh) | لمبودر | ← | (belly) | اُدر | + (long) | لَمب |

| | | | | | | |
|---|---|---|---|---|---|---|
| | **[e]** | **اُے** | **←** | **ای** | **+** | **اَ** |
| (the supreme lord) | پرمیشور | ← | (lord) | اِیشوَر | (highest) + | پَرَم |

اَ + اِ ← ـُے **[e]**

نَر (man) + اندر (lord) ← نَریندر (lord of men; king, prince)

*A. Combine the words on the right to form the names or epithets of deities and give their literal meanings. Note that these names are also commonly used as personal names. Assume words end in ˊ [a] unless otherwise indicated.*

| | | | | |
|---|---|---|---|---|
| ا۔ | راکا | (full moon) | ایش | (lord) |
| ۲۔ | کَپی | (monkey) | ایش | (lord) |
| ۳۔ | پَنچ | (five) | آنَن | (face) |
| ۴۔ | پُرَجا | (children; subjects) | اِیش | (lord) |
| ۵۔ | اکِھل | (all) | ایشور | (lord) |
| ۶۔ | پُرُش | (man, being) | اُتّم | (best) |
| ۷۔ | مہا | (great) | ایش | (lord) |
| ۸۔ | ہیم | (gold) | انگ | (body) |
| ۹۔ | مُنی | (saint, ascetic) | ایش | (lord) |
| ۱۰۔ | وَجر / بَجَر | (hardy) | انگ | (body) |

*B. Read the following Sanskrit compounds aloud. Then use the chart above to separate them into their component parts. Finally, use the given meanings to estimate the meanings of the component parts.*

| | | | | | |
|---|---|---|---|---|---|
| ا۔ | ہیمیندر | (lord of gold) | ۲۔ | گجانَن | (elephant-faced) |
| ۳۔ | ویدوکت | (learned in the vedas) | ۴۔ | ہماچل | (mountain of snow) |
| ۵۔ | پرماتما | (the supreme spirit) | ۶ | | |

## 5.3.2 Sandhi of Consonants

A second set of rules governs the combination of consonants.

Study the following, chart, which has been adapted from the work of the Hindi scholar, Rupert Snell. The consonant or vowel resulting from the combination can be found by locating the point at which horizontal and vertical lines intersect inside the chart. For example, to find how a word ending in ک combines with a word beginning with گ, find the point of intersection between ک on the horizontal axis and گ on the vertical one. The chart is not exhaustive, but does give the most common forms found in Urdu.

| First Word: Final Letter ک | ٹ | ت | پ | (ہ ر س) | اَہ | Second Word: Initial Letter |
|---|---|---|---|---|---|---|
| گ | ڈ | د | ب | ر | و[o] | all vowels & گ د ب یَہ وَر |
| ک | ٹ | چ | پ | ش | اَش | چ ش |
| گ | ڈ | ج | ب | ر | و[o] | ج |
| ک | ٹ | ٹ | پ | ش | اَش | ٹ |
| گ | ڈ | ڈ | ب | ر | و [o] | ڈ |
| ک | ٹ | ت | پ | س | اَس | ت |
| ن | ن | ن | م | ر | و[o] | ن م |

Note the regularities in the pattern. In most cases, the final letter of the first element in a compound will retain its site of articulation and will be voiced or unvoiced according to the quality of the letter that begins the second word in the compound. To put it formulaically: site of articulation of the final letter of the first element + voiced/unvoiced character of the initial letter of the second second element = the letter at the site of combination. Thus, پ combined with ج yields ب [b] (the voiced counterpart of p); and ک combined with ڈ yields گ [g] (the voiced counterpart of k). Here follow examples.

1. Unaspirated, voiceless consonants change to their voiced counterparts when followed by any vowel or by the voiced counterpart of themselves:

ب ← پ

(water-born; lotus) اَبج ← (born of) ج (water) اَپ

ڈ ← ٹ

(the six systems of philosophy) شڈدرشن ← (system) درشن (six) شٹ

گ ← ک

("lord of speech"; eloquent person) واگیش ← (lord) ایش (speech) واک

د ← ت

(ruler of the world) جگدِیش ← (lord) اِیش (world) جگت

2. Unaspirated, voiceless consonants change to nasals of the same site of articulation (e.g. the bilabial پ changes to the bilabial nasal م) when followed by nasals. In Nagari, these nasals are represented by different characters. In Urdu, they are simply represented as ن or ں and م.

| | | | | | | |
|---|---|---|---|---|---|---|
| | | | | ں | ← | ک |
| (literature) | وانے | ← | (comprising) | ے | (speech) | واک |
| | | | | ن | ← | ٹ |
| (six months) | شنماس | ← | (months) | ماس | (six) | شٹ |
| | | | | ن | ← | ت |
| (lord of the world) | جگنناتھ | ← | (lord) | ناتھ | (world) | جگت |

3. The rules governing changes to ت are regular, but complicated. When ت is followed by گ د ب یہ ر و or any vowel, it changes to د. Note that all of the above are voiced sounds. When it is followed by چ or ج, ت assimilates and the چ or ج is doubled. When it is followed by ہ, ت changes to د and ہ changes to the aspirated ھ. When followed by ش, ت changes to چ and ش changes to چھ. The same rule applies to all voiceless non-aspirate consonants, which change to their doubled form followed by an aspirate.

| | | | | | | |
|---|---|---|---|---|---|---|
| | د | ← | | | | ت |
| (virtue) | سدگن | ← | (quality) | گن | (true) | ست |
| (gentleman) | سجّن | ← | (person) | جن | (true) | ست |

There is a large number of similar rules governing the combination of other letters. When چھ follows a vowel, it changes to چّھ. (This is not properly a sandhi rule, but rather an orthographic convention.) If م is followed by a consonant, it assimilates to the appropriate nasal ں. If م is followed by a semivowel or sibilant (ش س ہ), then it changes to ں. Here follow some typical changes encountered in Sanskrit vocabulary.

If ش is followed by ت, then ت becomes ٹ.

| | | | | |
|---|---|---|---|---|
| (drawn, attracted) | آکرشٹ | ← | ت | کرش |
| (asked, questioned) | پرشٹ | ← | ت | پرش |

If س is followed by چ, it becomes ش.

| | | | | | | |
|---|---|---|---|---|---|---|
| (not deceitful) | نِشچھل | ← | (deceit) | چھل | (not) | نِس |

If س is followed by اَ or any voiced consonant, then it becomes و [o].

| | | | | | | |
|---|---|---|---|---|---|---|
| (born of a lake; lotus) | سَرُوج | ← | (born of) | ج | (lake) | سَرَس |
| (entertainment, pleasure) | منورنجن | ← | (pleasing) | رنجن | (mind) | منس |

If س is followed by any vowel other than اَ or آ or precedes a voiced consonant or a vowel, then it becomes ر.

| | | | | | | |
|---|---|---|---|---|---|---|
| (medical science) | آیُرْوید | ← | (knowledge) | وید | (life) | آیُس |
| (wretch) | دُرجن | ← | (person) | جن | (bad) | دُس |

*A. Given the meanings of the words on the right, give the literal meaning of the word on the left.*

| | | | | | | |
|---|---|---|---|---|---|---|
| بہروپ | ← | (form) | روپ | (many) | بَہُ | ۱۔ |
| پرجاپالک | ← | (protector) | پالک | (subjects) | پرجا | ۲۔ |
| منوج | ← | (born of) | ج | (mind) | منس | ۳۔ |
| سرواتما | ← | (spirit) | آتما | (all) | سرو | ۴۔ |

*B. Combine the following elements to form the Sanskrit word. Then give the literal meaning.*

| | | | | |
|---|---|---|---|---|
| (worry; thought) | چِنت | (without; no, not) | نِس | ۱۔ |
| (capturing) | ہر | (mind) | منس | ۲۔ |
| (strength) | بل | (poor, bad) | دُس | ۳۔ |

## 5.4 Vowel Elongation and Word-Derivation: گن and وردھی [Guṇa and Vṛiddhi]

An important part of derived adjectives and nouns in Sanskrit is the elongation or alteration of vowels. English vowels undergo similar changes with suffixation or changes to parts of speech. For example, compare the sound of the letter a in "nature" with its sound in "natural." Sanskrit grammarians refer to this process using the terms guṇa (quality) and vṛiddhi (growth, expansion). This is also sometimes called internal sandhi. In this system, guṇa is a medial stage, whereby a vowel is implicitly altered to produce a predictable change according to the same set of vowel patterns covered in our discussion of *sandhi*. Study the following chart.

| (vowel sound in the derived word) | وردھی | | گن | | Vowel in the Base Word |
|---|---|---|---|---|---|
| [ā] | آ | ← | ا / آ | + | ا / آ |
| [ai] | اَے | ← | اُے [e] | + | اِ / ای |
| [au, ava, āva; (in the final position)] | اَو | ← | اَو | + | اُ / اُو |
| [ār] | ار | ← | اَر | + | ر |

In Urdu, we most commonly see the resulting vṛiddhi form, not the guṇa, and that is what we will focus on in this section.

## 5.4.1 Derived Nouns and Vṛiddhi

In Sanskrit, guṇa and vṛiddhi are applied across a range of contexts. In Urdu, we typically encounter vṛiddhi derivatives as relative nouns or adjectives that connote abstraction (often nominalized), belonging, progeniture, or relation. Among the common vowel changes is the lengthening (or "strengthening") of the vowel in **the first syllable** of the word, though vṛiddhi may involve changes to other vowels in the word, too. The same changes are sometimes necessitated by suffixation; for example, the suffixation of ـیہ to شور (see below). The following examples survey common vṛiddhi derivatives and their meanings.

| | | | | |
|---|---|---|---|---|
| **[ā]** | **آ** | ← | **[a]** | **ا** |
| (Durga [lit. daughter of the mountain]) | پاروتی | ← | (mountain) | پَروَت |
| (made of honey; sweet) | مادھَو | ← | (honey) | مَدھُو |
| | | | | |
| **[ai]** | **اَے** | ← | **[i]** | **اِ** |
| (Vaishnava, devotee of Vishnu) | وَیشنَو | ← | (Vishnu) | وِشنُو |
| (Shaiva, devotee of Shiva) | شَیو | ← | (Shiva) | شِو |
| | | | | |
| **[au]** | **اَو** | ← | **[u / ū]** | **اُ / اُو** |
| (Kaurava [descendants of Kuru in the Mahabharata]) | کَورَو | ← | (Kuru) | کُرُ |
| (heroism) | شَوریہ | ← | (hero) | شور |

The same elongation of vowels is also used to indicate a related quality:

| | | | |
|---|---|---|---|
| (nocturnal) | نَیش | (night) | نِش |
| (solar) | سَور | (the sun) | سُور / سُوَر |

*A. Given the meaning of the word or name on the right, guess the meaning of the word or name on the left.*

| | | | | |
|---|---|---|---|---|
| آدِتیہ | ← | (mother of the Gods) | اَدِتی | ۱۔ |
| مانَو | ← | (Manu [progenitor of mankind]) | مَنُو | ۲۔ |
| راگَھو | ← | (Raghu [great-grandfather of Ram]) | رَگھُو | ۳۔ |
| واسُدیو | ← | (Vasudeva [father of Krishna]) | وَسُدیو | ۴۔ |
| وَیدیہ | ← | (learning, scholarship) | ودیا | ۵۔ |
| لاگھو | ← | (light [adj.]) | لَگھو | ۶۔ |
| گَورَو | ← | (guru, heavy) | گُرُو | ۷۔ |
| اوچِتیہ | ← | (proper) | اُچِت | ۸۔ |

*B. Derive the relative vṛiddhi word from the following nouns and give its meaning. Required suffixes have been given.*

| | | | | | | | |
|---|---|---|---|---|---|---|---|
| [-ik] ک | (world) | لوک | ۲۔ | | (the mind) | مَنَس | ۱۔ |
| [-ya] یہ | (lord) | ایشور | ۴۔ | [-ik] ک | (world, universe) | سَنسار | ۳۔ |

## Note on Sanskritic Registers

The proliferation of Sanskritized Hindi-Urdu at the end of the nineteenth century, later associated exclusively with Hindi, resulted in an unprecedented degree of contact with tatsam(a) Sanskrit vocabulary in Hindi-Urdu. Direct borrowings of Sanskritic vṛiddhi forms, in particular, were less common in Urdu prior to that time. The following chart compares the Sanskritic forms with the Prakritic Urdu ones.

| | Urdu | | Urdu | | Sanskrit, Urdu (rare) | | Sanskrit, Urdu |
|---|---|---|---|---|---|---|---|
| (grandson) | پوتا، پوترا | (grandson) | پوت | (grandson) | پَوتر | (son) | پُتر |

The first of these words, پُتر [putr] (which is often pronounced putar or puttar in Urdu following standard patterns of vowel infixation), has been in use in Urdu since at least the nineteenth century. The Sanskritic vṛiddhi form پَوتر is extremely rare in Urdu. By contrast,

پوت and پوترا have been used since at least the seventeenth century; the former is common in compounds (e.g. Rajput). But the most common of all of them is پوتا.

## 5.5 Sanskrit Prefixes

Sanskrit, like other Indo-European languages, builds a large amount of vocabulary by prefixation and suffixation. The following section reviews Sanskrit prefixes commonly encountered in Sanskrit and Prakrit vocabulary in Urdu.

### 5.5.1 Spacio-Temporal and Relational Prefixes

| | | | | | |
|---|---|---|---|---|---|
| پر | **[par-]** | | **(distant, remote; other)** | | |
| دیش / دیس | (country) | پردیس | (foreign) | | |
| لوک | (world) | پرلوک | (the next world; heaven) | | |

| | | | | | |
|---|---|---|---|---|---|
| پر | **[pra-]** | | **(forward, exceeding)** | | |
| کریا | (action) | پرکریا | (process) | | |
| دھا | (to set, put) | پردھان | (foremost) | پردھان منتری | (prime minister) |

This prefix is a fine lens through which to observe the relationship between Sanskrit and Persian. Consider the etymological relationships between the elements in the Persian word فراہم.

پر (forward) سم (together) ← فراہم (put together; gathered, provided)

| | | | |
|---|---|---|---|
| وِ / بِ | **[vi-, bi-]** | | **(apart, away; difference, distinction; intensive)** |
| لگ | (connection) | ولگ / بلگ | (disconnected) |
| دیش / دیس | (country) | ودیش / بدیس | (foreign country) |
| جے | (victory) | وجے | (great victory) |

| | | | |
|---|---|---|---|
| اَو | **[au-/ava-]** | | **(down, off, away; negation, deprivation; intensive)** |
| گن | (quality, attribute) | اوگن | (fault; vice; wretchedness) |
| ستھا | (standing, existing) | اوستھا | (situation, state; story) |

| | | | |
|---|---|---|---|
| **اتی** | **[ati-]** | | **(beyond; excessive; very much)** |
| آچار | (conduct; propriety) | اتیاچار | (an action that is opposed to decency or morals) |
| بل | (power, strength) | اتی بل | (very powerful) |
| **اد** | **[ud-]** | | **(upwards; over; away from)** |
| آشا | (hope) | اداس | (despairing) |
| یوگ | (joining, engagement) | ادیوگ | (effort) |
| **اُپ** | **[up-]** | | **(near; subordinate, inferior to, at the service of)** |
| منتری | (minister) | اپمنتری | (sub-minister; deputy minister) |
| کار | (task, work) | اپکار | (favor; aid) |
| **پرَتِ** | **[prati-]** | | **(again; against; towards; near; about; for; in exchange; counter-, re-)** |
| کار | (karma) | پرتکار | (retaliation; compensation) |
| پالن | (protecting) | پرتپال | (protection) |
| **انتر** | **[antar-]** | | **(inner-, interior; intermediate)** |
| جات | (birth) | انترجات | (in-born) |
| دوار | (door) | انتردوار | (inner, private, or secret door) |
| **نِ** | **[ni-]** | | **(in, into; back; upon; positive intensive)** |
| یم | (restraint) | نیم | (restriction, rule; custom; religious observance) |
| یوگ | (joining) | نیوگ | (attachment; task; use; command; authority; effort) |
| **انُ / انو** | **[anu-]** | | **(after; similarity; according to, with regard to)** |
| سار | (use) | انسار | (in conformity with; according to) |
| مان | (notion) | انمان | (inference; estimate; opinion) |
| **پورو** | **[pūrva-]** | | **(prior, pre-; east-, eastern)** |
| ج | (born of) | پوروج | (ancient, former; first-born) |
| گیان | (knowledge) | پوروگیان | (foreknowledge) |

*A. Combine the prefixes with the words on the left to form vocabulary and guess the meaning of the resulting words. Check your guesses in a dictionary.*

۱۔ پَرَ گتی (movement)
۲۔ اَنُ بھو (being)
۳۔ بِ / وِ چر (moving, acting)
۴۔ نِ کام (desire)
۵۔ پرَ چار (motion)
۶۔ پَر ارتھ (purpose, advantage)
۷۔ اَو تر (to cross) (lengthen vowel)
۸۔ وِ / بِ یوگ / جوگ (union; alignment [of stars])
۹۔ وِ بھاشا (language)
۱۰۔ اتی سندر (beautiful)
۱۱۔ اُد آہرن (taking)
۱۲۔ اُپ راشٹرپتی (president)
۱۳۔ پرتِ کار (action)
۱۴۔ پورو کال (time, age)
۱۵۔ انتر آتما (soul)

## 5.5.2 Prefixes of Negation

**نِر / نِس / نِش [nir-, nis-, nish-] (absence, lack; away, out; utterly)**

انتر (rift; difference) — نرنتر (continuously, always)
تر (to cross) — نستار (liberation, deliverance)

**ا / ان [a-, an-] (un-, in- [negation])**

کھنڈ (segment) — اکھنڈ (continuous)
انگ (body) — اننگ (bodiless)

*A. Use the given prefix of negation to negate the noun and give the meaning of the resulting noun or adjective.*

۱۔ نِر روپ (form)
۲۔ نِر گُن (quality, attribute)
۳۔ نِر آش / آس (hope)
۴۔ نش کپٹ (falseness, deceit)
۵۔ نش چِنتا (worry) (drop ا)
۶۔ ا پار (side)
۷۔ ا بھاو (being)
۸۔ ان آد (beginning)
۹۔ اَن انت (end)

*B. Read the following epithets of deities, all of which negate some quality.*

۱۔ اَجا (unreality of the universe, illusion)
۲۔ اَجر (imperishable; ever youthful)
۳۔ امر (immortal, undying)
۴۔ اَچیُت (immortal)

| | | | | | |
|---|---|---|---|---|---|
| ۵۔ | اکام | (without desire) | ۶۔ | اگن | (without attribute) |
| ۷۔ | آننت | (without end) | ۸۔ | اجے | (unvanquished) |

## 5.5.3 Prefixes of Emotion and Attitude

| | | | |
|---|---|---|---|
| سُ | [su-] | **(good)** | |
| روپ | (form, face) | سروپ | (handsome, beautiful) |
| میل | (meeting) | سمیل | (sociable) |

| | | | |
|---|---|---|---|
| دُر / دُس / دُش | [dur-, dus-, dush-] | **(difficulty, painful; hard; deterioration; evil, bad)** | |
| جن | (person) | دُرجن | (scoundrel) |
| گم | (to go) | درگت | (bad circumstances, misfortune) |

| | | | |
|---|---|---|---|
| کُ | [ku-] | **(bad, deficient)** | |
| کرم | (karma) | کُکرم | (evil deed) |
| روپ | (form) | کُروپ | (ugly, deformed) |

| | | | |
|---|---|---|---|
| اَپ | [ap-] | **(contrary; inferior)** | |
| مان | (belief; respect) | اپمان | (affront, insult; disgrace) |
| کار | (work, undertaking) | اپکار | (harm, loss; hindrance) |

*A. Use the following prefixes of negative emotion or attitude to negate the nouns and estimate the meaning of the resuting word.*

| | | | | | | | |
|---|---|---|---|---|---|---|---|
| ا۔ | اپ | کرم | (karma, action) | ۲۔ | دُر | دَشا | (state, condition) |
| ۳۔ | سُ | گندھ | (smell) | ۴۔ | کُ | چال | (movement, manner) |

## 5.5.4 Prefixes of Classification and Comparison

| | | | |
|---|---|---|---|
| سَ | [sa-] | **(with)** | |
| گُن | (quality) | سگن | (having attributes; virtuous) |
| کُل | (family) | سکل | (of one family) |

| | | | |
|---|---|---|---|
| سن / سم | **[sam-]** | | **(-with; union; completeness; like Latin con-)** |
| گیت | (song, singing) | سنگیت | (music) |
| یوگ / جوگ | (joining, union) | سنیوگ / سنجوگ | (connection; occasion; intercourse) |

| | | | |
|---|---|---|---|
| سہ | **[sah-]** | | **(with, together)** |
| ج | (-born; born of) | سہج | (innate; simple, easy; natural; of one race, family, species) |
| پاٹھ | (lesson, class) | سہپاٹھی | (classmate) |

| | | | |
|---|---|---|---|
| سم | **[sam-]** | | **(same, equal)** |
| درش | (to look at, see) | سم درشی | (seeing all equally; gnostic) |
| روپ | (form) | سروپ | (of the same form) |

The sa- prefixes, all of which convey a sense of togetherness, are all etymologically related to the first component of many Urdu verbs that express the idea of togetherness, combination, or completion. Consider the following:

| | |
|---|---|
| سکڑنا | (to draw together, to contract, shrivel) |
| سمانا | (to be held or contained) |
| سنبھالنا | (to support, maintain; manage; to pull together) |
| سمٹنا | (to be collected, condensed, crumpled; to be recoiled) |
| سمجھنا | (to understand; from sambuddh [enlightened]) |
| سنوارنا | (to decorate) |
| سونپنا | (to consign, to entrust) |

| | | | |
|---|---|---|---|
| سو | **[sva-]** | | **(one's own; self-)** |
| دیش | (country) | سودیشی | (of one's own country) |
| تنتر | (authority) | سوتنتر | (independent, autonomous) |

*A. Use the following prefixes of comparison and classification to form words and give their meanings.*

| | | | | | | | |
|---|---|---|---|---|---|---|---|
| ۱۔ | سَن | پھل | (fruit; reward, upshot) | ۲۔ | سَن | پورن | (filling; satisfying) |
| ۳۔ | سَن | گم | (to go) | ۴۔ | سوَ | راج | (rule, governance) |
| ۵۔ | سہ | اُدر | (womb, belly) | | | | |

## 5.6 Sanskrit Suffixes

Just as Sanskrit derives and builds vocabulary by prefixation, it also derives vocabulary by suffixation. Some suffixes require vriddhī changes to vowels, others do not. Also note that the rules of sandhi apply to the site of suffixation. This is why the suffixation of ج [-aj] to منس [manas(a)] yields منوج [manoj], and so on. The most common Sanskrit suffixes encountered in Urdu are surveyed here. Note that some of these are suffixes proper, some are verbal suffixes, and others are nominal and adjectival forms. Four the sake of simplicity, they will all be treated together here.

### 5.6.1 Adjectival and Adverbial Suffixes

The first set of suffixes that we will consider is used to form adjectives and adverbs. Keep in mind that, in some cases, these words may also be used as nouns.

Most Sanskrit suffixes do not require any change to the internal vowel patterns of the root word. The suffix ک [-ik(a)] is an exception, since it requires the application of vṛiddhi to the first syllable. It is also among the most common Sanskrit adjectivizing suffixes in Urdu.

| | | | |
|---|---|---|---|
| ک | **[-ik]** | | **(adjectivizing [-al, etc.], adverbializing [-ly])** |
| دِن | (day) | دَینِک | (daily) |
| دھرم | (dharma) | دھارمک | (righteous) |

The remaining suffixes discussed here do not require any vṛiddhi changes.

| | | | |
|---|---|---|---|
| ت | **[-t(a); -it(a)]** | | **(adjectivizing (-ed, -ous, etc.); typically passive)** |
| پات | (decline) | پاتت | (declined; defeated, depressed) |
| پرسار | (going forth; extension, spreading) | پرسارت | (held out; expanded; spread) |

| | | | |
|---|---|---|---|
| ل / لو | **[-lu/lū]** | | **(adjectivizing; being susceptible, sensitive to something)** |
| ندرا | (sleep, drowsiness) | ندرالو | (sleepy) |
| تندرا | (exhaustion) | تندرالو | (exhausted) |

**پورک** **[-pūrvak]** **(adverbializing, adjectival; -ful; -fully)**

شانتی (peace) شانتی پورک (peaceful, peacefully)

**مان / متی** **[mān (m.); -matī (f.)]** **(possessed of; adjectives of character)**

بُدھ (wisdom) بدھ مان بدھ متی (wise, intelligent)

شری / سری (dignity) شری مان / سری مان (sir) (honorific) شری متی / سری متی (madam) (honorific)

**وان / وتی** **[-vān (m.); vatī (f.)]** **(possive adjective; possessed of)**

دھن (wealth) دھنوان دھنوتی (wealthy)

گیان (knowledge) گیانوان گیانوتی (knowledgable)

**وت** **[-vat]** **(adjectivizing, adverbializing; possessed of; -like)**

مت (intoxicated) متوَت (like an intoxicated person)

دند (stick) دندوت (saluting or prostrating by lying flat [like a stick])

**ونت** **[-vant]** **(adjectivizing, adverbializing; possessed of; -like)**

دھن (wealth) دھن ونت (wealthy)

دھرم (virtue) دھرم ونت (virtuous, righteous)

**دا** **[-dā]** **(denoting time)**

سدا (always)

تدا (at that time)

Some suffixes are made from verbal stems:

**ج** **[-j, -aj, -ja]** **(-born; born of)**

جل (water) جلج (lotus)

منس (mind) منوج (born of the mind; Kamdev)

*A. Form adjectives from the following nouns using the suffix or suffixes given to the left. Then give their meanings.*

| | | | | | | | |
|---|---|---|---|---|---|---|---|
| ۱۔ | اتہاس | (history) | ک | ۲۔ | وید | (veda) | ک |
| ۳۔ | لوک | (world) | ک | ۴۔ | دکھ | (pain) | ت |
| ۵۔ | وِکاس | (opening) | ت | ۶۔ | بل | (power) | وان |
| ۷۔ | دیا | (mercy) | لو | ۸۔ | کرپا | (kindness) | لو |
| ۹۔ | نیر | (water) | ج | ۱۰۔ | بھاگ | (lot, fortune) | متی |

## 5.6.2 Nominal Suffixes

The most commonly encountered Sanskrit nominal suffix in Urdu is تا [tā]. All words ending in this suffix are grammatically feminine in Urdu.

| | | | |
|---|---|---|---|
| **تا** | **(-tā)** | | **(abstract nouns; -ness)** |
| ویر | (hero, warrior) | ویرتا | (heroism, bravery) |

A related suffix forms masculine abstract nouns. Note that this is also applied to Perso-Arabic vocabulary, such as ہندو [hindū], in Urdu.

| | | | |
|---|---|---|---|
| **تو or توا** | **[-tva]** | | **(abstract nouns; -ness, -hood, etc.)** |
| مہت | (great, glorious) | مہتو | (greatness, majesty) |
| ہندو | (Hindu) | ہندوتوا or ہندتو | (lit. Hindu-ness; Hindutva) |

| | | | |
|---|---|---|---|
| **ک** | **[-ak]** | | **(forms agentive, diminutive, and relative nouns)** |
| انت | (end) | انتک | (ender, death) |
| پُتر | (son, boy) | پترک | (little boy) |
| روپ | (form) | روپک | (likeness, form) |

When the root ends in a long ā, an intervening y ی may be placed before the suffix:

| | | | |
|---|---|---|---|
| گا | (singing) | گایک | (singer) |

The following words, built on the root *sev* (serving) show the relationships among the root, a verbal noun, and the agentive noun formed with the suffix ک.

| | | | | | |
|---|---|---|---|---|---|
| سیو | (serving) | سیوا | (service) | سیوک | (servant) |

| | | | |
|---|---|---|---|
| **پاتر** | **[pātr-]** | | **(vessel; recipient; object of)** |
| پریم | (love) | پریم پاتر | (beloved, the object of one's love) |
| مایا | (power, wealth) | مایا پاتر | (wealthy person, powerful person) |

| | | | |
|---|---|---|---|
| **پتی** | **[-patī]** | | **(-master)** |
| دھرم | (righteousness) | دھرم پتی | (a righteous man) |
| گج | (elephant) | گج پتی | (elephant-keeper; a very large elephant; a king) |

Sometimes the suffixes are made from verbal stems:

| | | | |
|---|---|---|---|
| **د / دا** | **[-da, -ad; -dā (f.)]** | | **(-giver, -giving)** |
| سکھ | (pleasure) | سکھ دائی | (pleasure-giver, pleasure-giving) |
| جل | (water) | جلد | (a cloud) |

| | | | |
|---|---|---|---|
| **دھر** | **[dhar]** | | **(keeper)** |
| مرلی | (flute) | مرلی دھر | (floutist; Krishna) |
| یم / جم | (death) | جمدھر | (a special kind of dagger) |

*A. Using the given suffix, form nouns from the following adjectives and give their meanings.*

| | | | | | | | |
|---|---|---|---|---|---|---|---|
| ۱۔ | گمبھیر | (profound, serious) | تا | ۲۔ | ادھک | (additional, more) | تا |
| ۳۔ | سندر | (beautiful) | تا | ۴۔ | ست | (real, virtuous) | تو |
| ۵۔ | راج | (rule, reign) | پتی | ۶۔ | دُکھ | (pain) | دائی |

In the following two examples, lengthen the short vowel in the initial syllable:

| | | | | | | | |
|---|---|---|---|---|---|---|---|
| ۷۔ | پَل | (guarding) | ک | ۸۔ | پچ | (cooking) | ک |

## 5.6.3 Comparative and Superlative Suffixes

Two common comparative (English "-er") and superlative (English "-est") suffixes are تر and تم.

| | | | |
|---|---|---|---|
| تر | **[-tar]** | | **(comparative)** |
| مند | (slow) | مندتر | (slower) |
| اُد | (up) | اُتّر | (upper) |

| | | | |
|---|---|---|---|
| تم | **[-tam]** | | **(superlative)** |
| پریا | (beloved) | پریتم | (dearest, most beloved) |
| اُد | (up) | اُتّم | (highest; best) |

A second set of comparative and superlative suffixes is also used.

| | | | |
|---|---|---|---|
| یس | **[-(ī)yas]** | | **(comparative)** |
| کنین | (young) | کنییس | (younger) |

| | | | |
|---|---|---|---|
| شٹھ | **[-ishṭh]** | | **(superlative)** |
| کنین | (young) | کنشٹھ | (youngest, smallest) |
| پرتی | (towards) | پرتشٹھ | (prominent, famous) |

*A. Form the comparative and superative adjectives of the following using the comparative and superlative suffixes in parentheses. Then give their meanings.*

۱۔ دھنوَت (wealthy) ← دھنَت (تر) ۲۔ ست (true, virtuous) (تم)

*Review Exercise. Read the following names of famous Urdu writers aloud. Note any instances of sandhī, vṛiddhi, prefixation, or suffixation. Separate the constituent parts of the names and use a dictionary to learn their meanings.*

اپیندرناتھ اشک سمپورن سنگھ گلزار دھنپت رائے پریم چند جگن ناتھ آزاد رگھوپتی سہائے فراق گورکھپوری

سریندر پرکاش جَینت پرمار رتن ناتھ سرشار نریش کمار شاد راجندر سنگھ بیدی

## 5.7 Sanskrit Proverbs and an Introduction to Sanskrit Grammar

Sanskrit proverbs are used far less frequently in literary Urdu than Arabic and Persain ones, but it is still useful to be familiar with them. To appreciate the literal meaning of Sanskrit proverbs requires a basic familiarity with Sanskrit grammar, which is notoriously complicated and can take years, if not decades, to master. An amusing joke intended to illustrate the complexity of the language and the extraordinarily length of time required to learn it goes something like this: They asked a man facing execution for his last request. He paused and, after a bit of consideration, responded, "Sir, before I die, I'd like to master Sanskrit!"

Students interested in highly Sanskritized registers of Urdu will also benefit from studying the Nagari script. Just as the Arabic script facilitates mastery of the Arabic element in Urdu, the Nagari script gives readers access to aspects of Sanskrit morphology and grammar that have not historically been developed in Nastaliq. For example, just as Nastaliq distinguishes between عام (general) and آم (mango) where Nagari does not (both are spelled आम), Nagari distinguishes between letters such as ष and श, both of which are typically written as ش in Nastaliq and pronounced sh in Urdu. (Note that ष is written and pronounced کھ (as in بھاکھا or بھاشا) in some registers of Urdu.)

Of course, there is no reason why Sanskrit phonemes could not be written in Nastaliq. After all, Sanskrit has been written in many scripts throughout the centuries, not just Nagari. But because Sanskrit has not generally been written in Nastaliq, there is no universally (or even generally) acknowledged system for writing those aspects of the script and language that are, at present, not easily represented in it. It bears repeating that there is nothing necessary about the Nastaliq script that prohibits the kind of distinctions that one finds in Nagari (e.g. one can imagine a system whereby the palatal/retroflex sibilant ष is distinguished from श / ش by shifting the dots below the letter; such a character has precedent in the Persian manuscript tradition, anyway, in which it is used to distinguish س from ش) or the use of a fourth dot on ش, since retroflex consonants have been written this way in Urdu before (e.g. ٹ as ٿ in Platts). Yet because of this lack of standardization, the relatively recent history of direct borrowing from Sanskrit, and the longer history of using Prakritic forms in Urdu, when Urdu authors write Sanskrit vocabulary and phrases, they often do so by approximating the sounds and spellings of Sanskrit and adapting them. While this is not a problem in principle, it does mean that students of highly Sanskritized registers of Hindi-Urdu will find it more challenging to work with them exclusively through Nastaliq, just as students of highly Arabicized registers will find it easier to work in Nastaliq and more challenging in Nagari.

Orthographical issues aside, as this unit has shown, Sanskrit remains an integral part of the Urdu linguistic, literary, and cultural world. Indeed, it is difficult to spend more than a small amount of time in most of the major Urdu-speaking cities in India without hearing the Gayatri Mantra or some Sanskrit verses recited at temples or at religious and cultural ceremonies like weddings. In this section, we will closely examine two Sanskrit proverbs that students may encounter in contexts in which Sanskrit registers are used in Urdu. Our purpose in doing so will be to gain familiarity with several basic points of Sanskrit grammar and to facilitate comprehension of Sanskrit phrases and quotations used in Urdu. It is hoped that this brief introduction will encourage students to study the language further.

## 5.7.1 Sanskrit Proverb One

۱۔ وِناش کالے وِپریت بُدّھی (In a time of ruin, wisdom is upended.)

The first word in our proverb comprises two parts: the intensive prefix وِ [vi-] and Sanskrit ناش (ruin). The latter is typically used in its Prakrit form in Urdu, ناس (ruin), as in the commonplace idiom ستیا ناس (total ruin).

The second word کالے illustrates an important point about Sanskrit grammar. Like Latin, but unlike English and Urdu, Sanskrit (typically) uses cases rather than prepositions or postpositions to express location ("in, at") (Urdu: میں / پر), instrument ("by, through") (Urdu: سے), and so on. One common locative suffix in Sanskrit is ے [-e]. Here, we see it suffixed to the word کال (time, era), which is a commonly used Urdu word with a wide semantic range (famine; scarcity; death; time). Thus:

| | | | |
|---|---|---|---|
| کال | (a time) | کالے | (in/at a time) |

The third word in our proverb is rare, but attested, in Urdu, in which it is used in its Prakrit form بپریت (opposite, reversed, inverted). It begins with the prefix وِ(away), which is affixed to پَریت (turning, moving round), that is, turned the wrong way or inverted. Incidentally, وِپَریت has been borrowed into English as part of the name for a yoga pose (viparita dandasana) in which the practitioner assumes an inverted position.

The fourth and final word, بُدّھی (understanding, wisdom) is cognate with the English Buddha. Note that there is no verb for "to be" in the proverb, since it is implied. Putting it all together, we have:

وِناش کالے وِپریت بُدّھی (In times of ruin, wisdom is upended.)

## 5.7.2 Sanskrit Proverb Two

۲۔ وِدیا وِنیین شوبھتے (Learning is beautified by humility.)

Our second example begins with وِدیا (learning or wisdom), which is a common Urdu word in both its Sanskritic and Prakritic ( بِدیا ) forms. One Sanskritic word in which it is found is وشوودیالے [vishvavidyāle], which is a calque of the English "university." The Hindi-Urdu word literally means a place (آلے) of universal ( وِشْو ) learning ( وِدیا ) and is ubiquitous in highly Sanskritized registers of Urdu.

The second word in its basic form is ونے [vinay], whose meanings include humility, modesty, courtesy, and refinement. It is also a common personal name. Here, we find it in the instrumental case (cf. English "by, through"), which is marked by the suffix ین [-en(a)], hence وِنَیین [vinayen(a)]. Thus, "by or through courtesy" or "by or through humility."

The third and final word is the present-tense, singular, middle form (a kind of passive or intransitive form) of the verb شُبھ (to shine; to be beautiful; to suit). This form is characterized by the ending تے [te]. The verb شُبھ is related to a handful of common Urdu words: شُبھ (good, fine), as in آپ کا شبھ نام کیا ہے (What is your good name?); and شُوبھا (beauty). Here, it might be translated as "is beautified," "shines," "is adorned."

(Learning is beautified by humility.) وِدیا وِنَیین شوبھَتے

## 5.8 Suggestions for Further Study

The following works include a great deal of Sanskrit and Sanskritic vocabulary and are therefore recommended for further reading. Maikash Akbarābādī, *Naqd-e Iqbāl* (Agra: Agrah Aḳhbār, 1952); Nārā'in Prasād Betāb, *Patnī Pratāp*; Bābū Bhagvān Dās Bhārgav, *Bhagvat Gītā Urdū* (Lucknow: Naval Kishor, 1945 [3rd printing]); Firāq Gorakhpūrī, *Gul-e Naġhmah* (Allahabad: Idārah-e Anīs-e Urdū, 1959); Pyārelāl, trans., *Tarjumah-e Jog Bashishṭh*, 2 vols. (Lucknow: Naval Kishor, 1904, 1905 [3rd printing]); Qurrat ul-'Ain Ḥaidar, *Āg kā Daryā* (Lahore: Matkabah-e Jadīd, 1959); Taḥsīn ud-Dīn, *Qiṣṣah-e Kāmrūp o Kalā* (Paris: 1835); Yasavantasinha Varma Tohanavī, *Āryah Sangīt Rāmāyan* (1915); Sajjād Ẓahīr, *Pighlā Nīlam* (Delhi: Na'ī Raushnī Prakāshan, 1964).

# Appendix I
# Arabic Verbal Noun Charts

The charts on the following pages survey the Urdu words derived from some of the most common Arabic roots, Persian verbs, Hindi verbs, and Sanskrit roots. Glosses for the words are given in the first few charts, then the words alone are given to encourage practice. Broken plural forms are given, but standard suffixational forms (e.g. ات for Arabic nouns ending in ہ or ت; ین [īn] for human plurals) are not. Estimate the meanings of familiar words or words built from familiar roots and patterns. Then estimate the meanings of unfamiliar words. Check your estimations in a dictionary. Add any related words not listed here and use the charts as models for your own charts of roots and verbs that you encounter repeatedly in your reading. Record derived or related words along with notes about their meanings.

# نظر

(to see)

## Form I (Root) Nouns

| | | | | | | |
|---|---|---|---|---|---|---|
| نظر | (ج۔ انظار / نظرات) | (sight) | نظّاره | (seeing; scene) | نظارت | (supervision) |
| نظریہ | (ج نظریات) | (perspective; theory) | نظریاتی | (theoretical) | | |
| نظری | | (speculative) | نظراً | (apparently) | | |
| نظیر | (ج۔ نظائر) | (likeness; nadir) | نظیراً | (by way of example) | نظیره | (imitative likeness) |

## Nouns of Place and Instrument

| | | | | | |
|---|---|---|---|---|---|
| مَنظر | (ج۔ مَناظِر) | (scene) | | | |
| مِنظار | (ج۔ مناظیر) | (telescope; microscope; stereoscope) | مِنظر | (ج۔ مناظِر) | (spectacle; telescope) |

## Verbal Nouns and Participles

| Form | Noun | | Participles | | | | |
|---|---|---|---|---|---|---|---|
| I | | (see above) | ناظر | (ج۔ نُظّار / ناظرین) | (viewer, reader; pl. viewership, viewers) | | |
| | | | منظور | | (seen; (that which is) seen; desired; accepted) | | |
| II | تنظیر | (analogy) | مُنَظِّر | | (analogizing, analogizer) | | |
| III | مناظره | (debate) | مُناظر | | (debator) | | |
| IV | انظار | (astrological reading) | | | | | |
| V | تنظّر | (state of expectation) | مُتَنَظِّر | | (expectant) | | |
| VI | تناظر | (perspective; symmetry) | متناظر | | (symmetrical, symmetry) | | |
| VII | | | | | | | |
| VIII | انتظار | (expectation, waiting) | منتظِر | | (expectant; expected) | منتظَر | (expected) |

# علم

(to know)

Form I (Root) Verbal Nouns

| | | | | | |
|---|---|---|---|---|---|
| عِلم (ج۔ علوم) | (knowledge; science) | عَلَم (ج۔ اَعلام) | (banner) | عَلامت | (sign, symbol) |
| علّام | (all-knowing) | علّامہ | (very learned) | | |
| علیم | (omniscient) | اعلم | (more, most knowledgeable) | | |

Nouns of Place and Instrument

مَعلَم (ج مَعالِم) (sign, token; the world)

Verbal Nouns and Participles

| Form | Noun | | Participles | | | |
|---|---|---|---|---|---|---|
| I | | (see above) | عالِم (ج۔ علما / علماء) | (scholar, intellectual) | | |
| | معلوم | (known) | معلومات | (information) | | |
| II | تعلیم | (education, instruction) | معلِّم | (educator) | معلَم | (educated) |
| III | | | | | | |
| IV | اعلام | (announcement) | | | | |
| | اعلامیہ | (official announcement; communiqué) | | | | |
| V | تعلم | (instruction, awareness) | متعلم | (student) | | |
| VI | تعالم | (state of knowing all) | متعالم | (knowing or familiar with all) | | |
| VII | | | | | | |
| VIII | | | | | | |
| X | استعلام | (seeking or gaining knowledge) | | | | |

# حکم

## (to judge, to rule)

### Form I (Root) Nouns

حُکم (ج۔ احکام) (command) حکمت (ج۔ حِکَم) (wisdom) حکومت (governance, government)

حَکَم (ج۔ حُکّام) (arbitrator) حکیم (ج۔ حکماء) (philosopher; physician)

احکم (greatest ruler; most authoritative; most solid)

### Nouns of Place and Instrument

محکمہ (ج۔ محاکم) (bureau; office [legal, governmental]; department)

### Verbal Nouns and Participles

| | | | | Participles | | | Noun | Form |
|---|---|---|---|---|---|---|---|---|
| (ruled, governed) | محکوم | (ruler, governor) | (ج۔ حُکّام) | حاکم | (see above) | | | I |
| (authorized, authoritative) | محکَّم | (authority) | | محکّم | ([allocating] authority) | تحکیم | | II |
| | | | | | (trial, arbitration) | محاکمہ | | III |
| (stabilized, stable) | محکَم | (stabilizer) | | محکِم | (stabilization; pillar) | اِحکام | | IV |
| | | (domineering; ruler) | | متحکم | (domination) | تحکم | | V |
| | | | | | (arbitration, investing authority) | تحاکم | | VI |
| | | | | | | | | VII |
| | | | | | | | | VIII |
| | | (stable, firm) | | مستحکَم | (stability, steadfastness) | استحکام | | X |

# ملک

(to possess; to own; to control)

## Form I (Root) Nouns

مُلک (region, country) — مَلَک (ج۔ مَلائِک) (angel) — مَلِک (ج۔ مُلوک) (king) — مَلِکہ (queen)

مَلَکوت (kingdom; world of angels) — ملوکیت (monarchy)

مِلک (ج۔ اَملاک) (property) — مِلکِیت (possession; property) — مَلَکہ (aptitude)

مِلاک (basis)

مَلّاک (great possessor or owner; God) — ملیک (ج۔ مُلَکا / مُلَکاء) (king; God)

## Nouns of Place and Instrument

مملکت (مَمالِک) (reign; region)

## Verbal Nouns and Participles

| Form | Noun | | Participles | | |
|---|---|---|---|---|---|
| I | | (see above) | مالک | (ج۔ مُلّاک) | (owner) |
| | مملوک | (owned; slave) | مملوکیت | (slavery) | |
| II | تملیک | (claiming or assigning ownership) | | | |
| III | | | | | |
| IV | اِملاک | (property; putting in possession) | | | |
| V | تملک | (ownership) | | | |
| VI | تمالک | (self-control, self-possession) | | | |
| VII | | | | | |
| VIII | | | | | |
| X | استملاک | (the ability to be owned as property) | | | |

# قوم

(to rise, to stand)

## Form I (Root) Nouns

| | | | | | |
|---|---|---|---|---|---|
| قوم (ج۔ اَقوام) | (community, nation) | قومہ | (standing in prayer) | قامت | (stature) |
| قیمت | (value) | قِوام | (prop, support; confection [medicine]) | قیام | (residence; standing) |
| قیامت | (doomsday) | قیُّوم | (very stable) | قیِّم | (self-sustaining; God) |
| قویم | (right; stable) | اقوم | (most (or very) correct, stable) | | |

## Nouns of Place and Instrument

مقام (ج۔ مقامات) (place; station)

## Verbal Nouns and Participles

| Form | Noun | | Participles | | | |
|---|---|---|---|---|---|---|
| I | | (see above) | قائم | (standing, erect) | قائمہ | (right angle; pillar) |
| II | تقویم | (establishing; almanac) | مقوِّم | (establisher, founder; distinguisher [logic]) | | |
| | (ج۔ تقاویم) | | مقوَّم | (someone for whom a confection has been made) | | |
| III | مقاومت | (competition, opposition) | مقاوِم | (competitor, opponent) | | |
| IV | اقامت | (residence) | مقیم | (residing, staying) | مقیمیہ | (residency) |
| V | | | متقوم | (valuable, precious) | | |
| VI | | | | | | |
| VII | | | | | | |
| VIII | | | | | | |
| X | استقامت | (erectness; rectitude; stability) | مستقیم | (upright, straight; stable) | | |

# عمل

(to act)

## Form I (Root) Nouns

عمل (ج۔ اعمال) (act, action) — عملہ (staff [of an organization])

عملاً (practically) — عملیت (practicality) — عمالہ (allowance)

## Nouns of Place and Instrument

مَعمل (factory; workspace; laboratory) — مَعمِلت (work, action)

## Verbal Nouns and Participles

| Form | Noun | | Participles | | | |
|---|---|---|---|---|---|---|
| I | | (see above) | عامل (ج۔ عُمّال) | (doer, worker; ruler) | | |
| | | | معمول | (enacted; [regular] action) | معمولی | (ordinary) |
| II | تعمیل | (activation; enaction) | معمِّل | (activator; enactor) | معمَّل | (activated; enacted) |
| III | معاملہ | (business, dealing) | | | | |
| IV | اعمال | (application) | معمِل | (applier) | معمَل | (applied; worn out) |
| V | تعمّل | (effort, endeavor, exertion) | | | | |
| VI | تعامل | (interaction, reaction) | متعامل | (interactive, reactive) | متعامِلہ | (reactor) |
| VII | | | | | | |
| XIII | | | | | | |
| X | استعمال | (use, utilization) | مستعمل | (used, utilized) | | |

# قدر

(to decree; to have power; to be capable; to have value)

Form I (Root) Verbal Nouns

قدر (ج۔ اقدار) قُدرت

قدیر

Nouns of Place and Instrument

مِقدار (ج مقادیر)

Verbal Nouns and Participles

| Form | Noun | Participles | |
|---|---|---|---|
| I | (see above) | قادر | مقدور |
| II | تقدیر (ج۔ تقادیر) | | مقدَّر |
| III | | | |
| IV | | | |
| V | تقدر | متقدِر | |
| VI | | | |
| VII | | | |
| VIII | اقتدار | مقتدِر | |
| X | | | |

# حق

(to be true, right; to be due; to have a right, be entitled)

Form I (Root) Verbal Nouns

| | | | |
|---|---|---|---|
| حق | (ج۔ حُقوق) | حقہ | حقانی |
| حقیق | حقیقت | احق | |

Nouns of Place and Instrument

Verbal Nouns and Participles

| Form | Noun | | Participles | |
|---|---|---|---|---|
| I | | | | |
| II | تحقیق | (ج۔ تحاقیق) | محقق | محقق |
| III | | | | |
| IV | احقاق | | محق | |
| V | تحقق | | متحقق | متحقق |
| VI | | | | |
| VII | | | | |
| VIII | | | | |
| X | استحقاق | | مستحق | |

# قرب

(to be near)

Form I (Root) Verbal Nouns

قرب قربت قرابت قُربان

قریب (ج۔اقرِبا) اقرب

Nouns of Place and Instrument

Verbal Nouns and Participles

| Participles | | Noun | Form |
|---|---|---|---|
| | | | I |
| مقرِّب | (ج۔تقاریب) | تقریب | II |
| | | مقاربت | III |
| | | | IV |
| متقرب | | تقرب | V |
| متقارب | | تقارب | VI |
| | | | VII |
| مقترِب | | اقتراب | VIII |
| | | | X |

# وقع

(to fall; to occur)

Verbal Nouns (Root)

وقعت    وقوع    وقوعہ

Nouns of Place and Instrument

مَوقع / موقعہ    (ج مواقع)

Verbal Nouns and Participles

| Form | Noun | Participles | | |
|---|---|---|---|---|
| I | | واقع | واقعہ | موقوعہ |
| II | توقیع | | | |
| III | وِقاع | مُواقع | | |
| IV | ایقاع | | | |
| V | توقع | متوقع | | |
| VI | | | | |
| VII | | | | |
| VIII | | | | |
| X | | | | |

# Appendix II
# Persian Verbal Noun Charts

## خواستن

(to desire)

| Past Stem | Present Stem |
|---|---|
| خواست | خواه |

### Simple Nouns—Present Stem

| | | | | | | | |
|---|---|---|---|---|---|---|---|
| (desirous) | خواهان | (desirer) | خواهنده | (desire) | خواهش | (desire; if, whether) | خواه |

### Simple Nouns—Past Stem

| | | | | | | | |
|---|---|---|---|---|---|---|---|
| (desired; desire) | خواسته | (request for marriage) | خواستاری | (desirer) | خواستار | (desire) (archaic) | خواست |
| | | (request or appeal [especially for marriage]) | | | خواستگاری | (suitor) | خواستگار |

### Compound Nouns—Present Stem

| | | | | | |
|---|---|---|---|---|---|
| (retaliator; bloodthirsty) | خون خواه | (satisfactory) | خاطرخواه | (ill-wisher; rival, enemy) | بدخواه |
| | | (seeker after praise or justice; claimant) | دادخواه | (well-wisher; friend) | خیرخواه |
| | | (apologetic; apologizer) | عذر خواه | (favored, cherished; beloved) | دلخواه |
| | | (apologetic; apologizer) | معذرت خواه | (money-lender) | قرض خواه |
| | | (well-wisher, friend) | هواخواه | (involuntarily, unintentionally) | ناخواه |

Compound Nouns—Past Stem

درخواست (application) باز خواست (inquiry)

Phrases and Idioms

خواہ مخواہ (like it or not; needlessly) خدا نخواستہ (God forbid!) خواستہ نا خواستہ (willed or not)

# داشتن

(to have)

| Present Stem | Past Stem |
|---|---|
| دار | داشت |

**Simple Nouns—Present Stem**

دارا (possessor; Darius)    دارنده (possessor)

**Simple Nouns—Past Stem**

داشت (care, upbringing; protection)

داشته (kept, protected, cared for; a concubine)

**Compound Nouns—Present Stem**

آبدار (lustrous)    حصه دار (shareholder)    خبردار (beware!)

**Compound Nouns—Past Stem**

برداشت (tolerance)    بے داشت (uncared for, neglected)

چشم داشت (desire, hope; trust)    خاطر داشت (care, attention; service)

عرض داشت (appeal)    نگاه داشت (care, supervision)    یاد داشت (memory; note)

**Phrases**

دار و گیر (interference, seizure)    داشت و پرداخت (caretaking)

ندارد (absent, empty, nill)    جواب ندارد (no response)

# دانستن

(to know)

| Present Stem | Past Stem |
|---|---|
| دان | دانست |

### Simple Nouns—Present Stem

دانا (knowing, wise) — دانائی (wisdom) — دانش (wisdom, knowledge) — دانندہ (knower)

### Simple Nouns—Past Stem

دانست (a person's knowledge, understanding) — دانستہ (knowingly)

### Compound Nouns—Present Stem

اردوداں (Urdu scholar [knower]) — تاریخ داں (historian) — حساب داں (mathematician)

رازداں (confidant) — ریاضی داں (mathematician)

زبان داں (knower of a language) — قدرداں (connoisseur; patron)

نکتہ داں (discerning, penetrating) — غیب داں (knower of hidden or otherworldly things)

ناداں (naive, ignorant) — ہمہ داں (all-knowing, very knowledgable)

### Compound Nouns—Past Stem

دانست دار (intelligent) — دانست کار (wise, intelligent) — نادانستگی (ignorance)

### Phrases and Idioms

دانا بینا (knowing, aware) — دیدہ و دانستہ (knowingly and willingly) — ہیچ مداں (a know-nothing)

# رفتن

(to go)

| Present Stem | Past Stem |
|---|---|
| رو | رفت |

Simple Nouns—Present Stem

روا (permitted (thing); right; current)
روان (current, flowing)
روانی (fluency)
رونده (traveler, wayfarer)
روش (style, manner)

Simple Nouns—Past Stem

رفت (going [usually in compounds])
رفته (apologetic; apologizer)
رفتگاں (the departed)
رفتار (speed)

Simple Nouns—Verbal Infinitive

رفتنی (fleeting)

Compound Nouns—Present Stem

خود رو (automatic)
پیش رو (leader)

Compound Nouns—Present Stem

پیش رفته (advanced)

Phrases and Idioms

از خود رفته (ecstatic)
رفته رفته (slowly, gradually)
یاد رفتگان (memories of the departed)
آمد و رفت (traffic; coming and going)
روان دوان (quickly)

# کشیدن

(to pull, draw tight)

| Present Stem | Past Stem |
|---|---|
| کش | کشید |

Simple Nouns—Present Stem

کش (drag) (e.g. of a cigarette)
کشش (attraction)

Simple Nouns—Past Stem

کشید (pull; distillation)
کشیدہ (tense)
کشیدگی (tension)

Simple Nouns—Infinitive

کشیدنی (fit to be drawn)

Compound Nouns—Present Stem

محنت کش (hard-working; hard worker; laborer)
منت کش (indebted, obliged)
دل کش (attractive, appealing)
فاقہ کش (starving)

Compound Nouns—Past Stem

کشیدہ خاطر (disturbed)
کشیدہ قد (tall)

Phrases

کشاکش (struggle)
کشمکش (struggle)

# خریدن

(to buy)

| Present Stem | Past Stem |
| --- | --- |
| خر | خرید |

Simple Nouns—Present Stem

Simple Nouns—Past Stem

خرید　　خریده

خریدار　　خریداری

Compound Nouns—Present Stem

Compound Nouns—Past Stem

خریدنامه　　زرخرید　　خوش خرید　　بی زر خریده

Phrases

خرید و فروخت

# گذشتن / گذاشتن

(to pass / to pass (transitive))

Present Stem　　Past Stem

گذر / گذار　　گذشت / گذاشت

Simple Nouns—Present Stem

گذر　　گذراں

گذارش　　گذارا　　گذارانہ　　گذارہ

Simple Nouns—Past Stem

گذشتہ

گذاشت　　گذاشتگی

Simple Nouns—Infinitive

گذاشتنی

Compound Nouns—Present Stem

امانت گذار　　حق گذار　　خدمت گذار　　کار گذار　　گذار گر　　گذارش پذیر　　گذارہ دار　　شکر گذار

در گذر　　رہ گذر

Compound Nouns—Past Stem

سر گذشت

فرو گذاشت　　واگذاشت

Phrases

گذاشتنی اور گذاشتنی　　رفت و گذشت

# یافتن

(to find)

| Past Stem | Present Stem |
| --- | --- |
| یافت | یاب |

Simple Nouns—Present Stem

یابنده

Simple Nouns—Past Stem

یافت

Simple Nouns—Infinitive

یافتنی

Compound Nouns—Present Stem

باریاب دستیاب سزایاب فیض یاب کامیاب کمیاب نایاب

Compound Nouns—Past Stem

دریافت بازیافت تعلیم یافته تربیت یافته تهذیب یافته سزا یافته صحت یافته سند یافته

Phrases

جوینده یابنده

# Appendix III
# Hindi Verbal Noun Charts

## ہونا

(to be)

| | | | | | |
|---|---|---|---|---|---|
| ہونہار | (promising; soon-to-be [archaic]) | ہونی | (fate [usually negative]) | انہونی | (the impossible) |
| ہوتا | (relative) | ہوتوں سوتوں | (relatives, friends, and so on) | | |
| ہوتو | (fate, destiny) | | | | |
| ہونی ان ہونی | (unexpected, suddenly) | ہونی بلوان ہے | (there's no escaping fate) | | |
| ہونی شدنی | (fate, destiny) | | | | |

## کرنا

(to do)

| | | | |
|---|---|---|---|
| کرنہار | (doer, maker; creator) | کرنی | (action, deed) |
| کرتا | (maker; boss, owner, lord) | کرتاپن | (makership; bosshood) |
| کرتار | (creator; God) | | |
| کرنی کا پھل | (reward [especially punishment] for one's deeds) | | |
| جیسی کرنی ویسی بھرنی | (you reap what you sow) | | |
| کرنی کرتوت | (one's deeds, actions) | | |

## جانا

(to go)

| | |
|---|---|
| جانہار / جانہارا | (going, passing; dying; passer-by) |

## دینا

(to give)

دیا (given, gift)   دیوا (giver)   دین (gift, giving)   دہنار / دہنارا (giver)

لین دین (business, dealings)

## رکھنا

(to keep)

رکھوال / رکھوالا (guard, keeper)   رکھوالی (guardianship)

رکھائی (keeping)   رکھ رکھاؤ (formalities; safekeeping)

رکھا رکھایا (saved, kept back)

## آنا

(to come)

آہٹ   آن   آئی

آن بان   آتا جاتا

آئی گئی   آئی ہوئی

آئی کا شریک   آئی کو ٹالنا

## کہنا

(to say)

کہا   کہانی

کہا سنا   کہا سنا معاف کرنا

## لینا

(to take)

لین　　لیا دیا

لین دین　　لے دے

## دیکھنا

(to see)

دکھاؤ　　دکھاؤُ　　دکھاوا　　دکھاوٹ　　دکھائی

دیکھا دیکھی　　دیکھا ان دیکھا

دیکھ بھال　　دیکھا بھالی　　دیکھا بھولی

دیکھا نہ بھالا صدقے گئی خالہ

## چلنا

(to move)

چال　　چالا　　چالو　　چالی　　چالیا　　چلاؤُ　　چلاوا　　چلت　　چلتی　　چلن

چلاچلی　　چل چلاؤ　　بول چال

چال چلن　　حال چال　　چال ڈھال　　چال باز

# Appendix IV
# Sanskrit Roots

The following sections survey Urdu vocabulary derived from Sanskrit as well as Urdu vocabulary related to these Sanskrit roots that is found in other Indo-European languages.

## بھُو

(to be)

ہونا (to be)

بھَو (existence) | بھُو (the world) | بھاو (existence; nature, character)

اسمبھو (impossible; improbable) | سمبھو (possible)

وبھو / ببھو (extraordinary power) | وَیبھو / ببیھو (power, majesty) | وِبھُوتی / ببھُوتی (power)

بھوَن (building; being; birth)

## کرِ

(to do)

کرنا (to do)

کر (hand) | کار (work) | اکارت (useless)

کرِت (done) | کرتب (feat, achievement) | کرتوت (deed, doing) | کرم (karma)

اکھڑّ (crude)

کردار (role, character) | کردن (to do [Persian]) | گر / گار (-er)

## یُج

(to join)

جگانا (to arrange)

جوتا (shoe; pair of shoes)

یوگ / جوگ (yoga) | جوگ (worthy) | یوگی / جوگی (yogi)

جُنگ (emotion, impulse) سنیوگ / سنجوگ (connection) ادیوگ (effort)

جوش (passion; boiling) بجوگ (separation; misfortune; loss; death)

جُت (suffix [-endowed with]) جُڑنا (to unite, join) جلاہا (weaver)

## رَکْش

(to keep, preserve)

رکھنا (to keep, preserve)

انگرکھا (tunic, angarkha) راکھی (rakhi)

## کَتھ

(to say)

کہنا (to say)

کہاوت (saying, idiom)

کتھا (story, tale) کتھانک (story) کتھک (narrator; name of a narrative dance form)

## دھی / دھیے

(to perceive / to think)

سُدھ (thought, perception) دھیان (meditation; focus)

دیدن (to see [Persian])

## دُرِش

(to see)

دیکھنا (to see) دیسنا (archaic) (to appear)

درشن (visitation) درسی (vision) آرسی (mirror, looking-glass)

ادرسا (lit. “unseen”; a special kind of thin cloth) آدرش (message; purpose; example; mirror)

# چل

(to move)

| | | | |
|---|---|---|---|
| چلنا | (to move) | نِچلا | (motionless; quiet) |
| چالاک | (clever; deceitful) | سنچل | (footfall; dreams) |

# Bibliography

Aḥmad Dihlavī, Sayyid (1908). *Farhang-e Āṣafiyah*. 4 vols. Lahore: Rifāh-e ʿĀm.

Ahmed, Hasanuddin (1973). *Urdu Word Count*. Hyderabad: Villa Academy.

Akḥtar, Salīm (2015). *Iṣṭilāḥ-sāzī: Tārīḳh, Maśā'il, Mabāḥiś*. Lahore: Sang-e Mīl Publications.

Apte, Vaman Shivaram (1957–9). *Revised and Enlarged Edition of Prin. V. S. Apte's The Practical Sanskrit-English Dictionary*. 3 vols. Poona: Prasad Prakashan.

Barker, Muhammad Abd-al-Rahman, Hasan Jahangir Hamdani, and Muhammad Shafi Dihlavi (1969). *An Urdu Newspaper Word Count*. Montreal: Institute of Islamic Studies, McGill University Press.

Barker, Muhammad Abd-al-Rahman, Hasan Jahangir Hamdani, Khwaja Muhammad Shafi Dihlavi, and Shafiqur Rahman (1975). *A Course in Urdu*. 3 vols. Ithaca, NY: Spoken Language Services.

Beams, John (1872). *Comparative Grammar of the Modern Aryan Languages of India*. Vol. 1, *On Sounds*. London: Trübner & Co.

Bukḥārī, Suhail (1989). *Urdū Zabān meñ Alfāẓ-sāzī*. Islamabad: Muqtadirah-e Qaumī Zabān.

Cannon, Garland Hampton and Alan S. Kaye (1994). *The Arabic Contributions to the English Language: An Historical Dictionary*. Wiesbaden: Harrassowitz Verlag.

_____ (2001). *The Persian Contributions to the English Language: An Historical Dictionary*. Wiesbaden: Harrassowitz Verlag.

Corriente, F. (2008). *Dictionary of Arabic and Allied Loanwords: Spanish, Portuguese, Catalan, Galician, and Kindred Dialects*. Leiden: Brill.

Coulson, Michael (1976). *Sanskrit: An Introduction to the Classical Language*. Sevenoaks: Hodder and Stoughton.

Crowley, Terry (1997). *An Introduction to Historical Linguistics*. New York: Oxford University Press.

Daryush, A. A. (1934). *Persian Words in English*. Oxford: Clarendon Press.

Dās, Śyāmsundar (1965–75). *Hindi Śabdsāgar*. Kāśī: Nāgarī Pracāriṇī Sabhā.

Dihḳhudā, ʿAlī Akbar (1946–). *Luġhatnāmah*. Tehran: Dānishgāh-e Tehran.

_____. *Luġhatnāmah*, <https://www.parsi.wiki> (last accessed 31 July 2020).

Editors. *The Oxford English Dictionary*. Oxford: Oxford University Press (Online), <www.oed.com> (last accessed 31 July 2020).

Editors. *Urdu Luġhat*. Karachi: Urdu Lughat Board, <http://udb.gov.pk> (last accessed 31 July 2020).

Fallon, S. W. (1879). *A New Hindustani-English Dictionary*. London: Medical Hall Press; Trubner and Co.

Ganesan, S. N. (1972). *Semantic Variation of Some Sanskrit Words in Hindi and the Major Dravidian Languages*. Madras.

Hāshmī, ʿIshrat Jahān (2012). *Urdū Muḥāvarāt*. Lahore: Dār ush-Shuʿūr.

Hillmann, Michael Craig (2007). *Persian Vocabulary Acquisition*. Hyattsville: Dunwoody Press.

Hisamuddin, A.A. (1906). *A Guide to Persian-Arabic Roots and Plurals*. Poona: Munshi Muhammad.

Jain, Madiayal (1966). *Hindī Śabd-racnā*.

Jeffery, Arthur (1938). *The Foreign Vocabulary of the Quran*. Leiden; Boston: Brill (1st impression).

Kellogg, Samuel Henry [1875] (1938). *A Grammar of the Hindí Language*. London: Kegan Paul, Trench, Trubner and Co. Ltd (3rd edn).

Lazard, Gilbert (2006). *Grammaire du Persan Contemporain*. Tehran : Institute-Français de Recherche en Iran.

Lo Bello, Anthony (2013). *The Origins of Mathematical Words: A Comprehensive Dictionary of Latin, Greek, and Arabic Roots*. Baltimore: The Johns Hopkins University Press.

Macdonell, Arthur Anthony (1929). *A Practical Sanskrit Dictionary with Transliteration, Accentuation, and Etymological Analysis Throughout*. London: Oxford University Press.

Mace, John (1998). *Arabic Grammar: A Reference Guide*. Edinburgh: Edinburgh University Press.

McGregor, R. S. (1993). *The Oxford Hindi-English Dictionary*. Oxford and New York: Oxford University Press.

Malik, Qayyum (1979). *Urdū meṅ ʿArabī Alfāẕ kā Talaffuẕ*. Karachi: National Book Foundation.

_____ (1995). *Urdu meṅ ʿArabī aur Fārsī Alfāẕ o Murakkabāt*. Lahore: Maktabah-e Karvān.

Mangrio, Riaz Ahmed (2016). *The Morphology of Loanwords in Urdu: The Persian, Arabic, and English Strands*. Newcastle upon Tyne: Cambridge Scholars Publishing.

Munīr Lucknowi and Muḥammad Munīr (1924). *Mulk kī Zabān, al-Maʿrūf bah Muḥāvarāt-e Hindūstān*. Kanpur: Maṭbaʿ-e Majīdī.

Muqtadirah-e Qaumī Zabān (2004). *Urdu-Angrezī Mushtarak Zak̲h̲īrah-e Alfāẕ*. Islāmābād: Muqtadirah-e Qaumī Zabān.

Naim, C. M. (1965). *Readings in Urdu: Prose and Poetry*. Honolulu and Chicago: East-West Center Press, South Asia Language and Area Center, University of Chicago.

_____ (1975). *Introductory Urdu*. Chicago: Committee on Southern Asian Studies, University of Chicago.

Nayyar, Nūr al-Ḥasan (1924). *Nūr al-Luġhāt*. Lucknow: Nayyar Press.

Pāl, Keśav Rām (1964). *Hindi meṅ Prayukt Sanskrit śabdoṅ meṅ Arth Parivartan*. Merut: Praci Prakaśan.

Phillott, D. C. (ed. and trans.) (1912). *K̲h̲azīnah-e Muḥāvarāt or Urdu Idioms*. Calcutta: Baptist Mission Press.

Platts, John T. (1884). *A Dictionary of Urdu, Classical Hindi, and English*. London: W. H. Allen & Co.

Quraishī, Sharīf Aḥmad (2016). *Urdū Kahāvateṅ*. Jhelum: Book Corner.

Riẓvī, Sayyid Masʿūd Ḥasan (1958). *Farhang-e Amṡāl*. Lucknow: Kitāb Ghar.

Schmidt, Ruth Laila (1999). *Urdu: An Essential Grammar*. London, New York: Routledge.

Shackle, Christopher and Rupert Snell (1990). *Hindi and Urdu Since 1800: A Common Reader*. London: School of Oriental and African Studies.

Singh, Rajendra and Agnihotri, Rama Kant (1997). *Hindi Morphology: A Word-Based Description*. Delhi: Motilal Banarsidas Publishers.

Snell, Rupert (1991). *The Hindi Classical Tradition: A Braj Bhāṣā Reader*. London: School of Oriental and African Studies.

_____ (2000). *Teach Yourself Hindi*. Lincolnwood, IL: Teach Yourself Books.

Srivastava, Murli Dhar (1995). *Essentials of Hindi Grammar*. Lincolnwood, IL: Passport Books.

Steingass, Francis Joseph (1982). *A Comprehensive Persian-English Dictionary*. London: Routledge & Kegan Paul.

Taylor, Walt (1933). *Arabic Words in English*. Oxford: The Clarendon Press.

Thackston, Wheeler M. (1993). *An Introduction to Persian*. Bethesda: Iranbooks.

_____ (1994). *An Introduction to Koranic and Classical Arabic*. Bethesda: Iranbooks.

Thomas, Lewis V. (1967). *Elementary Turkish*. Rev. and ed. Norman Itzkowitz. Cambridge, MA: Harvard University Press.

Tishnah, Naẕīr Aḥmad (2008). *Urdū Ẓarb ul-Amṡāl*. Lahore: Maqbūl Academy.

Tivārī, Bholānāth and Kiraṇ Bālā (1985). *Hindī Bhāṣā kī Śabd Saṃracnā*. Delhi: Sāhitya Sahakār.

Turner, R. L. (1962–6). *A Comparative Dictionary of Indo-Aryan Languages*. London: Oxford University Press. (Supplements published 1969–85), <http://dsal.uchicago.edu/dictionaries/> (last accessed 31 July 2020).

ʿUmar, Muḥammad bin (1954). *Purtugālī Zabān kā Aṡar Urdu Zabān Par*. Hyderabad: Kitāb Khānah.

______. *Urdu meñ Dāḳhil Yūrapī Alfāẕ* (1955). Hyderabad: Maṯbaʿ-e Ibrāhīmiyah.

Wehr, Hans (1976). *A Dictionary of Modern Written Arabic*. Ithica: Spoken Language Services.

Wickens, G. M. (1980). *Arabic Grammar: A First Workbook*. Cambridge and New York: Cambridge University Press.

Zaidi, Shamshad (1989). *Studies in Urdu Linguistics*. Patiala: Husna Publications.

# Index

## English Index

## Urdu Index